Ex<

CW01430139

5-

OUR INIS EOGHAIN HERITAGE

By the Author
Where Aileach Guards
That Audacious Traitor
Derry: An Outline History of the Diocese
The Homeland of Ó Dochartaigh

OUR INIS EOGHAIN HERITAGE

The Parishes of Culdaff and Cloncha

BRIAN BONNER

The Bookshop
Carndonagh, Co. Donegal

This edition published 2009 by
© The Bookshop
Mart Road
Carndonagh
Co. Donegal
Tel: 074 9373 369 or 086 8349 373
info@booksofireland.com
www.booksofireland.com

Offset from the original
edition first published 1972 by
Foilseacháin Náisiúnta Teo.
Áth Cliath I.

Printed by Impact Printing,
Ballycastle, Co. Antrim.

ISBN: 978-1-906689-13-1

TIOMNÚ

Do m'Athair agus do mo Mháthair.

Pádraig Ua Cnáimhsighe

as

Dún an Ghrianáin

agus

Maighréad Nic Cuaig

as

Baile Uí Ghormáin.

A FHRÉAMHAIGH BUANGHRÁ DAINGEAN IONAM

DO MO THÍR DHÚCHAIS

AGUS

A ROINN GO FRAS LIOM A MBARRSHAMHAIL

GO MBEADH ÉIRE

Saor, Aontaithe, Gaelach

CONTENTS

Post Office and Communications
Police Barracks
Garda Stations
Dispensaries
Loan Fund
The Coastguard Service
Roads
Meteorological Station at Malin Head

ILLUSTRATIONS

ACKNOWLEDGEMENT

NO WORK of an historical nature can reach completion without the co-operation of others. This publication is no exception.

As a considerable portion of the material in this book was the result of much field-work, my thanks are due in the first place to the ordinary people of Inis Eoghain. Courtesy, assistance and interest were experienced everywhere throughout the peninsula.

To the members of the staff of the National Library, Kildare Street, and at the Royal Irish Academy, my sincere gratitude is hereby expressed.

Finally, a special word of appreciation to Breandan Mac Cnaimhsighe, M.A., for his abiding interest in the preparation of this work and for acting as consultant on those points within his field of specialisation.

BRIAN BONNER

Brian Bonner was born on 27 February 1917 in the townland of Meenawarra, two miles from the village of Culdaff in Co. Donegal. Following his primary education at Ballyharry N.S., the Salesian College, Pallaskenry and Shrigley College, Macclesfield, he found employment in Dublin as an accountant. In his spare time, he visited the National Library, the State Paper Office in Dublin Castle and the Public Record Office, making notes in pencil in a large blue ledger. These handwritten pages formed the basis of the trilogy of Inishowen history he planned to publish; it was a labour of love and as the work increased, he found that even his lunch hour was taken up with research. Once he examined the British Parliamentary Papers, he discovered a wealth of material about his native peninsula that few historians had uncovered. In 1969, Brian contacted Donegal Historical Society and presented an extract from his research to the Editor of *Donegal Annual,* Fr. Paddy Gallagher, also a noted historian who published an article under the title "Distilling - illicit and otherwise in Inihowen". Brian was overwhelmed with the positive response from his readers and in 1970, he submitted a second paper on a subject close to his heart - Early Christian history entitled, "Sidelights of the Parishes of Culdaff and Cloncha". Within two years, he had found a Dublin publisher, Foilseacháin Náisiúnta Tta. (FNT) eager to bring his work to a national audience, with the support and encouragement of a close friend and Irish scholar, Breandan MacCnaimhsighe. In 1972, without any fanfare, Brian's first book, *Our Inishowen Heritage, The Parishes of Culdaff and Cloncha* was available in the bookshops. By1974, FNT published Brian's second book, *Where Aileach Guards,* followed in 1975 by *That Audacious Traitor.* It was a dream fulfilled and the trilogy he envisaged was a reality.

In 1984, a paperback edition of *Our Inishowen Heritage* appeared under the imprint of the LImerick based Salesian Press Trust, Followed in 1991 by a hard-back version published by Pallas Publications, also from Limerick. With some additional material, Brian added three appendices, one relating to a community study of Culdaff and the others containing documentation on the assassination of Norton Butler together with a poem by Culdaff poet Séamas Mac Reannacháin.

Sean Beattie

PREFACE

THE FORMATIVE forces which have created and enriched the cultural heritage and traditional way of life of any long-established and distinctive community are the work of many generations. The mature and well-balanced members of such a group of people will, in each generation, treasure and safeguard the culture and tradition of their ancestors. All that is best is eagerly retained and dearly cherished. Each successive generation will make its own contribution and it will, consequently, hand on an augmented and enhanced cultural heritage to the people of the future.

The person fully in touch with life in the peninsula of Inis Eoghain knows how rich is the culture of its inhabitants. Here is a tapestry complex, ornate and variegated. It has been a long time in the making. Many were the hands that held the woof, many were the fingers that spun the weft and many, many were the generations that operated the treadle of the weaving loom—a treasure beyond price.

The lover of Inis Eoghain notes, however, with concern and even trepidation, that all which is distinctive of the "island of Eoghan" is now in danger of extinction. Modern communications are creating among its people a new and superficial sense of values. There is a great danger that the old and precious order of things will be rejected. A new and materialistic culture devoid of spiritual values may be substituted. The community of Inis Eoghain will thus become part of that pagan, de-Christianised society which is a disturbing feature of the present day elsewhere.

This book is written to let the people of Inis Eoghain know something of their past. It is aimed to make them aware of the achievements, the sufferings and the heroism of their ancestors. These helped to mould them and to make them what they are. The example of the past generations will, it is hoped, help them to retain a true sense of values and so stimulate a better informed line of action in the community of to-day.

The earnest hope is that the present inhabitants of Inis Eoghain will become more fully aware of their rich inheritance and appreciate adequately its great and unique character. They will then, no doubt, take steps to restore what has been lost and retain, from deep conviction, what is best in their traditional mode of life. A renewed and dynamic community will be the result. Inis Eoghain will thus be able to make a major contri-

1

bution to the whole Irish nation in the coming years, as it did so effectively once before, in the period following the introduction of Christianity.

PREFACE TO SECOND EDITION

The present demand for a second edition of this book highlights the marked change towards local history which has taken place over the past two decades. In the early sixties the person engaged in field-work relative to local history was regarded as somewhat eccentric and was consequently dismissed with a charitable nod as a "duine le Dia". Nowadays the interest in ones roots is as strong among the people of the area as it is in the visitor from abroad.

This new edition is substantially the same as the original apart from a 1982 study of the parish of Culdaff and two documents relative to the assassination of Norton Butler. There are also a few minor corrections of printer's errors, a more detailed index and an updating of census information.

PREFACE TO THE THIRD EDITION

The continuing demand for this work has induced the publishers to issue a third edition. At their request the author has updated as relevant and has also made emendations in the light of further research. A 'List of Protestant Householders' for 1740 has also been added. Otherwise the original edition remains intact.

DESCRIPTION OF
CULDAFF AND CLONCHA

THE PENINSULA of Inis Eoghain lies at the extreme northern tip of the country and is bounded on the east and west respectively by the Foyle and the Swilly. On the north-eastern end are situated the parishes of Culdaff and Cloncha.

The parish of Culdaff has a total of 20,089 acres, divided into 25 townlands. The townland of Ballymagaraghy is divided between the parishes of Culdaff and Moville. The Culdaff portion lies along the sea. It is entirely detached from the remainder of the parish. A small stream which flows through the townland forms the boundary between the two parishes.

The parish of Culdaff is divided into two sections, *viz.*, the area surrounding the village of Culdaff and an area extending from Tirmacroragh to Drumaville and around to Cashel. Part of the townland of Carrowblagh belonging to the parish of Moville juts into Culdaff and extends as far as Kindroyhad.

The total acreage of the parish of Cloncha is 19,643, divided into 42 townlands. This parish begins at Redford-Glebe and extends in a narrow strip through Glacknadrummond, Knockergrana, Larrahirrel and Cloncha to Malin Head. It thus divides the parish of Culdaff in two sections.

The largest townland in the area comprising the two parishes is Moneydarragh, with 2,596 acres, and the smallest—excluding the *goirt*—is Drumballycaslin, consisting of 53 acres.

These two parishes are part of the county of Donegal. With the rest of Inis Eoghain they were at first incorporated into the diocese of Raphoe, but in 1261 A.D.[1] the peninsula was transferred to the see of Derry, where it has remained up to the present time.

The parishes are bounded on the north-east and north by the sea, on the west by Straghbreggagh and the parish of Donagh and on the south and south-east by Moville. A long and rugged coastline starts at Crodubh and extends for over twenty miles until it terminates at the southern tip of Straghbreggagh near Malin Town.

The physical lay-out of these two parishes is somewhat mixed geographically, as already indicated. In the post-Reformation period the Catholic authorities re-defined the area of each. The townlands of Redford-Glebe, Glacknadrummond, Larrahirrel, Knockergrana, Dunross and Cloncha were transferred from Cloncha to Culdaff. In exchange Culdaff yielded Glengad, part of Carthage and Lower and Upper Balleighan. Moville ceded part of Carrowblagh to Culdaff. The result was a more compact unit for the administration of each parish.

The Protestant Church retained the old divisions; hence the strange situation by which the two rectories lay within a half of a mile of each other—the Cloncha rectory at Redford-Glebe and the Culdaff rectory at Culdaff-Glebe in the neighbouring townland.

The earliest reference to the parish of Cloncha is found in the Ecclesiastical Taxation of Ireland in 1302 A.D.[2] Culdaff is first mentioned in 1367 A.D., by Colton.[3] The early references[4] to Cloncha indicate that the correct rendering was *Cluain Catha* —the meadow of Catha. In the case of Culdaff,[5] the references show that the place-name had a vowelised ending. An examination of the spot which gave rise to the name shows a sort of corner in the angle of a river lying between two fords. A suggested derivation is *Cuil da Ath*—corner between fords.

THE ORIGIN OF THE PARISHES

Ireland, after the arrival of St. Patrick, developed a distinctive form of Church government which lasted until the twelfth century. Then this country fell into line with the European form of ecclesiastical administration, which consisted of parish units. These merged into the diocese, with the bishop, as head, exercising full powers of orders and jurisdiction.

In the older system the monastery was the real centre of authority and each monastic unit had its own area of influence. Small hermitages and small monasteries were often founded under the direction of the large monastic centre. These smaller units remained within the sphere of control of the large monastery.

When the Irish Church was re-organised, the largest monasteries became the diocesan centres, the principal monastery in each local area became the parish centre and its area of influence the parish unit. This re-organisation was a gradual process and was probably generally established throughout the whole country in the early part of the thirteenth century.

The parishes of Culdaff and Cloncha date from the first half of the thirteenth century and each parish represents the area formerly under the control of a larger monastery.

The foundation at Cloncha had been a monastery of some standing. Over the centuries from its establishment it gradually extended its control from its own immediate area towards Malin Head. All the smaller monasteries in this area, including Greallach, were subject to it. In the re-organisation, Cloncha became the parish centre, giving its name to the whole area now known as Cloncha parish. Greallach[6] became a perpetual vicarage subject to the rector of Cloncha.

The parish of Culdaff is made up of two separate units, each of which was formerly the area of influence of an important monastic centre. These two monasteries were closely associated—hence the merging of the two areas into one unit. The district around Culdaff was within the control of the foundation known as St. Buadan's. The other portion was in the sphere of influence of the older monastery of Both Chonais at Carrowmore. Monks from Carrowmore had been associated with the Culdaff foundation, and the links between the two remained close throughout the centuries.

When the re-organisation took place in Inis Eoghain, Moville became the parish and Culdaff, embracing the two districts mentioned, became a perpetual vicarage[7] subject to the rector at Moville. This arrangement lasted until the seventeenth century, when Culdaff was first established as an independent parish. The name given to the parish was Culdaff, despite the fact that Both Chonais was the older and more important centre.

As already mentioned, each large monastery had smaller units founded by its monks and established at various points within its area of control. The implication is that one such hermitage was sited by the sea at Ballymagaraghy. This would explain the retention by Culdaff of this detached segment when the parish area was defined.

OLD DIVISIONS

The pre-plantation division known as the *tuath*[8] was Malin in the case of Cloncha. Culdaff was included in Bredach. The exact demarcation lines of these Gaelic divisions are not now clear.

Following on the forfeiture of the barony of Inis Eoghain, the English authorities divided the area for administrative purposes into four units called the "Manors"[9] of Elagh, Buncrana, Greencastle and Malin. This arrangement was made around 1609

5

—the year following the death of Cahir O Doherty, the ruler of Inis Eoghain.

Greencastle Manor included the parish of Culdaff and the narrow strip of land running from Redford to Cloncha townland in the parish of Cloncha. The Manor of Malin corresponded exactly to the remainder of the parish of Cloncha. Some doubts about the location of the island of Inistrahull caused its inclusion in the Manor of Greencastle.

ELECTORAL DIVISIONS

The Electoral Divisions were formed in the nineteenth century and are as follows: —

1. *Gleneely:* Aghaglasson, Aghatubrid, Baskill, Carrowmore, Cashel, Dristernan, Drumlee, Freehold. Kindroyhad, Moneydarragh, Ourt.

2. *Ardmalin:* Ardmalin, Ballygorman, Ballykenny, Bree, Dunagard, Inistrahull, Keenagh, Knockamany, Knockglass, Kullourt, Meedanmore, Umgall.

3. *Carthage:* Balleighan Lr. in Cloncha Parish, Balleighan Upper (*do.*), Balleighan Lr. in Culdaff Parish, Balleighan Upper (*do.*), Carthage, Glengad.

4. *Culdaff:* Cloncha, Culdaff, Culdaff-Glebe, Drumaville, Drumballycaslin, Dunross, Glacknadrummond, Gort Cloncha, Gort Culdaff, Knockergrana, Knock, Larrahirrel, Muff, Redford-Glebe, Templemoyle.

5. *Malin:* Ballagh, Ballellaghan, Ballycrampsey, Carrowmore, Drumavohy, Drumcarbit, Drumnaskea, Drung, Goorey, Killin, Lagg, Lougherbraghey, Magheryard, Norrira, Tullybeg, Tullymore, Urblereagh.

6. *Termone:* Ballyharry, Ballymagaraghy, Drumaville, Leitrim, Tirmacroragh, and four other townlands in the parish of Lower Moville.

GEOGRAPHICAL AND GEOLOGICAL FEATURES

The 40,000 acres which constitute the parishes of Culdaff and Cloncha include a long coastline, many lakes, a few rivers, much upland, extensive bogs and distinctive geological features. While there is some fertile land, there is a big proportion of untillable territory.

Coastline

The sea-bounded area starts at the base of Straghbreggagh adjacent to Malin Town and extends north-westward to Malin Head. From here it goes south-eastward to meet Moville parish at Ballymagaraghy. From Malin Town the coastline is low until Lagg is reached. Here the cliffs begin at Knockamany Bens and extend to the bay at Kullourt. The elevated coast starts again at Ardmalin until Inverin Bay, where the cliffs again appear and extend through Polliffrin to Dunaldreagh. From Portmore to Malin Well the coast is low. At Ballygorman the cliffs again commence and extend as far as Portaleen, with a few small ports in between.

Along this section are the Bengorms, which rise steeply from the sea and present an awesome appearance when viewed from the top of the cliffs. Portaleen has a reasonably safe harbour. From this point the cliffs again commence, passing the Claggan Bens until Bunagee is reached. Culdaff Bay is spacious and is at times a safe anchorage for ships. The rugged high coastline commences again and extends to Ballymagaraghy, with ports such as Portawad, Termone and a few smaller ones here and there along the coast. To appreciate fully the impressive coastline one must travel by boat from Malin Head to Moville.

Straghbreggagh is a large bay with a narrow entrance to the sea. The tides are rapid and there are many dangerous rocks. Large vessels avoid this hazardous area.

At the extreme northern tip of the area is Polliffrin, or Hell's Hole. A frightening, yawning chasm extends into the land for over ninety yards, with a width of about three. At the land-end is a cavern through which the agitated waves pass and return. The cliffs to each side rise over a 100 feet from the water.

A journey round the coast from Malin to Malin Head and thence to Ballymagaraghy is a pleasant and exhilarating experience for the discerning tourist and the nature-loving resident. On a clear day, in a north-easterly direction, can be seen the island of Islay, the Paps of Jura and other areas of Scotland. Seawards, further east, Fair Head in Antrim and Rathlin Island are visible.

A Decade of Lakes

In Dunagard near Malin Head there is the sacred lake called Cruckalough and on the borders of Carrowmore and Lougherbraghey is situated Lochbellthick. Between Drumlee and Dristernan is Drumlee Loch and between Drumlee and Carrowblagh there is the mysterious lake called Callybear. In Leitrim is found Effish Lough and on the borders of Leitrim and Carrowblagh, the Black Lough.

On the southern tip of Culdaff, on the border between Culdaff and Moville, there are situated two lakes, Loch Fad and Loch-na-Stackan. The first-named is a sheet of pure water surrounded by bogland. Four townlands converge in the centre of Loch Fad: Moneydarragh, Tullyalley, Tullynavin and Carrickmaquigley. Loch-

7

na-Stackan, a grass-grown shallow lake, lies on the borders of Moneydarragh and Tullyalley.

On the borders of Leitrim and Lecamy, to the left of the road between Bellnacrea and Falmore, lies a small sheet of water also called Loch-na-Stackan. One lake has disappeared. A record of the seventeenth century shows the existence of a lake in Glacknadrummond, near where this townland meets Redford-Glebe. No trace of this lake can now be found.

Rivers

Owing to the short distance to the sea from any part of this area, there are no rivers of note. The river known variously as the Gleneely River and the Culdaff River rises at Crucknanoneen and flows into the bay at Culdaff near to Bunagee. This river was formerly known as the Deel and it gave the district of Gleneely—*Gleann Daoiligh*—its name. There are also the Ballyboe River, which flows through Drumcarbit into the bay of Straghbreggagh, and the Keenagh River, which empties into the bay at Kullourt. There are, in addition, many streams, and as an indication of this the word *sruthan* occurs often in place-names here.

Mountains

The visitor who approaches from the Glackmore side will first enter Culdaff at the elevation called Crucknanoneen. From here to his left he can see Clonkeen and on the north side Carthage mountain is visible. Further on there is Glengad mountain, with its summit known as the Cruach. The elevations known as Knockamany and Knockbrack lie nearer to the northern portion. Finally, we have the Ardmalin ridge at the extreme north. The whole area has many other elevations of varying heights. Apart from rough grass and heather all these elevations are bare and exposed. In no case is the elevation high enough to justify the name of mountain. Indeed the Irish word *sliabh* is not used at all in this area.

Bogs

Nature was indeed very generous in allocating bogland to this northern outpost. For unnumbered generations the fuel for heating and cooking was produced in the extensive bogs found in almost every area. In the course of cutting turf, many tree trunks have been found. Fir was found most frequently and oak less so. Yew has been found on rare occasions. These trunks were used for roofing houses and for firewood.

The presence of these remains of trees is evidence of the existence here in a remote past of great forests of fir and oak. It is worthy of note that at Malin Head, where no trees can now grow, large tree trunks have been found buried in the bogs close to the edge of the sea. A major climatic change has evidently taken place since pre-historic times.

The great increase in the population from 1750 A.D. onwards augmented the demand for turf to such a degree that almost all the bogs were cut out. The residents now have to use an alternative type of fuel or go outside the parishes to cut turf.

Rock Formation

The geological map[10] of the area shows quartzite at Malin Head, sand dunes at Lagg, schist in a belt from Glengad to Straghbreggagh Bay, crana quartzite in the area from Portaleen to Culdaff Bay and extending to Malin, limestone in veins extending from Culdaff through Dunross, Glacknadrummond, Cloncha, Larrahirrel and Cashel to Carndonagh, and slate in an area extending westwards from Dunmore. Grits are shown in the district from Dunmore to Termone Bay, extending westwards through Gleneely.

The Culdaff limestone is for the most a typical coarsely-crystalline marble, with large crystals of black calcite. Sometimes pebbles of quartz occur in it. In the area adjacent to the village of Culdaff the dark rock contains in some places radiating, vein-like marks of white calcite.

Part of the rock formation at Dunglass in Redford-Glebe is worthy of special mention. The rocks at this point dip very steeply, and are beautifully exposed on the wave-washed face at the bottom of the cliff. The series is thinly bedded, and bed after bed is graded. They *young* consistently to the north-west, except in one intercalated slab, that measures two feet across and fifteen feet along the strike, before it is lost inland under soil. In this particular slab there are many graded beds and for the most part they young to the southeast, in opposition to the rule that holds in the rocks on either side. There is sufficient marginal folding in the slab to make it self-evident that there has been inversion at some time, and the question arises as to whether the inversion occurred upon the sea bottom or, later, during the folding that has steeply tilted the sediments as a whole. The former alternative appears to be demonstrated by the occurrence of veins of sand injected across the bedding of the inverted slab. It seems necessary to suppose that the slab was turned over and its cracks injected with quicksand on the sea bottom. The magnitude of the phenomenon and the absence of accompanying landslip debris point to an earthquake as responsible for the disturbance.

A point of particular interest here is that in prehistoric times the tide met between Culdaff Bay on the east and Straghbreggagh Bay on the west. This low neck of land is now overlaid with peat, but is has a deeper stratum of sand, silt and gravel. The area to the north consisted of an island—hence the reference to *Oilean na Malann* which is made at times in older records.

At Dunmore in Redford-Glebe are found slates, which have been quarried for various purposes. There is also a good quarry for building stones at Tirmacroragh. Limestone was quarried extensively for lime in Glacknadrummond and elsewhere up to recent years, but the burning of limestone in local kilns has now ceased.

The visitor to Malin Well shore will notice vast quantities of pebbles. Here are found agate, coral, cornelian, jasper and opal. In the past these stones were polished and used in the making of ornaments such as necklaces, rings and seals. There is material here for a profitable souvenir industry. Coral is also found elsewhere along this coastline.

The island of Inistrahull is a place of special geological interest.[11] The rock formation is entirely different from that on the mainland of Inis Eoghain. The Inistrahull formation is composed of Lewisian gneiss. It bears a close resemblance to the Archaean rocks of Sutherlandshire and is the same as the Lewisian outcrop of the Rhinns of Islay.

Towns

The natural tendency among the people here was to build their dwelling houses in groups known as *bailte*, hamlets. Examples of these natural growths can be seen at Ballymagaraghy, Ardmalin and Glengad. Such groups of houses developed in a haphazard and unplanned manner. The wags here in the earlier part of this century told how beggars doing their rounds in Ballymagaraghy often called two or three times on the same house because of the confused building pattern !

Two villages, however, developed on a planned basis, Malin and Culdaff. Each of these grew up in the eighteenth century and each was built adjacent to the landlord's house. The landlord in each case organised the building for his tenants.

MAP OF INIS EOGHAIN

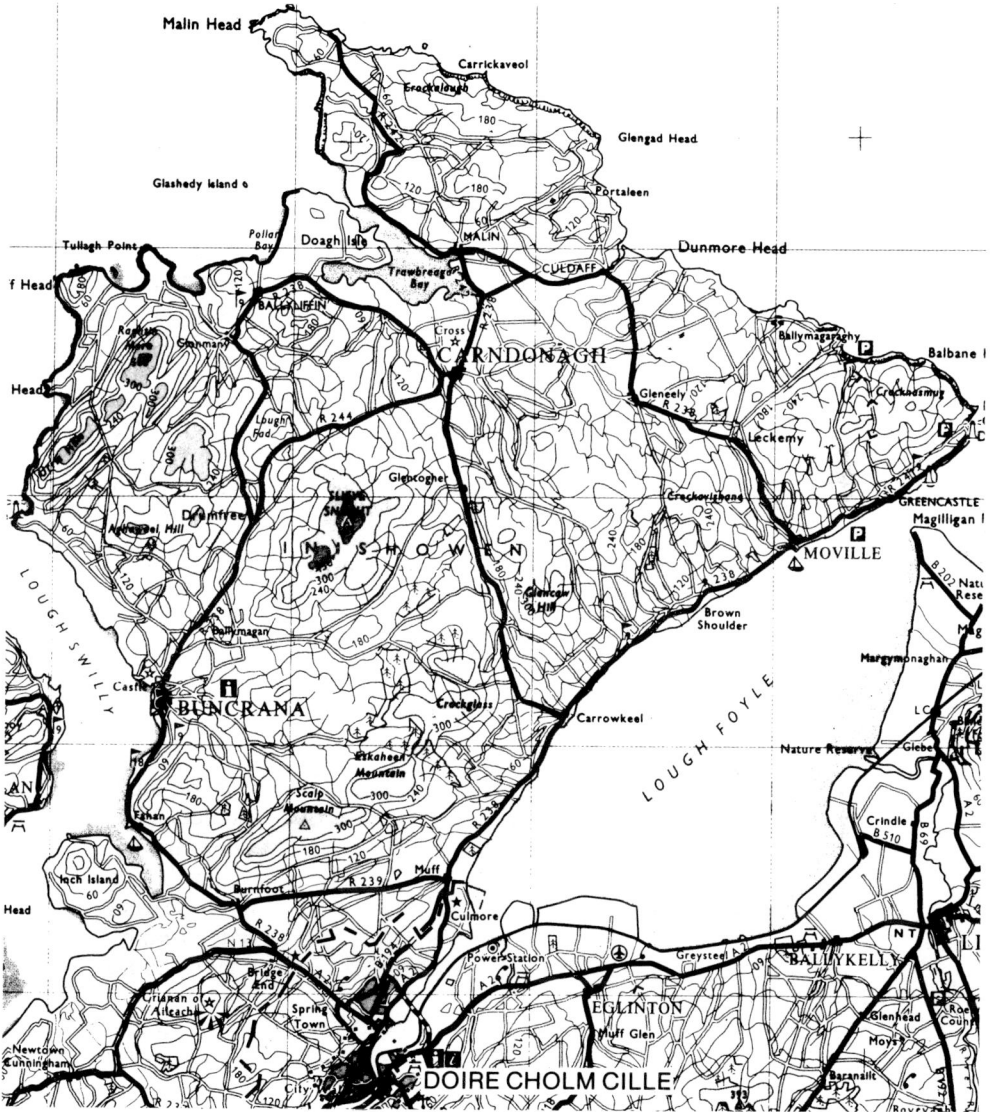

Malin Head

Carrickaveol

Erackalough

180

Glengad Head

Glashedy Island

120

180

Portaleen

Tullagh Point

Pollan Bay

Doagh Isle

MALIN

Dunmore Head

f Head

BALLYLIFFEN

Trawbreaga Bay

CULDAFF

Cross

CARNDONAGH

Ballymagaraghy

Balbane

Rockstown

Clonmany

Head

Gleneely

Crackavanny

Lough Fad

R 244

Leckemy

GREENCASTLE

Glencoghe

Drumfree

SLIEVE SNAGHT

I N I S H O W E N

Crockalishane

Magilligan

Nature Reserve

Mindoel Hill

MOVILLE

300

240

Glencole Hill

Brown Shoulder

LOUGH SWILLY

Ballymagan

Margymonaghan

Castle

Crockglass

LOUGH FOYLE

BUNCRANA

Carrowkeel

Nature Reserve

Glebe

Crckaheel Mountain

Scalp Mountain

300

Crindle

B 510

Fahan

300

Inch Island

60

180

120

Muff

R 239

Head

Burnfoot

R 239

Culmore

NT

BALLYKELLY

Power Station

Greysteel

LI

Grianan of Aileach

Bridge End

Spring Town

EGLINTON

Glenhead

Newtown Cunningham

City

DOIRE CHOLM CILLE

Muff Glen

Moys

Bovenagh

11

Malin, situated in the townlands of Carrowmore and Drum-carbit, is sited at the entrance to the Harvey estate and close to Straghbreggagh Bay. The roads from Culdaff to Malin Head and from Carndonagh to Glengad pass through this town. The town itself is built around a well-kept green, which gives it a distinctive and pleasant appearance.

The general appearance of this town reflects credit on the original planners—the Harvey family—and on the present inhabitants, who have maintained a high standard of order and tidiness. Malin has twice secured first place in its own category in the Tidy Towns competition run by Bord Failte, and in 1970 it secured first place in all Ireland.

Culdaff is built around the site of the old monastic foundation of St. Buadan and on the banks of the Culdaff river. The roads from Gleneely to Malin and from Gleneely to Glengad pass through this village. It is located in the townland of Culdaff.

The population data[12] for the two villages are set out in the following table:

YEAR	CULDAFF	MALIN	YEAR	CULDAFF	MALIN
1821	—	307	1891	106	105
1841	135	205	1901	110	114
1851	136	244	1911	104	129
1861	100	200	1951	83	100
1871	113	189	1956	96	105
1881	—	156	1961	108	164

1. *Medieval Religious Houses Ireland*, Hadcock and Gwynn, P.67.
2. *Calendar of Documents Ireland, 1302-1307.*
3. *Acts of Archbishop Colton's Visitation of Derry, 1367.*
4, 5, 6. *Calendar of Papal Registers, 1417-1486.*
7. *Analecta Hibernica*, Vol. 12—The O Kane Papers: Bishop Montgomery's Survey of Derry diocese, *circa* 1605.
8. *Book of Inishowen*, H. P. Swan.
9. MS.14, C.9, State Papers. Royal Irish Academy.
10. *Proceedings of the R.I.A.*, Vol. XLII: "The Metamorphic Rocks of Inishowen, Co. Donegal," William J. McCallien.
11. *Geol. Mag.*, LXVII, P.542: "The Gneiss of Inishtrahull, County Donegal," W. J. McCallien.
12. *Census of Population.*

2
TRACES OF THE PAST

ANYONE ACQUAINTED with the parishes of Culdaff and Cloncha cannot fail to notice the numerous monuments of different kinds which dot the landscape. Everywhere, to the discerning eye and to the enquiring mind, is evidence of the older civilisations which existed here since man, in the Neolithic Age, first set foot in this part of Inis Eoghain.

The people of these parishes, on the whole, have had a great reverence for these relics of the past. Their survival over the centuries is confirmation of this. The Irish in general have always had a profound regard for the last resting-place of their dead—mixed, no doubt, with a superstitious fear that ill-luck may follow interference with any ancient stone or fort. Around the firesides in the winter evenings many tales are told of the evils which befell the greedy farmer who, to clear his land, removed an old grave or some other relic. Crops failed, cattle died and illness befell the farmer himself or the members of his family. The moral was clear: respect the relics of the past. Whatever the motivation, most people did so.

Nevertheless, many monuments of the past in our area have perished. The ravages of time and the greed and ignorance of a minority have done much damage. Over the past century we have evidence of the disappearance of old graveyards, standing stones and other monuments.[1] It is gratifying to note that public opinion is against such vandalism and serves as a useful deterrent. These monuments serve to remind people that they are heirs of an ancient civilisation. There is an obligation on all to preserve the monuments as did past generations. As superstitious fears cease to influence it is important that the present and future generations are fully aware of the cultural and historical value of these monuments, so that respect for them will ensure their continued survival.

The earliest colonists came to a land of forests and marshes. Drainage has changed profoundly the face of the lower areas since the days of Neolithic man. The first inhabitants lived along the coast and in the higher areas. For religious rites and the burial-places of their leaders the tops of hills were chosen. Hence the presence of so many monuments on the elevated areas. One ridge may be particularly noticed: the plateau stretching from

13

Caragh Hill to Deen.[2] The abundance of monuments here suggests an area of particular importance to the early settlers. One can safely assume that we have here to-day only a remnant of the original monuments.

Despite the richness of the two parishes in archaelogical remains, it is disappointing to note that very few finds have been recorded. This may mean that there is much yet undiscovered or alternatively that many finds were made by people who did not perceive their real significance. Much, no doubt, went unrecognised during the period of intensive cultivation in the last century, when the population was at its maximum.

BURIAL MOUNDS

There are two kinds of burial mounds found in this country. Where the mound is of earth it is known as a tumulus; if it is built of stones the name cairn is applied. These mounds may be chambered or unchambered. The last-named will usually contain a cist wherein the remains will repose. This cist is a box-like construction of stone slabs.

The cists are of two kinds. The short ones are two or three feet across and are square, while the long ones are two feet wide by six feet long. In the long cists the remains are extended full length while in the short ones they are found in a crouched position. The short cists belong to the Bronze Age and generally the long ones are of a later date. They belong to a period following the end of the Bronze Age and extending into the early Christian era. However, some long ones may refer to the Neolithic Age.

In dealing with cairns care should be taken to avoid confusion with recently formed heaps of stone arising out of the common Irish custom of placing a stone when passing the location of some notable event. Again, where a standing stone was placed in the middle of a field farmers placed around it loose stones collected from the area. Over a period a substantial collection of stones was formed, to which the name cairn was given. The cairn shown on the Ordnance map for Drumaville, Culdaff, is probably an example of the cairn formed by a collection of stones off the surrounding area.

Cairns are found at Cashel, Killin, Knockglass and Umgall. Burial mounds are found along the stream which flows through the south-western section of Lougherbraghey. This area is regarded with respect by the inhabitants. It would seem to have been the site of an old pagan burial-ground and has yet to be fully examined. It has not been established whether the mounds are chambered or not or whether in fact they really are of a megalithic structure.

A few years ago, while widening the road through Lagg, workers found four cist-graves side by side. In each was a crouched skeleton.

At Stragilla in Moneydarragh there is beside a stream a spot which is regarded with respect. Here is a holly-bush and a flat stone. It is probably an old burial site.

" BRU " AND " BRUION "

These terms occur often in place-names throughout the whole country. The term *bruion* is more frequently found. Both words have roughly the same meaning—a royal residence, a great habitation, a house of public hospitality. In more recent times the story-teller has tended to apply the word *bruion* to a fairy palace, as the people believed that the old forts were the dwelling-places of the fairies. The good *seanchai* localised his tale and often the word used in the story was applied to a local site by his listeners.

In the townland of Templemoyle there is a hill called Cruckavreen—*Cnoc na Bruine* ? Here was sited, no doubt, an old fort or residence of some kind.

The terms *bru* and *bruion* go back to the pre-Christian era.

CIRCULAR BUILDING AT BALLELLAGHAN

This primitive structure is roughly rectangular in shape and measures eight feet by five feet. In one wall is a small door about one and a half feet wide and three feet high. In the other side is a small window. It is built of dry masonry up against an overhanging rock. Within, at the base of the rock, is a rough bench of stones, which served the occupant as a seat by day and a bed by night. The roof consists of long stone slabs, which slope down radially from the rock. A hole is left in the top centre to serve as a chimney.

Tradition states that *circa* 1630 A.D. this cell was inhabited by a hermit called Cathal Dubh O Dochartaigh. The name " Friar's Cell " is often applied to it by the local people. The Black and Tans damaged the structure during a raid—perhaps the I.R.A. had used it as a hiding place for arms.

" GRIANAN "

The basic meaning of this word is " a sunny spot ". It is a derivative of the word *grian*, " sun ". In a topographical sense it means a royal seat, a regal residence, a summer palace. The word is found frequently in place-names. In our area Grianan at Ourt and Dun an Ghrianain, the old name for Redford-Glebe, are the only examples recorded.

" CLOCHAN "

In place-names this term may mean a row of stepping-stones across a river, a stone castle, or a stone house of bee-hive shape. The bee-hive-shaped house is found frequently along the west and south-west of the country, and is at least as old as the first century of the present era. We have Clochan at Carthage and Cloghandubh at Kullourt Bay.

MEGALITHIC TOMBS

The chief feature of this type of tomb is the size of the stones used in its construction. Originally these stones were covered with soil or pebbles, which gave the whole the appearance of a great mound or cairn. These monuments are variously called giant's grave, cloghogle and *Leaba Dhiarmada agus Ghrainne.*

There are two main groups, gallery graves and passage graves. The former is characterised by a long, narrow chamber in which the burials were placed. The gallery graves may be sub-divided into court cairns, southern wedge-shaped galleries and northern wedge-shaped galleries.

Passage graves consist of a burial chamber which is entered by a long, narrow passage, the whole being covered by a round mound usually surrounded by a kerb.

The gallery graves of the court-cairn type are neolithic and are found mainly in the northern part of the country. The passage graves are of a later date.

The more usual burial rite in the Irish tombs of the megalithic type was cremation, though other kinds of burial are also found. This kind of tomb can be regarded as one of the earliest signs of colonisation in Ireland. It is almost the only sign left of the first arrivals over four thousand years ago.

There is also the portal dolmen, which is a tomb of simple construction. The essential feature is a number of upright stones capped by a large st ne.

The area under discussion has many tombs. Single-chambered ones are found at Carthage, Drumaville-Malin, Templemoyle and Drumcarbit. Multiple-chambered ones are seen at Muff, Cashel, Drumaville-Malin, Larrahirrel, Baskill, Knockglass and Umgall. There is a giant's grave in Aghaglasson. This grave is surrounded by a circle of stones laid in the ground.

16

At Ballagh there was a sort of dolmen which is described as a large coffin-shaped stone resting on three uprights. A local family, who required the stones for building, destroyed this monument about 50 years ago.

OGHAM MONUMENT

" Maghtochair,"[3] writing *circa* 1860, states that there was at that time an ogham monument in the parish of Culdaff. The stone was ornamented by a circle, within which was incised a cross of a type found in the Book of Kells. The monument had the stem line and the four different groups of incised strokes: lines to the left, lines to the right, longer strokes crossing obliquely, and small notches on the edge itself. The inscription was read as: *nocati maqui maqui ret*—"(this is the stone) of Nocat the son of Mac Rethe ". The subsequent history of this stone is unknown. It cannot be traced in the area to-day. One report indicates that it was in the vicinity of the old church at Claggan but was later taken away.

RING FORTS

There are two kinds of forts to be found throughout the country, hill-forts and ring-forts. The type found in our area is the last-mentioned and is the only one with which we are concerned.

The ring-fort may be simply defined as a space surrounded by a bank and fosse. The bank was usually formed by the soil obtained by digging the fosse, but it may also be partly or wholly of stone. The stone bank often occurs where the fosse is quarried out of the solid rock. Consequently, the ring-forts may be subdivided into earthen and stone-built.

In Irish the names *lios* and *rath* were applied to earthen forts while the words *cathair* and *caiseal* meant stone forts. More accurately, the word *lios* referred to the inner enclosed area on which the house was built, while the term *rath* was applied to the surrounding earthen wall.

Within the district under discussion the *rath* is found only once. A hill in Ballagh is known as Knockrath (*Cnoc Ratha*)— the hill of the fort. *Cathair* does not occur, while the term *caiseal* is found twice only. The word *lios* is found more frequently. The following examples may be noted: Liscomfort in the townland of Drumcarbit, Lisdarrigan in the townland of Cloncha, Listarrigan in the townland of Culdaff-Glebe, Listallaghan in the townland of Ourt, The Lios in the townland of Knock.

17

Investigations show that forts were in use in Ireland from the Late Bronze Age. They were used as dwelling-places and were fortified as a means of protection against wild animals and robbers. Forts were occupied in some cases up to the eleventh century. Indeed, the one site could have been used successively for upwards of 2,000 years. The date of any particular fort can only be determined by on-the-spot examination.

Forts were located as follows: Drumballycaslin (1), Carrowmore (2), Balleighan Lower (1), Cashel (2), Drumlee (1), Leitrim (1), Ourt (1), Baskill (1), Aghaglasson (1), Aghatubrid (1), Dristernan (2), Culdaff (2), Glacknadrummond (1), Templemoyle (2), Goorey (1), Knock (1), Drumcarbit (1), Culdaff-Glebe (1), Cloncha (1), Drumaville-Malin (1), Tullymore (1).

A stone fort is found at Cashel, while a fort at Carrowmore is known as Caiseal Ban. The fort at Tullymore was called Cranagh Fort. The area around abounded in trees, evidently.

SOUTERRAINS

The souterrain is an artificial cave or set of caves. It is often found in association with a fort and dates back to the Late Bronze Age. Souterrains were built up to the early Christian period.

These artificial caves were used as a place of refuge from attack. Some were used as habitations and others as storage depots. Indeed, any souterrain could have been used at different times for all three purposes.

The caves were cut out of the rock, usually of a soft type, and different chambers were formed. These were connected by tunnels or narrow entrances.

To date, three have been found in our area — at Baskill, at Kullourt and at Norrira.

The souterrain at Baskill was discovered in 1863, when men were quarrying in the area. This one has four compartments. The entrance is through a circular opening, three feet in diameter, leading downwards from the surface. The opening was sealed with a flag-stone. The first cave, of irregular shape, is ten feet long, seven feet broad and five feet high. A narrow entrance of about two feet in height and of similar width leads into a second cave 30 feet long, ten feet wide and six feet high. The entrance into the other caves is similar. No remains of any kind whatsoever were found.

The souterrain at Ballylin, Norrira, is made up of five circular chambers each ten feet in diameter and connected by tunnels. All were cut out of the soft rock.

The one at Kullourt was cut out of a small hillock close to the area. It is at present blocked by large stones.

STONE CIRCLE AT GLACKNADRUMMOND

The hill-top on which the stone circle stands is popularly known as the "Mass Hill". Its correct and older name was Banchan.[4] There is a commanding view from the summit. Carndonagh, Straghbreggagh Bay, Malin and Glengad meet the eye along the horizon. The open Atlantic and, if the day is clear, the hills of Scotland complete the panoramic view.

This spot about 4,000 years ago was the scene of intensive activity over a considerable period. A large group of men were at work erecting circles of large stones, which they placed in the ground at intervals, according to a set plan. Around, later, were built houses of wood, where the political, cultural and religious leaders could dwell. For the civilisation which existed at the time in North Inis Eoghain, this was a centre of great importance and all the people in the area looked to it for leadership and direction. It is estimated that there were here formerly four concentric elliptical formations of upright stones, numbering· 30 stones in all. In 1815 [5] there were 12 of these stones still in position; ten remained in 1891[6] and to-day there are only eight left. The inner circle had a diameter of about 60 feet.

Local farmers who required stones for particular purposes removed some of them. As the demand for land increased in the early part of the last century, an attempt was made to reclaim this hill-top and a number of the stones was buried. This was the easiest way to remove the stones, which the owner regarded as obstructions. Many finds of archaeological value were made but the undiscerning failed to report them. Much valuable evidence has therefore been lost to us.

What exactly did these circles of stone mean and for what were they used? Authorities[7] date the erection of this type of circle early in the Bronze Age and state that they had a ritual significance in the religion practised at that time. One authority[8] sees in the arrangement of the stone circle an orientation towards Farragan Hill about five miles away and a connection with the line of the sunset on the day of the summer solstice, when from the circle the sun will be seen setting over the summit of the hill mentioned. Does this indicate that these early inhabitants were sun worshippers?

Banchan was also a favoured burial place for the dead of this early period and graves have, in the course of the years, been found here.[9] In these were found earthen urns presumably containing the ashes of the dead. The urns mouldered away quickly, however, and none has survived. There is a possibility that these urns were really food vessels placed in the graves of the dead.

STANDING STONES

This type of monument consists of a stone placed upright in the ground. The terms *gallan, dallan* and *liagan* are applied in Irish to stones of this type, while in English we have monolith and menhir. It is difficult, without investigating in each case, to define the use or age of any stone.

These monuments date from the Bronze Age up to the Early Christian Era and were to some extent forerunners of the stone crosses which are a feature of Ireland in the Christian period.

Their uses are various. Some mark burial spots, some mark the location of great events and others indicate the lines of an ancient roadway or the gate-posts of the entrance to an old fort. In later times some were erected as scratching stones for cattle. Again, some stones became the focus of a religious cult.

Within the parishes of Culdaff and Cloncha standing stones are found in the following places: Drumaville-Culdaff (1), Inistrahull Island (1), Norrira (2), Drumcarbit (1), Balleighan (1), Glengad (1), Tirmacroragh (1), Cashel (3), Knockergrana (1), Ballymagaraghy (1), Ballyharry (2), Gort at Muff (1), Redford-Glebe (1), Killin (1).

A standing stone at Ballyharry was removed by the farmer who owned the land.

The field on which the cairn and standing-stone were placed in Drumaville is known as the *leacht*. This Irish word means a grave mound or cairn. A number of years ago the farmer who owned the land decided to remove the cairn. When he had cleared the loose stones away he found a standing stone beneath the pile. He removed the stone and placed it in the wall at the end af the field, where it still stands. On the stone can be seen a rough drawing somewhat like a Celtic cross. It is not clear whether the cairn was part of the original *leacht*.

Stone alignments are found throughout the country. There is one example in the pair of standing stones at Ballymagaraghy.

The standing stone at Killin is in the centre of the great stone circle which is found on the top of Knockraw. The area around abounds in loose stones and it is clear that the circle was formed from stones collected in the surrounding hill. Up to recently, the local farmers were careful not to interfere with the circle.

STONE BUILDINGS

The word castle as used nowadays is defined as a " large fortified building or set of buildings, a stronghold". Within our area there was no building which justified the name of castle as defined. The terms *dun, lios, rath, caiseal* and *cathair* refer to a different type of structure.

The Irish word *caislean* means " castle", "fort," " stronghold". It is doubtful whether it has exactly the same meaning as the English word castle.

The word *caislean* is found a couple of times in the area. The townland of Drumballycaslin has traces of a large circular building which was evidently made of material other than stone. It was probably a very large fort. In Lower Balleighan is the site of a fort called Caislean an Naoimh.

The material used for house building by the ordinary people in our parishes was not of a durable nature until modern times. Earth and timber were evidently generally in use. As the cabins so formed fell into disuse, the ruins soon merged into the ordinary soil, and after a few years no trace remained.

Buildings of stone were rare and, consequently, where these occurred they were noted. A tower[10] is shown in the Malin area in certain seventeenth-century maps. There is a tradition that a castle stood on the site of Malin Hall. However, this is not substantiated by any record.

Some old maps show two towers at Culdaff, while the Montgomery Visitation of 1606 refers to a stone house near the church in Culdaff.[11] The Hearth Money Roll record from 1665 indicates the existence at Curt of a large house with three hearths. Here lived a man called John Bunbury.[12] All the other dwellings refered to had only one hearth.

THE SWEAT-HOUSE

The modern sauna bath had its equivalent in Ireland from the earliest times up to the last century. This form of steam bath was called in English " the Sweat House " and was used as a cure for rheumatism.

The bath was a small bee-hive-shaped house built of stone and with a very low entrance. A fire of turf was lit inside and kept burning until the whole interior was thoroughly heated. Then the remains of the fire were quickly cleared out and the patient, wrapped in a blanket, went in and sat down. The entrance was sealed up and a slight aperture left to admit air. The stones retained the heat and after some time the patient was taken out and dipped in a nearby stream. This treatment was repeated until the patient was well. After each treatment the patient got an intensive rub-down to restore warmth to his body. There are two sweat houses in our area; one between Tirmacroragh and Ballyharry at the Orable and the other on the hill at Dreenagh near Malin Town.

SITES OF EARLY COASTAL DWELLINGS

Around the coastal area of the northern part of Ireland there is abundant evidence in certain places of early settlements. Flints, middens and the foundations of round huts indicate that from the neolithic age onwards people lived close to the sea in colonies and depended on sea-foods for their sustenance. The middens are merely the places where the refuse was dumped. An examination shows that these middens contained bones, shells, old flints and bits of earthenware.

In the townland of Kullourt, a kitchen midden was found in conjunction with a souterrain. Among the finds were pieces of pottery and an urn.

A sort of shell-mound was found some years ago at Portaloran in Ballyhillin, in the townland of Ardmalin. Nearby is the site of an old church and burial ground.

RECORDS OF FINDS

Urns were found in the townland of Kullourt near Malin

Head. It is not clear whether these were food vessels or proper sepulchral urns.

A gold ornament—a small dress fastener—was found in 1853. It is stated to belong to the Late Bronze Age. This ornament was found by a farmer. While working on his land he found a flat stone and resting on it an object like a horse shoe. Without realising its value, he brought it to his house. It was shown to the neighbours and finally to a man of experience. On the advice of the latter the ornament was sent to the Royal Irish Academy, which gave the farmer a reward of £5 for the fibula.

While reclaiming land, a farmer in the townland of Redford-Glebe found a wooden sword. On taking it to his home in Meenawarra he left it in an outhouse and during the night it was stolen. It was never afterwards traced.

Bog-butter has been found at a spot in Culdaff-Glebe called Listarrigan.

An inscribed stone was found at the beginning of this century when digging a foundation on the island of Inistrahull. The stone, resembling a Brazil nut, was found at a depth of eight feet. On the flat side is inscribed a circle nine inches in diameter. Within this circle is a four-leafed pattern in the form of a cross, with expanding arms with curved sides. From the rim of the circle a shaft or staff design runs to the long end of the stone.

The inscribed cross suggests a Christian association. A memorial stone in Scotland bearing the same device has also the words *Petri Apostoli* inscribed. Had the device shown on both these stones a special meaning to the early Christian peoples who dwelt in Ireland and Scotland?

A similar stone was used elsewhere in Donegal as a "cursing stone". It is possible that it had the same use in Inistrahull for a time. It was probably brought here from Scotland, which is only thirty miles away. Its burial suggests the influence of a Catholic priest, who had it disposed of as an object of superstition.

———————————✠———————————

1. See Ordnance map, **1835.**
2. In the townlands of Knockergrana and Larrahirrel respectively.
3. *Inishowen*, "Maghtochair".
4. *Bainseachan:* pasture-land.
5. *Mason's Statistical, Survey,* 1816: "Culdaff and Cloncha," E. Chichester.
6. *Inis-owen and Tirconnell,* **William James Doherty.**
7. *Antiquities of the Irish Countryside,* Sean P. O Riordain.

23

8. *Royal Society of Antiquaries of Ireland, 1929:* "Culdaff Stone Circle," Vice-Admiral Boyle Somerville, C.M.G., F.R.S.A.I.

9. *Mason's Statistical Survey,* 1816: "Culdaff and Cloncha," E. Chichester.

10, 11. *Twixt Foyle and Swilly,* H. P. Swan.

12. Leslie's *Derry Clergy and Parishes* records a man named John Bun bury as rector of Clonmany and Donagh from 1630. Is this the mar who had property at Ourt?

24

3
INTRODUCTION AND DEVELOPMENT OF CHRISTIANITY

AN EXAMINATION of the evidence available shows that the area comprising the parishes of Culdaff and Cloncha was inhabited from 2000 B.C.[1]—that is, 2,500 years before Christianity reached Ireland. During this long period a pagan civilisation flourished, with its own distinctive religion. Traces of the temples still remain in the area. The beliefs of those early inhabitants and their form of worship cannot now be determined.

The introduction of Christianity here was a slow and uphill process. The old way of life and the pagan practices entwined with it were deeply entrenched. For generations both religions existed together and, indeed, the careful investigator will find in certain areas here traces of paganism in the beliefs and practices of the people at the present time.[2] And such, fifteen centuries after St. Patrick visited this corner of the island!

ST. PATRICK'S VISIT

In the course of his missionary journey, St. Patrick travelled northwards and came to Aileach, where he was received by Eoghan, son of Niall. With the approval and support of the ruler of Inis Eoghain, Patrick came into the peninsula to evangelise the people.

Tradition asserts that the missionary travelled along the west side of the peninsula, passing through Burnfoot, Fahan and Buncrana.[3] At Bun na Cille in the townland of Kinnego he stopped and founded a church at a spot still known as Sean-Domhnach. Later he went to Donagh, where he founded another church and left a bishop in charge.

Patrick then proceeded to the north-west, stopping probably at Carrowmore. Here was land owned by a brother-in-law of the Apostle. Then, if Colgan's suggestion is correct,[4] Patrick went to the present site of the old church at Cluain Catha. Here he founded a church which was known as Domhnach Catha. Patrick then proceeded to Cooley at Moville.[5]

While Patrick remained in the area which now corresponds to the parishes of Culdaff and Cloncha, he preached the Gospel to the residents. It is interesting to note that the first contact with Christianity in this area came, most probably, through Patrick himself. As the great missionary went his way, his words,

25

and the strange party which acccompanied him, must have left a vivid impression on the minds of the people here.

The pagan priests who watched the group pass and heard the reports of their strange doctrine felt no uneasiness. Was not their cult now secure after 25 centuries? The people were faithful and the Druidic grip very strong indeed. However, the seed sown that day by St. Patrick did not perish, but grew and increased like the mustard seed of the parable. Paganism was soon to meet its first challenge. The old order would fight long and valiantly, but Christianity was fated to be the victor.

ON THE NATIONAL LEVEL

Before examining the development of Christianity here in North Inis Eoghain, it is well to survey briefly the national progress in the introduction and spread of Christianity.[6] This will set in correct perspective progress in our own area.

The missionary activity of the fifth century was directed to the conversion of all the people, beginning with the leaders. The aim was to establish an organisation consisting of bishops and priests with definite areas of responsibility, on the lines of the countries of Western Europe. Persons who had taken monastic vows were introduced almost at the beginning, and these men often became the Gospel messengers to people in remote areas such as the north of Inis Eoghain.

In these early days the area governed by a bishop corresponded to the lands of a particular *tuath*. The ordinary was the spiritual head, with full authority in his area. However, the peculiar Irish way of life modified and soon tended to alter this manner of Church organisation.

By 550 monastic foundations had begun to establish a wide area of influence through new houses founded as off-shoots of the parent monastery. The abbot was head and he exercised full authority in both the spiritual and material order over all these scattered houses.

The monastic way of life so appealed to the Irish that, in addition to the great numbers of entrants, local people of means made grants of land to the monastery. A very close relationship developed between the laity and the monastic settlements. The monastery became the centre where people worshipped, where they were educated, where medical remedies were available and, finally, where a peaceful and blessed last resting-place was found.

The power and influence of the territorial bishopric declined

26

but did not entirely disappear. However, the monastic *paruchiae* continued to gain in power and influence up to the beginning of the twelfth century. In most cases the bishop was subject to the abbot and concerned only with the administration of sacraments reserved to the episcopal office.

As the lives of the great monastic founders such as Colm Cille and Columbanus show, the Irish were soon attracted to the ascetical life. Contemplation, prayer and fasting (the essentials of the spiritual life) were practised with great zeal by the monks. Many took to the heroic life, and they gave themselves whole-heartedly and with complete self-surrender.

The typical monastic establishment which evolved had its abbot, its bishops, its men of learning and its ordinary members, and there were also the men who were called " monks ". These were not men in vows and subject to a superior. They were in fact a sort of monastic tenants who held land and stock on a rental basis from the abbot. These men were married and the custom was to give the first-born son to the monastery for an ecclesiastical education. Was Maol Iosa, who entered the monastery of Both Chonais at seven years of age, the son of such a " monk "? It seems very likely.

The means of education provided by the monastery had been unknown in the pagan society which Christianity replaced. As a result, in the area surrounding a monastery an educated and literate laity evolved and so a very close relationship was established between the clergy and the people.

The early fervour of the Irish lasted over a century and a half but the beginning of the eighth century saw a decline. At no time did the practice of asceticism disappear, however. It merely suffered diminution.

The end of the eighth century saw a revival of spiritual fervour. The hermit who withdrew from the distractions of the world to find a proper environment for prayer and contemplation was always a feature of Ireland from the coming of Christianity. In the end of the eighth and during the ninth centuries the number of hermits increased in a marked manner. In the new awakening these men tended at times to form into small groups with the same ideals. The effect on the Irish Church as a whole was beneficial and the general level of spirituality was raised.

Ireland was now, however, to endure a reign of terror and destruction which was to interrupt the development of both the

Church and the State. For the 200 years from 800 A.D. Viking raids were to become a feature of Irish life. In 798 these barbarians, from their bases in the Western Isles of Scotland, began surprise raids on the coast of Ireland. As time passed, they grew bolder and advanced inland to raid the great monasteries. Finally they established bases in Ireland.

Inis Eoghain was raided by the Vikings on many occasions. One such raid was recorded in 919 A.D.[7] The monastery at Moville was plundered and burned in 812 A.D.[8] by a body of Danes who sailed up Lough Foyle. Many other, unrecorded raids took place in Inis Eoghain, no doubt.

The ascetical revival to which reference was made earlier had spent itself by the end of the tenth century. The disturbed state of the country arising from the Viking invasions was doubtless a major contributory factor. Nevertheless, Christianity was still a potent factor in Irish life.

The victory of Brian Boru over the Danes made possible the restoration of the Church as an organising factor in the country. Contacts with Western Europe were renewed and strengthened. New ideas began to permeate the country and churchmen in Ireland became more and more aware of the wide differences between the structure and practices of the Irish Church and those obtaining on the Continent.

The twelfth century was a time of reform and re-organisation in the Irish Church. Following the Synod of Rathbrasil in 1111 A.D. the reformers established dioceses and parishes. A number of the great monasteries became the bishops' seats and lesser monasteries became parish churches. In fact, the ecclesiastical organisation with which we are now familiar began to emerge. In 1152 a synod was held at Kells, where a papal legate, Cardinal John Paparo, presided. He had brought from Rome the *pallia* for four Irish archbishops, those of Armagh, Cashel, Dublin and Tuam.

CHRISTIANITY IN CULDAFF AND CLONCHA

The development at national level of Christianity between 450 A.D. and 1150 A.D. has been sketched in brief. Now attention can be directed to North Inis Eoghain, to determine how the general trend was reflected here.

The first contact with the Gospel here was through the direct action of Patrick himself. The small centres at Cluain Catha and Carrowmore helped, in conjunction with the churches at Donagh

Ecclesiastical divisions before British Occupation
(prior to 1610 a.d.)

1. Part of Cuil da Ath (part of Magh Bhile)
2. Part of Cluain Catha
3. Cuil da Ath, part of Magh Bhile
4. Na Minte—common to Cluain Maine & Teampall Mor
5. An Greallach, part of Cluain Catha
6. Inis na nOisri, part of Teampall Mor.

and Moville, to carry on the evangelisation of the northern portion of Inis Eoghain.

The period up to 550 A.D. can be regarded as the time of direct Patrician influence. In the three generations followings Patrick's death, the new religion began to permeate the society here. The pagan cult as an organised religion was almost supplanted.

A century and a half of intense monastic activity followed. Cluain Catha and Both Chonais at Carrowmore began to develop as great monastic foundations. Possibly one other centre was established further north. This was the period when the Columban influence began to manifest itself and to replace gradually the Patrician.

The foundations mentioned continued to have a powerful impact here during the eighth century, when there was a period of stagnation in the Irish Church. However, the end of the eighth century saw the beginning of a movement which was to have a profound effect on this area. The district we now know as the parishes of Culdaff and Cloncha was, during the centuries following 800 A.D., to become a great centre of monastic activity and the seat of many foundations.[9]

By the end of the eighth century Carrowmore had established a new site at Culdaff. Along the valley of the Deel from Cashel to Moneydarragh hermitages were founded. Further hermitages were sited in Ballyharry and Ballymagaraghy.

The same thing was taking place in the area beginning at Cluain Catha and extending out to Malin Head. The principal ones were at Greallach, Malin Well and Kullourt. There were many others.

The period from 800 A.D. saw at national level an awakening of strong religious fervour, with emphasis on the hermitage. This type of site began with one or a few who isolated themselves from human contact so as to attain the highest degree of spiritual contemplation possible. The wild, desolate and partially inaccessible area in the north of Inis Eoghain was the ideal environment and many monks came to find peace and solitude.

A survey of the whole peninsula shows that of the total known monastic sites in it, half were located in the area comprising the parishes of Culdaff and Cloncha. The effect on the life of all here was profound.

As one goes back in time he can see here an area of great intellectual activity, in which the laity were involved. The means of learning were available to all. Through the marvellous communication system which operated between the monasteries new ideas were interchanged. All Ireland was thus in contact and the result was a quickening of life at the spiritual, the intellectual and the cultural levels. The community of Culdaff and Cloncha participated to the full, and the result was a golden age not equalled before and not exceeded since.

Contact with western Scotland was maintained and missionaries from here assisted in the conversion of the Scots. St. Buadan's at Culdaff was closely associated with this work of evangelisation.

It is interesting to note that the cult of St. Patrick seems to have had no deep roots here. There was evidence of some devotion to him at Cruckalough in the townland of Dunagard, at Ballyharry and some association with him at Cluain Catha. However, the Columban influence was stronger, so that from the death of Colm Cille the people looked to the man from Gartan as the great father-figure.

The extension of monasticism here, as in the rest of Inis Eoghain, was largely the work of the disciples of Colm Cille. The parish of Cluain Catha had him as patron.[10] In the folklore and devotion of the people here Colm Cille remained up to the beginning of this century the great saint with the lovable human traits. He was a fellow Donegalman whom all took to their hearts.

St. Brigid, through the influence of the monasteries, became a saint to whom there was also a very special devotion. She was the refuge of all who were sick. Brigid was to the people here, up to recently, a living, vivid personality who had an attentive ear for the sick and the lonely.

The powerful and beneficent influence of Cineal Eoghain should be carefully noted. Eoghan had given Patrick his full support in the evangelisation of Inis Eoghain, and the descendants of Eoghan continued to help the development of Christianity here. In our area can be found strong evidence of the patronage of this powerful family in the centuries which followed the death of Eoghan, son of Niall.[11]

The Norse raids had harmful effects on the spiritual and intellectual life of the nation. While there is no direct evidence of the effects of raids in our area, it can be assumed that life here did not continue without some interruption. Nevertheless, there is evidence that monastic life continued to operate here up to the eleventh century[12] and perhaps later.

The re-organisation of the Irish Church in the twelfth century had its repercussions here early in the thirteenth century, when the parish pattern we know to-day was established.

Each parish had its rector, its vicar and its *airchinneach*. The last named was a layman who had the responsibility for the administration of the material affairs associated with the parish church. The vicar was a fully ordained priest who conducted the services. The rector was at times a layman and at times a priest.

An examination of the *Calendar of Papal Registers*[13] for the fifteenth century in respect of Culdaff and Cluain Catha shows a number of interesting points. Cluain Catha is mentioned as being subject to the canons of Derry. Indeed, all the available documents show a close association with Derry and in particular the monastery there.

The documents are addressed to various people for action. Two are directed to the abbot of Macosquin, a Cistercian foundation situated near Coleraine and founded in 1218 A.D. This monastery had been granted lands in Inis Eoghain at Kullourt and Burt.

A number of documents is directed to the abbot of Derry. This is understandable because of the pre-eminence of that monastery in this area. The Bishop of Derry is directed to act on only one occasion. Both these parishes were in his diocese.

THE BRITISH OCCUPATION

While the Normans and their followers had been in occupation of part of Ireland since 1170 A.D., this northern part of Inis Eoghain had remained unaffected until the beginning of the seventeenth century. As the year 1601 heralded the beginning of a new century, it seemed that the old order would continue without any interruption. People who stand at the threshold of change seldom are aware of the real significance of events at the time. Here also, no doubt, this principle was true and the residents were totally unaware of the great changes pending.

The English had already had greedy eyes on the lands here. The rebellion of Cathaoir O Dochartaigh provided the pretext for action and the whole area was annexed to the Crown. The church-lands became the property of the Protestant Bishop of Derry. In a few years the meaning of the annexation became evident to all the native Irish living in Culdaff and Cloncha.

By 1620 A.D. the churches at Lagg, Greallach, Culdaff and Cloncha, together with all the churchlands, were taken over by the Established Church. A Protestant rector was in residence in each parish. For the Catholic Irish it meant that the places of worship sanctified by over a thousand years of prayer were now in alien hands.

THE LAST MASS AT ST. BUADAN'S

As has been said, the people who live on the eve of change are rarely aware of the drastic alteration about to take place. Such was the case in the parish of Culdaff on a Sunday morning in May in the early part of the seventeenth century.

On that May morning the sun shone from a sky which was unmarred by cloud. A gentle wind blew from the southwest. It was just sufficient to cool somewhat the strong rays of sunshine which beat down on the landscape. The crops were appearing above ground. Wild flowers were blooming profusely. The occasional lowing of a cow, the buzz of a bee or the bark of a dog was the only sound heard. It was a morning of peace and beauty.

The people of the parish walked in groups on their way to early Mass at the spot between two fords—St. Buadan's of Culdaff. They came from Cashel, from Gleneely, Ballyharry and Ballymagaraghy, from Glengad and Ballycarron. Their feet trod the paths which their ancestors had worn even from the days when Buadan himself had fasted and prayed at the spot which was their destination today.

As these people walked their way they unconsciously felt that the general order of things which they now knew was as changeless as the sun in its course or as the waves which rolled ceaselessly to the shore at Culdaff. Nothing could interrupt the normal flow of events. The well-known trends of seasons, of birth and death, were accepted.

The many streams of people converge at the focal point. The sound of salutations in Irish can be heard as the people meet at the entrance to the church. As all kneel in readiness An tAthair Padraig O Cearnaigh[14] enters, takes his place at the altar and the Mass begins. The well-known and familiar ritual proceeds as on so many other occasions. The sermon is preached in mellifluous Irish. Yet this is a distinctive, unique and tragic occasion.

Sons and daughters of Culdaff, you are on the eve of great and terrible events. The link with your fathers is about to be broken.

The old order is changing. The Gael is about to give way to the Gall; the Celt must yield to the Saxon and the old religion to the new. This day you have attended the last Mass at St. Buadan's. The Mass will be replaced by a new, strange liturgy. The Bell of St. Buadan is sounding here for the last time.

For forty generations your forebears lived as freemen in this land. They loved its language, its culture and the faith of Patrick. For six generations your children and theirs will live in bondage. Land, language and culture will be lost, though all will retain deep in their hearts the faith of the wandering stranger who passed this way in the fifth century.

In the hills and in the glens, by the sea-shore and by hidden mountain stream, your people will meet in secret to hear the Mass and be renewed in faith.

As to-day you hear the *Ite Missa Est* and take your leave, you go for the last time. No more will you worship here. Return you will to this hallowed spot after death to leave your remains with those of your beloved kindred. This at least the usurping Saxon will permit.

Yet at a time in the distant future justice will be done. Many angry northern gales will beat against unyielding Dunmore. Many, many stormy waves will race to death on Culdaff strand. The time, nevertheless, will come when peace and justice will come in the fair land of Eire. Your descendants will come again to this spot by the river side. One in language and in culture with you, they will renew in the same Sacrifice their loyalty to the same faith as yours. They will profess again their allegiance to the faith that Patrick brought, the faith that mighty Eoghan embraced and that your spiritual father Buadan lived. Have patience, justice will be done.

THE PERIOD OF PENAL LAWS

The period from 1620 A.D. to 1780 A.D., spanning five generations, marked the era of Penal Laws for Catholics. The manner of life of the Catholic Irish in Culdaff and Cloncha was profoundly affected during those eventful years. The main provisions of the Penal Laws were:

1. All Catholic bishops were to leave the country. £50 reward was given to anyone securing a Catholic bishop.
2. No Catholic could own a horse worth more than five pounds.
3. Catholics were forbidden to go abroad for education and not allowed to have a school at home.

34

4. Attendance at the State Church was made compulsory on pain of a fine for each Sunday's absence.

5. An oath of supremacy acknowledging the British monarch as head of the Church was imposed on all holders of office in Church and State.

6. Catholics could not become members of Parliament because of the nature of the oath required on entry.

7. Catholics were forbidden to carry arms.

8. Catholic clergymen were required to register and take an oath of allegiance. An unregistered priest was liable to the same penalties as those for treason.

9. A Catholic coud not inherit land belonging to a Protestant and could not purchase land.

10. The right of Catholics to practise their religion in any way in public was severely restricted.

In practice the Catholics of Culdaff and Cloncha were not allowed to have churches and their priests were not allowed to practise as such save under government permission. The means of education were denied to them because no Catholic schools could be opened in the area. To go abroad for education was forbidden. The land-owning limitations meant that Catholics could not really own land at all. The native Irish were thus reduced to the position of ignorant serfs, used to serve the privileged minority of Protestants who had been planted in the area.

The law which required the registration of priests was ignored by some and observed by others. The records[15] show that some priests in our area took the necessary oath and were given a limited freedom. Owen McCoole, who was born in 1650 and ordained in 1672 by Oliver Plunkett at Dundalk, appears in the " Register of Popish Priests " compiled in 1704. He was parish priest of Cloncha. In Culdaff there was Dermot O Meely, who was born in 1659 and who was ordained by the Bishop of Clonfert at Derry in 1684.

The loss of their churches meant that the people had no place to meet for Divine Worship. To meet in the houses of the people could incur the landlord's anger and lead to the eviction of the owner. The Mass Rock in the open was the solution. Early on Sunday morning, at a secluded spot, the people gathered in great secrecy. The time and place were made known to the initiated only. The life of the priest and their own security were at stake. Discretion was needed. On the hill nearby one person stood on guard to give warning of the approach of the priest-hunter and the English soldiers.

Mass Rocks are found in Carthage, Keenagh, Tirmacroragh,[16]

Carrowmore, Muff, Glacknadrummond, Bootagh and Ballyharry. There were, no doubt, many others whose location is now forgotten. It should be noted that after 1780, when the Penal Laws were relaxed to allow Catholics the right to worship, these altars were still used pending the erection of churches. The practice was to say Mass in turn at an altar in each end of the parish on consecutive Sundays.

While the Catholics worshipped in hidden glen and mountain recess, the small Protestant community enjoyed the protection of the churches at Culdaff and Cloncha. The churchlands, once the property of the Catholic Church, helped to maintain the Protestant clergy. In addition, each Catholic land-occupier throughout the two parishes paid tithes[17] yearly to ensure that the rectors of the Established Church lived in luxury. This was indeed an anomalous situation. The majority which refused to conform and which never received any service from the Protestant rector was compelled to maintain him. Tithes were an irritant which served to remind the Catholic community of the injustice perpetrated by England and perpetuated by her unjust laws.

Despite the Penal Laws, the Catholics continued therefore to practise their religion. In the field of education the native Irish here refused to be kept in ignorance. The hedge schools[18] which were established at various places throughout the area provided some education, but those who sought a better education were compelled to go abroad.

How vigorously were the Penal Laws enforced in the area ? It is clear that the ascendancy group ensured that the laws were enforced so that their own privileged position might be fully maintained. Two cases which support this view were reported during the eighteenth century.

Toirealach O Dochartaigh, a native of Cashel in the parish of Culdaff, went to Spain, where he was ordained. He returned to Inis Eoghain to minister to his people. Found offering Mass in the district of Muff, he was arrested and would have experienced the full penalty of the law but for the good offices of a friend who had influence with the army officer in charge.[19]

The Bishop of Derry, Dr. McColgan, had to carry out his duties in secrecy and surrounded by many hazards. For a time he had to take refuge in a lime-kiln and only escaped the military through the kindness of a Presbyterian farmer.[20]

The laws preventing Catholics worshipping and organising schools were of course rigorously enforced.

1780—1850: A TIME OF CATHOLIC REVIVAL

By 1780 the Penal Laws were being less stringently enforced, so that the Catholics began to come into the open after 160 years. The years between 1780 and 1850 were for them ones of intense organisation, and this despite the period of serious unrest in Inis Eoghain at the beginning of the eighteenth century. The priests and people did great work to ensure that fitting places of worship were available and that the means of education were provided for the children.

An act was passed in 1778 permitting Catholics to take leases for any term of years not exceeding 999 provided that an oath of allegiance was taken in accordance with an act of the Irish Parliament passed in 1774. Among those who attended at Derry Assizes to take the oath on the 15th September, 1785, was Charles O Donnell, " Popish " priest of Cloncha.[21] Had this any connection with the securing of a lease for the church at Lagg ?

The first church built in the peninsula for Catholics was the present church at Lagg. It was built in 1784. Charles O Donnell was probably the driving force behind this project. In 1805, during the pastorate of Denis O Donnell, the church at Bocan was built for the people of Culdaff. This church stands in the townland of Dunross, which is in the parish of Cloncha.

The next church built was the present edifice at Aghaclay. This building was erected in 1837, probably during the pastorates of Neil O Flaherty and Francis McHugh. The church at Malin Head, known as the Star of the Sea, was built in 1847, when Philip Porter was parish priest in the parish of Cloncha.

The parish of Cloncha has three churches, while Culdaff has one. It is worthy of note that all the new churches built after the Penal Laws were sited close to the pre-Reformation churches. The weight of tradition was evidently very strong. The church at Malin Head is in the same townland as Drumnakill and the church of Lagg is beside the old church of Grainseach. Aghaclay church is adjacent to Greallach. Finally, Bocan church stands midway between and close to the old foundations at Cloncha and Culdaff. On the day that the church at Malin Head was opened a major step had been taken towards the undoing of the injustice of the Reformation in this area; these four churches were in full operation so close to the ancient and honoured foundations of olden days.

While the churches were being built steps were being taken to provide schools also. Before the operation of the act of 1832, the priests had already opened schools. These were built by the people and the teachers were paid by voluntary subscriptions. The Catholic clergy co-operated fully with the Government schemes from 1832 onwards, and as a result every child in the two parishes had the opportunity to get the rudiments of learning. The literacy ratio among Catholics rose steadily as the nineteenth century advanced.

PROSELYTISING IN CULDAFF AND CLONCHA

Missionary activity is an essential note of Christianity. To bring the Gospel message to all who do not possess it is seen as the duty, the obligation, of the sincere believer, irrespective of the division of Christianity to which he may belong. If, however, the economic plight of the poor is used to force them into a religious denomination to which they would not otherwise give any allegiance it is a different matter and such action is truly reprehensible.

From 1620 A.D. for over two hundred and fifty years, Catholicism was to a great extent a religion under siege in this area, and indeed throughout the whole country. Ignorance and poverty were the hallmarks of the Catholics in parishes like Cloncha and Culdaff. The promise of learning and better economic conditions were the inducements used by various Protestant organisations to encourage Catholics to conform to the new religion. It is well to point out that there is little evidence of real involvement in this type of activity by the Protestant clergy resident here.

At any time during the period referred to above, any Catholic who wished to conform would have been rewarded with a better and larger farm and would have been admitted into the select group making up the Protestant community. These enjoyed not only a better standard of living but also a higher social status.

Towards the end of the eighteenth and at the beginning of the nineteenth century a number of societies became active. These societies opened schools and promised the means of education to the poor. Bibles were distributed. These organisations were proselytisers and they had substantial funds available for their work. From about 1790 to 1830 " The Association for Discountenancing Vice and Promoting the Knowledge and Practice of the Christian Religion " and " The Hibernian Sunday School Society for Ireland " were active in the parishes of Culdaff and Cloncha. The last-named founded seven schools in each parish and these schools were attended largely by Catholics. The Catholic clergy founded schools in opposition and discouraged attendance at these proselytising schools, and by 1830 the activities of these societies had ceased in this educational guise in our area.

As late as 1848 there is evidence of a proselytising campaign among her tenants directed by Mrs. Young of Culdaff House.[22] The information available regarding this case is quoted *in extenso*:

Date, 14.1.1848. **Letter from George Young, Culdaff House, Carndonagh, forwarding copies of information** lately sworn before him about books taken by Revd. Mr. McKeague, C.C., Malin, who forcibly carried away a number of books and assaulted Eleanor Bradley while endeavouring to prevent him. The persons who have sworn the informations are chiefly Irish Scripture readers and all well-conducted men.

Information of Patrick Bradley of Carthage Mountain, who said that on the 4th January, 1848, a number of books, his property, consisting of Irish and English Bibles, Testaments, *etc.*, value for £2 and upwards, together with some rent receipts and other papers — including a few books which had been lent to him — were forcibly carried out of his house by Revd. Mr. McKeague, curate of the Revd. Mr. Porter, P.P. Malin; that the books referred to consisted of one large Irish Bible value 10/- at first cost, one large English Bible value 8/-, an Irish Grammar value 5/-, 4 Irish Testaments value 6/-, three English Testaments value 6/-, three English Testaments value 3/-, about a dozen of portions of Irish Scripture value 5/-, an Irish prayer book value 5/-, an Irish Dictionary which had been lent to him value 7/6 with a variety of small books and tracts value 2/6 at least.

Sworn before me at Culdaff House, 5.1.1848. Eleanor Bradley stated that Fr. McKeague came to the house at 12 o'clock and forcibly carried off books and assaulted her twice — when she tried to prevent him — and with so much violence the second time that she fell on the dunghill just outside the door.

Edward Bradley, son, saw priest strike mother in the shoulder with his fist and also said that he — the priest — would break Edward's nose because he requested him to leave the house until his father came.

Information of Patrick Bradley of Carthage Mountain, who said that on Monday, January 3rd, 1848, he was present at a station held by Revd. Philip Porter, P.P. Malin, in the house of James Farren of Trianatobair in the townland of Carthage. Fr. McKeague, curate, was also present; that Revd. Mr. Porter on entering house said "I hope there is none of you here this day that has anything to do with this Anti-Christ that lives at Culdaff. I am told that he keeps a bad house and that he keeps an Orange Lodge, a Ribbon Lodge and a Freemason Lodge. I am told he sometimes reads Irish and sometimes English". Fr. Porter, not knowing his name, asked Patrick Bradley and he replied the name was "Keegan". Fr. Porter then said in presence of all "My curse and God's curse be

39

upon him and on everyone that has anything to do with him or that goes into his house".

Fr. Porter then rang the bell, repeated the curses and added "I authorise the people to put Keegan out of their houses like a dog, to spit on his face and to scald him if he refuses to go out". Denis McKinney, Neil McColgan, Patrick McLaughlin of Trianatobair, Pat Farren of Doon and many others were present at the time. Sworn 4th January, 1848, by Patrick Bradley before George Young.

Information of John Keegan of Culdaff said on oath: In consequence of the threats and denunciations which he had heard and believes were made against him by the Revd. P. Porter, P.P. Malin, at a station in Trianatobair and which were afterwards proved on oath by Patrick Bradley of Carthage Mountain before George Young, Esq., J.P., in the presence of the informant, he has strong reasons to fear a serious injury may be inflicted on himself, his family and his property by night or by day and therefore prays that such steps may be taken by those in authority as would ensure protection to all concerned. Sworn in the presence of George Young, 5.1.1848.

Sworn Statement of Shaun McGonigle of Doon: That having heard this morning from Edward Bradley of Carthage Mountain that Fr. McKeague, curate to the Revd. P. Porter . . . had entered his house in his presence and carried off a number of books, his property. Informant proceeded to the house of the Widow McGuinness of Keidycarragh accompanied by the said Edward Bradley having understood that Mr. McKeague was there and asked him to return the books. This he refused to do and said that he would burn them. He stated that it was better they should be burned than that the informant himself to burn in the flames of Hell; that about this time Fr. Porter entered the house. Fr. McKeague told the parish priest that the defendant was looking for his books. Fr. Porter immediately took hold of informant by the collar and kicked him out of the house. When the defendant came to the street, Fr. McKeague followed him and taunted him about going away without his books. Fr. McKeague asked the others present to throw dirt or clabar at him. The people refused and then Fr. McKeague himself threw several lumps of dirty clay and mire at him. Informant then lifted a stone and threatened to strike Fr. McKeague if he did not stop. Fr. McKeague then struck the informant a severe blow on his left ear with his fist and immediately afterwards gave him a severe kick on the thigh.

Shaun McGonigle 4.1.1848.

The tradition among the people supports the report sent to Dublin Castle by Young. The parish priest, Fr. P. Porter, and the curate, Fr. John McCaig, had found that Mrs. Young's agents had left Bibles and Protestant tracts in all the houses in Glengad, Carthage and other areas. In addition to the action recorded above, Fr. McCaig went round each house accompanied by Philip Crampsey of Doon carrying a creel on his back. As the priest went from house to house he collected the Bibles, etc., and threw them into the creel. At the end of the tour Philip Crampsey had a full load. Fr. McCaig and his helper returned to Doon, where, on the top of the Hill of Doon, in the sight of all, the books were burned. The fire could be seen at Culdaff House.

The law advisers[23] replied to Young and informed him that since intention to steal could not be proved, there were no grounds for a court action.

Young was the landlord in this area and he held his lands in part from the Bishop of Derry and in part from the Marquis of Donegall. His lands included the townlands of Glengad, Carthage, Balleighan, Dunross, Cloncha, Larrahirrel, Glacknadrummond. Mrs. Young was therefore in a strong position to exert pressure on her tenants. These people were thus placed in a dilemma. If they took a firm stand against the proselytising agents of Mrs. Young, the rents were liable to be increased and they might even suffer eviction from their holdings. On the other hand, if they co-operated with Mrs. Young they acted against their consciences and incurred the anger of the priests.

The story told in the parish of Culdaff regarding one case will illustrate with a touch of humour the problems facing people in those days of persecution. Dualtach Mac Reannachain lived in the townland of Cloncha. He had a large family of ten children and a small farm of bad land. Life was difficult. His only cow, on which his family depended for milk, had difficulty in those land-hungry days getting enough to eat. The landlord was passing through the townland with his wife. Dualtach humbly saluted and in the course of the conversation he explained his problem regarding sufficient grass for his cow. The landlord's wife had been listening and she leaned out of the carriage window and said very sweetly, " You will have grass for your cow ". " But I have no money to pay any rent for the land you promise," said Dualtach. " You will not be asked to pay any rent. Take your cow to Banchan each day and let her graze to her satisfaction. I will ask you to do only one thing in return. Attend the evening service in Culdaff every Sunday." The Cloncha man listened in silence and the carriage proceeded on its way.

This matter required careful consideration. Dualtach took off his cap and sat down on the stone wall to think matters over. He was no theologian, but he knew that to go to the Protestant church was a serious step. His mind was in a whirl. Through it went the thoughts of a hungry cow and hungrier children, jeering neighbours and angry priests. A vision of hell came before his vivid Celtic imagination and in the midst, with hundreds of devils for company, sat a burning Irishman, Dualtach Mac Reannachain by name. The vision was too horrible to contemplate and he got up hurriedly, placing his cap on his head as he did so.

On his way he called at a neighbour's house, where the house-wife noticed that Dualtach " was not himself ". She gave him a good glass of poteen distilled in the bog below. The worried man drank gratefully, but he kept his silence, thanked the good woman and hurried home. His wife always had a solution. He would consult her. He had not married a Deen woman for nothing.

While the ten children slept in the corner of their one-roomed cabin, Malsi and Dualtach talked and talked and at last a conclusion was reached. Dualtach would each Sunday go to Bocan to Mass in the morning and to the Protestant church in Culdaff in the evening. The cow would get her grass and the children would get their milk.

A Sunday or two later Padraig Mor Mac Ciarain was standing at the gate of Bocan church as Dualtach arrived. Padraig Mor was the Mass server and having a certain status on this account he had the right to speak on matters pertaining to the Church. Padraig Mor looked at the approaching man and remarked: " Dualtach, where are you going this morning ? Is not Culdaff your destination ?"

Dualtach looked the Meenawarra man in the face: " It is like this, a Phadraig. I come to Bocan on a Sunday morning for the good of my soul and I go to Culdaff in the evening for the good of my cow ". The Cloncha man, as often before and after, had his answer for the Meenawarra man, so the saying goes.

What effect had the efforts made to induce Catholics to renounce their own creed and conform to that of the Established Church ? The activities of the proselytisers met with scant success. While there is no tradition of any family conforming, an examination of the Protestant records available shows a number of Irish names. Were these residents of the area or were they people who had conformed elsewhere ? Were they natives who conformed for a time and later returned to their own Church ?

In 1686 in Cloncha parish we find Hugh McLaughlin of Dun an Ghrianain and Brian O Laughlin of Duncorbek recorded as churchwardens.[24] The Protestant Parish Register for Cloncha shows the following names:

1710: John son to Duald O Doherty was baptised John O Doherty and Thomas Flynn godfather and Annie McKahy alias Noone as godmother.

42

1711: John McLaughlin had a son baptised called Hugh. John Flinn and Knoker McKala, Eleanor McLaughlin, Sara McKala Witnesses.

1711: Neil McGowan had a child baptised called Isobel . . .

1714: James McDevitt had a child baptised called John . . .

1714: William O Granachine had a child baptised called Patrick, Thomas Bradley and George O Galacher godfathers and Maeve O Quigley godmother.

1715: James McDaid had a son baptised called Daniel . . .

1717: John McDevitt had a child baptised called Mary . . .

1773: Margaret and Jane daughters of Owen Dougherty of Termacroragh.

1782: Sarah daughter of William McMonagle of Ourt . . .

1783: William son of James McGuinness and of Ann his wife of Leitrim . . .

1783: Mary daughter of Daniel McCann and of Rose his wife of Irish Ballyharry.

The list[25] of Protestant Housekeepers dated 1740 has the following:

Baskill: Donal McCalay, Michael O Carolan, Patrick O Carolan, John McCala.

Ballyharry: Thomas Magee.

Carrowmore (Gleneely): Samuel McCala.

Cashel: Thomas Morrison, Alex Morrison, Daniel O Carrolan.

Kindroyhad: Art O Gillin, Widow Gillin.

Bree: John Molloy, John Moore.

Carrowmore (Malin): Widow Moore.

Keenagh: William O Carolan.

In the Protestant records[26] for Culdaff parish we find that in 1661 Charles O Doherty was parish clerk and that John Moylline and Uffney Oge O Quilly were churchwardens. In 1718 William McGrenaghan and James McDevitt were churchwardens. In the following year we have as churchwardens William McGrenagh and John McDevitt.

Whatever conclusion may be drawn from the names given above, it is clear that not more than half a dozen families who were natives of the two parishes were involved. In view of the inducements held out to those who conformed, why did most of the people cling to their ancient faith and prefer to remain in poverty and ignorance? There was the great force of tradition, the strength of public opinion, the lack of enthusiasm among the clergy of the Established Church and finally, but most important, the influence of the Catholic clergy. In this area the continuity of the presence of the priest was never broken. He was always present to advise and to act where there was any threat to his flock.

A tribute is due to those priests who served here during the operation of the Penal Laws. These men had studied abroad and returned to a life of poverty and hardship. They lived in constant danger of imprisonment and even death. The names of some are unknown and many rest in nameless graves at Greallach, Lagg, Cloncha and Culdaff.

ACT OF EMANCIPATION, 1829

By the end of the eighteenth century conditions had begun to improve for the Catholic population here. The relaxation of the Penal Laws continued and in 1829 the Act of Emancipation removed almost all the restrictions. Locally the Protestant Community resented the change. George Young, the landlord at Culdaff, was deeply resentful of the freedom accorded to Catholics.[27] Another report[28] stated that on the Sunday in 1829 when the ministers of the various denominations (other than Catholics) announced the royal assent to the Act of Emancipation, the congregations were deeply disturbed and returned home in a state of anxiety. Perhaps they foresaw that the Catholics, by reason of their numbers, would in time become masters. The days of a minority which was privileged economically and otherwise were coming to an end.

DISESTABLISHMENT OF THE PROTESTANT CHURCH

The payment of tithes still remained and was deeply resented by the Catholic section of the community. In 1838 an act was passed which merged this obnoxious exaction in the rent. In 1869 an act was passed which disestablished the Protestant Church and left this institution on an equal footing with all other Churches. After two and a half centuries, Catholics in the parishes of Culdaff and Cloncha were once again free of many intolerable impositions.

THE STATIONS

The custom of holding " stations " in the houses of the people twice yearly still continues in these parishes. Each parish is divided into " station areas ", usually consisting each of two or three townlands. The parish priest and curate attend to hear confessions and say Mass. The station is held in the spring during Lent and in the late autumn, usually in October. Each house in the station area will have the station in turn. In practice, it means that the station will be held in each house once in say seven or eight years, depending on the number of houses.

The origin of this custom is related to the period of Penal Laws but it is not clear how it started. Owing to the risks involved the station could not have been held in private houses when the Penal Laws were rigorously imposed. The custom probably started around 1780, when the laws were relaxed. The purpose was to enable all, especially the older people, to attend Mass and receive the sacraments.

The people regard the station as a privilege and take great care to have their houses well prepared for the occasion. Up to the early part of this century all the neighbours gave a hand in the preparation of the house at which the station was to be held. A dance was held on the night of the station day and all who helped were invited to the festivities, but this custom has now died out.

OFFERINGS

The confiscation of the churchlands left the Catholic clergy without any source of income and consequently the priest had to depend on the contributions of the people. One means of support came from " offerings ". On the day of a burial the neighbours of the dead person each paid a small sum of money towards the support of the priest. The original intention was to share the contribution due to the officiating priest but the custom developed to a sort of " status symbol ". Where a neighbour paid at the burial of a member of the family of another neighbour the latter acted in the same way when a death occurred in the family of the former. Over the years there developed the practice whereby each family had an obligation to pay offerings on the death of anyone within at least eight or nine townlands. The total collected became a means of measuring the importance of the family of the deceased. The higher the amount of the offerings the higher the standing of the family in the community. The custom of offerings at funerals was abolished in the parishes of Culdaff and Cloncha from January 1st, 1970.

The other sources of income were the payments made at Christmas, the spring station and the autumn station. The spring contribution was known as the " stipend " and the autumn contribution was called the " stook "—a reminder of the days when the contribution was made in kind. Each family gave a stook of corn to maintain the horse belonging to the priest. The custom of making a contribution in kind still continues here in the case of fuel: each family leaves a load of turf in September at the residence of the priest.

THE PRIEST AND THE PEOPLE

The priest had an honoured place in the community in this part of Ireland. He was very often an adviser and helper in many spheres other than the spiritual. However, there is now a trend to confine the priest to his spiritual role.

Some of the people in this area had at certain times the strength of character to act independently of and even in defiance of the priest's direction in matters outside his spiritual office. This was particularly true in matters of politics.

A newspaper report in March, 1891, shows that during the Parnellite split, Fr. William McLaughlin, P.P. of Cloncha, denounced Parnell and his supporters from the altar at Aghaclay. He ordered the people to ignore a pro-Parnellite meeting due to he held outside after Mass. Later he came out to the meeting and asked the people to leave. A substantial number of the people ignored the priest and remained at the meeting.

During the period between 1917 and 1921 the clergy strongly supported the Sinn Fein party. In some cases men who were sought by the Black-and-Tans found refuge in the presbytery, where they stayed in security while the British Army raided all around the parish. Despite the strong support given to Sinn Fein by the clergy, however, a section of the parish continued its support for the Redmondite party.

When the Treaty was signed the parish priest of Culdaff was a strong and zealous Treaty supporter. He used his position to force the parishioners to take the same line as himself. A substantial section of the people refused, however, to be coerced and continued to identify themselves openly with Anti-Treaty activities. In 1927 the parish priest of Culdaff read from the altar the names of the Pro-Treaty candidates at the election to be held during the week. For this he was subjected to severe criticism by many of his parishioners. The priests in these parishes are to-day more mature and confine their admonitions and directions to spiritual matters.

To sum up in this regard, the people of these parishes have not been and are not unduly influenced by the Catholic priests. The charge made against the Irish of being a priest-ridden people is not true of the parishes of Culdaff and Cloncha. The people have sufficient judgement to enable them to distinguish between the priest acting in his spiritual capacity and the man who is merely expressing his own views or abusing his position.

CATHOLIC PLACES OF WORSHIP IN 1970

At present, the churches in use are those at Lagg, Malin Head, Aghaclay and Bocan. The last-named was originally a thatched building. This church was enlarged and renovated in 1846 when James McDevitt was parish priest. It was at this time, probably, that the roof was slated.

To finance this work, which was undertaken during the Famine, the parish priest secured a loan of £300 from the Commissioners of Public Works. The loan was repayable in five yearly instalments of £82.6.3 each.[29]

A bell was presented to the parish of Culdaff in 1929 by a native of the parish named Hegarty. This bell was originally erected in the open. In 1933 the church was re-roofed and the belfry was added.

The cut stones used in the belfry were produced by stone cutters in the quarry at Croragh. The repairs to the church were carried out during the pastorate of John H. McKenna.[30]

BURIAL PLACES

The Catholic burial grounds were formerly at the old churches of Cloncha, Culdaff, Greallach, Lagg and Malin Well. Cloncha and Culdaff continued as a burial place for Catholics until the first quarter of the nineteenth century. Then the new burial place at Bocan was used.

The first burial at Bocan was in 1815. The grave is situated near the vestry door and bears the inscription " Peggy Doherty 1815".

Malin Well was used up to the end of the eighteenth century. Lagg then became the burial ground for the people of Malin Head. It is interesting to note that Lagg is the only cemetery which has been used by Catholics without a break since the pre-Reformation era.

Greallach was used as a burial ground up to the early part of the nineteenth centry. People in this area now bury their dead in the graveyard adjoining the church at Aghaclay.

There is no burial ground adjoining the church at Malin Head, known as the Star of the Sea, but one priest was buried here.

THE CLERGY OF CULDAFF AND CLONCHA

Because of the destruction of the native records by the British, data are very scanty in respect of the pre-Reformation clergy. During the Penal Law period prudence demanded the minimum of written evidence, to ensure the safety of the clergy

47

in their hunted, secret lives. Hence the list of Catholic clergy is very incomplete for the years preceding the middle of the eighteenth century.

The list of Church of Ireland clergy is complete from the introduction of the new religion in 1620 up to the present. Adequate church records have been kept to enable the researcher to outline the progress of the Church of Ireland in the two parishes.

One may here rightly ask the question, how did the Catholic clergy receive education and what standard was maintained. The tradition of scholarship was kept up in certain families connected with the church in each parish. When the monastic institutions remained intact the means of study and teaching were available. In our area this was possible up to the end of the sixteenth century. The monastery at Derry was a focal point for Inis Eoghain.

An English writer,[31] referring to the clergy of Derry diocese at the end of the sixteenth century, shows that a number was well-educated and could speak three languages—Irish, English and Latin. At this time Irish students from Derry diocese were attending the University of Glasgow. This is another example of the close connection maintained from the earliest times with Scotland.

From the seventeenth century until the founding of Maynooth at the end of the eighteenth, students for the priesthood had to go to the Continent to complete their studies. The basics were learned in secret at home.

The Church of Ireland clergy were, as members of the Established Church, provided with every facility. From the middle of the eighteenth century we find that the rectors of Culdaff and Cloncha were graduates of Trinity College.

The break with the tradition of educating the Catholic clergy at home in native institutions was to have far-reaching effects on the cultural and devotional lives of Irish Catholics. The break with Ireland's cultural heritage prepared the way for the rejection of the Irish language and everything associated with the culture of the old Celtic order. The priest was enriched by his contact with the culture of France or Spain but was ignorant of the culture of his own land. Many devotions and other accidentals of Continental Catholicism were introduced to Irish parishes. Devotion to native saints practically disappeared and Irish prayers, the heritage of fourteen centuries, were allowed to lapse in favour of new ones from the Continent.

Thus Church and State were unwittingly at one in robbing the Irish people of their cultural heritage. With this formidable union the ordinary people knew no other way than to follow. The Anglicisation of the country was thus accelerated.

CATHOLIC CLERGY OF CLONCHA AND CULDAFF

PARISH OF CLONCHA[32]
Greallach:
1425: John O Gubuin would seem to have been vicar and resigned this year.
1425: Roger O Cnamhsi was vicar here for an unstated period. His death took place in this year.
1425: Patrick Loclannach was appointed vicar here this year by virtue of a decree of Pope Martin V, who directed the Bishop of Alet and the Abbot of Cella Nigra to see that the decree was carried out. Patrick Loclannach died at the Apostolic See, where he evidently had gone on pilgrimage. This cleric was also vicar of Culdaff.
1429: John Drover, vicar here, was, by virtue of a faculty given by the Pope to Donald, Bishop of Derry, promoted to Holy Orders without observance of legal time delay in the case of certain orders.
Cloncha:
14?: David O Murgisan, Rector, held this parish and also that of Clonmany. By decree of Pope John XXIII — anti-pope — he was deprived of Cloncha.
14?: Solomon O Brolcan, Rector, was rehabilitated in place of David O Murgisan. A clerk of the diocese of Derry, Luke O Molmochchair by name, claimed part of the income of the parish but the papal decree stated that Solomon was not bound to pay the moiety. About 1422 Solomon entered and made his profession as a canon of the Augustinian Monastery of Derry.
1419: Patrick O Molmocorig, holder of the vicarage of Cloncha, died this year.
1419: Solomon O Horchan is appointed perpetual vicar this year by virtue of a decree issued by the Holy See to the Abbot of Macosquin.
1422: Donald O Dubay took illegal possession of the parish after the departure of Solomon O Brolchan to Derry. On false information he obtained permission from Rome to occupy the rectorship.
1427: John O Gubuin was appointed Rector in place of the deposed Donald O Dubay. John had previously held the vicarship of Greallach and was Rector of Clonmany when appointed here. The last-named post he was directed to resign when taking possession of Cloncha. He had permission to retain the posts of rector at Moville in Derry diocese and of canonries and prebends in Limerick and Ossory. A short time later another papal decree gave him a canonry in each of the dioceses of Derry and Raphoe, with reservation of a prebend of each. John later became Bishop of Derry.
14?: John McColgan was vicar of Cloncha and in 1427 was appointed rector of Donagh parish.
1430: Felimus O Docharthaidh was appointed vicar of Cloncha.
14?: Henry O Marigesan (*sic*), the rector of Cloncha, was charged with misconduct on the evidence of Rory O Harcan, a priest of the

diocese of Derry. Henry had so many friends in his own diocese that it was necessary to appeal to Rome. Nicholas V authorised three canons of the neighbouring diocese of Raphoe to investigate. If the charge was found to be correct, Rory O Harcan was to be appointed Rector and Henry O Marigesan to be deposed. Roger or Rory O Harcan would seem to have proved the charges and got the right to the rectorship. For an unstated reason he did not have possession. By 1455 Henry O Murgessan (sic) was accused by a clerk, Patrick O Dubagay, of simony and persistence in a state of misconduct. The Abbot of Cella Nigra in the diocese of Derry was appointed to investigate. If the charge is found to be true. Patrick O Dubagay to be promoted to all Holy Orders and given the rectorship. As we shall see, he was appointed rector, the charges having been proved to the satisfaction of the Abbot.

Henry had been given a canonry at Derry when he was eighteen years. By 1440 a priest of this name held the perpetual vicarage of Domhnach Mor for two years against the wishes of his chapter. In 1461 he is a canon of Derry again.

14?: Rory O Harcan was rector but did not have possession.

14?: Patrick O Dubagay was rector and was charged by a priest named Bernard McColgan with perjury, simony and misconduct. The Abbot of Cella Nigra. was appointed to investigate. The charge of simony was related to a bargain between the above-named Patrick O Dubagay and his brother Cornelius in respect of the collation of the perpetual vicarage of Moville. If the charges proved, the said Bernard to get the rectorship. There is no evidence that he was ever in possession. A later document shows that Nicholas Bishop of Derry deprived O Dubagay of his benefice.

14?: Donald O Duby would seem to have been Rector according to a papal document of 1463.

1470: Comedinus O Murgissan, a clerk, was appointed rector. A direction was given to the Abbot of Derry and two of the canons of Derry to collate and assign the rectorship of Cloncha after admission to all orders of the priesthood.

1478: Magonius O Domnaill, a clerk aged 19 years, is given possession of the parish church at Cloncha with an income of nine marks. There is no mention of his admission to Holy Orders.

1486: Thomas Mumneath was unlawfully in possession of the perpetual vicarage of Cloncha.

1486: John O Lasci, a canon of Raphoe, was given the perpetual vicarage by virtue of a papal document authorising the removal of Thomas Mumneath.

1492: David O Moran [33] was appointed vicar of Cloncha. He was a deacon of the diocese of Raphoe.

1605: John O Lafferty [34] was Rector, Donald O Horcan was vicar.

1629, circa: Edmund McFeely. (Ref. *C.S.P. of Ireland*.)

1672: Owen McCoole, [35] born 1650, was ordained this year by Blessed Oliver Plunkett at Dundalk. It is not clear in what year he became parish priest. According to the "Register of Popish Priests" compiled in 1704 by a law of the British Government, he was then in possession of the parish and was in residence at Malin.

1780: Friar George O Doherty, [36] a native of the parish, was parish priest. He is buried at Lagg. See note on page 58.

1784: Dr. Charles O Donnell [37] acted as administrator during the last years of the life of Fr. George O Doherty. Dr. O Donnell did higher studies in Paris at the College of the Lombards, where he commenced on July 26th, 1777. He took the degrees of Bachelor of Divinity and

Doctor of Divinity at the Sorbonne. By 1784 he was living in the townland of Muff in the parish of Culdaff, in the house of a man called John Doherty. He became parish priest of the parishes of Culdaff and Cloncha. On the 15th September, 1785, he attended at the Assizes in Derry to take the oath required by law to enable a Catholic to take a lease. Had this any connection with the building of the church at Lagg? The edifice was completed about this time. Dr. O Donnell was also parish priest of Iskaheen and became Bishop of Derry in 1798. He ruled the diocese until his death in 1823.

17 ?: Fr. O Kane,[37a] a native of Tirscullion in the parish of Culdaff, succeeded Dr. O Donnell.

17 ? : Fr. Shiel [38] succeeded and was transferred to Clonmany in 1794.

1794: Fr. Philip Doherty,[39] a native of Priesttown, in the parish of Donagh, became parish priest this year. He died in 1806 and was buried at Lagg.

1806: Fr. Patrick McKenna,[40] a native of Maghera, followed. He was a student in Paris during the French Revolution. At his death in 1820 he was buried in Lagg.

1820: Fr. James O'Flaherty,[41] a native of Urney, followed and died in 1826. He was buried at Lagg.

1826: Fr. Neil O Flaherty,[42] came next. He was transferred to Longfield in Tyrone. He was born in Termonamongan.

18 ?: Fr. Francis McHugh[43] was the next occupant. After a short period he was transferred to Longfield like his predecessor.

1839: Fr. Philip Porter[44] succeeded. He died 3rd June, 1870.

1871: William McLaughlin[45] was then appointed.

1884: Jeremiah Quin[46] succeeded but after a short period died. 12th April, 1885.

1886: James Devlin[47] became parish priest. In 1893 he retired and John McCullagh was appointed administrator. Fr. Devlin died March 8th, 1897.

1898: John McCullagh[48] was the new parish priest, a position he occupied until his death on December 26th, 1902.

1904: James Morris[49] succeeded.

1921: John O Brien[50] became parish priest this year. He died on October 13th, 1952.

1953: B'é Colm Mag Ualghairg a chomharba. I mBun Cranncha a rugadh é. Chaith sé seal mar shagart in Albain, i nDroichead Lios na Caoraidheachta, i nDún Geimhin, i mBaile na Scríne agus i nDoire Cholmcille. Bhí sé ina riarthóir ar pharóiste an Túir Fhada. Fuair sé bás i mí na Bealtaine, 1968. Tá sé curtha sa Lag.

Note: See page 58

PARISH OF CULDAFF

Vicars:

14 ?: Sitrig O Brolchan, Vicar.

14 ?: Nemias O Dufaghy, Vicar.

1415: Arhalt O Dufaghy, a priest, had unlawful possession for more than ten years. He was deposed and replaced in 1425.

1425: Patrick Loclannach, the vicar of Greallach, to be appointed also perpetual vicar of Culdaff in place of the usurper Arhalt O Dufaghy. He was permitted to hold both together for life.

1429: Henry O Muirgissan was appointed to the perpetual vicarage of Culdaff. He was of noble blood according to the papal document which appointed him. For details of this cleric see Cluain Catha.

1431: Cornelius O Horstim, vicar, died this year.

1431: Philip O Dubaid succeeded as vicar. See *De Annatis Hiberniae 1400-1535,* Costello.

1605: Patrick O Kernie,[52] vicar. It is stated that he who is rector of Moville is also rector of this parish. Cornelius O Doherty was rector at this date of both Moville and Culdaff.

1684: Dermot O Meely[53] was parish priest in 1694 according to the Register compiled by the Government. He was born in 1659 and was ordained at the age of 25, at Creggan, by Thady Keogh, Titular Bishop of Clonfert. He resided at Balleighan. A monument in the graveyard at Culdaff bears the inscription: "This monument was erected by Darby Meeley, Priest of Culdaff, for his grand-uncle Edmund Meeley and his brother Manus Meeley, both priests and for himself also. A.D. 1713". It can be inferred that these three priests were buried here but there is no evidence of where Edmund Meeley and Manus Meeley were serving as priests. As Edmund Meeley was granduncle of Dermot Meeley, this date of birth could be placed *circa* 1600 — a few years before the English occupation.

1688: Dermot McFeely,[54] parish priest.

1690: Owen McColgan,[55] parish priest.

17 ?: Patrick O Doherty,[56] parish priest. He died 29th March, 1751.

17 ?: James Begley,[57] parish priest, died 10 June, 1766.

17 ?: Fr. Crampsey,[58] parish priest, was a native of the parish.

17 ?: Fr. Orr,[59] parish priest, was a native of the parish and died in 1783.

1784: Dr. Charles O Donnell,[60] later Bishop of Derry, was parish priest. See Cluain Catha.

17 ?: Manasses Divine,[61] parish priest, was a native of County Derry. He lived in Cashel.

17 ?: Denis O Donnell,[62] parish priest, was a native of Donagh. He died in 1807.

18 ?: Fr. O Kane,[63] parish priest, followed. He was a native of County Derry and lived at Ballinagran. In 1824 he exchanged his parish with Gerald Doherty for Moville.

1824: Gerald Doherty,[64] a native of Urney, succeeded but was parish priest for one year only. He died in 1825 and was buried at Drung.

1825: Fr. O Connor,[65] a native of County Derry, succeeded. He died in 1831.

1831: James McDevitt[66] became parish priest. He died on the 28th October, 1867.

1868: R. P. O Doherty[67] succeeded and continued as parish priest until his death in 1889. He was a native of Clonmany.

1889: William McGlinchey,[68] a nephew of Fr. James McDevitt, was appointed. He served as curate here previously. His brother James bought the property at Termacroragh from Major Murray. Here the parish priest lived with his brother and sister until his death on the 24th September, 1897. He is buried at Bocan.

1898: John O Kane[69] succeeded. He died on January 11th. 1907.

1908: Michael O Neill[70] was then appointed and remained one year. He was transferred to another parish.

1909: Francis McCullagh[71] succeeded.

1922: Bernard McWilliams[72] was next parish priest. He died on the ninth of August, 1926.

1927: Peter Tracy[73] succeeded. He was transferred to Desertegney and Lower Fahan in 1932.

1932: John Henry McKenna.[74] a native of County Derry, followed. He died on February 28th, 1941. During his pastorate the church at

Bocan was renovated. A new school was built at Bocan and the other schools in the parish were repaired.

1942: Walter Hegarty,[75] a native of Derry City, was the next parish priest. He died October 31st, 1950. He was a man rich in learning and Gaelic culture.

1951: Charles Byrne[76] succeeded. He died October 16th, 1958.

1959: John McGilligan,[77] born at Castlerock, Co. Derry in 1890, was ordained in 1915. He retired from the pastorate of Culdaff in 1974 and died July 10, 1977.

1974: Bernard Duffy, a native of Drumderg in the parish of Ballinascreen, was ordained in 1942. He served on the English mission from 1942 to 1946 and, on his recall to Derry Diocese, in Termonamongan, Drumragh and Maghera.

CHURCHLANDS IN CULDAFF AND CLONCHA

Over the centuries since the time of Patrick many grants of land were made by the rulers to those engaged in the service of the Church. These lands provided the means of support for the monasteries. When the parishes were established, the major portion of the lands was passed on to those involved in serving the spiritual needs of the people. Thus each parish had a number of townlands allocated to the service of the church and known as churchlands or *talamh eaglasta.*

Culdaff[78]

The churchlands of this parish were the townlands of Carrowtemple, Crancor, Knock and the *trian* of Dun an Ghrianain. The modern townland of Culdaff corresponds to the area which formerly comprised the townlands of Carrowtemple and Crancor. Culdaff-Glebe is the name of the townland known as the *trian* of Dun an Ghrianain. The *gort* of this parish is situated near Muff and it contains 1 acre, 3 roods and 19 perches.

At the Reformation the glebe of this parish was established in the townland of Culdaff-Glebe. The rector's residence was at Cregasole and the land-occupiers in this townland became his tenants.

The Ua Dubhaigh family were the *airchinnigh* of this parish. This family lived in post-Reformation times in the townland of Glacknadrummond and were the hereditary custodians of the Bell of St. Buadan. The last member of this family died at the beginning of this century.

In the pre-Reformation period the tithes collected over the whole parish were divided in three. One third was given to each of the following: the *airchinneach,* the rector and the vicar. The *airchinneach* paid ten shillings a year to the bishop out of his share of the tithes. The people paid the tithes in kind.

Out of the income of the churchlands, the *airchinneach* had that of one townland, and the bishop got part of the income of the other two. The *gort* belonged to the vicar and the townland of Dun an Ghrianain to the rector. The rector, the vicar and the *airchinneach* had joint responsibility for the care and maintenance of the church of St. Buadan's at Culdaff.

Pope Paul V,[79] in a Bull dated March 29th, 1609, granted to Aodh O Neill, then resident in Rome, the advowson of certain parishes in Derry and Clogher. Among these was the parish of Culdaff. O Neill never had the opportunity to exercise his privilege, as the old Gaelic order of things in Inis Eoghain was on the point of collapse in 1609. The three hundred years of British occupation were about to commence.

Cloncha[80]

There were eight townlands in this parish under the control of the Church. Five were associated with the church at Cloncha and three with the church at Greallach. To Cloncha belonged the *trian* of Dun an Ghrianain. Glacknadrummond, Dunross, Larrahirrel and Carrowtemple. The present townland of Redford-Glebe is the old division of the *trian* of Dun an Ghrianain and Carrowtemple is the townland now known as Cloncha.

The lands connected with Greallach were the townlands of Carrowtemple, Drumaville and Drumballycaslin. Templemoyle is the modern name of Carrowtemple.

The *airchinnigh* of this parish were the families of O Harkan and O Mollinogher serving in the Cloncha portion and the " Clanloughlangrillies " associated with the church at Greallach.

The general principle regarding the division of the tithes applying to Culdaff also applied here: one third to the parson, one third to the vicar and one third to the *airchinnigh*. A joint responsibility for the repairs and maintenance of the churches rested on those who shared the tithes: the parson, the vicar and the *airchinnigh*. The tithes were paid in kind.

For the purpose of assessing and distributing the tithes the parish was divided into two areas. The first was the section which corresponded to the old area of influence of the foundation at Greallach. In addition to the churchlands mentioned, there were also seven quarters of land. In this division the " Clanloughlangrillies " were the *airchinnigh* and received one third of the tithes of the seven quarters mentioned. This family was under obligation to pay out of such third a sum of 6/8d. yearly to the bishop.

The second area was the remainder of the parish. Out of the third of the tithes received by them, the O Harkans and the O Mollinoghers paid yearly a sum of twenty Irish shillings to the bishop. The O Harkans had two quarters of land and had to pay a yearly contribution to the upkeep of the bishop. The O Mollinoghers had also two quarters but there is no reference to any episcopal stipend. The " Clanloughlingrillies " held two townlands and out of these a yearly payment was made to the bishop of Derry.

There were four *goirt* in this parish—two belonged to the parson and two to the vicar. One *gort,* an acre in extent, was near the church at Cloncha and a second, of four acres and 37 perches, lies between the townlands of Dunross and Glacknadrummond. Are the other *goirt* mentioned the Glebe lands ? If so, one can be identified as the *trian* of Dun an Ghrianain, the modern Redford-Glebe. The fourth is not identified and may be the present townland of Drumballycaslin.

In 1469[81] Pope Paul II appointed three canons of Derry to investigate a petition sent by one William O Dulhardy in which it was stated that in the parish of Cloncha were two pieces of land called Larathomrill and Clonimmoluchuik. The document goes on to state that it was the custom that when the holder of these lands died without issue, the land became the property of the Holy See. The three canons were, after due investigation, to grant the land under the wonted yearly cess to the said William for himself and his father and their heirs. These two pieces of land corresponded respectively probably to the modern townlands of Larrahirrel and Cloncha.

At Kullourt there was an old monastery. The greater portion of the lands of this foundation was granted to the Cistercian abbey of Macosquin in County Derry. These lands consisted of two quarters, probably corresponding to the area covered by the present townlands of Kullourt, Knockamany and part of Lagg. The occupiers *circa* 1610 A.D. were the " Munterdowanes ", who paid to the abbey of Macosquin a yearly sum of 6/8d. Irish and to O Dochartaigh four meathers of butter and eight of meal.[82]

As monastic lands, the Kullourt townland paid no tithes to the rector of Cloncha either before or after 1610 A.D.[83]

Included in the present townland of Lagg is an area of 58 acres approximately surrounding the present church. This division

55

was called Grainseach [84] and it was tithe-free up to the abolition of the tithe system in the last century. This land was probably retained in 1218 A.D. when the remainder of the monastic lands of Kullourt was given to the Cistercian foundation at Macosquin. This spot marks the site of an older foundation. Here is found a church in the early seventeenth century.

The Protestant rector of Cloncha lived at Redford-Glebe— Dun an Ghrianain.

GENERAL

Regarding the payment of tithes, an interesting feature arises which refers to both parishes. The townlands of Moneydarragh, Drumley and Dristernan paid two thirds of their tithes to the parish of Culdaff and one third to the parish of Cloncha.[85]

What is the explanation of this ? These three townlands were divided between the parishes of Cloncha and Culdaff. The implication is that the foundation at Cloncha had founded one or two hermitages here *circa* 800 and had retained its control up to the establishment of the parishes. In the thirteenth century Cloncha's right to possession was recognised and a portion of each of these townlands was given to Cloncha parish. The exact portion was clearly defined, as can be seen from an examination of the Hearth Money Rolls in 1665.

With the defeat of O Dochartaigh, King James I confiscated all the lands of Inis Eoghain. The churchlands were granted to the Protestant church and the right to the tithes was granted to the Protestant rector of each parish. In 1828 the Protestant rector of Cloncha enjoyed an income from tithes amounting to £555 per annum and his equivalent in Culdaff had £482. Very often the rectorship of the two parishes was held by one man, who enjoyed the combined income. It was a substantial sum in those days.[86]

Apart from the two glebes, the other churchlands were leased by the Protestant Bishop of Derry to the Young family at Culdaff. This family collected the rent from the tenants and in turn paid an annual charge to the bishop.

The fishery rights of Culdaff river belonged to the monastery of St. Buadan's and later to the rector of Culdaff. At the confiscation of the land of Inis Eoghain this right was claimed by the Bishop of Derry.[87] The fishery was leased to the Young family.

1. There are burial sites in this area belonging to the Neolithic and Early Bronze Ages.
2. Of many such customs one may be mentioned: when churning in certain areas, a hare's skin is placed on the half-door to guard against ill-luck.
3. *The Life and Writings of St. Patrick*, Healy.
4. *Tripartite Life*, Colgan, P. 271.
5. *The Life and Writings of St. Patrick*, Healy.
6. *The Church in Early Irish Society*, Kathleen Hughes.
7. *Annals of the Kingdom of Ireland.*
8. *Inishowen*, "Maghtochair".
9. See Chapter 4.
10. O Donovan Letters 1835 regarding Culdaff and Cloncha: "Ta Cluain Catha ag Colum Cille . . ."
11. See Chapter 4.
12. Ref. *Annals of the Kingdom of Ireland*: Maol Iosa of Both Chonais was of the eleventh century.
13. *Calendar of Papal Registers, 1417-1486.*
14. The O Kane Papers: Bishop Montgomery's Survey of Derry diocese, *circa* 1605, records this priest as vicar of Culdaff.
15. *Irish Catholic Directory*: The Register of Popish Priests — 11th Jan., 1704.
16. Seamas Mac Lochlainn (1837-1927), a former resident of Meenawarra, stated that his grandfather had attended Mass at the Altar Hill in Termacroragh. Afterwards he took part in a game of *caman* which his townland played against a neighbouring townland. Mass was said at this open-air altar until the early part of the nineteenth century.
17. In Culdaff there is still related the incident regarding Ned McDaid of Meenawarra. This man had to pay tithes to the Protestant rector of Cloncha, living at Redford. The tithes were paid in kind. Ned was due to leave a hen at the Rectory on a certain morning. He did not arrive until the afternoon and was challenged for the delay by the rector who was walking in the grounds with an English visitor. "Sorry, Sir," said Ned "but I had to wait until the hen laid so that my wife could buy salt for the children's dinner."
18. Local tradition tells of such schools in Glacknadrummond and Culdaff-Glebe.
19, 20. *Inishowen*, "Maghtochair".
21. *Catholic Qualification Rolls, 1778-1790.*
22, 23. State Paper Office: Outrage Papers, 1848.
24. *Derry Clergy and Parishes*, Leslie.
25. Genealogical Office, Dublin Castle — MSS. 539-539A.
26. *Derry Clergy and Parishes*, Leslie.
27. *Three Hundred Years in Innishowen*, Young.
28. Told by Catherine Magee of Culdaff-Glebe as heard from her mother, Mary O Doherty (1814-1907).
29. *P.P. 1849*, Vol. 23.
30. The visitor to Bocan will notice two stones inset in the wall to the left of the entrance gate. One bears the date 1836. The other bears the date 1846. The former was found in the wall above the door of the north side and the latter above the door of the west side. That some alterations took place in 1836 is indicated.
31. *Analecta Hibernica*, Vol. 12, P. 99.
32. The source record for the years up to 1486, except where otherwise stated, is *The Calendar of Papal Registers, 1417-1486*.
33. *Derry Clergy and Parishes*, Leslie.

34. *Analecta Hibernica*, Vol. 12 — The O Kane Papers: Bishop Montgomery's Survey of Derry diocese, *circa* 1605.
35. *Irish Catholic Directory*: The Register of Popish Priests, 1704.
36, 37, 37a, 38, 39, 40, 41, 42, 43. *Inishowen*, "Maghtochair".
44, 45, 46, 47, 48, 49, 50, 51. *Irish Catholic Directory*.
52. *Analecta Hibernica*, Vol. 12 — The O Kane Papers: Bishop Montgomery's Survey of Derry diocese, *circa* 1605.
53. *Irish Catholic Directory*: Register of Popish Priests, 1704.
54, 55, 56, 57. *Memorials of the Dead of Ireland*, Vol. V.
58, 59, 60, 61, 62, 63, 64, 65. *Inishowen*, "Maghtochair".
66, 67, 68, 69, 70, 71, 72, 73, 74, 75, 76, 77. *Irish Catholic Directory*.
78. Inquisitions of James I: Appendix for Donegal.
79. *Archivium Hibernicum*, Vol. 1.
80. Inquisitions of James I: Appendix for Donegal.
81. *Calendar of Papal Registers, 1417-1486*.
82. Inquisitions of James I: Appendix for Donegal.
83, 84, 85, 86. Tithe Applotment Book: Cloncha, 1828.
87. *Analecta Hibernica*: Ulster Plantation Papers, 1608-1613, Vol. 8, P. 292.

Note: See page 50:

George O'Doherty was born in 1721 and became a postulant, in the Order of Preachers, in his late teens. He was professed in 1741. On his ordination he was assigned to the monastery at Derry. Records show he was there in 1762.

The more intensive application of the Penal Laws forced the Dominicans and other Orders to leave the city. Fr. O'Doherty, at the request of the Bishop of Derry, went to serve in Cloncha, his native parish. The date of his death is not known.

Reference:

Hibernia Dominicana by Thomas De Burgo 1762 see page 281.

Note: See page 51:

1968: Patrick Joseph McKenna, born at Eden, Dungiven in 1910, was ordained in 1935. He served in Nigeria, United States and Derry City. On his retirement in 1985, he served as a curate for two years. He died in August 31, 1989 and is buried at Lagg.

1985: Charles Campbell, a native of Ballinascreen, Draperstown, Co. Derry, succeeded. He was ordained in June 1955 and served successively at Termonamongan, Carndonagh, Plumbridge & Limavady.

4
INTRODUCTION AND DEVELOPMENT OF CHRISTIANITY (CONTINUED)

IN THE previous chapter the rise and development of monasticism at national level from 550 A.D. to 1150 A.D. were sketched. How the parishes of Culdaff and Cloncha were influenced has been indicated and how they made a noted contribution in this golden age of monasticism was outlined in brief. Now the foundations themselves in our area can be examined, insofar as information is available.

The religious sites in the area can for convenience be divided into four categories: those of national repute and standing, the lesser foundations which are evidenced by a strong and enduring tradition, the small hermitages whose existence is certain but about which little is known and finally those sites of which further evidence is required before they can be correctly classified.

Both Chonais, mentioned in many of the Annals, belongs to the first division. The foundations at Cluain Catha, Culdaff, Greallach and Teampall Muirdhealaigh enjoyed a strong and enduring tradition as centres of worship and devotion. Of the remaining 25, more than a dozen can be included without any doubt in the third category, the small hermitages.

An examination of the information available in respect of the others shows that they may have originated as pagan burial grounds. Alternatively, some may have been old forts which were used as burial places for unbaptised children. No local tradition exists to help in establishing a clearer classification.

The evidence available as a whole is sufficient to prove beyond doubt that here was a remote corner of Ireland where monasticism flourished during Ireland's Golden Age. Many of the sons and daughters of the Gael found here the correct environment for giving full expression to their intense desire for a higher spiritual life. A greater and closer union with God was made possible by the peace and solitude found in this secluded area.

Among the religious centres in our area two were outstanding in the popular devotion, Tobar Muirdhealaigh and Linntreach Buadain. The local folklore contained more information about these two centres than about any of the others. Why ?

Medical skill, with its reasonable assurance of a remedy for every illness, is a modern development. In the past, up to say one hundred years ago, people had not the doctor or the veterinary surgeon to consult in case of illness of man or beast respectively. That hope of recovery so necessary to maintain the mental tone of the ill and of their relations was sustained by the curative waters of centres of devotion such as Malin Well and Buadan's Pool.

The lapse of time dimmed the memory of other centres. In due course their story was forgotten and people ceased to frequent the once hallowed spots. The abiding presence of human ills ensured, however, that in each generation places like the two mentioned continued as places of pilgrimage for the sick and needy almost to the present time.

A more sophisticated society here has now forsaken all the old centres of pilgrimage. The doctor and the hospital services are substituted for the saving waters of Drumnakill and Culdaff.

AGHAGLASSON

In the valley of the Deel, near the stream flowing between the townlands of Ourt and Aghaglasson, there is a well-respected burial ground. There is evidence of the existence of a circular building, and many stones are strewn around. Have we here the site of an old fort converted to a burial place for children, or the site of an old hermitage associated with the monastic foundation at Carrowmore nearby ? The latter is highly probable.

BALLELLAGHAN

By the side of a stream, in a very secluded and sheltered spot, there is a well-preserved and ancient graveyard called locally the " Keldra ".

BALLYHILLIN

Close to the sea there is the site of an old burial ground. The port close by is called Portaloran—*Port Chill Orain*. Old residents here say that this site was known to them in their early days as Ceall Orain—the church of Oran. St. Oran was a disciple of Colm Cille. This saint had also a church and foundation at Binion in Clonmany.

The area now is merely a patch of sand by the seaside. Nearby a small stream flows into the sea, and a skull was found here some years ago. Sand was taken from here for the building of the tower nearby. While removing the sand a midden of *bairneach* shells was found, indicating human habitation of some form.

In this spot there was a monastic foundation with its church.

Later the site was used as a burial ground. The church is remembered in the name of the area—Ballyhillin, or in Irish *Baile an Chillín*.

BALLYMAGARAGHY

The portion of this townland running along the sea is part of the parish of Culdaff. A glance at the map will indicate that this section of the townland is detached from the rest of the parish to which it belongs. It is a sort of island surrounded by the sea and the parish of Moville. It is suggested that here was the site of a hermitage founded by Both Chonais and retained within its area of influence when the parishes were delimited.

BOTH CHONAIS

To the left of the road which passes through Gleneely to Carndonagh, near where the road junctions off towards Culdaff, can be seen two stone crosses. These stand on the side of a hill and they mark the location of one of the oldest and most important monastic foundations in Inis Eoghain. Here, in the townland of Carrowmore, is the site of Both Chonais.[1]

It is highly probable that St. Patrick passed this way on his journey from Donagh towards Moville. The land here at Carrowmore belonged to Conas,[2] the second husband of Darerca, who was a sister of Patrick. Hence *Both Chonais*—the cell of Conas.

In St. Patrick's lifetime a small church was probably built here by Conas. It was, however, the coming of Comhghall, a member of the influential Cineál Eoghain, that enhanced this foundation so that it was known throughout the whole of Ireland for the sanctity and learning of its community.

Along the valley of the Deel around 650 A.D. came Comhghall[3] in search of a place to establish a monastery. This was the first period of monasticism and the great descendant of Eoghan selected this spot above the river as the site of his foundation. It was a fertile spot, well-watered and commanding a good view of the surrounding district. Through the influence of Comhghall, lands were granted. A church and cells were erected. The most learned in Ireland were invited here to teach and to train the aspirants to the spiritual life in the art of prayer and contemplation. So were laid the beginnings of Both Chonais, which for five hundred years was to be a shining light to illuminate the area.

Despite the fluctuating tone of monasticism between 650 and 1150 at national level, Carrowmore maintained a high standard in both learning and spirituality. It extended its immediate area of influence and control from Cashel, in the environs of Donagh, to Ballymagaraghy, on the eastern side. In the monastic developments which tended towards the setting up of hermitages and small foundations, the area was dotted with off-shoots from Both Chonais. The monks who sought a higher degree of sanctity set up small hermitages at different points along the valley of the Deel and further. These were almost all subject to Carrowmore. A visit to this area around 800 A.D. would have shown a scene of great monastic activity. Here was a place of prayer, of culture and of learning.

The greatest and most important foundation sponsored by Both Chonais was the monastery of St. Buadan at Culdaff. Here, by the side of the same river which flowed past Both Chonais, was established an important seat of missionary activity. The annalists[4] mention this foundation at Carrowmore on a number of occasions. In 852 is recorded the death of Ceannfaeled, son of Ultan, "wise man of Both Chonais," the death of Dubhdabhairenn, *airchinneach* of the monastery, in 988 and the demise in 1049 of Tuathal Ua hUaill. In the same century the monastery is referred to in connection with the death of Maol Iosa O Brolchain,[5] a man whose learning and piety highlighted, as late as the eleventh century, the continuing high standards at Both Chonais.

It is clear that Carrowmore was still a very important seat of learning in the eleventh century but the circumstances in which it ceased to function are vague and uncertain. One tradition states that when the Ui Dhochartaigh took possession of Inis Eoghain their chief demanded tribute from the abbot. The payment was refused and O Dochartaigh burned the foundation. However, this story is open to question.

When the parish areas were established and defined in the thirteenth century, the foundation at Culdaff became the centre of this parish and gave it its name. The area of influence of Both Chonais became part of Culdaff. If Carrowmore then existed as a monastic centre it would have had pre-eminence and would have become the centre of the parish.

In the fourteenth century records there are references[6] to Culdaff, Cloncha and Greallach. Both Chonais is not mentioned. The implication is that this monastery had ceased to exist much earlier. It is highly probable that Both Chonais ceased as a foundation in the twelfth century. The decline of monasticism generally may have been the cause, or perhaps a raid may have resulted in the burning and pillaging of this sacred foundation.

There is no indication as to how the lands of the monastery were disposed of. De Burgo got some of the monastic lands of Inis Eoghain,[7] but there is no evidence that he secured these.

The site of the ancient foundation continued to be a place of pilgrimage. There was a holy well here and a *turas* was made to it up to the end of the last century. Nearby, when the Penal Laws forbade the Catholic community the right of public worship, Mass was said in the glen.

To-day the visitor to Teampall Mor can see the old graveyard overlooking the Carrowmore river. Here lie the remains of many of the people of Inis Eoghain. Both Chonais as a burial place was to the people of this peninsula what Clonmacnoise was to the people of Ireland, a place of honour and holiness to await the resurrection hour.

Two fine crosses, standing ten feet high, dominate the site.

There is also an irregularly shaped stone on which is carved a small cross. There is evidence of the existence of another cross within the graveyard area. These works of stone indicate the existence of a high degree of craftsmanship among the monks. There is little doubt but that many more crosses existed here when the monastery functioned in full.

Oral tradition regarding this place is very scant. The break in oral tradition and our defective educational system have left people generally very ill-informed about their great heritage.

At the beginning of this century the parish priest at Bocan held a service on Sunday afternoons at this spot in order to foster interest in and to restore respect for the foundation. The parochial hall for the parish of Culdaff is known as St. Comhghall's. This is the only reference to the founder of Both Chonais in the area. Some, however, would see in the name " Bocan " a corruption of the original name of the Carrowmore foundation.

The full story of this monastery has yet to be written. Some day perhaps the site will be explored under the direction of a competent authority and some of its storied past revealed.

CARRICK

By the side of a stream in the valley of the river Deel part of an old burial ground can still be seen. Some years ago the owner ploughed part of this site but desisted from tilling the whole area because of the disapproval shown locally. This site was used as a burial place for unbaptised children up to the middle of the last century. Here, most probably, was a hermitage founded by the monastic community at Both Chonais.

CASHEL

In Upper Cashel, midway between the upper and lower roads to Carndonagh, there is an old graveyard known locally as the " Caldragh ". The site is well-respected by the present owner of the land. The burial ground is grown over by a clump of bushes and there are many stones strewn around. A close examination shows a small pillar and evidence of a circular building.

The late Fr. W. Hegarty stated that there was a Columban stone here.[8] This suggests a small church and perhaps the site of another hermitage associated with Both Chonais. The foundation is sited in the fertile valley which runs from Gleneely along the banks of the Deel.

KILMURRAY

In the townland of Kullourt, by the side of the river which

flows into Kullourt Bay, was situated an old burial ground. A former owner of the land tilled the site and no trace remains today, but tradition still indicates the hallowed spot.

That an old and important monastery existed in this townland is beyond doubt. Local tradition is strong. No tithes were paid by the tenants of this townland, because it was monastic property.[9] Records show that this area was granted to the Cistercian monastery in 1218 A.D.[10]

Was this foundation established and endowed by Muireadach, son of Eoghan ? Cill Muireadaigh ? The area under the influence of this monastery extended most probably as far as Lagg. The thirteenth century was a time of great change in church organisation. The parish units were defined and monastic lands disposed of. The monastery at Kullourt lasted probably up to the eleventh or twelfth century.

CILL PHADRAIG

In the area which lies seawards from Cruckameal in the townland of Ballyharry is a spot by the sea known as Cill Phadraig. Have we here the hermitage site of Achadh Drumman associated with St. Patrick's missionary journey in the north ? Fr. Hegarty so suggests.[11]

This is one of the few sites in Inis Eoghain dedicated to St. Patrick. The Columban cult, by design or by accident, was the dominant one in this area.

CLUAIN CATHA

To the left of the road which connects Bocan church with Carrowmore, and near the point at which the road from Larrahirrel abuts, can be seen the ruins of an old church. Here, in a pleasant meadow, was sited the important monastic foundation known as Cluain Catha. The modern English name is Cloncha.

It is probable that this spot had religious significance from the time of St. Patrick. One authority suggests that here may have been located the Patrician foundation called Domhnach Catha.[12] It is reasonable to assume that St. Patrick, as he journeyed from Donagh to Moville, would have taken every opportunity to preach to the people. To ensure continuity of contact some sort of centre of worship would have been necessary. The establishment of some simple form of church here in the fifth century is therefore probable. The evidence is slender but should not be dismissed altogether.

This foundation was developed during the first phase of

monasticism, that is within the years 550 A.D. to 700 A.D. Columban influences were at work, however, and this monastery fell into the orbit of the disciples of the man from Gartan. Any Patrician cult that existed was quietly eliminated. Here it is interesting to note that in contrast Both Chonais and Culdaff maintained an independent existence and did not fall under the sway of the followers of Colm Cille. As well as at Cluain Catha, the Columban influence affected most of the area now known as the parish of Cloncha. Greallach, Cill Orain and Teampall Muirdhealaigh are examples.

It was the coming of Breacan[13] and his disciples that led to the development of Cluain Catha as an important foundation. Breacan was of the powerful Cineal Eoghain. This ensured for Cluain Catha a grant of lands, and men skilled in learning and the spiritual life. The community grew in strength.

The importance of the foundation can be appreciated from the extent of its lands, amounting to a total area of 2,800 acres. The actual monastic foundation was much wider than the area now enclosed within the graveyard wall. In the early thirteenth century the foundation became the parish centre and gave its name to the whole parish. Cluain Catha was closely associated with the foundation at Derry during the succeeding centuries. The first reference to this parish is found in 1302.[14] It is mentioned again in 1367[15] and frequently in the fifteenth century.[16]

An indication of the greatness of Cluain Catha can be seen in the stone-work, some of which dates back to the year 800 A.D.[17] It must be recognised that only a fraction is now left.

A fragment of a stone on the side of the church bears part of an inscription in Irish: . . . *an O Dubhagan do ri-nne-* . . . *og so do Domnall On . . . Sunn.* Evidently it is part of a gravestone left after the builder's hammer had moulded it for its place in the wall of the church. The device of a mallet and chisel can be seen above the inscription, which may mean " Brian O Duagain made this stone for Donall O Neill ".

The remains of a high cross now stand outside the enclosure wall. The portion of the shaft now erect measures about ten feet in height and sixteen inches by eight and a half. For an unexplained reason some recent writers describe this as the " Cross of St. Buadan ". There is no evidence that St. Buadan had any connection with this foundation. Authorities say that the cross was divided into panels and carved with figures representing

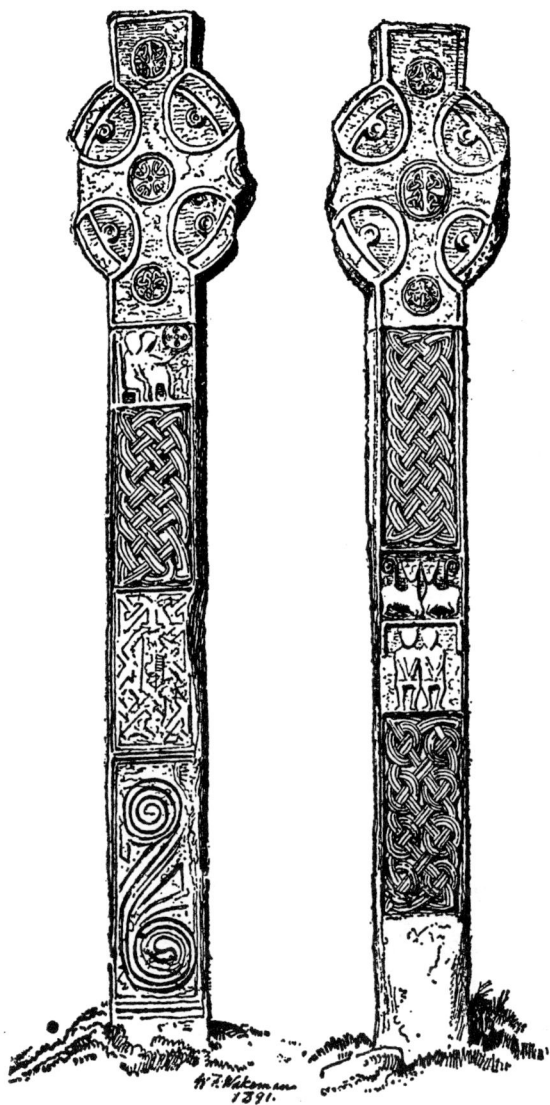

Biblical subjects, after the style of the Monasterboice crosses. The figures sculptured on the cross at the top are said to represent St. Paul and St. Anthony, the founder of monasticism, dividing the bread brought to them by a raven. Below can be seen a panel of plait-work, a panel of diagonal fret and a large spiral or trumpet pattern. The west side shows at the top a panel filled by a plait formed of double bands. Below these are two animals crouching, with human heads and tails coiled over their backs. Next to them are two human figures side by side and below the latter is a long panel of interlaced bands crossing diagonally through axes. There is also a large cross-head which has a solid recessed ring of three feet eight inches in diameter and is decorated with plain mouldings and flat bosses or roundels containing interlaced patterns. The remainder of the cross cannot now be traced.

Within the church, near the sanctuary, can be seen a work of surpassing beauty, exhibiting the skill of a worker of exceptional ability. A piece of local limestone, it is beautifully carved, with a divisional cross, which commences by turned serpent's heads, extending so as to form by graceful curves the terminations of the head and arms of the cross. The foot of the cross ends in various floral embellishments, possibly emblematic. On the right of the cross is a double-headed sculptured sword, full size, with ornamental pommel and recurved guard. Alongside the sword is the outline of a *caman* and *sliotar*, or possibly a sort of golf club and ball. On the left-hand side of the slab is a curved spray of flowers extending over the surface, as a counterpoise to the *caman* and sword.

The stone bears an inscription in Irish. On the right, reading from the centre, is: *FERGUS MA ALIAN DORISTEN*. On the left, reading towards the centre: *MAGNUS MACORRISTIN IAPOTKISE*. Part of the inscription is worn away. A suggested rendering is: *FERGUS MAC ALIAN DO RIN IN CLAG SO. MAGNUS MAC ORRISTIN IA FO TRI SEO.* (Fergus Mac Alian made this stone. Magnus Mac Orristin of the Isles under this mound.)

The singular beauty of this stone was no doubt the reason for its preservation when the church was re-built. Indeed, it was probably within the sanctuary of the old pre-Reformation church and was left there undisturbed—a lone survival of the stone workers' skill, of which there must have been many other examples in the old monastic foundation.

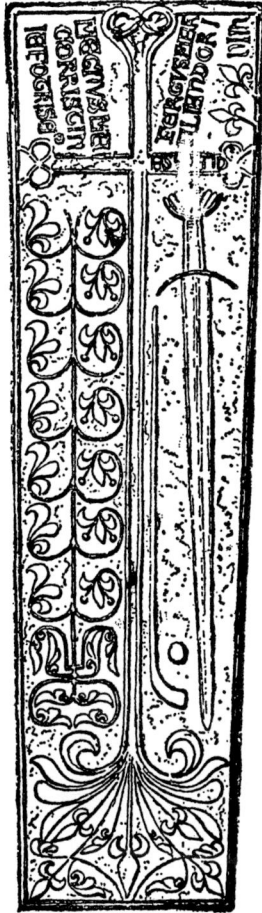

We have now no information regarding either the stoneworker or the person buried here. There was, down the centuries, the closest contact between Inis Eoghain and the west of Scotland. All the Columban foundations here maintained close links with Iona, and there were trading and inter-marriage connections.

The people in both areas had much in common: they were both of Celtic stock and they spoke the same language.

There is also a small, very ancient and rudely shaped cross about twenty inches high and a foot from the extremity of one limb to that of the other. It used to be in the gable.

With regard to the highly ornamented stone over Magnus Mac Orristin, there is a story told that some fishermen from Culdaff were driven by storm to the Western Isles. Seeking ballast, they entered a graveyard and took back this stone. It was left on the shore at Culdaff. Later, when a member of the Young family was buried in Cloncha, this stone was taken up to the burial-ground and used to mark the grave. This is a *deus ex machina* type of story, invented by those who had no knowledge of the historical background of the area. It should, therefore, be regarded as a mere fabrication.

There are also the remains of another high cross in a field near the road. It is fallen down. The base in which it was set can be also seen.

At the left angle of the road between Larrahirrel and Bellnamona made by the inter-section of the road from Bocan to Carrowmore there was a clump of stones. About thirty years ago the owner decided to remove the stones and found a small stone cross buried in the centre. The cross was taken to the presbytery at Culdaff.

In the early seventeenth century, when the lands and churches here belonging to the Catholic community were confiscated, Cloncha was given to the Protestant Church. For a time the building fell into decay. In 1622 we find a report that the " Church of Cloncagh is fallen down and altogether decayed ".[18]

About the middle of the seventeenth century the church was re-built. It was during this period that wholesale vandalism took place. The new occupiers of this ancient and hallowed spot knew nothing of and cared little for the culture of a thousand years. In the course of building most of the stone crosses and other ornamented grave stones were destroyed. Fragments of them can be seen in the walls of the old church. The lintel is evidently part of the older building.

The re-built church measured about 47 feet by 20 feet. It was used for worship up to 1827, when the present church in Malin Town was built. In 1880 the church and burial ground were declared a National Monument and thus, after two and a half centuries, it passed out of the control of the Protestant Church.

In this sacred spot lie the remains of forty generations of the people of this district. Evidence of its desirability as a last resting place is the fact that a bishop of Derry selected it for his grave, out of all the sites in his diocese. Opposite the church door there is a broad slab of unpolished stone covering a vault. Beneath lie the remains of Dr. J. McColgan,[19] a native of Carndonagh in the parish of Donagh. He ruled his see of Derry from 1760 to 1769, amid dangers and privations. He died in Omagh in 1769 and was buried here at his own request.

Within this graveyard, in an unmarked grave, was buried sometime in the eighteenth century Fr. Sheridan. This priest was closely associated with the House of Stuart.[20] Here also rests, beneath a fine tombstone, William Elwood, the first Protestant rector to live at Redford.

The burial ground at Cloncha continued to be used by both Catholics and Protestants up to 1820. When the church at Bocan was built Catholics began to use the present burial ground there. Protestants continued to bury at Cloncha up to 1935, but the graveyard is now closed.

The church and its environs are now empty and silent. The story of this foundation is known to only a few. It is, however, important to note that this area was once a seat of great learning and a place of prayer. Here was a place of culture which moulded the minds of many generations and raised the tone of intellectual life for many of our ancestors to a high level.

CRAIGAJANNY is an old burial place for unbaptised children. It is located at Bootagh in the townland of Tirmacroragh.

CRAIGMORE, in the townland of Ballygorman, is a site used for a purpose similar to the foregoing.

CRUCKALOUGH is a lake in the townland of Dunagard. Here was located a hermitage associated with Bee-ella (?), about whom little is known. A *turas* is made here and St. Patrick is honoured. It is a wild and desolate place on the summit of a hill overlooking the sea. Heather, bog and stones abound—an ideal place for prayer and contemplation.

CUIL CHILL NA gCORP is situated by the seaside at Portaleen in the townland of Glengad. This burial ground for unbaptised children is located on the top of a plateau. The summit is marked by a standing stone and many other stones are strewn around.

Here was located an ancient hermitage. It is a spot of peace and wild beauty. The beat of the waves and the call of the seabirds are the only sounds which disturb this haven by the side of the Atlantic.

CULDAFF

By the side of the river which drains the valley of Gleneely, and near the point where it reaches the sea, stands the village of Culdaff. To this spot many centuries ago came Buadan to seek a place of solitude and peace. Here he founded a monastery, which became a centre of culture and missionary activity.

When Buadan came to this place in the distant past he saw a corner of land located in the loop made by the river. The recess was completely wooded and the river was at certain places much wider. On the top of the height now known as Ardmore he cleared the trees and shrubs, and a crude form of shelter was built. Later a church and other buildings arose. A distinctive feature of the place was the two fords located so closely together. The people who lived around had noted this and gave the place the name which it still bears, *Cuil da Ath*—the corner of the two fords.

Buadan was a native of Inis Eoghain and was probably born within the area now known as the parish of Culdaff. He was educated at Both Chonais and Bangor and became actively involved in the evangelisation of his kinsmen in Scotland.[21] Some time in the eighth century he left Carrowmore with a group of followers. He came to Culdaff and founded a missionary springboard for his work in Scotland. From here to the nearest point in Scotland is a mere forty miles.

One can easily imagine the constant flow of traffic from Culdaff to the west coast of the neighbouring country. Fruitful association was maintained between the monasteries, the Gaelic rulers and the ordinary people.

In the decline of monasticism in the twelfth century Culdaff continued as a place of worship for the people of the district. One relic of the old monastery survived, the Bell of St. Buadan, a ninth century production. When the re-organisation resulting from the reform movement in the Irish Church took place, in the early thirteenth century, Culdaff became a perpetual vicarage subject to the rector of Moville. The district under the control of the vicar corresponded to the older monastic areas of both Both Chonais and Buadan.

72

It is interesting to speculate as to why Culdaff was attached to Moville. Cloncha had fallen under Columban influence early. It would seem that Buadan's and Comhghall's maintained their independence. Moville and Both Chonais had close association with St. Patrick. Did this mean that these two sites maintained close links in the succeeding centuries, so that the grouping of Culdaff with Moville was a natural development ?

Culdaff is mentioned in 1367[22] and in the Papal documents of the fifteenth century.[23] In 1605 the parish is mentioned in Bishop Montgomery's Survey.[24] There is mention of a stone house here then.

In 1622 the Protestant Bishop of Derry reported that " the parish church had very good walls standing, fit to be built on but not covered ".[25] The new rector was building a house and later the church was repaired and made suitable for worship. This report indicates that after the church and lands had been confiscated from the Catholics a decade before, the building was allowed to fall into disuse for a time. Indeed, the new rector had little use for a place of worship, as he had not a single person of his own religious persuasion in the area at this time.

Bishop Nicholson, the Protestant ordinary at Derry, found in 1739 that the church was again in a ruinous and decayed state.[26] He ordered that the old building be pulled down and a new one built. The episcopal instructions were carried out and a new church arose on the old site in 1747. A tower was added in 1828, and the structure has remained unaltered since that date.[27]

The original graveyard extended from Ardmore, where there are the remains of the old burial ground, across the road running through the village to where the church now stands. This was confirmed in the last century, when road-workers found human bones in the soil while road-widening. Both Catholics and Protestants used the graveyard here during the seventeenth and eighteenth centuries. Many parish priests of Culdaff in the post-confiscation period were buried there.

Of the many religious foundations in the parishes of Culdaff and Cloncha this site has the unique record of being the only one which continued as a place of worship from the eighth century until the present day.

As happened in many other areas, the re-building of the church effaced not only the older structure but all evidence of the early stone-work. The vandalism here was complete. There is not to-day a single vestige of the stone crosses which were a feature of these old foundations. Masterpieces of early Irish art perished at the hands of unfeeling Saxons.

The boat, the well and the station of St. Buadan still remain to remind all that here there was once a flourishing and influential monastery. The great force of the father and founder is evidenced by the survival of devotion to him even until the present.

As the Protestant population in this parish continues to diminish can one hope that, in the spirit of ecumenism and as a gesture of reparation and reconciliation, the Protestant authorities will return this church and burial ground to the Catholic community, from whom the property was unjustly taken by the decree of an English monarch in 1609 ?

DRUMACROSS is the name of a ridge in the townland of Ballygorman. It is not far from Teampall Muirdhealaigh. There is no tradition to indicate the nature of the holy place situated here.

DRUMCARBIT: Here is located a burial ground on the banks of the river Ballyboe. There is no tradition to indicate the existence of any foundation. There may have been an old fort here.

DRUMNAKILL is in the townland of Ballygorman.

Near where Malin Head juts out into the Atlantic there is a quiet spot by the sea, known far and wide in its day as a religious centre. The place is now known as Malin Well — the *Tobar Muirdhealaigh* of Irish-speaking times.

Nature was in an austere mood when her hand formed this spot. Landwards, giant, gaunt cliffs stand as mighty, unyielding sentinels. No tree casts its shade here. On the shore lie thousands of pebbles, large and small, and of many hues, showing the results of the rushing waters over millions of years. The mighty rock bastion of Doon stands seawards, ensuring that the wild sea will keep its proper bounds and leave the spot untouched.

A little further out are Inis Ban, Inis Glas and Inis Boillscinne —a trinity of islands standing stark and naked, braking somewhat the violence of the sea in its rush to meet the land. This sacred spot, this focal point, is *Droim na Cille*—the ridge of the church.

When the Celt in his island home first received the Christian revelation he interpreted the message as a call to prayer, fasting and contemplation. For such, solitude was essential. A serious young man sought the proper environment and found it at Malin

74

Well. The immanence of God in nature could never be forgotten here. Such was the beginning of Drumnakill. The example of this early anchorite influenced others to come and share his life, and in time a community was formed. A church was built and cells for the large and growing membership were added. Who was this first arrival whose example was so powerful and compelling ?

In attempting to answer this query some attention should be given to the saints associated with this foundation. Three are mentioned, Gorman, Machar and Muirdhealach.

It has been the custom to refer to the building here as the " Gorman Church ". This gave rise to the idea that St. Gorman was venerated at Drumnakill. This is an error. The Gorman reference is associated with an old and respected family in the townland of Ballygorman who had a special connection with Malin Well. (This point will be dealt with later.)

Machar or Mochonna was, according to tradition, honoured here and is credited with the building of the church. This saint had a close association with Scotland.

St. Muirdhealach is referred to in the *Martyrology of Donegal*: " Muirdeathair, son of Cranna of the race of Irial, is called Muirdhealach at the present day and in Inis Eoghain his church and holiday are ". This is a reference to the saint's cult at Malin Well. In the tradition of the people in Malin Head up to the present day, Muirdhealach has survived as a real living person. He is and was the saint regarded by the local residents as the one most closely connected with the religious centre at Malin Well. Therefore, in answering the query posed above regarding the identity of the first hermit, it can be asserted that, while it is unlikely that Muirdhealach himself was here, the first arrival was a close disciple of this saint.

One of the families who have had a long association with Ballygorman, the townland in which Drumnakill is situated, is that of O Gormain. This family is mentioned in the Hearth Money Roll for 1660.

The last member of the family, Padraig O Gormain, told an interesting story regarding the Holy Stone of Malin. The stone had been given to the O Gormain family by the " Saint " of Malin Well. The holy man promised that no member of the family would ever be lost at sea while the stone was kept in its possession. The Holy Stone had also a curing effect. Anyone seeking a cure called on the O Gormain family, who applied the stone to the part affected. The possession of the relic was regarded as a great honour and this led to a dispute in the early part of the last century. The O Gormain sept had a number of branches and among these was one family in Ballyhillin, in the neighbouring townland of Ardmalin. A member of this family stole the stone, and the owners went in strength to Ballyhillin and recovered it by force. As a result of the fracas the parish priest, Fr. Neil O Flaherty, became involved. To settle matters finally he took the stone, and since then no trace of it can be found.

On the edge of the sea, in a sheltered spot, stand the ruins of the old church. The original building measured about 35 feet by 15. Nowadays one gable wall and part of two side walls are all that remain. The walls are faced with large stones and packed inside with small stones, without mortar. On the end of the angle of the wall at the land side there is a stone with the outline of a face cut into it.

A close examination of the surrounding area shows the site outline of other buildings. One of these may have been the inn referred to by some writers.

The "Well", famous for its curative waters, has been described as a natural basin of fresh water formed in the rock and covered by the sea at high tide. It was, according to tradition, blessed by St. Muirdhealach. He imparted to its waters the supernatural qualities which drew pilgrims from many places. The person making the station here bathed in the sacred waters.

Nearby is the "Wee House of Malin". It is a sort of cave in the face of the cliff. Local tradition says that the "House" will hold all who go into it.

The most sacred spot in this holy area is the saint's grave. Its exact location is now in doubt as there was a land subsidence, and the grave was comple tely covered in the fall of earth. The name of the saint is unknown.

Tobar Muirdhealaigh was a famous place of pilgrimage. People came here not only from the whole of Inis Eoghain but also from the rest of Donegal and from Derry and Tyrone. Two days of special devotion were held here, the eve of the Feast of St. John the Baptist and the Feast of the Assumption. Locally, up to recently, the last named feast was called La 'le Muire.

The crowds who gathered here came not only to make the

station but also to sing and dance. Prayer and entertainment were combined. The festivities on the eve of the Feast of St. John ceased in the last century but the commemoration of August 15th continued up to the beginning of the present century. The station is no longer made here.

The earliest extant reference to Malin Well was made in 1669. In the confirmation by Charles II of the lands of Inis Eoghain to Chichester is mentioned "an ancient chapel, called Templemurgalla, reputed parcel of Ballygorman."[28]

Reports written by various visitors to Drumnakill during the eighteenth and early nineteenth centuries give interesting details regarding the pilgrimage here. All were written by hostile observers.

Describing a "Journey to Ye North" in 1708, Dr. Thomas Molyneux says:[29]

> **Tuesday: We were invited to dine with Major General Hamilton,** who lives at a place called . . . within two miles of Newtown, on the road to Derry. Mrs. Hamilton here told me of a very famous Well in Enishowen, in C. Donnegall, which is a Vast Peninsula of Land between Loughfoile and Swilly, all belonging to . . . called Mallinwell. Here the sick came from all parts to be cured by going into it, yet has the Waters of it no particular virtue, for it seems to be only a hollow in a Rock where one may sit and let the Waves beat clear over you. However, the Coldness of the Water has surely had good effects. She told me she had been in it several times, but has not found much benefit . . .

In 1739:[30]

> Malinhead was much visited in Summer for the sea-bathing, especially by invalids, the water being reckoned to have here a more than ordinary virtue in strengthening and restoring weak limbs. The bathing place was a deep cave under the cliff . . .

Richard Pococke, an Englishman and Bishop of Ossory, passed this way during his Irish tour in 1752. His observations were as follows:[31]

> Coming near the sea cliff I looked for the house I was going to and could see none, but came to a passage down the cliff where I found the house on the beach under the rocks, and enquiring for the well, they showed me a hollow under a rock at the south end of a high small rocky Island, which at low water is a peninsula. Here people bathe with great success, the water being very salty as not mixed with fresh. And the Roman Catholics plunge in with superstitious notions that the water received some virtue from the Saint (Terence Marialla) who lived in a cave in a rock of the cliff, where poor people lodge who come for cure. The house for accommodation is exceeding bad . . .

Another visitor was James McParlan. In 1801 he reported the following:[32]

It probably, however, is near this old church, or the site of it, that a famous pilgrimage is performed, on some certain day in Summer, at a creek of the sea, which comes in among the rocks of Mawlin-head, by dropping a great number of beads; some walking on their legs, some on their knees and some stationary, all vehemently whispering prayers; but the ceremony finishes something like the Indian Tamarodie, by a general ablution in the sea, male and female, all frisking and playing in the water, stark naked and washing off each other's sins.

Dr. McParlan was evidently referring to the different spots visited during the station which were associated with the saints.

The very active pen of the Protestant rector of Cloncha, Edward Chichester, wrote in 1815:[33]

Near Malin Head is a small hollow in a rock which is filled with sea water at every tide; it is reputed to possess a miraculous power of curing diseases, and is consequently a serious nuisance to the neighbourhood for it invites strollers and mendicants of the worst description from the three adjoining counties who infest the neighbourhood by their numbers and corrupt it by their example. The patron days of the place are Saint John's Eve and the Assumption of the Virgin, and they are celebrated there by the most disgusting drunkeness and debauching, under pretence of paying adoration to Saint Moriallagh the patron of the Well. This saint is not acknowledged in the calendar: and the clergy of the Church of Rome have very promptly forbidden the offensive orgies by which he is worshipped: it is, however, to be regretted that his votaries have not attended to the salutary advice of their pastors on this subject.

The burial place at Drumnakill was used up to the early part of the last century. The last adult buried here was a male member of the O Gormain family.

Here it may be asked what special connection had the O Gormain family with this ancient foundation. They were custodians of the Holy Stone, the church was known as the Gorman Church and for this family Malin Well was the desired place of burial long after others had changed to Lagg. It is highly probable that the O Gormain family held the position of *airchinnigh* in earlier times here.

There is no doubt that there was a very early Christian foundation here, dating back to a period even earlier that 800 A.D. There is also the implication that Malin Well was originally a pagan centre of worship. The early hermits came and Christianised the cult.

The people of Malin Head still have a deep and abiding reverence for this saced spot. For centuries their ancestors came to worship at this church. Each generation found in turn a holy and peaceful resting place here by the side of the monks who had served them in life. It is fitting then that the people who live here to-day still honour the sacred spot.

The discerning visitor of to-day cannot fail to be impressed by the beauty and solitude of the place. If he has imagination he can picture the days of its glory, when it pulsed with life. He will hear again the chanting of the psalms of David, the tinkle of the Mass Bell and the sweet sound of our native language above the roaring of the waves.

FAHAN is the name of a district in the townland of Drumaville. Has the following entry in the *Martyrology of Donegal* any connection with the district mentioned above?

Colman Iomhramha — Colman Eirmer Marian — of Fathan Beg in Inis Eoghain. He is of the race of Cairpre Riada, son of Conaire, who is of the race of Heremon.

Investigations carried out on the spot fail to establish any oral tradition.

GREALLACH

Close to the southern tip of Straghbreggagh Bay, amid bogs and hills, there can still be seen an old graveyard and the ruins of a building. The site is located in a fertile oasis chosen many centuries ago by monks who sought a place for prayer. Here, in the townland of Teampall Maol, is the location of the ancient foundation known as Greallach.

The name Greallach is applied to-day to the spot where the old monastery stands. However, the area of Greallach was much wider in former times.[34] In 1829 the name applied to the modern townlands of Teampall Maol, Drumaville and Drumballycaslin. When Greallach functioned as a centre of worship its area included at least ten townlands extending from the borders of Culdaff parish towards Malin.

The foundation at Greallach was dedicated to St. Eunan,[35] the abbot of Iona. The strong devotion to him here suggests the influence of Columban monks and implies that this was a Columban foundation. With the decline of the monasteries Greallach became a perpetual vicarage subject to the rector of Cloncha.

In the fifteenth and sixteenth centuries there are references to this site in Papal and other documents.[36] By the early seventeenth century it ceased to exist as a vicarage, though the church-lands were still part of the church property in the parish of Cloncha.

There was a *turas* here in honour of St. Eunan. The devotion continued here up to the beginning of the present century. Two holy wells associated with the *turas* are located on the left-hand side of the road running between Culdaff and Malin, at the angle formed by the road between Aghaclay and Drumaville.

The visitor to Greallach to-day will see an old graveyard surrounded by a wall and overgrown by cherry trees. Burials took place here up to the beginning of the last century. Outside, a heap of stones, a small cross and the outline of a circular building are all that remain of the old foundation.

The local people, while ignorant of its history, still revere Greallach as a sacred spot. Under the Penal Laws their ancestors often gathered near here on a Sunday morning in secret to hear Mass. When the harsh laws were relaxed the site chosen for the new church was at Aghaclay, a short distance away. A person going to Mass at Aghaclay to-day walks on ground sanctified by the feet of worshippers for well over one thousand years.

KILLIN is the name of a townland in the parish of Cloncha. Here were located a small church and hermitage. No trace of them can be found to-day. Because of the plantations, the continuity in oral tradition was broken.

KILMAROO: Here was located a church dedicated to Mael Rubha. He was of Cineal Eoghain. No trace of the church exists to-day. Local tradition is meagre. This place is located in Larrahirrel, adjacent to the famous foundation at Cluain Catha.

KILNOXTER is situated in the townland of Umgall. An old burial ground is located beside the river flowing towardh Kullourt. This area was. known to the older generation as *Cill an Chnoic*. Here was sited a small church. The area lies in the shelter of Knock-raw, where there are an old burial site and a holy well.

KILLYCOOLEY is in the townland of Dristernan. An old burial ground was located near the present school-house. The field in which it was sited was tilled, and so to-day there is no trace of it. Close by is Killycooley, the site of a church and hermitage.

This foundation lies in the valley of the Deel, not far from Both Chonais.

KNOCKAMANY is a townland adjacent to Kullourt. Was there at *Cnoc an Mhanaigh* a hermitage under the control of the large monastic foundation in Kullourt? There are many traditions in this area regarding an old monastery.

LAGG

On the left of the road which runs from Malin Town to Malin Head, by the side of Straghbreggagh Bay, a church can be seen amid the sand dunes. It is the Catholic place of worship for the people of this area. An examination of the burial place which adjoins it shows the site of an older church. A map of Inis Eoghain prepared about 1660 indicates that a church existed at this spot at that time.

The place surrounding the church was known as "Grainseach".[37] This area consisted of 60 acres approximately and was tithe free. The word *grainseach* occurs frequently in place-names and it is defined as a monastic granary.

According to the oral tradition, Lagg was the site of a monastery. The land around was once very fertile, and wheat was grown to fill the monastic granary. One day the monks saw a ship in the Bay of Straghbreggagh. The arrival of these strangers heralded an attack, because at the time Inis Eoghain was subject to many raids. The monks gathered in the monastic church and prayed for protection. A great sandstorm arose and the ship was lost. The land around was, however, severely damaged by the heavy coating of sand and it ceased to be capable of producing wheat.

The name, the oral tradition and the fact that the land remained tithe free indicate that the area was closely associated for a long time with the Church. Was there here an old monastic foundation or was this place associated with the foundation at Kullourt? There is a possibility that when all the monastic lands at Kullourt were disposed of this portion called Grainseach was retained as a site and as a support for a church to serve the people. A hermitage set here in solitude among the hills may have been the first ecclesiastical association of this place.

A reference occurs to a church here in 1605.[38] Another document mentions a church probably here and named Caldynalle (*Ceall Dun Aille*, the church of the cliff fort?).

This area, more than any other in the parish, has suffered through the plantations a break in oral tradition. The native Irish were driven out. Thus the normal accompaniments of an old foundation, such as the *turas* and the holy well, are absent. NA REILIGI at Ballyharry is situated near Termone at a spot overlooking the sea. There is at the place an old and revered burial ground. Is this the Baile Brighde mentioned by Symmington and regarded by the late Fr. W. Hegarty[39] as evidence of a Brigidine foundation near the border between Culdaff and Moville? Here was probably the site of an old church and hermitage.

NA REILIGI, at the Orable in the townland of Ballyharry, is the site of an old burial ground about which little is known.

SCREEN, on the border between Culdaff-Glebe and Glacknadrummond, is the site of an old shrine. Fr. Hegarty suggests that here many be the *scrin* of Dacuaillen, a saint associated with Derry and Colm Cille.[40]

NOTE:

A fragmentary alphabetical list of Irish placenames prepared in the seventeenth century and now in the custody of the Franciscans at Killiney contains this entry: *Cill Ultain in diocesi Derens I a d-Tuarmhoin, in parrochia de Magh Bile*. The letters "cap" are appended, denoting a chapel.

The reference relates without doubt to the area close to Falmore school and the site of St. Ultan's Well. This confirms the tradition that there was a church here founded by Ultan himself or by one of his disciples. The writer is correct in placing the area in the parish of Moville. Culdaff was part of that parish in pre-Reformation days. The district now called "Termone" had a wider area in earlier times than to-day.

Refer to *Celtica*, Vol. I .

SAINTS ASSOCIATED WITH CULDAFF AND CLONCHA

In this section are noted in brief the names and activities of saints associated with our area. Some of these have been connected with the religious foundations previously discussed. Others, for various reasons, enjoyed a special cult in this district. In the introduction and fostering of these devotions the old monastic foundations played a big part.

BREACAN was associated with the development of Cluain Catha and was of the Cineal Eoghain. He lived in the seventh century. He was abbot of Moville and bishop of Ard Bhreacain in County Meath.[41] His feast-day is July 16th. There is no popular devotion to him.

BRIGID OF KILDARE was revered by the people here up to the early part of this century. Devotion to her was widespread, and many traditions were associated with her feast-day. Her power, in the judgment of her devotees here, was ever used to alleviate human suffering in all its forms.

ST. BUADAN

This saint is very closely associated with the parish of Culdaff and his feast day is July 22nd. At Culdaff village was a church dedicated to him; in the river is a large stone known as Buadan's Boat; there is a holy well associated with him and his bell is still kept in the parish, of which he is the patron.

The Ulster Visitation Book of 1622 records that there were then rude steps down to the well or *linntreach* which, according to the writer, was cut out of the solid rock. It goes on: " it was considered a meritorious act for the Roman Catholics to pray on these steps, holding up the bell of St. Buadan ".

Chichester, writing in 1815,[42] states that it was the custom to bring sick cattle to the *linntreach* and plunge them in. St. Buadan was at the same time invoked in prayer to secure a cure.

The *Turas Buadain* continues even to the present day. Local people say that water taken out of the *linntreach* retains its freshness indefinitely. Many cures have been attributed to him.

Local tradition states that St. Buadan blessed the port of Bunagee, situated at the mouth of Culdaff river. It was held that no boat putting out from this port was ever lost. The belief was so widespread that boats were brought overland from Malin and other places to be launched here, so as to obtain the results of the blessing.

Tradition asserts that St. Buadan crossed from Scotland on the stone " boat " which still bears the mark of his five fingers. The story goes on to state that St. Buadan was one of the two saints who accompanied Colm Cille to the top of Cnoc na Naomh when he wished to lift the spell off Tory as a preliminary to sending missionaries in to convert its people. Buadan and Colm Cille crossed to Scotland on a missionary tour but the fierce Scots chased them. Colm Cille reached the boat and his oarsmen went off at speed, leaving Buadan behind to the mercies of the Scots. Buadan, standing on the edge of the cliff, shouted in terror. Colm Cille looked back and seeing Buadan's plight told him to have faith. Meantime, Colm Cille prayed and the portion of the rock on which Buadan was standing broke away. He landed safely on the water and sailed straight to Bunagee and up the Culdaff river to the spot where the boat now rests.

In the last century a local man, so the story is told, interfered with the " boat " and as a result incurred a disability from which he suffered until his death.

The story about the boat, in connecting Buadan with Scotland, enshrines an historic truth, but it errs in connecting this Buadan with the disciple of Colm Cille who bore the same name.

A St. Buadan is venerated at Tamney, St. Johnston, Meath, and at Laragh in Wicklow. It is not clear whether this is the saint honoured at Culdaff.

The cult of St. Buadan was very strong here, and the traditions are still recounted by the local people. In addition, his is almost the only *turas* still made in the area. It is interesting to note that the devotion continued despite the take-over of the site by the Church of Ireland.

CATHA

Some authorities see in the name Cluain Catha a reference to this saint, whose feast-day is September 8th. There is no clear evidence to connect him with the area.

COLMAN was of Dal Riada and had some Inis Eoghain associations. His feast-day is July 8th. If, as one authority suggests, the Fathain Beag mentioned in the *Martyrology of Donegal* is the present district of Fahan in Drumaville Malin, Colman would have a direct connection with our area. There is no local devotion at present to the saint.

COLM CILLE, the man from Gartan, was taken to their hearts by the people here. He was a man of their own kith and they were proud of his achievements. In the folklore Colm Cille featured in many stories as a very human and lovable man. The parish of Cloncha was dedicated to him.

COMHGHALL was associated with the development of Both Chonais. His feast is kept on September 4th. A member of Cineal Eoghain, he was a brother of Christicola and his period was the seventh century.

DACUAILEN was a contemporary of Colm Cille and was left in charge of Derry by him. He was the patron of the Ua Fearain family, who were associated with Scrin Dacuailen. Was this shrine located at Screen in the townland of Glacknadrummond ?

EUNAN, the biographer of Colm Cille, had a church dedicated to him at Greallach.[43] Here also were a holy well and *turas* in

84

honour of this saint. A descendant of King Niall, he became abbot of Iona. His feast is held on September 23rd.

GORMAN is associated by some with Drumnakill. There is no reliable evidence to support this. Confusion has arisen between this saint and the O Gormain family whose members were associated with Tobar Muirdhealaigh.

MAOL IOSA was a native of Culdaff and a student of Both Chonais. His feast is kept on January 16th. He was of Cineal Eoghain and lived in the eleventh century. *The Martyrology of Gorman* speaks of him as "diligent and very chaste". Colgan says that he was a man of miracles, of virtue and of holiness of life.[44] As a poet and learned man he is dealt with elsewhere in this work.

MAOL RUBHA was born in what is now County Derry in the seventh century. He became abbot of Bangor and later went on the Scottish mission. His feast-day is April 21st. A member of Cineal Eoghan, he was associated with the parish of Cluain Catha. There was a church dedicated to him at Kilmaroo in the townland of Larrahirrel, and he was also venerated at Malin Head.

MUIRDHEALACH is associated with Malin Well, where he was venerated for many centuries. He came from Limerick and was brother of Forannan, another saint. His feast is kept on November 3rd. His name is mentioned at Malin Head even to the present time.

ORAN was one of the twelve disciples who accompanied Colm Cille to Scotland. His name is associated with the Isle of Oransay and also with Iona. In Inis Eoghain he was honoured at Binion in Clonmany and at Ballyhillin in Ardmalin. A church was dedicated to him at each of these places.

PATRICK, the Apostle of Ireland, was honoured at Cruckalough in the townland of Dunagard and at Cill Phadraig in Ballyharry. Tradition states that he destroyed two dangerous serpents which lived in Cruckalough. St. Patrick never enjoyed the warm, spontaneous devotion given to Brigid and Colm Cille in this area, however—his was the formal devotion of the Church.

RONAN: Fr. Hegarty suggests that Port Ronain at Malin Head is the place from which Colm Cille's first boat was launched and that the port was associated with St. Ronan.[45]

ULTAN is revered at Falmore, where there are a holy well and *turas* in his honour. As there are at least twenty saints of this name, it is difficult to determine which one is venerated here.

This *turas* was frequented by sick children: Ultan, the successor of Breacan of Ard Breacain, had a special care for children. In view of Breacan's close association with this area, it is highly probable that his successor was the saint honoured at Falmore.

HOLY WELLS IN CULDAFF AND CLONCHA

The holy well is a good example of how pagan cult was merged into the Christian way of life. The well was a centre of worship in Druidic times. When Christianity was introduced, people still visited the old place, but gradually the practice was Christianised and a saint substituted for the pagan deity.

The number of holy wells is small in this area. There is no doubt that formerly there were many more, but their story has been lost. The ones listed here continued as places of pilgrimage up to the early part of this century.

CARROWMORE, Gleneely, was the site of a holy well to which pilgrimages were made up to the early part of the present century. The name of the saint associated with it is not known. It was located close to the monastery of Both Chonais.

GREGASOLE in the townland of Culdaff was the site of a holy well associated with a cure for ailments of the eye. The well is still in use.

CULDAFF: Here was located the holy well associated with the cult of St. Buadan.

DRUMAVILLE-MALIN: At the foot of Dunkintra, near Straghbreggagh Bay, there are three wells. A *turas* was made to these, but nothing further is known about them.

FALMORE: In the townland of Leitrim, close by the spot where the school at Falmore formerly stood, there is a hollow in the stream at the foot of a waterfall. This was known as the Well of St. Ultan. It was a place of pilgrimage for those suffering from any illness. It was specially frequented by sick children. On the hill behind stood an ancient cross which has now disintegrated. In the last century the local landlord, a benevolent man, had a new cross cut and erected here to honour the saint and the *turas*. Local tradition says that the saint lived here for a time. Perhaps there was here an ancient hermitage.

MALIN WELL was a famous place of pilgrimage. Here was a well blessed by Muirdhealach.

TEMPLEMOYLE had two holy wells dedicated to St. Eunan.

UMGALL had two holy wells. One is situated on the summit of Knockrath. The well is closed in with stones and is well protected. It is located on the edge of the famous circle of stones marking an ancient grave. The second well is in the detached portion of Umgall and close to a large cairn. The well was dedicated to St. Oisin, and was a centre of devotion up to the second quarter of this century.

THE BELL OF ST. BUADAN

The area comprising the modern parishes of Culdaff and Cloncha was the site of many religious foundations. Nevertheless, apart from a few stone crosses, very little evidence is left of the handiwork of the monks.

There is no doubt that they produced many works of art, but time and wars have destroyed almost every vestige of these. However, there is still preserved in the parish of Culdaff an important link with the days of its monastic glory. It is the Bell of St. Buadan, which is now in the custody of the parish priest at Bocan, the parochial church of Culdaff.

The members of the Ua Dubhaigh sept were the *airchinnigh* of Culdaff and were mentioned in the Inquisitions of James I of England. This family was the hereditary custodian of the bell.

They lived in the townland of Dunross, where they had a farm. The last member of the family was Sorcha Ni Dhubhaigh, who died about the end of the last century.

The bell was then handed over to the custody of the O Doherty family of Glacknadrummond. Charles O Doherty's mother was a member of the Ua Dubhaigh family. At the death of Charles O Doherty the bell was given to a nephew, William O Doherty, who lived in Cashel. At his death in 1928 the bell became the property of the parish. It now rests in the sacristy, safe among the church vessels.

The bell has been examined by a number of authorities and it is stated that its construction indicates that it belongs to the ninth century.[46] It is made of bronze and is cast in one piece. The bell measures eleven inches in height and the mouth, elliptical in form, is eight and a quarter inches by five and a quarter inches in its major and minor axes. There is a circular hole, half an inch in diameter, at a height of four inches from the mouth. The clapper of the bell is now missing. The projection at its inner apex indicates the loop from which it was suspended. The handle springs from the crown of the bell in two stems of bronze, each half an inch in diameter, shaped with a swelled division in the lifting bar to fit the fingers.

The bell has a beaded rim that curves out from the upright on the outside of the mouth. This rim projects about half an inch beyond the sides. The shape of this bell, while it retains some of the quadrangular form of the earlier bells, is formed by easy curves. One of the sides is straight and the bell is narrower on that side than on the opposite by about $1\frac{1}{2}$", indicating that the model had been irregularly formed and shaped without accurate measurements.

The circular holes cast or drilled in each side may have been made to improve the sound by allowing the sound waves to escape without being impounded by the narrow surface of the crown. The bell at present produces a full mellow tone, though the abrasions at one corner interfere with its sound.

The Bell of Armagh, made about 900 A.D., and the Bell of St. Finian of Moville are similar to this bell, which is considered to be the oldest in Inis Eoghain. Indeed, it is stated to be the only ancient monastic bell to survive here.

The bell was regarded with great respect by the people of the area and was used in conjunction with the Well of St. Buadan in Culdaff for " curing " purposes.

A local tradition held that if the bell ever passed out of the ownership of the name Ua Dubhaigh the family of the new owner would soon become extinct. The believer of this tradition no doubt saw the fulfilment of the prophecy when the O Doherty family of Glack and later the O Doherty family in Cashel each became extinct soon after the custody of the bell passed into their hands.

———————————◦❖◦———————————

1. *Adamnan's Life of St. Columba,* edited by William Reeves. While there is not conclusive evidence regarding the exact location of Both Chonais, the view of Reeves, an eminent authority, is accepted as reliable.
2. *The Life and Writings of St. Patrick,* J. Healy.
3. *Acta Sanctorum Hiberniae,* Colgan.
4. *Annals of Ireland* in 852, in 988 and in 1049.
5. I, *The Annals of Clonmacnoise;* II, *The Annals of Ulster;* III, *Acta Sanctorum Hiberniae,* Colgan.
6. *Acts of Archbishop Colton's Visitation of Derry, 1367.*
7. *Rotulus Patens de Annis 3 & 4 Edw. II.*
8. *Book of Inishowen,* H. P. Swan.
9. Tithe Applotment Book, 1828 — Culdaff and Cloncha
10. Inquisitiones Derry, Tempore Jac. I, Regis.
11. *Book of Inishowen,* H. P. Swan.
12. *Tripartite Life,* Colgan, P. 271.
13. *Martyrology of Donegal;* "Brecan of Cluain Catha, in Inis Eoghain, Bishop of Ardbrecain and abbot of Magh-bile, of the race of Eoghan son of Niall".
14. *Calendar of Documents Ireland, 1302-1307:* "Ecclesiastical Taxation of Ireland, 1302-1306".
15. *Acts of Archbishop Colton's Visitation of Derry, 1367.*
16. *Calendar of Papal Registers, 1417-1486.*
17. *Irish Times,* Oct. 1970: "The Cost of Culture," Liam de Paor.
18. Ulster Visitation Book: Bishop Andrew Knox, 1622.
19, 20. *Inishowen,* "Maghtochair".
21. *Book of Inishowen,* H. P. Swan.
22. *Acts of Archbishop Colton's Visitation of Derry, 1367.*
23. *Calendar of Papal Registers, 1417-1486.*
24. *Analecta Hibernica,* Vol. 12 — Bishop Montgomery's Survey of Derry diocese, *circa* 1605.
25. Ulster Visitation Book: Bishop Andrew Knox, 1622.
26. Bishop Nicholson's Visitation Book, 1739.
27. *Derry Clergy and Parishes,* Leslie.
28. *Historical Notices of Old Belfast and its Vicinity,* R. M. Young: "Confirmation of the Chichester Patents 1669".
29. *Historical Notices of Old Belfast and its Vicinity,* R. M. Young: "Journey to Ye North by Thomas Molyneux".
30. *Donegal Annual,* Vol. IV, 1960, No. 3.
31. *Dr. Pococke's Journey.*
32. *Statistical Survey of County Donegal,* 1801, James McParlan, M.D.

33. *Mason's Statistical Survey,* 1816: "Culdaff and Cloncha," Edward Chichester.
34. Tithe Applotment Book, 1829: Culdaff and Cloncha.
35. *Acta Sanctorum Hiberniae,* Colgan, P. 387.
36. *Calendar of Papal Registers, 1417-1486.*
37. Tithe Applotment Book, 1829: Culdaff and Cloncha.
38. *Analecta Hibernica,* Vol. 12. — The O Kane Papers: Bishop montgomery's Survey of Derry diocese, *circa* 1605.
39. *Book of Inishowen,* H. P. Swan.
40. *Twixt Foyle and Swilly,* H. P. Swan.
41. *Martyrology of Donegal.*
42. *Mason's Statistical Survey,* 1816: "Culdaff and Cloncha," Edward Chichester.
43. *Acta Sanctorum Hiberniae,* Colgan, P. 387.
44. *Acta Sanctorum Hiberniae,* Colgan, P. 108.
45. *Twixt Foyle and Swilly,* H. P. Swan.
46. *Inis-owen and Tirconnell,* W. J. Doherty.

INTRODUCTION OF THE ESTABLISHED CHURCH AND OTHER PROTESTANT DENOMINATIONS

IN THE previous chapters, the introduction and development of Catholicism were discussed. The religious pattern in our area remained unaffected by the profound changes of the sixteenth century in England and on the Continent. The Reformation had as yet no impact in Inis Eoghain.

The English occupation of Inis Eoghain, however, in the early part of the seventeenth century changed completely the old established way of life of the people of Culdaff and Cloncha. Among many changes was the denial of religious freedom to Catholics. The Protestant Church became the established religion. Other Protestant denominations were later introduced.

The introduction and development of these new religions are now to be discussed.

THE ESTABLISHED CHURCH

As has been pointed out elsewhere, the rebellion of the ruler of Inis Eoghain gave the English the opportunity which they sought to occupy the whole peninsula. James I granted[1] to John Bishop of Derry and his successors for ever " the termon or erenagh land of Cloncagh and Grillagh containing six quarters . . . the termon or erenagh land of Cooledagh containing three quarters . . ." Thus the new Church started off with the advantage of substantial property and an assured income.

BEGINNINGS AND GROWTH

Within a few years of the grant the representatives of the Established Church began to occupy the buildings and lands which had been confiscated from the Catholic Church. By 1620 Edward Bowker,[2] the first Protestant rector, was resident in the parish of Cloncha and the parish of Culdaff was under the control of Robert Kane,[3] the rector of Moville. By 1630[4] Edward Bowker was also rector of Culdaff.

The Ulster Visitation Book[5] reported that in 1622 the church at Culdaff was roofless and that the incumbent was building near to the ruins of the old church a small building of stone. For what purpose it not stated. The same source stated that the " church of Cloncagh is fallen down and altogether decayed ". Greallach and Lagg were not mentioned. These buildings were also in decay and were never used as places of worship at any time by the Established Church.[6]

A PARADOXICAL POSITION

By 1635 each parish had its own rector. Here was a paradoxical position. The Protestant rectors had good incomes, churches of a kind and no parishioners, while the Catholic clergy had no income, no property and all the natives of the parishes as parishioners. In the background was the occupying power, ready to take action if any attempt were made to remedy this anomalous situation.

For the first fifty years these rectors lived in isolation. The churches were empty and it is doubtful whether any service at all was held. If these men preached or held any service the congregation consisted of members of their own households. Frustrated by living in such an environment, the rectors no doubt took steps to encourage the immigration of planters of their own denomination from England and Scotland. By 1665 there were six Protestant families in Culdaff and two in the parish of Cloncha.[7]

By 1694 conditions in the parish of Culdaff had improved for the Protestant rector. A letter[8] written by Pat McLachlan to the Bishop of Derry contained the following postscript:

Mr. Younge, whofe cares I frequently suplyed, has of our highlanders now in his parish twixt Ballinagarrighy, Keramenagh, Ballincarry, Drimbill, Leitrim, Monedarragh, Arhaglaffan, Tnamore, the number of 22 families whose names I can give yourly att demand . . .

The Protestant community in each parish was increased to a small extent by the conversion of a few native families who, at least for a time, conformed to the new religion.[9]

In 1740 the list of Protestant Householders[10] for Culdaff shows 58 families and that for Cloncha 112.

While these totals include Presbyterian families for each parish, it is clear that during the period from 1665 to 1740 great efforts were made by the Protestant rectors to organise a viable community for the Established Church.

In 1815[11] there were 58 families professing the Established religion in Culdaff and 49 in the parish of Cloncha. From the census,[12] which provided data on a denominational basis, we have the following numbers for the Church of Ireland:

	CULDAFF		CLONCHA	
Year	No.	% of total	No.	% of total
1815	319	6	270	5
1861	386	8	317	5
1881	329	8	245	5
1891	295	8	220	5
1901	280	8	219	5
1911	236	8	197	5

Combined figures for the two parishes for 1926 and 1936 are as follows:

Year	No.	% of total
1926	343	5
1936	272	5

The above figures show that members of the Established Church formed only a very small section of the whole community at any time. A steady decline in numbers set in around 1870 and has continued up to the present time. The beginning of the downward trend in numbers coincided with the disestablishment of the Protestant Church in 1870.

CHURCHES ORGANISED

The first task which faced the officials of the Established Church was to secure a viable community. As this problem tended towards solution through the plantations, the provision of churches and schools became a pressing matter. The churches at Culdaff and Cloncha were repaired to provide a place of worship for the small community of Protestants. In 1739[13] the church at Culdaff was in complete decay. This suggests that no service at all was held in Culdaff for a period. By 1747[14] the church was re-built. The church at Cloncha was also re-built during the seventeenth century, but the exact date is not clear. By 1827 a new church was built at Malin Town and the church at Cloncha was closed.

The re-siting of the church at Malin for Cloncha parish was a logical step, as the old one was situated at one end of the parish and within a mile of the church at Culdaff.

SCHOOLS

By the end of the seventeenth century the two parishes had a school each. In 1686 in Culdaff[15] the rector was schoolmaster

93

and in Cloncha the rector in 1693[16] was warned to appoint a schoolmaster. Thus early steps were taken to provide a means of education for the children of Protestants.

Later there were six schools for members of the Established Church in the parishes of Culdaff and Cloncha. These were at Cloncha,[17] Malin (a school for males and one for females), Gleneely and Culdaff (a school for males and one for females).[18] To-day (1971) the decline in numbers of all Protestant denominations can be seen from the fact that there is now not a single Protestant school in this area. The last school, which was at Culdaff, was closed in 1970.

THE GLEBES

In the allocation of the churchlands a glebe was provided for each parish. The two glebes were situated together in the district of Dun an Ghrianain. The Culdaff glebe was situated in the townland which now bears the name and the Cloncha glebe was in the townland of Redford-Glebe. Edward Bowker built a house near to the old church in Cloncha.[19] By 1735 William Elwood had built a house at Redford,[20] where the successive rectors for Cloncha lived until 1870. The building is now a ruin. A new rectory was later built at Malin Town.

The rectory for Culdaff probably was situated near the church for the period during which the rectorship was held by members of the Young family. Around 1710 the rector had his house within the parish glebe. It was situated at Cregasole and is mentioned in 1769.[21] The glebe house was re-built in 1877. In 1923 the house and lands were sold to a local farmer when the rector moved to Gleneely.

CHURCH AT GLENEELY

In 1856, through the influence of Miss Catherine Ball of Grousehall, a church was built at Gleneely. In the following year a rectory was built for the resident perpetual curate. In 1961 the rectory was sold when this area was united with the parish of Moville.

RE-ORGANISATION OF PARISHES

The two parishes of Culdaff and Cloncha *together* constitute a compact geographical entity but *separately* the parishes are geographically very much inter-mixed. From 1620 to 1847 they were united intermittently for a period of over a hundred years. During such times the one rector held both parishes.

In 1923 the glebe and rectory at Cregasole were sold and

this section of Culdaff was again united with Gleneely, where the rector lived until 1961. In 1961, as a result of a re-organisation, the Gleneely portion of Culdaff was united with Moville. The rector of Moville had now the care of this portion of the former parish of Culdaff.

Donagh and Cloncha were united under the care of the rector of Clonmany in 1925. In 1961, as a result of reorganisation, Donagh, Cloncha, Clonmany and the remaining portion of Culdaff were all united under the one rector. In 1963 Carrowbeg was added to the care of the same rector.

To-day (in 1971) the organisation set out above obtains. It is significant that by 1961, for the first time since 1620, there was no resident rector in either Cloncha or Culdaff. A declining Protestant population, reasons of economy, a scarcity of clergymen and easier means of transport all combined to bring about the new arrangement.

THE RECTORS

The office of rector in a parish such as Culdaff or Cloncha in the seventeenth, eighteenth and nineteenth centuries was pleasant, modestly comfortable and not too demanding. Those families which had sufficient influence with the person who had the right of presentation kept the Church in mind as a career for at least one son. The possession of a comfortable post rather than any particular zeal was the motivating factor in the selection of such a career by the young man on the threshold of life. The men[22] who held the position in Culdaff and Cloncha were quiet, peace-loving gentlemen of good education. They were not notorious for missionary activity and do not seem to have been deeply involved in any of the proselytising activities which took place from time to time. In some cases the rector did not reside in the parish at all. Through influence more than one benefice was held and the additional one was served by a poorly paid resident curate. Arthur Hyde, who held the rectorship of Culdaff from 1757 to 1769, and Arthur Champagne, rector of Cloncha from 1786 to 1891, were pluralists.[23] These men sought incomes rather than the spiritual well-being of their subjects.

On the whole, these rectors left no bitter memories in the the minds of the subject people. Indeed, one could say that their memorial is oblivion. If they did no particular good, they left no rancorous memories because of any evil-doing.

THE FAILURE OF THE ESTABLISHED CHURCH

When the devout Anglican Gladstone introduced and carried through the Act of Disestablishment in 1869 the Protestant Church ceased to function in Ireland as a privileged body. The British Prime Minister recognised that as far as Ireland was concerned the attempt to force the people to accept the reformed religion had failed completely. The Established Church failed at national level in her mission despite wealth and power. What was true at national level was even more so when the parishes of Culdaff and Cloncha are considered. In relation to these two parishes we can ask, why was the mission so complete a failure?

To a great extent the Reformation was concerned with economics—not religion. The desire to acquire the Church property was strong in the motivation of the early reformers. The decline in spiritual zeal among the pre-Reformation clergy was a good plausible reason for action. The first Protestant arrivals in Culdaff and Cloncha had greed in their hearts, swords in their hands and a wealth of Biblical quotations on their lips. How could the native Irish be attracted to a religion whose exponents were the very people who had stolen their lands, who had profaned their holy places and who were now in wrongful possession of their churches ?

The Protestant leaders here, whether rectors or landlords, had no real desire to convert the people. Did not their privileged position depend on the continued existence of a substantial group of third-class citizens whose toiling and moiling were essential to providing the secure and liberal incomes which they enjoyed? Apostolic zeal was a stranger in Protestant circles in Culdaff and Cloncha.

Between the native Irish and the English and Scottish planters there was a wide cultural and social gap. The planters regarded the natives of Culdaff and Cloncha as barbarians steeped in ignorance, superstition and idolatory. On the other hand, the Catholics regarded their new neighbours as heathens utterly bereft of any true religion. The two sections lived, in a certain sense, far apart from each other. Lack of any contacts, whether social, cultural, educational or religious, widened and made permanent the division. They had little chance to know each other and thus based their views of each other on prejudice and ignorance.

In the spiritual order, the native Irish here were never without the priest, who was always their guide and mentor. The survival of Catholicism in the area is due in great measure to the unbroken line of priests who served here during the period of persecution.

Finally, the strong traditional attatchment of the people here to the old way of things made them loath to accept a new cult which, among other things, rejected the Pope and discouraged respect for the Mother of God, for whom the people had so great a respect and for whom the Irish language has even a special name.[24]

CLERGY OF THE CHURCH OF IRELAND

The names of the clergy of the Established Church in Cloncha and Culdaff are set out below. The first clergy of this denomination entered the area about 1620 A.D.

CLONCHA

1620: Edward Bowker was the first rector. There are no data available regarding his origin. He found the glebe lands at Dun an Ghrianain too distant from the church at Cloncha and consequently built a house for himself at the *gort* adjacent to the church. Bishop Knox in his visitation report[25] for 1622 stated that "the incumbent is Edward Bowker, clerk, an honest man, but no licensed preacher, notwithstanding fit to catechise and to speak and read Irish and sufficient for a parish wholly consisting of Irish". His duties were indeed light as records show there was not a single Protestant in the area at this time. His death took place about 1639 or 1640. There is a rock at Culdaff shore called Bucker's Rock. Has it any association with this clergyman?

1640: Robert Young, a progenitor of the family who were later landlords at Culdaff. During the Commonwealth this rector would seem to have conformed to the religion of the Government and received a pension of £30 per year.[26] This did not, however, deprive him of his rectorship after the Restoration.

1668: Robert Young,[27] son of the above-named. He was instituted February 26th, 1668.

1706: Peter Ward.

1721: Robert Gardiner. Records show that his will was admitted to probate in 1735. He was a direct descendant of the Colonel Gardiner mentioned in Sir Walter Scott's novel *Waverley*.

1732: William Elwood, who was born in 1695 and died November, 1785. He is buried at Cloncha where his grave is marked by a fine tombstone. This rector was the first to reside in the glebe at Redford, where he built a house which served as a rectory from 1735 to 1870.

1786: Arthur Champagne, who was installed on March 17th, 1786. He was married to a daughter of Rev. Philip Homan. It is doubtful that he ever lived in his parish. He was a pluralist of note.

1791: William Chichester, instituted April 27th, 1791. See special note on Chichester family.

1800: Edward Chichester was instituted as rector 27th February, 1800. See note on Chichester family.

1823: Richard Hamilton, son of James Hamilton of Sheephill. James married three times and had 39 children. His son was known throughout the diocese as "one of the thirty-nines". He lived at Redford and took a

97

keen interest in the improvement of agriculture. During his rectorship the church at Malin was built and the church at Cloncha ceased to be used. His daughter married John Lawrence, Viceroy of India.

1847: Richard Homan served as rector for 25 years and was the last to live at Redford. He died on the 23rd December, 1871, in his ninety-first year and was buried with the other members of his family at Rathfarnham, Dublin, where a headstone marks his grave.

1872: Gregory St. Lawrence Cuff.

1874: Edmund Maturin. Tradition states that this rector became a Catholic for some time.

1897: Laurence William Rutledge. He resigned in 1899 for an appointment at Tamlaghtard.

1899: William Ralph.

1903: John Curtis Steele.

1908: William Jeffares. He was transferred in 1925 when this parish was united with that of Donagh.

In the early years of the establishment of the Church of Ireland the number of adherents was small, *e.g.*, in 1665, when the Hearth Money Roll was compiled, we find only the following: Dunross—Robert Butler, Robert Wilson. Perhaps, apart from the rector and his family, not more than a dozen.

Three hundred years from the days of the first rector, Edward Bowker, we find that the parish no longer had a rector. By 1925 the rector of Donagh takes over this parish and has responsibility also for Clonmany.

CULDAFF

1620: Robert Kane, who was also in charge at Moville. At this time the Catholic rector at Moville was also rector of Culdaff. The Protestants may at the beginning have followed this arrangement. A contemporary report says that "he was a good preacher and a man of unblameable conversation".[28]

1630: Edward Bowker. He was also rector of Cloncha, which see.

1635: James Young.[29]

1635: John Coade.

1661: Robert Young. He was also rector of Cloncha.

1668: Robert Young, son of the foregoing, and like him rector of Cloncha also.

1706: Robert Gardiner. He held also the rectorship of Cloncha from 1721 until his death. He had successive curates: Michael Rankin, Andrew Leslie and William Browne. The last named served in this capacity until 1769.

1733: George Sandford was installed as rector 2nd November, 1733. He was later chaplain to the Irish House of Commons. The church at Culdaff was rebuilt during the tenure of this rector.

1757: Arthur Hyde. He does not seem to have lived in the parish. The spiritual needs of the parishioners were served by a curate called William Browne.

1769: Samuel Stone was instituted as rector on July 18th, 1769.

1798: Edward Chichester, also rector of Cloncha, which see.

1800: William Chichester, also rector of Cloncha, which see.

1807: Edward Chichester. He held this office previously in this parish and was also rector of Cloncha, which see. A complaint was made that he failed to pay his curate Lawrence McHenry, owing him 2½ years' salary.

1823: Richard Hamilton. See Cloncha, of which he was also rector. A tower was added to Culdaff church in 1828 during his pastorate.

1847: John Sheal. He was accused of simoniacally exchanging the parish with his successor.

1851: Moore O Connor. This colourful character gave rise to a *cause celebre*. See separate chapter on this case.

1857: Alfred Theophilas Lee. He was a very prolific writer on religion and matters pertaining to the Church of Ireland.

1858: William Tyrrell became rector and was described as "an old gentleman of a mild and gentle disposition". He died March 23rd, 1870, at the rectory and was buried in Culdaff. On his deathbed he was visited by the parish priest and tradition says he was received into the Catholic Church by him.

1870: Phineas Hunt succeeded and later resigned the rectorship to take up a similar position in Rathgar.

1875: W. H. Lang then became rector. Later he became Musical Canon of Christ Church Cathedral in Dublin, where he died in 1894.

1882: W. Doherty. He held the post for only two years and then emigrated to Australia. There are still many stories current about him. Visiting a local Catholic family, he discussed his dilemma of conscience. He was the rector of the Church of Ireland and believed that the Catholic Church was the true Church. Challenged by the woman of the house as to why he remained in the Protestant Church, he replied "a man has to do many a thing for bread". He was friendly with the local Catholic clergy. Finally, he made his decision to declare himself openly and on the following Sunday told his congregation in Culdaff Church. He then departed to start a new life in Australia. Later he presented a silver chalice to the church at Bocan.

1884: T. C. Huston succeeded and died in 1911. The Church was restored internally in 1887.

1911: W. H. Haslett was the last rector to live at Cregnasole. The residence was sold in 1923 when Gleneely was united with Culdaff. Mr. Haslett remained in Gleneely until 1944. During his rectorship the church was re-decorated and the churchyard enlarged.

1944: J. R. Sloane succeeded.[30]

1954: J. Bryans was rector until 1961, when Culdaff was divided between Donagh and Moville. The Gleneely portion was attached to Moville.

GLENEELY: PERPETUAL CURATES[31]
1856: John Samuel McClintock.
1862: William Sproale.
1911: Charles Smith, who resigned when Gleneely was united to Culdaff.

GLENEELY CHURCH[32]

This church, dedicated to All Saints, was built in 1855 and consecrated on March 27th of the following year. The glebe house was built the following year.

Miss Catherine Ball of Grousehall financed the building of

this place of worship and also that of the curate's residence. A local tradition says that she was impelled to this action by a dream she had. She is buried in the graveyard adjoining the church.

The parishioners of Culdaff parish in 1665 were few indeed. The Hearth Money Roll for 1665 has the following—Cashel: John Knighton; Ourt: John Bunbury; Ballycarron: Robert Fleming; Crancor: James Miller, John Intyre; Culdaff: George Butler. The entire congregation would not have been more than twenty.

The close association between the two parishes is evidenced by the fact that out of the 227 years from 1620 to 1847 both parishes were ruled by the same rectors for 102 years.

PRESBYTERIANISM

The founder of Presbyterianism was John Calvin, who from his interpretation of the Bible formulated the principles of the system. He directed the practice of these principles firstly at Geneva and later in other places. This religion spread gradually to other parts of Europe. Through the plantations Presbyterianism reached the north of Ireland about 1610. It established itself in the nine counties of Ulster and has had a great impact on the history of this province for the last three centuries.

ARRIVAL OF PRESBYTERIANS

Members of this persuasion reached north Inis Eoghain by the end of the seventeenth century. In 1694 there is a record of a complaint regarding the arrival of dissenters at Moville.[33] In May 1695 the congregation of Presbyterians at Donagh was large enough in numbers to have a probationer from the Lagan as their minister.[34] Before the end of the seventeenth century dissenters had begun to settle at Malin.[35]

FIRST MINISTERS

The first minister at Donagh was Robert Neilson. He was called in 1695 but, owing to the inability of the congregation to support him or build a meeting-house, left three years later.[36] In 1701 Thomas Harvey was ordained here and served until his death seventeen years later.[37]

The first minister of the congregation at Moville was Thomas Harvey, junior. He was ordained at Moville in 1715 and served here until a vacancy occurred at Donagh in 1718.[38]

The first minister of whom there is mention at Malin was John Harvey, junior. He was ordained in 1717 and served here until his death in 1733. John Montgomery succeeded in 1734 but his pastorate was not satisfactory. The presbytery of Derry was ordered to enquire into charges of non-attendance at public worship against Montgomery, who died in 1749. David Walker was ordained for this congregation in 1738 and served until his death in 1766. In 1768 another David Walker was ordained and he acted here until his death in 1782.

From 1782 until 1798 Malin was served by the minister at Donagh. James Canning discharged the duty of minister there from 1798 until 1830. John Canning, son of James, succeeded in 1832 and served until his death in 1877.[39]

John Montgomery and the two ministers named David Walker are buried in the graveyard at Lagg, adjacent to the Catholic church there.

THE ECCLESIASTICAL UNIT

The administrative units of the Presbyterian church in Inis Eoghain do not correspond with the old parish divisions. The Malin division lies north of a line between Portaleen Pier and the sea at Drumaville House. The remainder of the parishes of Cloncha and Culdaff lies partly in Carndonagh division and partly in Moville division. The portion which extends from a line drawn between Portaleen and Drumaville southwards to a line connecting Ballyharry with Gleneely crossroads and Lough Inn is in Carndonagh division. The remainder is in Moville division.

DEVELOPMENT OF THE COMMUNITY

The community of Presbyterians in North Inis Eoghain was faced with many problems. Firstly, immigration of sufficient numbers in each area was necessary to constitute a viable entity. The building of places of worship and later on the provision of schools were the next difficulties to be encountered.

The plantation of Culdaff and Cloncha proceeded at a relatively fast pace. By 1740 a list of non-Catholic householders in our area numbered 170 householders.[40] The breakdown between members of the Established Church and the Presbyterian Church is not given. However, as members of the latter Church tended to congregate to the west of the area extending from Malin Town to Malin Head, it can be safely estimated that, of the number mentioned above, at least seventy of the householders were of the Presbyterian persuasion.

The data[41] available regarding the number of Presbyterians in the parishes of Culdaff and Cloncha are set out in the following tables.

	CLONCHA		CULDAFF	
Year	No.	% of total	No.	% of total
1815	259	4	99	2
1861	622	10	178	4
1881	586	12	130	3
1891	508	11	117	3
1901	449	11	92	3
1911	419	11	77	3

Combined figures for both parishes:

Year	No.	% of total
1926	415	7
1936	330	6

The Presbyterians were and are largely found in the parish of Cloncha, in the area from Malin Town northwards. The decline in numbers commenced around 1865 and still continues, while the percentage is also steadily dropping. It may also be noted that in all the years for which data are available apart from 1815 the combined figure for Presbyterians in these two parishes was greater than the total of members of the Established Church.

CHURCHES AND SCHOOLS

The only Presbyterian house of worship in the area is situated in the townland of Goorey and is popularly known as "Lagg Meeting-House". The first building, with a thatched roof, was built here about the first half of the eighteenth century and was later replaced by the present building. Nearby is the burial ground. In the eighteenth century the Presbyterians buried their dead in the older portion of the cemetery which adjoins the Catholic church at Lagg. From the early part of the nineteenth century schools were organised for members of the Presbyterian Church. There were schools at Knockamany, Keenagh, Goorey and Malin. While these schools were attended at certain times by children of all denominations, the majority of the pupils were Presbyterians.

THE PENAL LAWS

While the full brunt of the Penal Laws passed by the British Government fell heavily on the Catholics of Culdaff and Cloncha, the Presbyterians had some grievances. The Civil Law regarded their ministers as laymen and thus invalidated all marriages performed by them. Tithes were extracted from Presbyterians for the upkeep of the clergy of the Established Church. For a time they were compelled to attend the Established Church services on Sunday, but this imposition was removed in 1719.

PATRIOTISM AND ITS DECLINE

For a time towards the end of the eighteenth century Presbyterians in general showed a strong patriotic trend. The union of Catholics and dissenters promised to bring about the end of British rule in Ireland and made many hope that all creeds would rejoice in the common name of Irishmen. The hope was short lived. In the early part of the nineteenth century the British Government, by giving generous salaries to Presbyterian clergymen, alienated their allegiance from Ireland so that they became loyal to the British connection. Bigots stirred up hatred against the Catholic community and a deep division on religious lines was created which has lasted to the present day.

The community in Culdaff and Cloncha was largely unaffected by national events. They lived with the minimum of restriction on religious grounds and there is no evidence of any patriotic manifestation during the 1798 period.

Presbyterians here have shown devotion to their religious principles. Honesty, hard work and frugal living have been distinguishing marks by which the members of this Church wielded for a time a definite but unobtrusive influence on the whole community of this area. To-day, however, they are a fast-dwindling group whose influence is scarcely felt.

THE METHODIST CHURCH

John Wesley had a profound effect on the religious life of eighteenth-century England. He was a man of great zeal who devoted all his energy and ability to the revival of Christianity among the people of his time. At first he aimed at a sort of reformation of the Anglican Church, of which he was a loyal member. When he met with opposition from the higher ranks of the Anglican clergy he decided to sever his association with the Established Church and found a new Church. Such is the origin of the Methodist Communion.

Wesley devoted considerable attention to Ireland and we find

103

that from 1747 to his death in 1791 he crossed the Irish Sea a total of 42 times. The first Irish Conference was held at Limerick on the 14th August, 1752.

However, another century was to pass before followers of Wesley began to work among the people of Culdaff and Cloncha. The Reverend William O Flaherty,[42] a native of Offaly, was the first missioner to operate in the area.

Mr. O Flaherty directed his attention to the building of a school.[43] He contacted George Young of Culdaff House and secured a site in the townland of Glacknadrummond. The next problem was the collection of money to pay for the proposed building. Mr. O Flaherty collected in Dublin and also secured contributions from America and in Inis Eoghain. The school was completed in 1857. It was capable of accommodating over two hundred pupils and included a residence for the teacher. The official opening took place on the 9th June, 1857. Mr. O Flaherty, in his address, stated that his hope was that the school might become a light to many who were still in darkness and that the day was not far distant when many sons and daughters would be brought to God in the school. A vain hope, as events proved.

A Presbyterian congregation at Stirling in Scotland offered to make an annual contribution of £30 *per annum* towards the payment of a teacher.

The area at this time was well provided with schools for Catholics, Protestants and Presbyterians. It would seem that as a result the Methodist school met with little success. A man named Lindsay taught here for a time but soon the school closed through lack of support. It was never connected with the National Board, as the carrying out of public worship in the school on Sundays made this impossible. The school building, however, continued to be used as a place of worship for the small congregation in the area. In 1882[44] the building was enlarged and continued to be used as a church until 1903. Then a new building was raised and called the McCandless Memorial Church as a tribute to Mr. Charles McCandless of Caragh House, a benefactor. Further improvements were carried out in 1930, when new stables and a boundary wall were erected.

The early Methodist missionaries met with stiff opposition from the Protestant clergy. On the other hand, the Presbyterian Church was friendly. The Methodists drew their converts from the Protestant section of the community. The names McCandless,

Norris, Elkin and Scott are found among the first converts. Young, the Protestant landlord at Culdaff, gave the site for the school and also a generous subscription. Members of the Catholic Church here were uninfluenced by the new religion.

The census[45] shows the following totals for membership of the Methodist persuasion in this area:

YEAR	TOTAL
1861	42
1881	58
1891	64
1901	58
1911	47
1926	52
1936	44

The majority of the Methodists lived in the parish of Culdaff. For administrative purposes, the whole of Inis Eoghain is divided into three centres, Moville, Whitecastle and Glacknadrummond. The last-named includes the area covered by the parishes of Culdaff and Cloncha.

FAILURE OF PROTESTANTS TO INTEGRATE

In the foregoing the introduction and development of the various Protestant religious denominations have been examined. The Catholics were the native Irish while the membership of the other persuasions consisted of planters from England and Scotland. It is relevant to ask, did a homogeneous community develop in this area? Was there ultimately a society which, apart from attendance at different churches, could be regarded as one in national outlook, one in culture and displaying a common attitude to all main issues affecting the parish and the nation? The answer is a definite negative. Religion was the basic divisive force and this scission begot many other divisions.

The members of the main protesting religious from the beginning had much in common with each other. They were all one in their attitude to Catholicism and to the native Irish. As foreigners, whether of English or Scottish origin, they faced similar problems. They were members of a minority and whether they professed the tenets of the Established Church or those of any of the other protesting sects, they were all aware that fundamentally the doctrinal differences were insignificant. Intermarriage could and did take place without any serious disapproval from members of the churches concerned. Often they attended the

105

same schools and on certain occasions the same services. Membership of the Orange Order and the Masonic Lodge was open to all the protesting churches and, in this area, all met in these organisations in fellowship. The result was that the members of the Established Church, the Presbyterians and the Methodists fused into a compact society and presented a united and hostile front to Catholicism and all that was associated with it.

Within the area consisting of the parishes of Culdaff and Cloncha two distinct communities evolved. Each had its own distinctive characteristics but nevertheless, on the whole, there was no serious cleavage to disturb the society. Happily, no Cook or Paisley was present to foment strife. The alignments which arose from a religious source thus developed into a cultural, social and political dichotomy.

If the planters had been of the Catholic religion like the native Irish, worship at the same altar, education at identical schools and participation in uniform social and cultural activities would have merged them into the native community in a short time and all differences would have disappeared. The wide divergence between Catholicism and the protesting creeds made this impossible.

The Catholics on the whole were aware from generation to generation that they were Irish and consequently became associated with the various national movements for self-determination. Whatever their differences they never ceased to rejoice together in the name of Irishmen. On the other hand, the Protestant groups identified themselves always with the British connection and were very hostile to every national movement. The signatories to the Act of Union memorial[46] in 1799 were almost all Protestants. In all the political movements up to the end of the occupation here the Protestants were almost all found on the side of the British Government.[47]

Like their ancestors in 1829 at Emancipation, the Protestant community here was profoundly disturbed by the restoration of liberty to the native Irish in 1922. A few decided to leave, but in time the remainder became resigned to the new order of things. The toleration and fair play of successive Irish governments have removed the pressing fears of the Protestants, though without changing the centre of loyalty for them. They still look to England as their motherland and they despise Ireland and its culture.[48] Can time re-educate these people and re-direct their loyalty to Dublin and Ireland, or will the serious decline in their numbers

106

here lead in a few generations to their complete extinction? The lapse of time has the final solution in one form or another.[49]

1. *Calendar of the Irish Patent Rolls of James I* — Patent 13.
2, 3. The Ulster Visitation Book — Bishop Knox, 1622.
4. *Derry Clergy and Parishes*, Leslie.
5. Ulster Visitation Book — report for 1622.
6. It may be noted, however, that while Catholics were deprived of their churches at Culdaff, Cloncha, Greallach and Lagg, they continued to bury their dead at these centres.
7. Hearth Money Roll, 1665: Culdaff and Cloncha.
8. King — Lyons Collection, 1693-1695, T.C.D. Letter, No. 401.
9. I, *Derry Clergy and Parishes*, Leslie; II, Registers of Culdaff and Cloncha.
10. Genealogical Office, Dublin Castle, MSS. 539-539A.
11. *Mason's Statistical Survey*, 1816: "Culdaff and Cloncha," Edward Chichester.
12. *Census of Population*.
13, 14. Bishop Nicholson's Visitation Book.
15, 16. *Derry Clergy and Parishes*, Leslie.
17. *Board of Education Report, 1809-1812*.
18. See *Reports of the Commissioners of National Education in Ireland*.
19. Ulster Visitation Book — T.C.D.
20. *Mason's Statistical Survey*, 1816: "Culdaff and Cloncha," Edward Chichester.
21. *Three Hundred Years in Innishowen*, Young.
22. *The Commonwealth State Accounts*, Vol. 15, dated 14.3.1658, stated that Robert Young of Cloncha was giving scandal by his excessive drinking and that he was negligent in his calling. An investigation was ordered. According to Mrs. Young's *Three Hundred Years in Innishowen*, the enquiry was unable to prove the charge.
23. *Derry Clergy and Parishes*, Leslie.
24. *Muire* — see Dinneen. "La Muire" is still, among the older people at Malin Head, the name applied to the Feast of the Assumption.
25. The Ulster Visitation Book, 1622.
26. *History of Congregations of the Presbyterian Church in Ireland*, Killeen.
27. Leslie, *Derry Clergy and Parishes*, for names and particulars of the clergy from 1640 to 1908.
28. *Derry Clergy and Parishes*, Leslie.
29. Leslie, *Derry Clergy and Parishes*, for names and particulars of the clergy from 1635 to 1911.
30. *Irish Church Directory* for names of clergy from 1944.
31, 32. *Derry Clergy and Parishes*, Leslie.
33. King — Lyons Collection, 1693-1695, T.C.D. Letters in No. 401.
34. Killeen: *History of Congregations of the Presbyterian Church of Ireland*, P.78.
35. In the old section of the cemetery at Lagg Catholic Church there is the following inscription on a tombstone: "Here lies the Body of Margaret Hart aged 81 years wife of Jonathan Bines who died February the 16th Day A.D. 1719. Jonathan Bines aged 75 who departed this life the 26th Day of October 1722". The family to which this inscription refers were Presbyterians who lived at Knockamany. It can be safely stated that the couple mentioned were in residence here before the end of the seventeenth century.

36. Killeen: *History of Congregations of the Presbyterian Church in Ireland*, P. 78.
37. I, *Ibid.;* II, *Records of General Synod of Ulster* states that "Mr Thomas Harvey son of James Harvey nigh Derry was guilty of uncleanness with Susan Hamilton". Susan Hamilton denied this accusation; III, In the early years of Presbyterianism in Donagh, Moville and Malin, the name Harvey features largely. Is there a connection with the Harvey family who were deeply involved in the siege of Derry and later landlords at Malin? The Harveys at Malin were Presbyterians but later became members of the Established Church.
38, 39. Killeen: *History of Congregations of the Presbyterian Church in Ireland*, P. 78.
40. List of Protestant Housekeepers, 1740. Genealogical Office, Dublin Castle. MSS. 539-539A.
41. *Census of Population* for the years 1861 to 1936 inclusive. The data for 1815 are based on an estimate by Edward Chichester in *Mason's Statistical Survey*, "Cloncha and Culdaff".
42. *History of Methodism in Ireland*, Crookshank.
43. *Derry Standard*, 11.6.1857.
44. Per Rev. G. W. Loane, Methodist Manse, Moville.
45. *Census of Population*.
46. *George Faulkner: The Dublin Journal*, 1799.
47. The writer is aware of only one Protestant family here which supported the movement for Irish independence.
48. As late as 1950 there have been incidents in this area where Protestants have refused to honour either the National Flag or the National Anthem.
49. The ethos of the Anglican community in the parish of Culdaff can be seen from the minutes of the Select Vestry Meeting, dated September 25 1869, held to consider the effect of the Disestablishment Act passed at Westminister 1869:

"At a Meeting of the Protestant Episcopalians of the Parish of Culdaff held in the Parish Church on Saturday the 25th. September 1869 - the said Meeting having been duly convened by Notices Signed by the Minister and Church Wardens - in compliance with a request from the Bishop of Derry for the purpose of appointing Lay Delegates to represent the Parishioners at a Diocesan Synod to be held in Derry on the 5th. of October (prox.) for the Discussions of various matters relating to the Re-construction of the Church of Ireland - which has lately been *Disestablished* by an Act of the Legislature.

The following Resolutions were passed unanimously -

1st.   That the Revd. William Tyrell Rector of the Parish should preside as Chairman.

2.   That although the Disestablishment of our Church may not be considered by many persons as likely to prove injurious in its results - *yet we have no doubt the immense amount of loss occasioned by its Disendowment - is generally looked upon as an act of great injustice -*.

3.   That in order to raise a sufficient sum to support the future ministers of our Church we are aware it will require a considerable amount to be made up by voluntary subscription to afford them even a very moderate income we therefore feel bound to contribute towards the maintenance of our Church as far as in our power, as soon as matters are satisfactorily arranged for its Reorganization.

Ref: Press Mark ML35/P/35 Royal Irish Academy

6
RAIDS AND DEFENSIVE MEASURES

A LOOK at the map will show that the peninsula of Inis Eoghain, by reason of its long coastline, was and is easily accessible by sea. Invaders could land, raid the area and make off before effective defensive action could be taken. If this is true of the peninsula as a whole, it is particularly true of the parishes of Culdaff and Cloncha. The long coastline from the base of Straghbreggagh Bay at Malin to Termone Bay near Ballyharry has many good bays and safe landing places for friend or foe. A system of defence along the coast was a necessary evolution.

Records show that in Inis Eoghain over the period from 900 A.D. to 1610 A.D. a total of 18 large-scale raids took place. It can be safely assumed that many other attacks took place before 900 A.D. and during the seven centuries following. Scant records survive and the reason is obvious.

Few of the raids mentioned are localised but nevertheless it can be inferred that within the area under review, because of its location, many direct attacks took place. All other raids would have had their repercussions in the north-eastern tip of the peninsula. Oral tradition states that the monastery of Both Chonais was burned during a raid on Gleneely by the O Doherty family. The old church at Lagg was sacked and burned in another attack. There is no tradition which identifies the invaders, who evidently came in by sea.

The invaders were in turn Danes, Norsemen, Normans, English, Scots and neighbouring Irish rulers. To complete the harassment of the people, we can add an occasional civil war caused by rival claimants to the lordship of Inis Eoghain.

If one realises that within the memory of each person in the seven hundred years before the English occupation a raid of some type took place, it is evident that a constant fear of attack must have permeated the community. The natural development would be to maintain a constant watch, especially on the seaward side, and establish places of refuge to safeguard people and store food and other valuables. The general tendency was to live along the coast and it was only in later times that the inland areas were inhabited. It is probable that refuges were established in inaccessible places inland as well as the forts strung along the coastline.

Details of the recorded raids[1] are set out below:

919 A.D.: A fleet of foreigners, consisting of 32 ships, at Loch Feabhail, under Olbh; and Inis Eoghain was plundered by them.

1031 A.D.: Inis Eoghain was plundered by Flaitheartach, son of Muireartach O Neill, and his son, Aodh.

1011 A.D.: A great army was led by Muireartach Ua Briain, King of Munster . . .across Eas Rua into Inis Eoghain, and burned many churches and many forts about Fathan Mura, and about Ard Sratha; and he demolished Grianan Ailigh in revenge of Ceann Cora, which had been razed and demolished by Donall Ua Lochlainn some time before; and Muireartach commanded his army to carry with them from Aileach to Luimneach a stone — of the demolished building — for every sack of provisions which they had.

1154 A. D.: A fleet was brought by Toirealach Ua Conchuir on the sea, round Ireland northwards . . . and they plundered Tir Chonaill and Inis Eoghain. The Cineal Eoghain and Muireartach, son of Niall, sent persons over the sea to hire — and who did hire — the fleets of the Gall-Ghaeil, Ara, of Ceann Tire, of Manainn and the borders of Albain in general . . . and when they arrived near Inis Eoghain, they fell in with the other fleet, and a naval battle was fiercely and spiritedly fought between them . . . The foreign host, however, was defeated and slaughtered.

1186 A.D.: Con O Breslin, ruler of Fanaid, the lamp of the hospitality and valour of the north of Ireland, was slain by the son of Mac Lochlainn and a party of the Cineal Eoghain, in consequence of which Inis Eoghain was unjustly ravaged.

1198 A.D.: The English then plundered Inis Eoghain, and carried off a great number of cows from thence and then returned. (This was an Anglo-Norman force under the command of John de Courcy.)

1208 A.D.: A prey was taken by Aodh O Neill in Inis Eoghain. O Donaill overtook him with his forces; and a battle was fought between them, in which countless numbers were slaughtered on both sides . . .

1211 A.D.: Thomas Mac Uchtry (Earl of Atholl) and the sons of Randal McSorley came to Derry with a fleet of 76 ships, and plundered and destroyed the town. They passed thence into Inis Eoghain and ravaged the entire island.

1305 A.D.: The Red Earl erected a new castle at Greencastle to check the incursions of the Scots.

1456 A.D.: War between O Donaill and O Neill. O Neill and Mag Uidhir went with the sons of Neachtan into Inis Eoghain.

1462 A.D.:[2] District of Gleneely in Culdaff raided and burned.

1522 A.D.:[3] Gleann Daoile in Culdaff raided.

1526 A.D.: O Dochartaigh — Eachmarcach — lord of Inis Eoghain, died: and a great contention arose among his tribe concerning the lordship and continued until Gerald, son of Donall, son of Feilim O Dochartaigh, was at last styled lord.

1527 A.D.:[4] Maghnus O Donaill went on a raid into Gleann Daoile on Aodh O Donaill the Tawny, and two young horsemen of the people of Maghnus, namely the son of Donall, son of Feidhlimidh, son of Aenghus Og O Gallchoir, and the son of Brian Blind-eye, son of Donall Mac an Deaganaigh, were slain.

1555 A.D.: The son of O Donaill, *i.e.*, Calbhach, went to Scotland, attended by a few select persons, and obtained auxiliary forces from Mac Ailin — Giolla Easpaig Donn — under the command of Master Arsibel. He afterwards came back, with a great body of Scots, to desolate and ravage Tyrconnell. It was on this occasion that he brought with him a gun called "Gunna Cam", by which Newcastle in Inis Eoghain (among others) was demolished.

1582 A.D.: Eoghan O Dochartaigh, son of Feilim, son of Conchur Carrach, lord of Inis Eoghain, died on the 26th May . . . His son, Eoghan Og, was elected in his place in preference to Cathaoir O Dochartaigh; in consequence of which the country was ravaged — crops, corn, dwellings and cattle alike.

1586 A.D.: A Scottish fleet landed in Inis Eoghain, O Dochartaigh's country, in the north-eastern angle of Tir Chonaill. These were the gentlemen and chief constables of that fleet: Donall Gorm and Alexander, the two sons of James, son of Alexander, son of John Cathanach, son of Mac Donaill;; and Giolla Easpaig, son of Dughall, son of Donncha Cam, son of Giolla Easpaig Mac Ailin — Campbell — with many other gentlemen besides. Their name and fame were greater than their appearance. They pitched camps in the country where they landed, where they had much flesh meat. The haughty robbers, the plunderers, the perpetrators of treacherous deeds, and the opponents of goodness of the neighbouring territories flocked to join them there; so that there was nothing of value in Inis Eoghain, whether corn or cattle, which they did not carry off on this occasion.

1601 A.D.:5 They — O Donaill and the English — marched forward until they came to Gleneely, in the Cineal Eoghain, and that place was completely plundered by them.

1608 A.D.:6 Extract from letter written by Sir Thomas Ridgeway, Treasurer of Ireland, to Salisbury: "From Elough they — the English — sent out a party by Phelimagh Reagh's town to Donnagh and Malyn, the one sixteen miles and the other twenty four miles from Elough, to scour the country and their creaghts. From their being advised by letters that Phelimagh Reagh was lurking about and that O Dogherty himself meant to set on them to rescue their prey, if they did not presently second and relieve them, they posted thither, leaving a sufficient number behind to defend the munition, carriages, etc., and to make good the place; whereafter they had increased the prey to 1,000 cows, between 2,000 and 3,000 sheep, and 300 or 400 garrans. They returned killing only some seven or eight swordsmen of the enemy, the rest not being found for love or money, no, not so much as in threatened fastness itself, the next day in their return back again".

The purpose of the raids could be any one of three: punitive, to secure food, or to steal valuables stored in the churches or monasteries. In most cases there was no desire to remain long, so that an element of surprise was the most important factor in success. However, in 1586 A.D. a particularly severe raid was directed by the Scots at Inis Eoghain and it would seem that some of the people of the areas contiguous to their camp assisted them. The invaders remained for some time before they were driven out.

Examining the coastline from Malin Town to Termone Bay we can still find traces of the forts—27 at least—which were established along the sea at points which had a certain natural advantage for defence. In addition, place-names are guides to the location of the fortified places in each district. The word *dun* signifies a fort or fortress.

In listing the forts in the area it should be noted that these were not all in operation at one time and that in many cases they were also used as ordinary places of residence in peace-time.

1. Doon — Townland of Drumaville Malin.
2. Doonkintra — also known as Greenhill — is situated at the base of Straghbreggagh Bay near the town of Malin.
3. Doon in the townland of Balleighan Lr., parish of Culdaff.
4. Doonmore in the townland of Balleighan.
5. Dun Droinge in the townland of Drung and commanding a good view of the bay of Straghbreggagh. There are still signs of the foundation of an old fortress.
6. Dunargus is a headland overlooking the sea in the townland of Kullourt. The site of this fort is a promontory approximately 100 feet across and bounded by a rock-ridge on the south. On the south and north sides there is a drop of over 70 yards direct to the sea. The entrance was in the north-west, by a narrow path between the cliff and the bog on the mainland side. It was further protected by an earthwork from sea to sea, with a trench inside which seems to have been improved, and behind it by the low cliffs of the promontory itself. From the earthwork one reached the interior of the fort by a ramp, on which can be seen charcoal, burnt earth and stones, chips of burnt bone and rounded pebbles which may have been sling stones. This ramp was later blocked by an earthen bank, and at its side an irregular tunnel, nine feet long, three feet wide and three feet high, was driven through the rock. Inside the fort to-day no structures are visible, but there are traces of refuse, such as sea-shells. The State Papers,[7] in a report dated 1600, state that there was in this area a fort by the seaside called "Don-Yrishe" held and inhabited by O Dochartaigh. While it is not certain, the fort is probably the one known to-day as Dunargus. If this deduction is correct, the fort was still inhabited at the beginning of the seventeenth century.
7. Doonmore — a hill in the townland of Kullourt.
8. The Doonans — the small forts — are situated in Ardmalin.
9. Dunaldragh in Ardmalin is an island separated from the mainland by a deep trench three feet wide through which the sea passes. Here nature provided a well-fortified base against any enemy from land or sea.
10. Doon is a rock about 30 feet high at Malin Well. The top comprises an area 50 feet long and varying from ten to 20 feet wide.
11. Dungolgan in Ballygorman is a steep headland approached by a narrow strip of land. There is to-day evidence of earthwork on the top of the promontory.
12. Doherty's Doon in Ballygorman is another promontory approached by a narrow tongue of land. There are signs of earthwork of various kinds in the area.
13. Dunagard — in the townland of the same name.
14. Doonilheagh — near Lougherbraghey.
15. Doonvihill is a hill in the townland of Glengad.

16. Doon — near Portaleen in the townland of Glengad.
17. Doondavy in Carthage.
18. Dunfort (*dunphort*), a promontory in the townland of Carthage.
19. Dunowen in the townland of Carthage is mentioned in the State Papers under the year 1600.[8] It was then inhabited by "Gartill Mc Shane Buidhe O Dogherty". Dunowen lies on the north side of the village of Culdaff. The site is a double promontory, the top of which is about 30 yards above sea level and approximately 20 yards above a stretch of marsh on the landside. On the elevation there stretches from cliff to cliff a dry-stone wall built on a base of large stone blocks. There are still signs of the entrance gate. The keep located in the centre is still marked by mounds of earth. The area itself is a natural fort, which required only some additions to withstand attack by land or occupation by sea.
20. Dunmore in the townland of Redford-Glebe is a large elevation with a flat top, part of which is a bog now cut out. Seawards there is a sheer drop to the sea, from which side the hill is practically inaccessible. There are no clear signs of any fortification here to-day, apart from the site of an old coastguard watch house erected around 1820. The hill gives a good view of Culdaff Bay and on a clear day the west coast of Scotland is visible.
21. Dunglass is a promontory situated in the townland of Redford-Glebe a short distance to the south-east of Dunmore. It is connected to the mainland by a neck of land, in the centre of which is a cave which drops steeply into the sea. The summit has a well defined plateau on which the original fort was located. Landwards the plateau is protected by a high cliff and seawards the land drops gradually to the sea. The top of the promontory has always been covered with verdure — hence the name.
22. Dun an Ghrianain is the correct name of the area at present comprising the townlands of Redford-Glebe, Culdaff-Glebe, Kindroyhad and Knockergrana. The fort was placed either on the Bishop's Hill or Cara Hill. The last-named has extensive signs of old ruins, which have not yet been investigated.
23. Doonane is a promontory in the townland of Ballyharry.
24. Deen is a hill in the townland of Larrahirrel. There is evidence of an old grave site here but none of any old fort.
25. Ardadunn in the townland of Dunross indicates the site of an old fortification.
26. Ardadunn, a hill in Glacknadrummond, marks the site of a fort. The hill is situated in the bog on the south-east side of the Bishop's Hill.
27. Duncorbek, situated in the parish of Cloncha, cannot now be traced.

It is interesting to note that the State Papers[9] for 1600 contain the following:

Beyond it — the mainland of Inis Eoghain — is another river of like nature, as I hear, but I have not seen it — as I have this — which cutteth off the far end of the country from all the rest; upon which standeth a wood and a pass, where into O Dogherty is now retired with all his people and goods. It is said to be the fertilist part of all the rest, *and hath upon it divers castles built of late years to resist the landing of the Scots,* and it is so full of poor Irish houses, as it seems all in a manner but one town.

113

Some English reports around 1600 refer to the area north of a line drawn from the base of Straghbreggagh to Culdaff Bay as an island. That it was so at an earlier time there is no doubt but at the time referred to it was connected to the mainland. Along the line mentioned there were bog and morass, which made a natural defence line, and O Dochartaigh availed of this.

If the report can be relied on there was still the threat of attack by sea, but the coming English occupation was soon to end all sea attacks. Instead, the Irish were to face a 300-year period of foreign occupation.

----------------·※·----------------

1. These are taken from *The Annals of the Kingdom of Ireland* (Four Masters) except where otherwise indicated.

2, 3, 4, 5. O Flanagan MSS.117-25, National Library.

6. *Calendar of State Papers, 1608:* Sir Thomas Ridgeway, Treasurer of Ireland, in a report to Salisbury.

7. *Calendar of State Papers, 1600:* letter from Sir Arthur Chichester to Robert Cecil. The report, insofar as it refers to the northern portion of Inis Eoghain, is vague. It is evidently based on hearsay.

8. *Calendar of State Papers, 1600:* Sir Arthur Chichester to Robert Cecil.

9. *Calendar of State Papers,* December 19th, 1600: Report on Inishowen.

7
A PERIOD OF TRANSITION: 1620-1800

BEFORE THE English occupation, the land of Inis Eoghain had been the cause of many battles between rival chiefs. The O Maol Fabhail, the O Diorma and the Mac Lochlainn families had surrendered to the more powerful Normans. The power of the De Burgos in time weakened and by the fourteenth century O Dochartaigh was lord of the principality. Apart from the occasional interruption of their lives by minor battles and raids, however, the ordinary occupiers of the land were usually left in peace. The early seventeenth century was to bring an end to the Irish form of ownership and with the change loss of security for the ordinary people.

The rebellion of Cathaoir O Dochartaigh gave the English the opportunity they had long hoped for. In the fourteenth century the Normans had established themselves in a strongly fortified spot in Greencastle. In time the O Dochartaigh family occupied this fort and managed to maintain their control over Inis Eoghain. O Dochartaigh had, however, given nominal obedience to Elizabeth I, who had in turn confirmed his possession of this northern outpost of Gaeldom.

THE PLANTATIONS

Years before the rebellion of Cathaoir O Dochartaigh the English had spied out the whole territory and had built up considerable data.[1] All that was needed was a pretext for confiscation. The rebellion and death of the ruler gave them this; James I declared the barony confiscated to the Crown. In 1609 James granted the greater part of the barony, to Arthur Chichester, the Lord Deputy of Ireland.[2] The balance was firstly the land belonging to the Catholic Church which was all granted to the Protestant Church and secondly a grant of 300 acres to the fort at Culmore.

One area, Kullourt, in the parish of Cloncha, requires special mention. Kullourt had been the property of the monastery of Macosquin in County Derry.[3] When this was confiscated, the townland of Kullourt was granted in 1604 by James I to George Carew, Knight, Vice-Chamberlain to the Queen.[4] From Carew it passed to Henry Docwra, Knight, who in turn sold it to William Sidney. Cathaoir O Dochartaigh, no doubt concerned that the English should not establish themselves in this outpost, bought

115

the land from Sidney. By a decree of James I the ownership passed temporarily to Randolph Bingley of Rathmullen. He[5] later surrendered it to Arthur Chichester.

In Culdaff and Cloncha the royal grant meant that all lands except the churchlands passed into the hands of Chichester. To the Protestant bishop of Derry passed the following townlands: Templemoyle, Drumaville-Malin, Drumballycaslin, Cloncha, Larrahirrel, Glacknadrummond, Dunross, Knock and Culdaff. The townlands of Redford-Glebe and Culdaff-Glebe became the glebe lands of Cloncha and Culdaff respectively.

No consideration was given to the native Irish in these two parishes. Their ancestors had owned and tilled these lands for many, many generations. Now their continued occupation depended entirely on the whim of an Englishman who probably knew very little of their existence. However, as the sequence of events will show, the Irish who lived in the northern tip of Inis Eoghain fared better than their compatriots elsewhere.

As the English took possession of the barony, what were their plans and intentions ? In granting the territory to Chichester King James directed him to divide the area into manors, to set up courts, to direct the holding of fairs and to arrange a division of the land among tenants. Finally, he was directed " to pursue the instructions of plantation in Ulster ".[6] To John, Earl of Annandale, whom James had appointed chief commander and governor of Donegal County, instructions were given " to reduce the inhabitants of the said county to civility of manners and good order according to the laws and statutes used in the English pale of our said realm of Ireland . . ."[7]

The Irish here were now without property. They lacked the means of education and were denied the right to practise their religion. The defeat of the O Dochartaigh family left them leaderless. This combination of unfavourable factors made the English plan seemingly easier to fulfill. The natives became third-class citizens in their own land and were to remain so for almost three centuries. They were, however, allowed to continue in occupation of the less fertile land.

It would seem that soon after he took possession Chichester granted some lands direct to the Irish.[8] Among others we find that Eugenius McShane Cugh McLaughlin was given land at Baskill " for ever, to be paid—to Chichester—thereout yearly 5/- money of England "; Richard O Dogherty, gentleman, got " the

116

whole quarter of Kenaughe . . . for the term of his life, to remain afterwards to certain of his sons and their heirs, for ever, to be paid thereout yearly to the said Lord Chichester 20/- —money of England ":

To an Englishman, George Cary, Esq., was granted among other lands the townland of " Monedaragh ".

Later the Irish who were granted land here were made tenants of William Usher and George Sexton.[9] The landlord—or middleman—pattern which was to last for over two and a half centuries was now evolving.

The first English resident in Culdaff and Cloncha was the Protestant rector called Edward Bowker.[10] He came around 1620. The plantation went very slowly here, as by 1665 there were only six Protestant families in Culdaff and two in Cloncha in addition to the rector.[11] No doubt it was the action of the Protestant clergy which encouraged the early planters. Courage was needed to come to this wild and inaccessible region and live among a people whose way of life was so far removed from that of the English.

The Commonwealth authority did not interfere with the lands belonging to Chichester. The churchlands belonging to the bishop were also left untouched in the hands of the original lessees.

Around 1655 Mrs. Sarah Babington is still[12] shown as the lease-holder of Knock, Culdaff, Cloncha, Dunross, Larrahirrel, Glacknadrummond and Drumballycaslin. James Downham is also still shown as the lease-holder of Templemoyle and Drumaville. The glebe lands of Redford-Glebe and Culdaff-Glebe were, however, confiscated and were recorded as belonging to the Commonwealth. Subsequently, these lands were returned to the Protestant Church.[13]

Between 1665 and 1740 the plantation proceeded at a fast pace. In 1694, in the area stretching from Ballymagaraghy to Carrowmore, there were 22 conformist families resident. It is of special interest to note that these planters were Gaelic-speaking Highlanders.[14]

The list of Protestant Householders in 1740[15] shows 58 households in Culdaff and 112 in Cloncha. The Church of Ireland adherents tended to settle in Culdaff parish while the Presbyterians settled in the Malin area, in Cloncha parish. It would seem that the landlord at Culdaff, Young, had arranged the immigration of those of his own persuasion to Culdaff, while the

Harvey family were responsible for the entry at Malin of the large contingent of Presbyterians.[16] Thus, within 80 years a substantial party of English and Scottish settlers was established in the area. It is clear from the location of these settlers that the better land was given to them. The native Irish were moved to other, less fertile soil. The bogs and mountains, in earlier times uninhabited, became now the refuge of the Catholics.

An examination of the list of Protestant Householders for 1740 shows a few Gaelic names, e.g., O Carolan occurs four times, McCauley three times and O Gillen once. This suggests that a few preferred their lands to their religion. It is not clear whether these householders came from outside the area or not. It may be noted that in the Hearth Money Roll dated 1665 for Culdaff and Cloncha, the names McCauley and O Gillen occur but the name O Carolan is not mentioned.

The first attempt at a census[17] in this area shows that in 1815 Culdaff had 893 families, of which 58 were Church of Ireland and 18 Presbyterian. Cloncha had 1,091 families; of these 49 were Church of Ireland and 47 were Presbyterian. In Culdaff there were 76 Protestant householders and in Cloncha 96, making a total of 172, compared with 170 in 1740. The total in Cloncha had decreased by 16 while in Culdaff there was an increase of 18 in the period of 75 years. It is evident from this census that the period between 1665 and 1740 was the time during which the organised plantation took place.

These early settlers must have faced many difficulties before they had formed an organised community. However, they had the backing of the landlords and the clergy. The best land was made available to them and in the early years organised help was given to the needy. House-building, tilling and seeding of their farms were priorities and essential to ensure their survival here.

A wide division existed between the natives and this alien minority. A different religion, a different language and a different culture marked the settlers as a people apart. To all this can be added the resentment felt by the Irish against these foreigners who had taken possession of the fertile lands. Indeed, the descendants of the settlers have never merged into the Irish community. Even to the present the Protestant community direct their loyalty and interest towards England rather than to their adopted land.

The social and cultural effects of the occupation and the plantations on the community as a whole were far-reaching and pro' found. The native Irish were dispirited and demoralised. This point is more fully discussed later.

What was the character, the type, of the early settlers from England and Scotland ? The answer is clearly given from a source which had no reason to decry the standing or to damage the image of these arrivals in Donegal and elsewhere in Ulster during the seventeenth century.

In *Historical and Literary Memorials of Presbyterianism in Ireland* by Thomas Witherow there is a note written by Andrew Stewart, a Presbyterian minister in Donaghadee during the years 1646-1671. The relevant extract, which is entitled " Character of the First Settlers ", is as follows:

> From Scotland came many, and from England not a few, yet all of them generally the scum of both nations, who for debt, or breaking and fleeing from justice, or seeking shelter, came hither, hoping to be without fear of man's justice in a land where there was nothing, or but little, as yet of the fear of God. And in a few years there followed such a multitude of people from Scotland that these northern counties of Down, Antrim, Londonderry, etc., were in a good measure planted, which had been made waste before; yet most of the people, as I said before, made a body (and, it is strange, of different names, nations, dialects, tempers, breeding, and, in a word, all void of godliness) who seemed rather to flee from God in this enterprise than to follow their own mercy. Yet God followed them when they fled from him — albeit at first it must be remembered that they cared little for any church . . .

Yet it was to these people and their descendants that many of the people of Culdaff and Cloncha turned as models in many spheres of life ! The heirs of the culture of Comhghall, Buadan and Muirdhealach had nothing to learn from these aliens. On the contrary, they had much to teach them.

Many of the Irish in our area, devoid of leadership, and ignorant of their own great culture and heritage, aped the ways of the planters. In the process they became a weak and slavish people, and unto the present the results can be seen in the community.

THE CHICHESTER FAMILY

It is fitting that this account should contain a note on the Chichester family. All Inis Eoghain was granted to Sir Arthur Chichester and later two members of this family were rectors in both parishes.

The first member of the family to appear on the Irish scene was Arthur Chichester. His life covered the years from 1563 to 1625—coinciding roughly with the reigns of the English sovereigns Elizabeth I and James I. He was the second son of Sir John Chichester of Rawleigh near Barnstaple.[18] As a young man he was involved in the robbery of one of the Queen's purveyors. To escape the penalty for his action he fled to Ireland, where he stayed for a time with an Englishman called George Bourchier.

Through the influence of friends he obtained the Queen's pardon and later we find him as captain of one of the best ships of the Queen's navy during the battle arising out of the threatened invasion by the Armada. Next he was appointed by Essex (during his Irish campaign) as governor of Carrickfergus and the area thereabouts. On February 3rd, 1605, Chichester was made Lord Deputy of Ireland by James I. He held this post until November 29th, 1614, when he was recalled. He lived at Carrickfergus and died there in 1625.

James rewarded his servant by granting him huge tracts of land in Ulster when the Irish owners were dispossessed. Among the grants was the peninsula of Inis Eoghain, the area confiscated after the rebellion of Cathaoir O Dochartaigh.

Chichester's attitude to the Irish is well illustrated in his letters. Early in the seventeenth century he wrote: —

We follow a painful, toilsome, hazardous and unprofitable war, by which the queen will never reap what is expected until the nation be wholly destroyed or so subjected as to take a new impression of laws and religion, being now the most treacherous infidels of the world, and we have too mild spirits and good consciences to be their masters . . . Our honesty, bounty, clemency and justice make them not any way assured of us; neither doth the actions of one of their own nation, though it be the murder of father, brother or friend. make them longer enemies than until some small gift or buying be given unto the wronged party.

In a later letter he wrote:

I wish the rebels and their countries in all parts of Ireland like these where they starve miserably and eat dogs, mares and garrons where they can get them. No course . . . will cut the throat of the grand traitors, subject his limbs, and bring the country into quiet, but famine, which is well begun, and will daily increase. When they are down, it must be good laws, severe punishment, abolishing their ceremonies and customs in religion, and lordlike Irish Government.

He was in this letter referring to and approving of Lord Mountjoy's manner of making war on the Irish nation. Such was the attitude of the first of the Chichesters to the Irish people, and it may be taken as that of his descendants.

120

Sir Arthur died without any direct heir to his title or his vast estates. Accordingly, he was succeeded by his brother Edward, who became the first Viscount Chichester. On the death of Edward, his son Arthur became heir and was created Earl of Donegall. In turn the Earl was succeeded by his nephew, who bore the same name and title.[19] With a brother named John of this second earl our story is now concerned.

Captain John Chichester had a son called William, who became a Church of Ireland clergyman. He was born in 1687 and died in 1736. William's son Arthur was also a clergyman, who as a curate served at Drumaul parish in Randalstown.[20] Nearby lived the O Neill family of Shane's Castle, who were direct descendants of the Irish High King Niall, from whom they could trace their descent through successive generations. Arthur Chichester, the curate in the nearby church, became acquainted with the O Neills and subsequently married Mary O Neill, daughter of Henry O Neill.[21] The union was of importance later when this branch of the O Neills became extinct.

Arthur served as rector in Clonmany parish from 1754 to his death in 1768. His son William succeeded in the same year.[22] William Chichester[23] was born in 1743 and after private tuition he entered Trinity College, Dublin. Here he took the degrees of B.A., M.A., LL.B. and LL.D. He was rector of Cloncha from 1791 to 1800 and of Culdaff from 1800 to 1807. He died August 31st, 1815, and was buried in his mother's tomb at Clonmany. William Chichester had married twice. His second wife was Mary Anne Hart of Kilderry. She bore a son, Edward, the next of the family with whom we are concerned.

Edward Chichester, who took the degrees of B.A. and M.A. at Trinity, was rector of Cloncha from 1800 to 1823 and of Culdaff for two periods, 1798 to 1800 and 1807 to 1823. He married Catherine, daughter of Robert Young of Culdaff House. Edward Chichester at this time lived at Redford in the Cloncha rectory. He later became rector of Kilmore near Armagh and was subsequently appointed Chancellor of Armagh, where he died in July, 1840, and was buried.[24]

Edward Chichester wrote, *circa* 1815, a " Statistical Account of Culdaff and Cloncha " for Mason's publication. During his rectorship the unrest associated with the action of the British Government in forbidding private distillation took place. As the parishes of Culdaff and Cloncha were centres of illicit distillation the people were well-nigh reduced to penury by the wholesale seizures of their property. The rector found that as a result the people were unable to pay their tithes to his support, and he was faced with a reduced income as a result.

He initiated a campaign against the Irish Revenue Officers and published a pamphlet entitled *Oppressions and Cruelties of the Irish Revenue Officers* in 1818. In this he detailed the abuses of the law arising from the corruption of the law officers. The Acting Inspector of Excise, Aeneas Coffey, replied in a pamphlet entitled *Observations on the Rev. Edward Chichester's pamphlet entitled Oppressions and Cruelties of Irish Revenue Officers*. To this document the rector of Culdaff and Cloncha replied in a further letter.

During these years the district was in a state of violent unrest. A local landlord was killed. A young man who was charged with threatening the life of Edward Chichester while this gentleman was executing a warrant for his arrest was hanged at Lifford. Martial law was declared and the British Army moved into the area. To the writings of Chichester we owe the detailed account of this area in the first quarter of the nineteenth century. He also published a theological work entitled *Deism compared with Christianity*.

At Redford on March 4th, 1813, to Edward Chichester and his wife Catherine was born a son who was named William, later Baron O Neill. Three other sons were born to them.

John Bruce Richard O Neill, third Viscount O Neill, died on February 12th, 1855. He had no direct heirs and left his estates to his cousin, the above-named William Chichester, then a clergyman at St. Michael's, Dublin. The Viscountcy became extinct.[25] William Chichester was created Baron O Neill of Shane's Castle by patent dated 18th April, 1868, taking the surname O Neill. His son Edward succeeded as second baron. The son and heir of the second baron, Arthur Edward Bruce, was killed in action on November 6th, 1914.[26]

Arthur Edward Bruce had three sons: Shane Edward Robert, who succeeded as the third baron; Brian Arthur, killed in Norway, 1940; and Terence Marne. The last named became Prime Minister at Stormont.[27]

The present holder of the title is Raymond Arthur Clanaboy, son of Shane Edward Robert. He is the fourth baron.[28]

With regard to the holders of the title of Earl of Donegall, we

122

find that the fourth earl died without issue and was succeeded by his nephew Arthur, who became the first Marquis of Donegall. Hence we find the title Marquis of Donegall occurring in the land records of Inis Eoghain in the eighteenth century. However, by the nineteenth century the name of the estate holder of the peninsula had again changed. The ultimate heir of the third marquis was an only daughter called Harriet. She inherited the estates, as her two brothers died without issue.

She married on the 22nd August, 1857, Anthony, eighth Earl of Shaftesbury.[29] On the death of the third Marquis of Donegall in 1883 the name in the land records was changed to that of the Earl of Shaftesbury, who was in possession when the British Government acquired the lands on behalf of the tenants under the Land Acts.

In conclusion, the question might be asked, " Why do we find members of the Chichester family in places as remote as Culdaff and Cloncha ?" The answer is found in the secure income arising from the tithes collected from the people. The less wealthy members of the notable Protestant families took Holy Orders and through influence were appointed rectors. The advowsons of the Inis Eoghain parishes were in the hands of the Earls of Donegall. Relatives were chosen to fill these positions as circumstances required.

THE YEOMANRY

The state which we know to-day, with its well-organised police force and its mobile army, is a relatively modern development. In Ireland there was no properly organised police force until around 1830, and the British Army was not so mobile as to ensure swift and effective action as required until comparatively recent times.

In such circumstances, a local organisation evolved in time of crisis to ensure the maintenance of control. Such was the yeomanry. This force was organised by the Protestant landed gentry for self-protection in the troubled years towards the end of the eighteenth century. Thomas Knox, the Knight of the Shire for County Tyrone, and W. Richardson of Trinity College, Dublin, were the pioneers in getting the force organised.[30]

The yeomanry was a partisan force somewhat like the modern " B Specials ". It was made up almost entirely of Protestants and its aim was to ensure the survival of the privileged minority. Wakefield, writing about 1812, shows that this army was the cause of idleness and much drinking. The local landlord used the men for his own purposes, such as planting or digging potatoes, and the men's pay was spent in the public house, in which the landlord or his deputy had a large interest.[31]

Because of its partisan make-up, distrust was generated among the majority who were Catholics. The ordinary Irishman saw it as an instrument of British injustice and secret societies were formed to afford some protection for the Catholics.

In the parishes of Culdaff and Cloncha the local landlords were active in forming and maintaining the force. Young of Culdaff House and Harvey of Malin Hall were both leaders.[32]

Around 1740, when the possibility of the restoration of the Stuarts to the English throne was a threat to the House of Hanover. Robert Young was a commissioned officer in the Donegal Militia.[33] About the same time John Harvey organised the Malin Volunteers.[34] No doubt the aim was to give support to King George, whose throne was in danger. With the defeat of Culloden the need for the volunteer force disappeared, however, and it would seem that the Malin Volunteers were disbanded.

Harvey's son, another John Harvey, had a very strong interest in the volunteer organisation which arose around 1780. He attended the Dungannon Convention and became acquainted with Lord Charlemont. At home he revived the Malin Volunteers, whom he recruited and trained at his own expense.[35] By the end of the century official recognition was given and the local forces were re-constituted under the names Malin Cavalry and Malin Infantry. Around the same time the Culdaff Infantry was established.[36] Later, these Culdaff volunteers became the Culdaff Corps of the Yeomanry.

Records show that on October 31st, 1796, Robert Young was commissioned as captain, John Young as first lieutenant and Thomas Harvey as second lieutenant, all in the Culdaff Infantry. On the same date, for the Malin Cavalry, were commissioned John Harvey as captain, John Montgomery as first lieutenant and Ralph Young as second lieutenant.[37]

There are indications that members of the Catholic population in the area were also active. In 1797 an incident took place in which a section of the Culdaff Yeomanry Corps was disarmed by what the writer[38] described as " rebels ".

The yeomanry were used locally for various kinds of duties. In Lent, 1789, we find Thomas Harvey, 2nd lieutenant of the

124

Culdaff Yeomanry, conveying prisoners to gaol.[39] In the efforts
which Young of Culdaff House made to suppress illicit distillation, he was supported by his yeomen.[40] In effecting the arrest
of McConnollogue, Edward Chichester was aided by this force[41]
and in a similar manner Young was helped in securing the arrest
of Daniel McGuinness.[42]

A list[43] of the parade attendance of the Culdaff Yeomanry
for the quarter ending September, 1828, includes the following
names:

Butler, Cane, Carney, Crumblisk, Danford, Doherty, Doran, Duncan,
Duffy, Faulkner, Farran, Hatton, Henderson, Knox, Lynch, Lyons, Long,
McCandless, McIntire, Mitchell, Mulhern, Platt, Wilkie, Sheals, Smith.

The names Hatton, Farran, McCandless, Lynch and Knox
occur twice, the names Henderson and Smith three times and
the name Doherty five times. An analysis of the names indicates
that a number of Catholics served in the yeomanry. Local tradition supports this conclusion.

In 1834 the " rebels " were again active, as a number of
houses belonging to the yeomen was raided and guns were taken.
Among the robbed we find the names of Robert Wallace and
James Long.[44] The guns were later returned to the owners.[45]

Around 1834 the force was disbanded and the regular police
soon began to operate in the area.[46]

THE ACT OF UNION PETITION[47]

In the last quarter of the eighteenth century, the British
Government became increasingly concerned about the threat to
imperial interests arising from the existence of a separate parliament in Ireland. The Cabinet in London noted with particular
attention the implications of the threat of a French invasion of
Ireland combined with a popular rebellion of the people. Government agents throughout the country fomented unrest to provide
a pretext to introduce proposals for the abolition of the Irish
legislature. The Rebellion of 1798 and the landing of French aid
gave the British Prime Minister the opportunity he sought. An
Act of Union was introduced and passed with the aid of bribery
and corruption. Potential opposition from Catholics was lessened
by the Government's promise to introduce a form of Catholic
Emancipation.

The supporters of the Union organised petitions which were
presented to the King asking for a legislative Union between Ire-

land and Great Britain. One such petition was presented from supporters in County Donegal. Among the petitioners were residents of Culdaff and Cloncha.
The text of the petition was as follows:

The subject of a Legislative Union between Great Britain and Ireland having undergone a full and extensive consideration, it is to be presumed that few Men are at this day undecided in their Opinions on that momentous subject. We, whose names are undersigned, take this method of conveying to the Public our sentiments on that most important Question.

We are not surprised that different opinions should prevail on a subject so interesting, and so extensive; we therefore hold the sentiments of such of our Fellow-Countrymen as happen to be different from our own, in that just respect that is due to their Characters and their Property in our Country. We deem it however right at this period to declare our own.

The principle of a Legislative Union between this Kingdom and Great Britain, founded on Equality of Trade, Equality of Protection, Equality of Constitutional Rights and Privileges, and Equality of Taxation, according to the respective wealth and resources of both Kingdoms, meets with our decided approbation.

But while we thus declare our approbation of the general principle, we are not to be understood to pledge ourselves to the detail. That detail we consider arduous and difficult. However, we do not think the apparent difficulty ought to discourage the efforts to accomplish an object that, in our opinion, will strengthen the Empire at large, allay private discontents and religious animosities in this Kingdom, and bury for ever the jealousies that are inseparable from a Federal Connection between different and independent Nations.

(The above Declaration has been signed by the following Noblemen and Gentlemen with about three thousand others whose Names we will insert when we can make room.)

The following, *inter alios*, signed the petition:

R. Harvey, Malin Hall; Thomas Harvey, *do.*; John Harvey, *do.*; Robert Hart, Cashel; R. Young, Culdaff; W. Chichester, LL.D., Rector, Cloncha; E. Chichester, Clerk, Rector, Culdaff; Jos. Curry, Umgal; W. McIntire, Bellieghan; Sam Latta, Ballagh; William Doherty, Killin; Sam Baird, Ballycrampsey; James Boggs, Lagg; Wm. Ringland, Malin Town; Jn. Hewston, Malin; R. McIntire, Malin Town; Rob Moore, Drumcarbit; J. McCanless, Carrimore; Ninian Boggs, Ballylin; J. Boggs, Sen., Ballylin; J. Carney, Cloncha-Glebe; Sam McInteger, Cloncha-Glebe; Owen Dougherty, Cloncha-Glebe; Jn. Faulkner, Glacknadrummond; George Reed, *do.*; T. Merchant, Cloncha; B. Gillin, Lisdarragan; Jn. Alcorn, Lisdarragan; J. Maginnis, Mallin Town; Wm. Starret, Killin; Edw. Harvey, clk. Cloncha; Tho. Russell, Ballylin; Jn. Fulton, Ballagh; Rob Harrett, Killin; T. Baird, Ballycrampsey; D. Fulton, Drumcrory; J. Dougherty, Malin Town; W. Young, Malin Town; *I.* Hill, Drumcarbett; Js. Wilson, Drumcarbett; Jn. Elkin, Drumcarbett; J. Moore, Carrimore; Sam Russell, Ballylin; Wm. Elder, Letterorr; R. McIntire, Malin; Walter McFarland, Culdaff-Glebe; John Clarke, Culdaff-Glebe· John Dougherty, Culdaff-Glebe; Michael Dougherty, Culdaff-Glebe; Denis Canny, Dunross; George Butler, Lisdarragan; John McConnologue, Cloncha; John Reed, Cloncha; Alex Moore, Bellelahan; Cha. Crow, Mallin Town.

This record shows that the petition in the parishes of Culdaff and Cloncha was supported in the main by the non-Catholic section of the community. The parish priests—Philip Doherty of Cloncha and Denis O Donnell of Culdaff—did not sign, though the parish priest of Clonmany did so.

———————◦▧◦———————

1. *Calendar of State Papers:* 19.12.1600. Sir Henry Docwra to Sir Robert Cecil.
2. *Irish Patent Rolls James I:* Patent 7.
3. Inquisitions—Derry.
4. *Repertory Patent Rolls James I.*
5. State Papers, MS.14C9—Royal Irish Academy.
6. *Irish Patent Rolls James I:* Patent 7.
7. *Irish Patent Rolls James I:* Patent 22.
8, 9. State Papers, MS.14C9—Royal Irish Academy.
10. *Derry Clergy and Parishes,* Leslie.
11. Hearth Money Roll.
12. Historical Manuscripts Commission: *Report on the Manuscripts of R. R. Hastings,* Vol. IV. A Rental for the Bishopric of Derry dated 1641. The names Babbington and Downham are associated with Culdaff and Cloncha in 1641.
13. *Analecta Hibernica,* Vol. 12: Ulster Plantation Papers.
14. King—Lyons Collection, 1693-1695. Letter, No. 401.
15. Genealogical Office Dublin: List of Protestant Housekeepers in 1740.
16. The members of the Harvey family were originally Presbyterian in religious persuasion. Members of this family took part in the siege of Derry and also gave a son to the Presbyterian ministry. This minister served the Presbyterians at Carndonagh and Malin at the beginning of the eighteenth century. The members of this family were very early in the Plantations associated with Malin, where they later became landlords.
17. *Mason's Statistical Survey,* 1816: "Culdaff and Cloncha," Edward Chichester.
18. *Dictionary of National Biography.*
19. *Burke's Peerage.*
20. *Three Hundred Years in Innishowen,* Young.
21. *Burke's Peerage.*
22, 23, 24. *Derry Clergy and Parishes,* Leslie.
25. *Dormant and Extinct Peerages,* Burke.
26, 27, 28, 29. *Burke's Peerage.*
30. *History of the Origin of the Irish Yeomanry,* W. Richardson, D.D.
31. *Ireland: Statistical and Political,* 1812, Wakefield.
32. *Three Hundred Years in Innishowen,* Young.
33. *Ulster Journal of Archaeology,* Vol. 3 and Vol. 4.
34, 35. *Three Hundred Years in Innishowen,* Young.
36. *Ulster Journal of Archaeology,* Vol. 3 and Vol. 4.
37. *A list of the Officers of the Several District Corps of Ireland together*

with the dates of their respective Commissions. Issued by Dublin Castle, 26.1.1797.

38. *Mason's Statistical Survey*, 1816: "Culdaff and Cloncha," Edward Chichester.
39. Grand Jury Presentments for County Donegal, Vol. 1.
40. *Three Hundred Years in Innishowen*, Young.
41. *Inishowen*, "Maghtochair".
42, 43, 44. *Three Hundred Years in Innishowen*, Young.
45. *The Derry Journal* dated 22nd April, 1834, reports: "We are happy to announce that, through the exertions of the Roman Catholics clergymen in Malin, the guns which were lately taken from the Culdaff yeomanry, have been restored to the Revd. Hugh Monaghan C.C. of Malin, and by him handed over to Richard Magann, Esq., Chief Constable of Police".
46. *Three Hundred Years in Innishowen*, Young.
47. George Faulkner: *The Dublin Journal*, No. 9212, Saturday, December 14th, 1799.

8
A PERIOD OF TURMOIL: 1800-1820

WHILE OUR general narrative is solely concerned with the story of Culdaff and Cloncha, it is necessary in the case of illicit distillation to deal with the subject on a more extended basis. If we are to see events in correct perspective and to assess this stormy period more accurately, it is not possible to isolate what happened in Culdaff and Cloncha from the remainder of Inis Eoghain. Hence this section deals with developments in the barony as a whole in outline and against this background events in the two parishes are related in more detail.

Inis Eoghain, an area of 200,000 acres, extends about thirty miles north of Derry city. The northern part lies less than 50 miles from Scotland. For example, Bunagee harbour at Culdaff is a mere 40 miles from Islay. The northern parts of Derry and Antrim are easily accessible by sea.

Because of its location and its long coastline, Inis Eoghain was easily approached by sea either from the northern coast of the country or from the west of Scotland. This factor was of great importance at the time to which this section refers. The roads were few and those few were mere tracks. The approaches by sea were relatively unguarded, as the coastguard service was not in operation here.

Inis Eoghain was therefore ideally situated geographically and admirably circumstanced by many factors to give those who wished to defy British law every opportunity to act with impunity in the early part of the nineteenth century.

IMPORTANCE OF DISTILLATION IN THE ECONOMY

In the early part of the last century Inis Eoghain was famous throughout the Three Kingdoms as the main centre of the illicit distillation industry. There was a number of special reasons for this.

Legal action against unlicensed stillers was becoming effective in many areas where Government control was strong. The demand for whiskey was great and customers, refusing to buy the legal spirits, turned elsewhere for supplies. Inis Eoghain was remote from irksome Government interference. The King's writ was generally ineffective in the area. The illegal stiller carried out his work openly and unmolested. As illicit distillation was curtailed in other areas, customers sought supplies in Inis Eoghain.

In addition, the whiskey produced here had already achieved a special status. The Inis Eoghain stiller was the heir of generations of experience and now was the time to commercialise his expertise.

The economy of Inis Eoghain was, and still is, largely based on the land. Distillation was closely associated with the produce of the soil and while the industry flourished it gave a great boost to the economy in general. All sections of the economy benefited during the period under review. This was a matter of special value at a time when the population was increasing at a fast pace.

The basic raw material was either barley or oats. The increasing demand for whiskey encouraged the farmers to a more intensive tillage. The demand could not be entirely satisfied locally. Prices rose and as a result the raw material was imported from places as distant as Scotland,[1] Antrim and Down. Boats came regularly from Scotland. A regular market for barley was held at Magilligan[2] in County Derry. The high prices attracted suppliers from all the neighbouring counties. Boats plied to and fro between Magilligan and Inis Eoghain.

There was a big demand for land for tillage. Rents were increased and so the landlords and Protestant rectors enjoyed a higher income. Thus they reaped a substantial share of the increase in the money which was circulating.

Many other associated activities were aided. The making of malt and the grinding of cereals meant extra income for the miller. There were at this time many mills in operation in the barony.[3] Most of their operative time was involved in the preparation of the raw material for stillers. The demand for utensils gave employment to the travelling tinkers. Stills at this time were usually made of copper, though sometimes tin was used.

In many cases each family made its own whiskey but there was a number who did not and who sought the service of others. A new professional class thus evolved. The full-time stiller who moved about from place to place offering his services was a familar sight in those days. He carried the necessary equipment on his back.

The clergy of all denominations participated in the general weal. They had a higher income and no clergyman was ever in want of his keg of Inis Eoghain whiskey. He thus could entertain his friends and have his nightly sleeping potion.

It is clear, therefore, that every member of the community

shared in the improved standard of living. The farmer, the landlord, the miller, the tinker, the professional stiller and the clergy
all had a better income. They all thus had a vested interest in
the continuance of illicit distillation.

Finally, if one may mention the indefinable and the immeasur-
able, the discerning customer throughout the land had his life
made happier by his regular glass of Inis Eoghain. Drooping
spirits were made to soar and flagging emotions were revived by
the magic nectar from the wilds of the island of Eoghan. Poteen
added zest to many a festive gathering and eased the pain of the
bereaved. It was in fact the panacea of its age in the barony and
elsewhere.

INFLUENCE OF THE LANDLORDS

In passing, it is important to note that the whole of Inis
Eoghain belonged to and was divided between two owners: the
Marquis of Donegall and the Protestant Bishop of Derry. The
former had the greater portion. Leases were given by the owners
to tenants who were known as " landlords ". These in turn let
the land to the farmers who actually tilled the soil.

During the early part of the nineteenth century, the landlords
and the Protestant rectors wielded a great influence over the
people of all denominations. They were also regarded by the
British Government as pillars and guardians of the law insofar as
action was required from time to time. In many cases each landlord had his own private army, recruited locally and maintained
by him. These were the yeomen. However, for a time, there was
a clash of interests between the Government and the landlords.

The source of conflict was the decision by the Government to
eliminate illicit distillation. The civil authority saw a loss of
revenue if the production of illicit spirits continued. On the
other hand, the landlords feared a decline in rent if it ceased.
Hence the vacillating policy of the landlord class.

THE ART OF DISTILLATION

It may be interesting to examine the art of distillation before
developing the narrative. What exactly is distillation ?

It is defined as the process of vaporising a liquid and subsequently recovering it by condensation. The liquid which is so formed is termed the " distillate ". The process of evaporation of
water from the sea, the formation of clouds and in due course
the falling of rain all exemplify in the natural order a form of
distillation.

Distillation and brewing have much in common. In both there is used at times the same kind of raw material. The processes of boiling and fermentation are similar. At this point however the resemblance ends.

The apparatus required for distillation in its simplest form consists of four elements. To contain the liquid while it is boiled a vessel called a still is used. The worm, usually made of a coiled length of hollow copper tubing, is used for condensing the vapour coming from the still. The head is an attachment to the top of the still to which the worm is fitted. The worm is placed in a vessel of cold water and a keg is placed at its outer terminal to receive the condensed liquid. Thus we have the familar terms used in the stilling world—the still, the head, the worm and the keg.

The art of distillation originated, it is said, among the Arabs. It reached Europe about the thirteenth century, when Genoese merchants introduced it into Italy. These merchants saw in the new art a source of profit and they began distilling on a small scale. The first distillate was called brandy. It was sold throughout Europe in small phials through chemist shops. It was regarded as a valuable balsam and was given the name *aqua vitae,* water of life. In Irish, whiskey is still known as *uisce beatha.*

Distillation took place at first from wine lees but later the enterprising merchants used fruit, and later again grain. Soon the art spread throughout Europe, so that by the end of the sixteenth century distillation was a general practice. The earliest reference to *aqua vitae* in Ireland is found in a record of the fourteenth century. In 1608 there is evidence of a restriction on the making of *aqua vitae.*[4] Sir Thomas Phillips was granted authority to forbid stilling save under his authority in the County of Coleraine. Corn was the raw material in use at the time.

It is thus evident that distillation had reached the north at least as early as the sixteenth century. When did the art reach the peninsula of Inis Eoghain ? From whence was it introduced ? There is no clear evidence to enable us to get a satisfactory answer to either of the questions posed. Most early writers say that the art was practised in the barony " from time immemorial ". Only vague hints are given regarding the source of introduction.

Inis Eoghain has had over the centuries close cultural and economic links with the west of Scotland—the kingdom of Dal-

Riada. The two countries were located close to each other. They were peopled by the same stock and they spoke the same language. There were close trading links. Inter-marriage and constant cultural contacts strengthened and sustained the relationships on both sides of the seas. 'New ideas flowed freely in both directions. It is highly probable that the people of Inis Eoghain got their first lessons in the art of distillation from their Scottish cousins. The people of Scotland had in turn acquired the knowledge from Continental contacts.

It can therefore be safely assumed that distillation was practised in Inis Eoghain as early as the sixteenth century. By the next century the art was widely known and the production of whiskey widespread.

INIS EOGHAIN WHISKEY AND ITS MARKETING

The foregoing shows that the art of distillation was an involved one requiring both time and skill. The people of Inis Eoghain had over their centuries of experience built up considerable expertise. They were as a result able to produce a high quality product, which was in great demand throughout the whole country and abroad. While allowance has to be made for the fact that the palate is trained to a certain taste and is not easily changed, there was among the people and especially the richer classes a marked preference for the illegal distillate simply because it was a better quality whiskey. Legal spirits were produced under severe government restrictions and were often adulterated. They were more expensive as well.

Among the various kinds of illegal whiskey that from Inis Eoghain had a special status. Reports from merchants in Dungannon[5] and Belfast show that among the upper classes the bottle of " Inishowen " had a special place. It was kept in the cellar and was produced only on great occasions and for the honoured guest. It commanded a price greater than legal whiskey and other illicit products.

An elaborate marketing system evolved to ensure that the Inis Eoghain product reached its customers at home and abroad. Boats from Scotland came over with barley, corn, herrings and ponies.[6] In exchange the Scots took back kegs of Inis Eoghain whiskey to give joy to the hearts of the Highland chief and his clan at every festive gathering. The city of Derry and the town of Strabane drew their supplies from the peninsula. The whiskey was transported thither on horseback. From Strabane it went to customers throughout Tyrone.

Twice weekly a whiskey fair was held in Bun an Phobail.[7] Here suppliers and buyers met in public. A fair took place also at Magilligan on the opposite side of the Foyle. Thither from the counties around came vendors of barley, which was bartered for whiskey or at times paid for in money. Indeed, the Foyle was full of small boats plying in both directions.[8] From Magilligan the whiskey was taken to Derry, Antrim and Down. Records show that Inis Eoghain whiskey even reached Dublin.[9] Indeed, at one investigation a highly placed official in the excise department stated that the whole country was supplied with it at one time. The northern coasts of Derry and Antrim were supplied direct from Inis Eoghain by boat.

A letter-writer in a Belfast magazine[10] in 1809 referred to the scenic view around Cushendall. In discussing the practice of visitors to this area climbing to the summit of Luirg Eadain he stated that at its base " resides a solitary female who compassionately regales the weary traveller with a glass of Inishowen to enable him to gain the summit of the steep ascent ".

The demand for the Inis Eoghain product was not confined to the poorer classes. The greatest and most consistent demand, as already noted, came from the more discerning palates of high ranking clerics, rich businessmen and the governing classes.

1810: A CONTEMPORARY ACCOUNT

The following letter, written on the 19th December, 1810, by William Gregory, a revenue official, to his principals, gives a vivid account of conditions in Inis Eoghain at the time: [11]

Gentlemen: I have deferred writing to you until I could collect sufficient information upon the subject of Private Distillation, as might enable me to form an opinion of the extent to which it is carried on and of the most probable means of suppressing it. I conceived the best method of ascertaining its extent was going into that part of the country where the distilleries are most numerous, from being most remote from any military stations. For this purpose I have made a circuit of the barony of Ennishowen, accompanied by a gentleman, who kindly undertook the journey to show me the roads.

Much as I had heard of the open manner in which this illicit traffic is conducted, yet the view of it astonished me. After leaving Buncrannagh a few miles, and entering into the mountains, there is scarce a village in which distillation is not carried on; this continues without interruption to the extremity of the coast at Malin and Culdaff. Near to the latter place I saw a vessel loading with spirits for Scotland; there I met a gentleman of the neighbourhood, who is a magistrate — as is also

134

he who accompanied me — and our presence gave no disturbance to the people bringing down their spirits to put on board. They fear no force but the military and that being the place where your officer Coffey, and the soldiers of the King's county were lately wounded they are become more confident even in their opposition to them. From thence around the whole coast to the entrance of Lough Foyle, near Greencastle, the same lawless trade is carried on with equal publicity. I have connected with those gentlemen to whom I have been made known, as to the best means of stopping private distillation in Ennishowen; and if once checked there the attention of the Board may be directed to other parts of the country. I shall therefore give you my opinion founded upon the result of those enquiries and the observations I have been able to make during the time I have been there. With the greatest military force, stationed as it is, I do not think any effectual impression can be made; the party at Buncrannagh have fourteen miles to march before they can arrive at that part of the country where the trade is most briskly carried on; the troops from hence twenty-two miles. As these marches must be conducted during the night through deep woods, the men are unfit for any active service when they arrive at the point of duty. Any set of men, as substitutes for soldiers would be totally useless.

The private distillers are principally yeomen, well-armed and would immediately resist any force but the military, in which they would be joined by nearly the whole population of the country. I should therefore recommend an officer and forty men to be stationed either at Malin or Culdaff, where accommodation can be procured, and they are both only three miles from Carn, a small market town. I should also advise a party of equal force at Green Castle, where accommodation can also be had. I think forces so placed would be sufficient for the interior of Ennishowen. Some few men stationed at Magilligan where there is now a vacant house, would annoy the trade on that side of the Lough Foyle. With these forces on land, and a revenue cruizer in Lough Foyle, with Captain Smith of the Annesley cutter in Lough Swilly, I am sanguine in my expectations of so harassing these illicit traders that they would be compelled to relinquish their business. The revenue barge in Lough Foyle is incompetent to the service. In this opinion I am fortified by the concurrence of the collector of the customs and Captain Smith of the Annesley, two gentlemen from which I have received much useful information and who are ready to give their assistance in co-operating with the officers of excise: exclusive of the unfitness of the revenue barge in Lough Foyle for this service, I am credibly informed that her crew are too much connected in the country. In the barony of Ennishowen are twentythree corn mills, which are employed four days in the week at least in grinding malt for the use of illicit stills.

I have directed the attention of the officers to the mills but they cannot venture to any distance without troops and therefore can only inspect them when out on other seizures. The necessity of placing millers under some check, to prevent their grinding malt for illicit purposes, may be worthy of legislative consideration. Barley is supplied from the neighbouring counties; some across Lough Swilly and Foyle, and much through the city of Derry; from Scotland the supply at present is but small, as they are apprehensive of loading their light vessels deeply at this season of the year; but about the month of March. they draw from thence great quantities, in exchange for spirits. Should the Government allow troops to be stationed at the places I have pointed out, and a revenue cruizer actively employed in each of the Loughs, much benefit would, in my mind, be the result. The garrison of Derry, together with the excise officers of the town might be sufficient — by patrolling the environs — to prevent the entrance of spirits into this city. As the season advanced, could another cutter be spared, to go round the headlands between Loughs Foyle and Swilly, the trade with Scotland would be completely destroyed.

With troops stationed in these remote places, I have no doubt of receiving the assistance of the few gentlemen who reside in the interior of Ennishowen but who, by their distance from each other, and from military aid, are unwilling to expose themselves to personal danger, where it could not be attended with any national benefit.

Should such regulations be adopted and the expected effects produced, I have reason to be satisfied a large public distillery would be established in Derry. A market would then be opened for the sale of barley, and the cultivators of that grain, finding the licensed distiller as good a customer as the smuggler, would be well pleased to bring their corn to him; and many landlords deluded with the idea that the high rents they received are kept by the consumption of barley in private distilleries would be equally gratified to find their incomes undiminished by their tenantry selling in obedience to the laws.

DISTILLATION WIDESPREAD AMONG PEOPLE

Illicit distillation was so widespread in Inis Eoghain that every stratum of society except the clergy was involved. In the early part of the nineteenth century, Major Bellingham Swan, the Inspector General of Excise and Licences of Ireland, reported that there were an estimated 3,000 private distillers in all Ireland.[12] Of these 43%, or 1,300, were based in Inis Eoghain. Another report stated that the people of this barony were smugglers and distillers from their cradles and added that they had " a bad and inveterate nature ".[13]

While the practice was widespread, there were areas in the peninsula of particular notoriety. Aeneas Coffey, Inspector General of Excise, reported *circa* 1810 that the townland of Moneydarragh in the parish of Culdaff was completely overrun by distillation.[14] Other places mentioned were Urris in the parish of Clonmany and Iskaheen in the parish of Templemore.

In view of the coming struggle between people and Government, it is well to furnish evidence regarding the people of the barony. Samuel Lumsden, an officer based at Grousehall in 1816, referred to the people as kind and responsive to any act of generosity done to them. Viewed from the wider conspectus of history, here was a people peace-loving, passive and even spineless. They had endured the English occupation without any resistance. They had been deprived of their lands. Denied religious freedom, they worshipped in secret and in fear. The law forbade them the means of education. All this was borne with what some interpret as heroic patience. Others see their docility as a sign of weakness and servility.

However, when the British Government began its campaign to eradicate the distilling industry it met with a fierce, bitter and bloody resistance which highlighted the land of Inis Eoghain throughout the Three Kingdoms. The years 1815, 1816 and 1817 were a time of battle, of blood and of suffering for the 48,000-odd citizens of this part of Ireland. It thus becomes evident that the very inmost core of their being was touched, so that a ruthless Government for once met with an equally ruthless resistance.

GOVERNMENT DUTIES

The action taken by the British Government to suppress illicit distillation was a matter of money, not morals. The Revenue Department was concerned with raising through taxation sufficient money to finance Government expenditure. A duty had been imposed on whiskey in Ireland for a long time. The first reference we can find is that a duty of 4d. per gallon was in force here in 1661, during the reign of Charles II.[15] By 1782 the rate had increased to 1/2. The rate kept increasing year by year, e.g., in 1802, 2/10¼; in 1820, 5/7½; and in 1860, 8/1.

In the second half of the eighteenth century legislation was passed which required a Government licence for distilling. To ensure the payment of duty the authorities had no option but to require that all distillers be registered and operate in a location and under conditions which would enable the gauger to know exactly the amount of spirits produced. In other words, the revenue official had to know who made whiskey, where it was made, when it was made and in what quantity, if the correct rate of duty was to be fixed and collected. Hence, the substance of the acts passed between 1760 and 1782 meant that distilleries could be sited in towns only where a gauger was located. The result was to make distillation illegal throughout almost the whole of Ireland and to bring all rural Ireland into direct conflict with the law.

Up to the end of the eighteenth century it would seem that matters continued throughout the country as before the enactment of the legislation. No serious attempt was made to interfere with the illicit stillers. Indeed, it would seem that the acts had a contrary effect in Inis Eoghain, where illegal distillation increased. At the beginning of the new century the authorities in

Dublin Castle began, no doubt under pressure from London, to become concerned. On the 30th September, 1801, the following letter was sent to the Commissioner of Revenue from the Chief Secretary's office:[16]

I am directed by the Lord Lieutenant to desire you will forthwith take into your consideration the subject of Illicit Distillation and report to Him, as soon as you conveniently can, your opinion upon the methods which may be most expedient to adopt for effectively preventing the same.

Thus the first shot was fired in the battle between the illegal distillers and the authorities. A spate of punitive legislation was soon to reach the Statute Book. As a result, the Lords and Members of Parliament in Westmister were now to become deeply involved in Irish affairs. The illicit distillation episode was but the beginning of over a century in which Ireland and her problems were to be discussed without intermission in the Houses of Parliament in London. Every noble lord and each honourable member knew a little more about Irish geography. Not one member of either House in the early years of the nineteenth century was ignorant of the existence and location of that part of His Majesty's realm known as " the barony of Inis Eoghain ".
PUNITIVE LEGISLATION
The standard government approach in devising legislation to discourage illegal distillation was that of fines and imprisonment. In practice it was so often impossible to determine the ownership of stills, etc., that legislation was passed to place fines on an area basis—at first the parish and later the townland. Where the stiller was not caught red-handed, the fine was imposed on the area in which the offence took place. The people as a whole were deemed to be guilty—those who stilled because they infringed the law and those who did not because they failed to inform the revenue officers. A dangerous reaction developed for the government, because the innocent preferred to make enemies of the officers by their silence than to be given the name of informer by their neighbours. As a result, the revenue officers and the law were regarded as the common enemy.
A flood of acts, some amending, some repealing existing laws, passed through the English House of Commons as the Revenue Commissioners met new difficulties. Indeed, so fast was the pace of change that it was well-nigh impossible to know at any given

138

moment what exactly the law specified. Events in Inis Eoghain can be said to have been the major influence in determining the trend of legislation at Westminster in the field of illicit distillation.

ACTION BY LANDLORDS

As already stated, both landlords and rectors had a vested interest. Consequently, at the beginning the land-owners were unhelpful to the authorities who were endeavouring to eliminate illicit distillation. As soon, however, as it became evident that the income from the tenants was endangered by the fining system the landowners of Inis Eoghain began to take action. The substantial flow of money which they got from their tenants was now to be diverted into the Government's coffers. To save their incomes the only course open was to discourage the making of illegal spirits until Government pressure eased off.

A meeting[17] of the landed proprietors of Inis Eoghain took place on April 21st, 1809, at Three Trees, Quigleyspoint. Among those attending were Robert Young of Culdaff, William Chichester, rector of Culdaff, and Edward Chichester of Cloncha.

They resolved, *inter alia*:

To use their influence to put down private distillation.
To refuse to renew leases of those tenants who engaged in illegal stilling.
To evict all tenants who persisted in the condemned activity.
To recommend that the individual engaged in illegal distillation be fined rather than the parish or townland. If this were not possible, the smaller area, *i.e.*, the townland, should be fined rather than the parish.
To request that care be taken to ensure that the correct townland be designated when an offence took place, by getting confirmation from one or two persons as required by law.

Five years later another meeting was held, at Letterkenny on April 4th, 1814.[18] This meeting was summoned by and presided over by Arthur Chichester, High Sheriff of County Donegal. The following action was decided:

Firm action to suppress all stilling; those present at meeting promised to avoid use of illicit spirits.
No lease of land to anyone engaged in stilling; no renewal of leases to stillers.
Every help to be given to the High Constable and his assistants in their efforts to collect fines.
Steps to be taken to prevent the kidnapping of state witnesses.
To ensure the backing of absentee landlords, a copy of the resolutions passed at the meeting to be sent to their land agents.

Resolutions to be inserted in the newspapers published in Strabane, Derry and Dublin.

Thus every effort was made to stand well with the government—now seemingly in control.

As well as resolutions and meetings, some of the landowners took active steps to prevent illicit stilling in their areas. Young of Culdaff, landlord of a substantial area in North Inis Eoghain, formed the Culdaff Yeomanry. The members were mostly local people and a major part of their duty was to suppress illicit distillation. Young paid fines of upwards of £2,000 on behalf of his tenants and then endeavoured to collect the money from them. He seized upwards of 100 stills. The indignant tenants attacked his dwelling at night and windows were broken. He was compelled to place an armed guard at night to ensure the safety of himself and his family.[19]

Some time later Robert Young presented a memorial to[20] the Revenue Commissioners of Ireland in the following terms:

Most humble sheweth
That your Petitioner has uniformly used his best endeavours to suppress private distillation on his property, in this barony, and at time, when the still fine laws were not in force, for which he received a letter of Thanks from your Honourable Board.

That some years ago the Petitioner let a house to the Government for a barrack, situate in the very centre of his lands, and was in hopes, from the residence of a Revenue Officer in it, that the illicit trade would have been suppressed in the places contiguous to it; that notwithstanding this, and the exertions of himself and his family, no less than 81 fines, for private distillation were imposed on your Petitioner's property at the Lent Assizes of the year 1815, shortly before the arrival of the honourable James Hewett in Derry for the purpose of enforcing the collection of the fines in this barony.

That in consequence of a proposal from Mr. Hewett to the landholders of Ennishowen to suspend all former fines, on payment of those imposed at the foregoing assizes, your Petitioner paid the whole of the 81 fines before mentioned, amounting to £2,139.15.0d., a sum more than six times as large as any other landholder in the barony paid; that the cattle of many townlands which were driven for the fines of the same assizes, were given back to the owners on their paying a very small proportion of them, one townland in particular paying only two fines out of seven. That the tenants of another paid in hand only the one half of their fines, and were allowed one or two years to make up the other half, but though this period has long since elapsed, this remainder has not been called for.

Your Petitioner therefore thinks it hard that after using his utmost exertions to suppress private distillation — by which he not only incurred the ill-will of his tenants, but rendered them less able to pay their rents — and after voluntarily paying the large sum before-mentioned, he should have suffered so much more seriously than those landholders

140

who have uniformly encouraged that unlawful trade, and who refused to pay any of their fines till compelled to do so.

That if the Petitioner had followed their example and suffered his lands to be distrained, he is convinced that from their remote and mountainous situation, and from the poverty of the tenants in general, not a fourth part of the money which he paid for them would have ever been collected.

Your Petitioner can with truth affirm that of the sum advanced by him he has not received more than one third part, and that he does not expect to be ever repaid by his tenants any part of the remaining two-thirds. He, therefore, prays such redress for the losses sustained by him as to your Honourable Board shall seem fit . . .

There is no evidence to indicate that Young received any compensation.

However badly Young fared, his neighbour and contemporary Norton Butler, who had property at Grousehall, experienced more drastic treatment, as can be seen later in this chapter.

George and Tristam Carey carried out a strong campaign against illicit spirits among their tenants in Upper Moville.[21] The house of George Carey was attacked in the daytime by infuriated tenants. Others in Inis Eoghain who took steps to discourage the stilling among their tenants were Edward Chichester, rector of Culdaff and Cloncha; Rev. Montgomery, rector of Moville; Austin, landlord at Ture; Harvey, landlord at Malin. The most successful action took place at Fahan under the direction of Spencer Knox, son of the Protestant Bishop of Derry, and Peter Maxwell.[22] The southern part of the barony as a result was less affected by illicit distillation. However, in general the landlords' action had no lasting effect.

EFFECT ON THE ORDINARY PEOPLE

The legislation passed in the 50-year period up to 1800 had little effect on Inis Eoghain. The people carried on their illicit traffic as before. Indeed, there was an increase because of the greater demand caused by Government action elsewhere. As the punitive laws were churned out from Westminster in the early part of the nineteenth century, the people were, if at all, only dimly aware of their nature or their possible effects. Newspapers were few and events in Dublin and London rarely reached the ears of the ordinary people of Inis Eoghain. Desultory attempts were made by revenue men here and there against illegal stillers. Now and again the army unit stationed at Buncrana took action. But in general the law was a dead letter in this barony.

The Government functioning from Dublin was a dim and dis-

141

tant institution which had never shown its hand in Inis Eoghain. The various rebellions had had no following here. The Government was neither feared nor respected. Its functions and methods of actions were unknown. The first quarter of the nineteenth century was to see a profound change in attitude towards the central authority and its agents, however.

As the new century passed on there were signs of increased activity. Seizures by revenue men became more frequent and fines were being imposed on a wide scale. Since no real effort was made to collect the fines, the people believed that no action would be taken. They were lulled into a false sense of security. The Revenue Commissioners pressed for action, to secure the collection of the fines. The forces of the Government went into action. A ruthless, relentless and devastating campaign against the people as a whole began. Innocent and guilty suffered alike because of the imposition of fines on an area basis.

The people were stunned and then alarmed as the full meaning of events became apparent. For the first time since the English occupation began 200 years before, the resentment of the people became a threat to the Government. A state of rebellion developed. The people, faced with destitution and famine, took determined and forceful action.

The army officer who was in Culdaff in 1816 wrote:[23]

> . . . Of all the miserable countrys and miserable peasantry I ever met my present situation affords me a view of the most so. I am here on detachment with another officer and thirtytwo men in an area twenty miles from Derry . . . except potatoes and eggs we cannot get an article of subsistence nearer than Head Quarters; our duty has been extremely severe, out every night searching for private stills and generally not in vain. The view of the country presents nothing to the eye save bog and mountain, illicit distillation appears the only means of subsistence and yet the fines arising from it have actually ruined them; in short, if every article they are possessed of and the principle of their property were sold it would not pay the fines to be levied — they are now desperate and if another law of felony is to be imposed it will be found insufficient to stop its progress for transportation cannot deter men who have a spirit of imagination, and who are conscious of their situation may be better but cannot be worse . . . I entered it with a disposition to esteem the inhabitants but these atrocious murders, etc., have jaundiced my mind against the bastardisation of a Scotch craft on Irish ferocity . . . This country is ruined; it is the station of poverty; all who can are flying from the approaching ruin and hope in America to find a home and plenty . . .

This officer was writing during the months when the battle between the Government and the people was at the point of crisis.

THE PEOPLE COMBINE

The threat to the well-being of the community united its members. An attack on one family was deemed an attack on all in the neighbourhood. The informer was given drastic treatment. Where no justice or law existed in the real sense, rough and ready " justice and law " were devised by the people.

As soon as the revenue men and the army came near an area a signal system warned the people. In Muff the bell of the Protestant Church was rung at the approach of the Government representatives. When the revenue authorities complained to the curate he replied that it was customary to ring the bell in times of common danger ! The threat to report the matter to the Protestant bishop at Derry stopped this method of communication.[24]

In other areas the warning was given by the blowing of a horn. While the stillers worked a watcher stood on the highest hill in the area. The " Cnoc an Amhairc " or " Watch Hill ", so familiar in every part of Inis Eoghain, was put to a new use. In former generations, the watchers kept vigil here while priest and people in a nearby glen united in the sacrifice of the Mass. Now the watcher kept his vigil to warn the stiller, so that all equipment could be dismantled and hidden before the revenue officers and their escort arrived.

Secret societies were formed. The will of the individual, however weak and vacillating, became merged into a ruthless, unflinching communal will. The result was that inoffensive and peaceful men became part of a vast organisation which carried out speedily and effectively the most atrocious acts which could be conceived. Vengence was wreaked where the leaders decided. Desperation had driven a peaceful, God-fearing people to actions which surprised all who had known them before. Such is the pattern of revolutions.

To realise the extent of the financial burden imposed on the people by the fining system, we can consider as a sample the amount of the fines in the parish of Culdaff as set out below: [25]

ASSIZES	NO. OF FINES	AMOUNT £
Spring, 1814	47	1,175
Summer, 1814	57	1,425
Spring, 1815	82	2,050
Summer, 1815	62	1,550
TOTAL:	248	£6,200

143

When one appreciates that the people were taxed to the limit of their resources by the payment of the rent to the landlord, it is clear that it was impossible to extract the money for the fines as well. The Government, however, made the effort and destitution was the result. Failure to pay the fines meant that all available assets were seized and sold at auction. Stocks of barley, oats and other farm produce, clothing, yarn and poultry were taken by the revenue officers under the protection of the forces of the British Government. As in the wake of a plague of locusts, when the seizers had completed their efforts in a townland nothing whatsoever was left. Men, women and children were left hungry. An artificial famine was imposed.

Eye-witnesses record many harrowing scenes. John Curry, the assistant barrister for Derry, stated that he had occasion to enter a house in the parish of Donagh.[26] There he found a man lying face downwards on the floor in a state of utter dejection. The man stated that he was not a stiller, yet because of the townland fining system all his property had been seized. His wife and seven children had now nothing left save a few potatoes.

Peter Maxwell of Fahan stated in evidence that the distress among the people in the barony was beyond all belief. Livestock seized by the revenue men starved to death in Derry while the owners and their families starved to death in Inis Eoghain. Property three times the value of the warrant was seized. Because of the general condition of misery and suffering, the witness had decided to leave Ireland and go to Switzerland.[27]

The Protestant rector of Cloncha, Edward Chichester, stated that when the cattle were seized in his area and driven to the pound at Carndonagh, the owners came and tried to feed them. Mothers with children in arms came to seek permission to milk their cows so that the slender thread of life remaining might be maintained unbroken for some time longer.[28]

Accounts like the foregoing could be multiplied from contemporary records. Inis Eoghain was now indeed a land of sorrow, suffering and destitution. The will to resist injustice was strong, but the lack of leadership made the efforts of the people ineffective. In the autumn of 1816 the people in the areas most affected hesitated to harvest their crops, as they knew that the Government forces would seize them. Reports reaching Dublin indicated that if corn and potatoes were not saved without delay there was the danger of a famine. The Excise Office issued the following statement: [29]

> The Commissioners of Excise and Taxes having been informed that the inhabitants of townlands and other districts subject to fines for illicit distillation, are abstaining from gathering in their corn and digging their potatoes under the apprehension that the same would be seized by the still fine. Collectors for such fines notice is hereby given that directions have been issued to the said Collectors to suspend the collection of the said fines for one calendar month from the date hereof; after which the said fines are to be levied off the property of the townland except corn and potatoes, the said townlands in all other respects strictly liable for the fines remaining unpaid; and to proceed with vigour to levy the same at the expiration of the above-mentioned period. By Order of the Commissioners . . . 16.10.1816.

The suspension of fine collection was extended later for two additional months.

A TRIAD OF CALAMITIES

The year 1817 was the high-water mark of disaster. Destructive Government action was at its peak. Famine was general throughout the whole country this year and Inis Eoghain shared in the national catastrophe. Disease completed the triad of misfortunes which befell the people of the barony. A contemporary account says of Inis Eoghain that in the following year—1818—the Board of Excise[30]

> recommenced its operations with an obstinacy unenforced by experience and a severity unrestrained by compassion. The dreadful famine which visited Ireland during the spring and summer of the last year was succeeded by a pestilence of a most malignant character and in no part of Ireland did these calamities press so heavily as in Inishowen, where the Excise laws had been so wantonly executed. While one half of the peasantry was afflicted with typhus fever; while entire families were suffering at the same moment and individuals dying unassisted and unnoticed, Excisemen were seizing their property and selling it for the payments of fines . . .

THE ARMY: INACTIVE

As already stated, there was in Inis Eoghain at this time no organised method for enforcing the law. Each landlord had his own private army made up of his henchmen and used for his own protection. The revenue officers when making seizures had the protection of the small body of soldiers stationed at Buncrana. The collection of fines was in the hands of the High Constable for the barony, who was paid on a commission basis.

The High Constable at the time was a noted illicit distiller,[31]

145

Porter by name. He made little effort to collect the fines and made the point to the authorities that in the turbulent state of affairs it was impossible to act without the backing of the army. The authorities acceded to Porter's request and sent in the spring of 1814 a force of approximately 300 men, who were stationed in a camp set up on the banks of the Culdaff river at Baskill near Gleneely.

The arrival of so great a force, fully armed and ready to assist in the prevention of illicit distillation and in the collection of fines, for a time frightened the people who had previously regarded the courts and the fining with contempt. Everyone now asked was the army going to collect all the fines due by force ?

Porter still made no effort to collect the fines and the soldiers settled down to a quiet, peaceful life in Culdaff. The people, when they observed the inactivity of the army, became friendly and soon they were all mixing without fear or suspicion. The soldiers were fond of the " wee still " and so as to ensure the availability of a ready supply an enterprising local set up a shebeen in the centre of the camp. Far from eliminating the practice of distillation, the army personnel became the best and most discerning customers for Culdaff whiskey ! Many of the local young men took the opportunity to get trained in the use of firearms and later bought guns and ammunition from the soldiers.[32]

The revenue officers observed the inactivity of the soldiers and reported to Dublin. Meantime, in the autumn the army left for winter quarters. The Board of Excise at the end of 1814 made representations to the British Government which now introduced legislation vesting authority to collect the fines in the hands of the revenue officers.[33] In future the army was to assist as required.

THE ARMY IN ACTION

The summer of 1815 saw a new and effective move against the stillers.[34] The High Constable was dismissed and a better-disciplined army stationed in the Culdaff area. The headquarters was at Grousehall in the townland of Aghaglasson. In addition, troops were placed at Carthage and Culdaff and other places.

Across the Foyle troops were based at Magilligan. The people were somewhat bewildered by events and did not realise that the Government was in earnest until the army and revenue officers began to seize property in the surrounding townlands where fines had been imposed in the Lent and Summer Assizes of 1814 and

Lent Assizes of 1815. The desolation described above now fell on the people and continued during the next few years.

RESISTANCE BY THE PEOPLE

The army met with resistance in many areas. The number of incidents during the early part of the eighteenth century was legion and a few cases are worth recording. The classical case of resistance took place in Urris in the parish of Clonmany.[35]

Urris is an area of poor land lying along the sea. Nature provided it with a natural defence on one side—the approach from Buncrana. There is a high ridge of mountains through which access is by means of a narrow pass known as the Gap of Mamore. Ignorance of the terrain left the military authorities unaware of the fact that entry could easily be made on the Carndonagh side. Before accurate maps were available it was thought that Urris was entirely surrounded by high mountains on one side and by the sea on the other.

The Hon. James Hewett, Commissioner of Excise in Ireland, related that from 1812 to 1815 Urris had existed as an independent state, a sort of " Poteen Republic ", where the King's writ had no effect.[36] Attempts made here to seize stills were defeated and the Government forces allowed out only on condition that the seized property was abandoned and that the intruders would not return.

The defenders of Urris had provided themselves with arms from three sources—the wreck of the *Saldanha* frigate, the auction of a local landlord's effects and the soldiers at Baskill.

During these years Urris became the refuge of stillers from other areas where the law was being enforced. These were admitted after paying a small sum of money and promising loyalty on oath.

Hewett stated that in 1815 the army discovered the easier entrance through the pass of Rockstown. The King's authority was again asserted and maintained to some extent in the succeeding years.

At Carthage, near the border of Glengad, Aeneas Coffey, later Inspector General of Excise, in November, 1810, was destroying an unlicensed distillery when he was attacked by a group of fifty men who suddenly appeared on the scene. In Coffey's own words:

They fractured my skull, left my body one mass of contusion and

147

gave me two bayonet wounds, one of which completely perforated my thigh. I owed my life to the rapid approach of the military party from which I had imprudently[37] wandered a few hundred yards . . .

A soldier was killed in Aghaglasson and buried by the banks of the stream called Struhan Menagh. In Moneydarragh the landlord, Norton Butler, was killed. In the townland of Cloncha on Christmas Eve, 1817, the normally peace-loving people attacked the officers who had entered the area to seize malt. The officers had to retreat and when they returned all evidence had been hidden.

CORRUPTION OF REVENUE OFFICERS[38]

Records of the early nineteenth century show that the lower ranks of the revenue officers were guilty of serious corruption in the carrying out of their duties. The law rewarded the officers when they were successful in capturing equipment and as a result many of them were able to retire early as rich men. To secure the necessary equipment the officers resorted to many devious ways. In addition, a form of blackmail was used to secure money from people who had been caught in the act of distillation. The officer desisted from legal action on payment of an agreed sum. Bribes were accepted to desist from interfering with certain stillers.

In December, 1817, Shane McCauly of Glack Culdaff swore an affidavit stating that he and Edward McColgan from the same townland had journeyed to Buncrana in 1808 to give a bribe to a named officer, who in return promised to refrain from making seizures in the townland of Glacknadrummond. James McColgan of Dunross swore that an officer had made part of a seizure in the townland. The officer then demanded from the witness the equipment necessary to complete the seizure, warning him that he would do the witness more injury than the worth of the equipment. The witness bought the items needed and gave them to the officer, who was then able to gain his reward. Brian Gillen of Lisdarrigan, Larrahirrel affirmed that an officer had agreed to forego a charge against him provided that the witness paid 1½ guineas per quarter, regularly gave a present of butter and performed certain work for him as required.

The actions of these and other officers were made public by the rector of Cloncha, Edward Chichester, in the pamphlet mentioned in Chapter 7.

148

AMUSING EVENTS

In the struggle between the people and the law some amusing incidents took place. Chichester related:[39]

> In the severe scrutiny for property at this time, a discovery of an extraordinary nature was made by one of the persons assisting in the levy of still-fines. In descending from an eminence he hurt his foot against a sharp projection which, on examination, proved to be the horn of a cow, which had been buried alive and in order to escape observation. On a further search several others were found concealed in a similar manner, the nostrils being kept above ground, that they might be enabled to breathe . . .

The residents of the area adjacent to the townland of Redford-Glebe, where the rector of Cloncha lived, hid their stilling equipment on the rectory lands. Seven stills were found here by the revenue men and no doubt the rector, Edward Chichester, a Justice of the Peace and a stalwart defender of the law, had a few embarrassing moments in explaining matters to the law officers.[40]

At Moville a servant of the rector—a noted enemy of illicit distillation—carried on a flourishing distillery in the basement of the Rectory, where he enjoyed for a long time a sort of diplomatic immunity. The rector was not aware of this until he left the parish.[41]

LICENSING LEGISLATION

It should be noted that for a time the Government did permit the operation of small stills under licence. Rigid rules applied, however, making economic production impossible. In addition, the competition from illicit distillers who paid no duty added to the problems of the licensed operator.

Records[42] show that one licensed stiller functioned at Bohillion, Burt, for two years, 1814 and 1815. The distillery was the property of William Leatham. It failed to function as a viable economic enterprise and closed at the end of 1815.

DISTILLATION AFTER 1820

The strong and ruthless action of the British Government reduced considerably the extent of illicit distillation in Inis Eoghain. It did not, however, eliminate the practice. Indeed, in the northern half of the barony stilling was widespread during the whole of the nineteenth century. One old man, a native of Termacroragh, told the writer that around 1870 he remembered seeing 40 stills in full operation during the daytime in the area comprising Tirmacroragh and Ballyharry.

Stilling generally was done in secret and during the night. The smoke of the fire tended to draw unwelcome attention from the law forces if stilling was carried on in the daytime. However, some stillers who resided in remote areas stilled in their own homes, sometimes in the daytime. During times of intense police activity, the stillers simply hid their equipment and desisted until the pressure eased. Then operations were resumed as before. This was the pattern of events from 1820 onwards.

Distillation got a boost during the First World War. There was a big demand. The whiskey was disposed of through the fishing trawlers operating off the coast of North Inis Eoghain. In turn the trawlers supplied the raw material. The spirits were also disposed of to publicans in various parts of the country.

As the law restricted the sale of yeast it became increasingly difficult to secure. One veteran stiller in Buiteog relates how he secured his supply of yeast through a travelling butcher. In a secret compartment of his horse-drawn van the butcher kept his supply of yeast and in the open portion he displayed the meat. He thus catered for all his customers, among whom were the local Garda sergeant. The law officer bought his meat weekly and never discovered the other line of business in which his butcher was engaged.

When the British occupation ended, the Gardai became active in the prevention of illicit distillation. The last years of British rule had seen a revival, because of the break-down of the administrative system. The new law officers soon took determined and generally effective action, although one enterprising stiller in Ballyharry claims he reached a *modus vivendi* with some of the local Gardai. When he made a "run" of poteen he left a pint of the spirits at an agreed spot close to a nearby crossroads. A Garda from the local station picked it up as he made his rounds, and the stiller continued his activity without molestation!

There was a steady decline from 1920 onwards in the number engaged in the illicit activity. In North Inis Eoghain the last areas involved in an extensive way were the townlands of Glengad and Ballyharry. Many factors contributed to this decline.

EPISCOPAL ACTION

The majority of Inis Eoghain people are Catholics and consequently the influence of the Catholic clergy was and is a powerful factor in any issue which may arise.

In 1892 the Bishop of Derry took firm action and promul-

150

gated a law making trafficking in poteen a reserved sin. This had the desired effect for a time, but the First World War created so great a demand for illicit spirits that the old stillers took out their utensils from the hideouts. Soon the industry was as rife ever.

In 1929 two stillers were killed in Glengad. The spot chosen for stilling was at the foot of the cliffs known as the Bengorms. When the men were climbing the cliff they slipped and were killed in the fall. Great publicity was directed to the area because of the deaths. This event was most probably the occasion, if not the cause, for the decision of the then Bishop of Derry to revive the law making trafficing in poteen a reserved sin in the whole of his diocese. Almost all the Catholics in Inis Eoghain obeyed the precept, but a number of Protestants continued to still.

In the post-war years the pastoral exhortation of the Bishop of Derry during his visitation of the Inis Eoghain portion of his diocese was always concerned with the evils of illicit distillation. Since 1931 he has been free to select another subject.

Owing to an erroneous interpretation of the bishop's edict, the Catholic laity assumed that anyone breaking the law against illicit distillation would have to go to the bishop himself for absolution. In this regard an amusing and probably apocryphal story has gone the rounds in Inis Eoghain.

Feidhlimidh Mac Ficheallaigh of Ballymagaraghy and Cathaoir Mac Seafraidh of Ballyharry had stilled for many years together at Craigcannon in the Ballyharry moss. A "run" was always made during the week before Christmas. In 1932 they were in a difficult position as Christmas drew near. They were, indeed, in a dilemma. On the one hand there was the episcopal edict and on the other hand the desire for a little "nourishment" during the Christmas season. "Christmas comes but once a year," said Feidhlimidh as he stood in the shelter of a haystack at Drumnagessan in the company of Cathaoir. The die was cast and they made the run of "wee still". The pair drank deep and rejoiced much during the season of Christmas.

The Lenten Station that year was held in Drumaville at the house of Seamas Mor O Ceallaigh. Here came the two stillers in fear and full of regret. Now they had to face "the music". An tAthair Sean Mac Cionaoith was a man to be feared. The people were already in line for confession, and Feidhlimidh and

Cathaoir joined the queue. Each in turn heard the same firm refusal. No absolution. Both must go to Derry and get absolution from the bishop. It was a moment of crisis for both.

A week later, starting at dawn, they walked to Moville and took the bus to Derry. They stepped out of the bus at Great James's St. and with much foreboding they climbed to the cathedral. Arriving at the palace door they rang the bell and were shown to the waiting-room by the housekeeper. In the room sat two fierce-looking men from Urris who were there for the same purpose. Soon a message came that the bishop was ready to see the penitents. No man wanted to be first. Cathaoir, a man of great courage who had in his day popped off a few Black and Tans, stood up and went right into the bishop's presence. The confession was heard, advice and absolution were given. Then the bishop warned Cathaoir not to discuss anything on his way out with those in the waiting room.

As the shrived penitent came out he was asked by one of the Urris men how he got on. Cathaoir pointed to his lips as an indication of silence. Feidhlimidh, a timorous man by nature, looked on in surprise. "Cathaoir," said he, "what penance did you get?" Cathaoir again placed his fingers on his lips and walked out of the room.

Feidhlimidh stood up and began to make his exit as well. "Why are you leaving?" said one of the Urris men. Feidhlimidh turned around and stood: "If the bishop made a 'dummie' out of that man, by G . . . he won't do the same with me!"

CESSATION OF ILLICIT DISTILLATION

At the time of writing illicit distillation, an industry associated with Inis Eoghain for so many generations, has entirely ceased. Indeed, for 40 years stilling has gradually been discontinued by all but a few. Now a generation has grown up to whom "wee still" is a mere name, mentioned only occasionally by an ancient reminiscing about the old days.

What was the cause of its decline and final elimination? The reasons were not one but many.

The extreme measures taken by the British Government in the early part of the last century were the first factor which discouraged many from the practice of stilling. While the pressure of Government action eased somewhat after 1820, many decided to seek an income from another source. In fact the making of illegal spirits never again attained its old popularity.

The next reason was an economic one. In the years following 1800 the population of Inis Eoghain was increasing very fast. Land was scarce and apart from fishing there was no other means than stilling to augment the small incomes of the people. Rent was high and money was also needed for clothing. Indeed, the problem of finding the means to pay the rent twice yearly was a constant anxiety to every small farmer in Inis Eoghain in those days. Eviction and the workhouse awaited the family which failed to pay promptly. A "run" of poteen earned a man one pound profit. The incentive to defy the law was very great indeed. As the nineteenth century advanced, however, emigration reduced the demand for land. More land was available for less people and rents were a lesser burden on those who remained. As the century advanced further, conditions on the land improved, so that by the end of the nineteenth century there was less and less need to supplement the income by making poteen. Emigrant remittances also became for many a welcome and steady source of additional income.

In time the subtle and powerful force of public opinion, together with a certain loss of status, made many give up entirely the making of poteen. It became associated with extreme poverty and with those who lived in backward, obscure places. It became the "not-done" thing.

The decision of the Catholic authorities to deny sacramental absolution to anyone who engaged in the making or handling of illicit spirits gave the final blow to an already declining industry. It is significant that the ordinary of the diocese took no drastic action during those years when there was a strong economic reason for the making of poteen. The bishop was prudent enough to impose no edict at a time when many of his subjects had no alternative to making and selling "wee still".

However, the chance to make a good profit caused many to ignore the bishop's edict. For example, the First World War tempted many. This should be kept in mind by those who to-day say that the industry finally died because of the episcopal prohibition.

CONCLUSION

The stilling industry has now been entirely eliminated in Inis Eoghain. A ruthless and unimaginative Government was solely concerned with the safe-guarding of revenue sources. Narrow-minded moralists who were out of touch with the real problems imposed burdens on the consciences of the people without due consideration. There was no one in authority who had the vision to view the problem as a whole and produce an acceptable solution.

Over the past century there has been a peculiar guilt complex regarding illicit distillation in the mind of the Inis Eoghain people. Church and State created around something which was in itself good an atmosphere of evil. The brow-beaten and drown-trodden people were unable to form their own judgement. Ignorance and fear were the sinister twins which dominated this society.

What was the correct solution? If the authorities in the civil and ecclesiastical orders had had the well-being of the people at heart, one could have seen in the early part of the last century or even later a committee made up of leaders of both orders. The function of the committee would have been to devise a system which would develop the stilling industry and at the same time safeguard the morals of the people and ensure an equitable revenue for the State. This was not done and the emigrant ships going down the Foyle took many an Inis Eoghain resident into exile who could have secured good and profitable employment at home.

The suggestion has been made from time to time that a more benign Government could have controlled distillation by issuing licences to the small stillers. This would have been an administrative impossibility and it would not have solved the moral dangers. The best solution would have been to set up a small distillery in each parish under rigid control. The opportunities for employment and the ready market for the raw materials produced in the area would have secured the full co-operation of the entire community. The problem was an economic one and it was in this field that the true and fair solution could be found. Such action was taken in other countries in similar situations and a valuable industry fostered and developed.

The foresight and planning mentioned above would have enriched our society. Inis Eoghain whiskey would to-day have its rightful place beside "Bushmills", "Powers" and other well-known brands in the home and foreign markets. That matters are otherwise is a scathing indictment of both Church and State over the past century and a half. The leaders failed and our society is impoverished as a result.

THE DEATH OF NORTON BUTLER

On the evening of Tuesday, July 2nd, 1816, between six and seven o'clock, Norton Butler of Grousehall in the townland of Aghaglasson,. parish of Culdaff, was attacked while walking in his garden after supper. He received serious injuries, which caused his death within a very short period.[43]

Norton Butler, who would seem to have been a native of the parish of Culdaff,[44] had lived in Grousehall from about 1800.[45] Formerly a captain[46] in the Donegal Militia, he had retired and taken up farming.[47] He was appointed Manorial Seneschal of the barony of Inis Eoghain. As landlord of the townland of Ourt[48] and receiver of rents for a number of absentee landlords in the area, he had a very deep interest in the ability of the tenants to pay their rents.

Directly south of Moneydarragh, over Crucknanoneen, there lies the townland of Tullyally in the parish of Lower Moville. In this townland there is a place called Glackmore—a deep glen through which a stream flows. To the right of this stream as one goes over Crucknanoneen there dwelt at the time a family called McGuinness. There were four brothers, Peter, James, Daniel and William. The father's name was Daniel.

A description of James[49] issued in 1816 states that he was "about thirty years of age, five feet seven inches in height, stout made, large head, round face, grey eyes, brown eyebrows, small nose and mouth, short neck, brown hair, round shoulders, proportionate arms, thick hands and thighs, long legs, small feet". He was stated to be a gardener. A similar description was circulated for Daniel McGuinness, excepting that he had lost part of one of his front teeth.

James had enlisted in the 21st Regiment of Dragoons under the name of "John Groves". He deserted at Palermo on the 21st June, 1812, and made his way back home again shortly afterwards.[50] The army training he received was imparted to his brothers. All became expert at handling firearms. In the locality these young men projected an image of courage and daring combined with good marksmanship. The trend of events was to involve them all in a most tragic manner.

Norton Butler, because of his duties as landlord and receiver of rents, had a most intimate knowledge of the surrounding area. He knew who was engaged in illict distillation, and when and where stilling took place. When he launched his campaign to eliminate distillation he became a formidable enemy. As a result, he was surrounded by hostility everywhere he moved in the locality. With a view to involving him with the law, people set up a private still near Grousehall.[51] Butler reported the matter to the revenue officers and demanded action. The corrupt officials saw an opportunity to secure the reward given for closing their eyes to the whole matter. Butler soon realised that bribery was the cause of inaction and he took direct action himself. He was attacked and beaten.

He took proceedings against the attackers and made a written statement. During the court proceedings, as Butler gave evidence on oath, the judge noted a substantial difference between the oral and written evidence, and the case was dismissed.

Norton Butler, evidently a man of great courage, continued his efforts to eliminate illicit distillation. As he moved about he carried a gun. This was an age when a man's life often depended on the possession and the quick, efficient use of firearms.

The townland of Moneydarragh was at the time a noted centre of distillation. Almost every family depended to some extent on income from making spirits. Here, in the midst of them, was an effective and formidable opponent of their way of life—Norton Butler. The words on everyone's lips were " Butler must be stopped ". Secret societies were very strong in the area and it was decided to frighten Butler. A collection was made and £40 was contributed by the people to secure the services of suitable and reliable men. The McGuinness family, because of their record, were chosen.

Butler's duties as Seneschal required considerable travelling. In September, 1815, as he made his way from Grousehall to Derry, he passed over Crucknanoneen and went towards the Foyle. His movements were quickly reported to Glackmore. James McGuinness and a man from Magheradreen called McConnollogue awaited Butler's arrival at a secluded spot about a quarter of a mile from the summit. As Butler approached a shot was fired and the horse fell dead.[52] It is not clear whether the ultimate intention was to injure Butler or whether he was merely being given a warning. Probably the latter was the aim, as the opportunity to mortally wound him was there on this occasion.

Butler would have been fully aware of the identity of his attacker, and James McGuinness knew this and hurried off to secure a place on a boat to America. He was kept hidden in a secluded spot until a friendly Inis Eoghain pilot brought him aboard a liner bound for the United States. James McGuinness[53] thus disappears from the narrative.

It was known that Butler would attend at Buncrana in February, 1816, in his capacity of Manorial Seneschal. A member of the McGuinness family made the journey in advance to await a suitable opportunity to deal with him. The court and its environs were crowded. As Butler emerged, a pistol was discharged in his face. The shot failed to go off and a sympathetic crowd ensured McGuinness's escape by closing in between Butler and his attacker.[54]

Despite the two attacks, Butler continued his efforts. In view of the weak and inadequate protection afforded to him by the Government, it was indeed rash and foolhardy to continue to provoke the people.

An assessment of events to date would indicate that the plotters against Butler had at first hoped to so frighten the landlord that he would desist from his endeavours and leave whatever action was necessary to the normal operations of the law. The first attack at Crucknanoneen was clearly to frighten. It is also probable that the attack in Buncrana was so planned that the shot misfired.

When it was clear that despite the two warnings Butler intended to pursue his ruthless and unceasing attack on the stillers, the final decision was made to kill him. At this stage it would seem that a further financial inducement was given to the McGuinness family.

After February, 1816, Butler travelled abroad less and less. He was aware of the conspiracy to kill him. Before long he remained in the safety of his own house and rarely went out. He was a man besieged and surrounded everywhere by enemies.[55]

Every move made by Butler was made known to those plotting against his life. Daniel and William McGuinness became aware of the fact that Butler, despite his state of siege, took a short walk after supper. The two, therefore, took up a position behind a wall near the house. On July 2nd, 1816, Butler ate his evening meal and came out of his dwelling as usual. He walked towards a paddock at the back of the house to view some cattle. The two saw the opportunity for which they had been waiting. A shot was fired, but Butler did not fall. Another shot came immediately after, but still Butler had not fallen. One of the attackers ran forward and, knocking the victim down, ran a bayonet into his belly. Withdrawing the bayonet, he ran it through Butler's thigh, pinning him to the ground. Butler put up a desperate resistance; according to one report, he disarmed one of the men during the struggle. A servant, hearing the noise, ran out to his master's assistance and the two attackers immediately retreated.[56]

It was a bright summer evening. People were working in the fields around, and many were witnesses of the struggle. One report[57] says that "This barbarous and cowardly murder was witnessed by many of the neighbouring cottagers and when Mr. Butler fell, some of them testified their satisfaction by cheers and exultations". Another[58] states that men cutting turf nearby, on seeing Butler's plight, ran to his assistance but were too late to save his life. It is probable that *both* these reports are correct !

Butler was immediately brought into his house and medical aid was summoned. The military at Carndonagh were also informed. The dying man made a clear statement and identified both attackers.[59] He died at midnight,[60] leaving his widow and eight children without any means of support.

The identity of the men who caused the death was not in doubt. Butler's dying declaration, confirmed by his servant, was on record and the people of Moneydarragh, already aware of the plan, saw in broad daylight the attack at Grousehall. Daniel and William McGuinness were now outlaws and their lives were in the hands of the ordinary people of the area.

The landlords and Protestant clergymen of Inis Eoghain, numbering eighteen in all, met at Muff on July 16th, 1816.[61] The Protestant Bishop of Derry presided over the meeting. As a privileged minority they were acutely aware of the serious danger to each one of them in the present unrest. The two men involved in Butler's death must be captured and hanged as a deterrent and a warning to all.

It was decided to place a notice in the local paper offering the following rewards: [62]

£68.5.0 for such information as would lead to the apprehension of Daniel McGuinness, Junior, charged with the murder of Norton Butler.

£50.0.0 for information leading to the capture of William McGuinness, "supposed to be concerned" in the murder of Norton Butler.

Apprehension of any deserter lurking in the barony: £11.7.6.

Secret information causing the apprehension of a deserter: £11.7.6.

For the discovery of persons harbouring or assisting William and Daniel McGuinness: £28.8.9.

158

Apprehension of a member of a secret meeting intended for the protection of disorder: £28.8.9.

The notice gave a detailed description of both James McGuinness and Daniel McGuinness, but no details respecting William. James was included as a deserter from the British Army.

A further reward was offered by the Lord Lieutenant and Council of Ireland as follows:[63]

£200 for the apprehension and lodging in gaol of Daniel McGuinness.
£200 for the discovery and apprehension of each and every person concerned in the murder.

.Thus Daniel McGuinness[64] was worth £268. 5. 0 to anybody who had the necessary information and the will to use it. On the head of William McGuinness was a sum of £250. At that time these sums were indeed very substantial, and doubly so in view of the dire poverty of the vast majority of the people. The outlaws had many loyal friends but in the circumstances only two false ones were needed to ensure success to those offering the rewards. Money was in truth the only factor that brought the attackers of Butler into the hands of the law officers.

It is clear that when the McGuinness family undertook the assignment to frighten and later to kill Butler they had no intention of remaining in the area long after the attack. James had fled soon after the attack at Crucknanoneen when Butler's horse was shot. Now, after the death of Butler, Daniel and William fled to the safety of friends pending an opportunity to get out of the country. The two men went into separate areas so as to more effectively elude the army.

There is a vast district of bog, mountain and moor lying to the south and west of Moneydarragh. To this day it is remote and largely inaccessible. In 1816 it was much more so. A stranger would venture into this area at his peril because of quagmires and dangerous bog holes. To the outlaws the area was well-known, so that even at night they could easily find their way whither they wished to go. Their movements were, of course, known to their friends. who were careful to maintain silence. The two men were never without a meal or a place to sleep at night. There was, however, a constant need for vigilance and for frequent changing of location.

Daniel had moved about to various locations in the parishes

of Culdaff, Moville and Donagh. One evening he directed his steps to a safe house in Gortayarn, where he was sure of a welcome from the Widow Mooney and her son. He got a meal and lay down by the fireside in his clothes, ready for action if the enemy should come this way.

George Balfour had been a member of the same secret society as Daniel McGuinness and shared with him all the secrets. Balfour one day became aware of the large reward given by the authorities to the person who would give the necessary information leading to the arrest of his friend. The large sum of money and all that he could do with it absorbed his mind day and night, so that be began to consider the means by which he could collect it. He kept in touch with Daniel's movements and was aware of the moment of the outlaw's entry into the house of Mrs. Mooney.

Tradition says that he entered the house and finding McGuinness asleep and Mrs. Mooney absent from the kitchen, where McGuinness lay, he rendered the pistol unusable. Then he went in haste to Culdaff House, where he informed Robert Young. Young and his sons summoned a party of Yeomen in haste and they proceeded on horseback, guided by Balfour, to the house of Mrs. Mooney. The sound of their approach alarmed the widow, who immediately roused McGuinness. As Young and his men entered, McGuinness raised his firearm but found that it was useless. He was arrested and brought to Culdaff, and later taken to Lifford gaol.[65]

On the first of September, 1816, a letter of thanks was sent from Dublin Castle to Robert Young to commend him for his diligence in capturing Daniel McGuinness. The text[66] reads:

Dear Sir,

As the exertions which have been made by yourself and other members of your family in co-operating in the arrest of a notorious offender of the name of McGuinness, have been made known to the Lord Lieutenant, he is desirous of returning his acknowledgements for them, and has commanded me to assure you that the splendid assistance given by your sons to Lieut. Plunkett on the occasion of the apprehension of McGuinness is considered by his Excellency very creditable to them. I have the honour to be, Sir,

Your most obedient servant,
Robert Peel.

William McGuinness, like his brother, had remained in the seclusion of the vast boggy area already mentioned. Near Lough Conn lived a small farmer called Shane McEleney. Here William deemed himself so safe that he helped in the seasonal work. At the time we refer to, McEleney and his helper were engaged in turf-cutting. Like Balfour, Shane McEleney had heard of the reward for the capture of his guest. As he pondered over the vast sum of money within his grasp he began to weaken, and the dreadful censure imposed on the informer ceased to worry him. An end to poverty was a great attraction. One afternoon, McEleney made the fatal decision and set out for the house of a neighbouring magistrate, Carey by name.

When night came a party under Carey, and guided by McEleney, entered the house where McGuinness lay. The outlaw was arrested and soon conveyed to Lifford gaol to join his brother.[67]

The authorities acted swiftly. Trial, sentence and execution followed each other rapidly. So ended the lives of these two young men from Glackmore.

As soon as the treachery of Balfour became known to the leaders of the secret society which operated in this area, a meeting was held. Apart from the betrayal of Daniel McGuinness, there was the danger that Balfour would disclose more information regarding the society. There was also the query in the minds of all, " Has this man been a spy since he joined the organisation ?" Before the meeting ended the execution of George Balfour was decided and a detailed method of achieving this arranged.[68]

Balfour lived in the Glenagannon district of Donagh. After the betrayal of Daniel McGuinness he was soon aware that his life was in constant danger. It is not clear whether he remained in hiding himself or was under the protection of the law. The secret society had gathered its members on five occasions[69] to kill him but was not successful. A man well-known to Balfour, a member of the society, but accepted by Balfour as a friend, visited him and as a result he agreed to come out in daylight and walk as far as Carndonagh village. It would seem that Balfour was assured there was no danger to his life.

The message that Balfour was in Carndonagh was quickly passed around. The members of the society gathered from miles around and met at a spot near Glenagannon Bridge. A man was placed in hiding along the road which Balfour and his companion were to come. Balfour's companion was informed that all was now ready, so he suggested that it was time to go home. The two

EXECUTION

ON Saturday last, Daniel Maginnes was convicted of
the Murder of Norton Butler, Esq. of Grouse-Hall—
and on Monday, the 31st day of March, pursuant to his
Sentence, was Executed in front of the New Gaol, Lifford,
at a few minutes past four o'Clock, afternoon. The unfortunate Man, though deeply affected, met his fate with
much fortitude and resignation. He fully confessed the
justice of his Sentence, and begged that his Relatives
would harbour no resentment against any individual, for
his fate. He has thus made the only atonement in his
power, to the offended Laws of his Country, and died an
example of the effect of unrestrained Passion.

We have been requested to publish the following Confession, to guard against the effect of mis-statement :

" Daniel Maginnes, this day, in presence of several Gentlemen, previous to the awful moment of his execution, acknowledged the justice of
his sentence, and that he had committed the crime for which he was to
suffer. He even added, that it was his anxious wish, that no person after his death, should suffer any injury in consequence.—He died, apparently, very contrite, possessed of much Christain fortitude, and in
peace with all mankind.

ARTHUR M'HUGH.,

Lifford, 31st March, 1817.

men walked briskly out from Carndonagh as the sun was setting. It was the 2nd October, 1816,[70] and exactly three months since the death of Norton Butler.

The pair went along the road and turned right towards Glenagannon. At an agreed spot Balfour's companion whistled a well-known tune, as arranged. A man sprang out at the bridge and felled Balfour with a bludgeon. As Balfour fell the attacker pierced him with a sword. A rope was tied around the wounded man who was then dragged to a spot where a large group of men was waiting.

The leader now supervised the " ritual " of ensuring that every man present had a hand in the informer's death. Each man passed by the unfortunate man and pierced him with a sword.[71] At the end the body, horribly mutilated, was thrown into a flax dam, and the men disappeared.

The fact of Balfour's death was soon known and the army began an intensive search for evidence which would lead to the discovery of the killers. Many were arrested and as the trial proceeded two men, Bradley and McEleney, were sentenced to death and executed. At this stage a witness, called Alexander McClure, stated on oath that he had been given a large sum of money if he would swear indiscriminately against selected men from among the accused. Major Dawson and Edward Chichester,[72] the rector of Culdaff, were stated to have been involved in this bribery. The judge immediately released the remainder of the accused and terminated the trial.

Tradition is silent about the other informer in this narrative —Shane McEleney of Meenamaddy. There is no record that he met a violent end. Perhaps he lived on unhappily, punished to the end of his life by the memory of his deed and the odium of his neighbours.

Norton Butler's property was not sufficient to clear off the stilling fines due,[73] and his widow and family were left in penury. Through the influence of friends her plight was made known to the Lord Lieutenant, Lord Whitworth. He authorised the payment of a yearly pension of £200 from public funds.[74]

One other tragic figure stands silent and unmentioned in the background—the mother of Daniel and William McGuinness. For her there was no Government pension nor any other public help. She had, no doubt, the kindness and sympathy of her neighbours and many friends but the anguish of her heart only death could assuage. Within one year she had been separated from her four sons—two by death and two by emigration.[75] The house at Glackmore was now lonely, and deserted save for the parents.[76]

THE STORY OF HUGH McCONNOLLOGUE[77]

A short distance from the large residence known as Grousehall, to the north side and just across the stream, there once stood a small thatched dwelling-house inhabited by a family called McConnollogue. Today the walls have disappeared but it is still possible to trace the outline of the site at the head of a green field. Here in the early part of the nineteenth century lived Hugh McConnollogue with his parents.

1816 was a time of revolt and unrest. Secret societies were active. Any young man who had an interest in the welfare of his community inevitably became involved in the struggle. Hugh became a member of the secret society which at that time had a wide membership in the parish of Culdaff. He was well acquainted with the McGuinness[78] family in Glackmore. Tradition states that he was the man mentioned as being in the company of James McGuinness on Crucknanoneen when Norton Butler was attacked. McConnollogue was involved in a robbery together with members of this famous Glackmore family.

A dispute arose over a grave in the burying ground at Cloncha. In the fight which took place McConnollogue was a participant and came under the notice of the local magistrate. Some time later Norton Butler was attacked at a still-house. Again McConnollogue was involved. Two warrants were issued for his arrest. One day Edward Chichester and a number of Yeomen went to Aghaglasson to arrest McConnollogue. He saw the party coming towards his house in Magheradreen and ran out in the direction of Carahunny carrying his gun.

McConnollogue discharged a shot. The exact circumstances are not clear but the firing of this shot became a crucial matter for Hugh. One version says that he fired his gun in the air and that it was not loaded with ball. Two witnesses supported this story on oath, saying that they were present when McConnollogue placed powder only in the gun. A second version, supported by another witness on oath, was that the defendant had taken deliberate aim at Edward Chichester but missed. The ball hit the ground near where the witness stood. The fact was, however, that Edward Chichester was uninjured.

McConnollogue[79] made good his escape to Greencastle and

here a friendly boatman took him across the Foyle to Magilligan, where he found refuge. *En route*, to ensure disguise, Hugh was dressed in female garb.

Two of his neighbours, Long of Carahunny and Sean Faulkner of Moneydarragh, were engaged in Hugh's pursuit. The two men crossed to Magilligan. One night shortly afterwards, a dance was held in the house of a family named Magee. To the dance came the three Gleneely men. Hugh was still in female dress, and as the dancing proceeded Long approached him and asked him to dance. During the dance Long recognised his partner. An early arrest was effected and McConnollogue was soon lodged in Lifford gaol.

At the trial the evidence of Sean Faulkner—the second version referred to above—was damning. Hugh McConnollogue was sentenced to death and executed. After execution the body was brought home and tradition says that as the horse-drawn vehicle came down from Crucknanoneen the horse stopped opposite the house of Sean Faulkner and the coffin burst open, thus fulfilling a threat made by McConnollogue to Faulkner.

Hugh McConnollogue was buried at Bocan at a spot behind the church and adjacent to the door of the sacristy.[80] The grave is marked by a large flat stone which as yet bears no inscription.

The execution of this young man and the accompanying circumstances excited the people, whose sympathy was with the victim. The story of his death is still remembered in the district where he was born, and the name of the man whose evidence led to his execution is still held in odium.

---

1. *Report on Distillation in Ireland,* 1813.
2. *P.P.: Second Report from Select Committee on Illicit Distillation in Ireland,* 1816.
3. *Report on the Distilleries in Ireland,* 1813.
4. Historical Manuscripts Commission: *Report on the Manuscripts of R. R. Hastings,* Vol. **IV**
5. *Report on the Distilleries in Ireland,* 1813.
6, 7. *Mason's Statistical Survey,* 1816: "Culdaff and Cloncha," Edward Chichester.
8, 9. *Report on the Distilleries in Ireland,* 1813.
10. *The Belfast Monthly Magazine,* July, 1809.
11. *Report on the Distilleries in Ireland,* 1813.
12. *Reports from the Committee on the Distillation of Sugar and Molasses,* 1808.
13. *P.P.: 1824,* Vol. II — *Commissioners' Reports:* Appendix to Tenth

Report of Commissioners of Enquiry into the Revenue arising in Ireland. Appendix No. 30.

14. *P.P.*: *Second Report from Select Committee on Illicit Distillation in Ireland*, 1816.
15. *Social Problems*, Vol. 1, 1834: Drunkenness.
16. *P.P.*: *1805* — Letters to Commissioners of Revenue.
17. *Oppressions and Cruelties of Irish Revenue Officers*, 1818, Edward Chichester.
18, 19. *P.P.*: *Second Report from Select Committee on Illicit Distillation in Ireland*, 1816.
20. *P.P.*: *1818* — Police Reports.
21, 22. *P.P.*: *Second Report from Select Committee on Illicit Distillation in Ireland*, 1816.
23. Letters of Samuel Lumsden, an Army Officer stationed at Grousehall, 1816. Belfast P.R.O.
24. *P.P.*: *Second Report from Select Committee on Illicit Distillation in Ireland*, 1816.
25. *Mason's Statistical Survey*, 1816: "Culdaff and Cloncha," Edward Chichester.
26, 27. *P.P.*: *Second Report from Select Committee on Illicit Distillation in Ireland*, 1816.
28. *Oppressions and Cruelties of Irish Revenue Officers*, 1818, Edward Chichester.
29. *P.P.*: *1818, Vol. 16* — Accounts and Papers.
30. *Oppressions and Cruelties of Irish Revenue Officers*, 1818, Edward Chichester.
31. *Observations on the Rev. Edward Chichester's Pamphlet entitled Oppressions, etc.*, Aeneas Coffey.
32. *Oppressions and Cruelties of Irish Revenue Officers*, 1818, Edward Chichester.
33, 34. *Observations on the Rev. Edward Chichester's Pamphlet entitled Oppressions, etc.*, Aeneas Coffey.
35, 36, 37. *P.P.*: *Second Report from Select Committee on Illicit Distillation in Ireland*, 1816.
38, 39. *Oppressions and Cruelties of Irish Revenue Officers*, 1818, Edward Chichester.
40, 41. *P.P.*: *Second Report from Select Committee on Illicit Distillation in Ireland*, 1816.
42. *P.P.*: *1818, Vol. 16* — Illicit Distillation.
43. *Derry Journal*, 9.7.1816.
44. Lumsden Letters, Belfast P.R.O.
45. *Three Hundred Years in Innishowen*, Young.
46. *List of the Officers of the Donegal Militia*, issued by Dublin Castle, 1.7.1799, shows Norton Butler as an Ensign commissioned 26th November, 1798.
47. *Mason's Statistical Survey*, 1816: "Culdaff and Cloncha," Edward Chichester. It is stated that Norton Butler was the first to drill potatoes in this district. Planting in ridges was the practice then.
48. *Mason's Statistical Survey*, 1816: "Culdaff and Cloncha," Edward Chichester.
49, 50. *Derry Journal*, July 30th, 1816.
51. *Oppressions and Cruelties of Irish Revenue Officers*, 1818, Edward Chichester.
52. I, *Ibid.*; II, *Inishowen*, "Maghtochair".
53. *Inishowen*, "Maghtochair". This author states that James McGuinness went off from Glengad. There is in Ballyharry a tradition that a pilot

named Roger McCann brought the fugitive out to a liner bound for the United States.

54, 55. *Oppressions and Cruelties of Irish Revenue Officers*, 1818, Edward Chichester.

56. I, *Derry Journal*, 9th July, 1816; II, *Oppresisons and Cruelties of Irish Revenue Officers*, 1818, Edward Chichester; III, *Inishowen*, "Maghtochair"; IV, Lumsden letters, Belfast P.R.O.

57. *Oppressions and Cruelties of Irish Revenue Officers*, 1818, Edward Chichester.

58. *Inishowen*, "Maghtochair".

59. *Oppressions and Cruelties of Irish Revenue Officers*, 1818, Edward Chichester.

60. *Derry Journal*, July 9th, 1816: Midnight is stated as time of death. "Maghtochair" in his record says eight the following morning.

61, 62, 63. *Derry Journal*, July 30th, 1816.

64. It is evident that Daniel McGuinness was considered by both the local landlords and the authorities in Dublin as the more guilty. It is probable that this view was based on Butler's statement before death. Daniel was probably the main attacker.

65. *Inishowen*, "Maghtochair".

66. *Three Hundred Years in Innishowen*, Young.

67, 68. *Inishowen*, "Maghtochair". This is the main sourse of the data on Balfour.

69. *Oppressions and Cruelties of Irish Revenue Officers*, 1818, Edward Chichester.

70. *Oppressions and Cruelties of Irish Revenue Officers*, 1818, Edward Chichester. "Maghtochair" gives August but I have accepted Chichester's date as he was writing at the time of these events. "Maghtochair" was recording the oral tradition fifty years afterwards.

71. Patrick Bonner of Meenawarra, Culdaff (1872-1958), told a traditional story regarding this participation in the killing by all. A man from Glack, Culdaff, called Carney was a member of the secret society and was present in the group of men. When Carney stabbed Balfour the victim emitted a groan. The memory of this remained vividly in Carney's memory until he died.

72. Local tradition includes Chichester.

73. *Oppressions and Cruelties of Irish Revenue Officers*, 1818, Edward Chichester. Butler's will was admitted to probate in 1817. Refer to *Irish Wills*, Vol. V — Derry and Raphoe. Edited by Gertrude Thrift.

74. *Oppressions and Cruelties of Irish Revenue Officers*, 1818, Edward Chichester.

75. Peter fled for safety to Connaught. Ref. "Maghtochair": *Inishowen*.

76. The farm occupied by this family passed later into the hands of James Bonner. It is now the property of a local family called Faulkner. It is related that when James Bonner took over the house he found equipment for counterfeiting money. There is no trace of the house now. The reward notice printed in the *Derry Journal* stated that James McGuinness was born in the town of Moville. Probably the family lived there for a time.

77. The main source of this story is "Maghtochair"'s *Inishowen*. Data from other sources are indicated.

78. "Maghtochair"'s *Inishowen* states that the bullets used to shoot Butler were made in the house of McConnollogue. Some years ago a man ploughing in the field opposite the site of the house of McConollogue found a mould which was used for making bullets.

167

79. For the additional information, I am indebted to Solomon Kavanagh of Aghaglasson.
80. Joseph O Cnaimhsi, the sexton at Bocan, indicated the exact location of the grave.

9

ESTABLISHMENT OF GOVERNMENT SERVICES

ADMIRALTY TOWER
The visitor to Malin Head will see a large building standing in a commanding situation at Ireland's most northerly point. Locally known as the Tower of Ballyhillin, this building is the ruins of the old Lloyd's signal tower and is situated in the townland of Ardmalin.

The tower was built by order of the Admiralty about 1805[1] to report all ships passing along this route. The Wireless Station, erected in 1902, superseded the tower, which fell into disuse from that date.

MALIN HEAD WIRELESS STATION
In the townland of Ballygorman, near the village of Sleebane, stands the Wireless Station with its 150-feet-high mast. It was built in 1902 by the Marconi Company as a coast station to communicate with ships. It had, at first, a range of 100 miles. In 1910 the Post Office took over. Its range of communication has now been considerably extended.

The first message ever transmitted was to the island of Inistrahull, in January, 1902.

POST OFFICE AND COMMUNICATIONS
One of the outstanding features of our present civilisation is the speed of communication. To-day there are television, radio, the telephone, the postal service and newspapers. Thus contact is maintained between peoples at the most distant ends of the earth. In the north of Inis Eoghain up to the beginning of the last century the system of communication was very primitive indeed. In this respect, the area was no different from any other part of rural Ireland.

Early in the last century post offices were established in Carndonagh[2] and Moville. From Carndonagh a foot post served Malin and the area lying northwards and in the same way the Culdaff area was served from Moville.[3]

Towards the middle of the century post offices were opened at Culdaff, Malin and Gleneely. Later Ballygorman and Culkeeny were added. Each of the post offices now has a telephone exchange. To-day postal deliveries are made to every part of the two parishes. A number of people has installed private telephones and the demand for this facility is increasing.

The citizen of to-day in our area enjoys the most up-to-date means of communication. The daily post, the telephone, radio and television are an essential part of modern life here. The impact on the social life of the people here is far-reaching.

POLICE BARRACKS

The disturbances in the northern part of Inis Eoghain early in the last century compelled the British authorities to take temporary steps to ensure the maintenance of peace. Army units were at first stationed here in strength and later, as conditions improved, constabulary were stationed at various points in the area. In 1827[4] a station was established at Culdaff and in the following year at the Crossroads in Gleneely. Later, stations were opened at Malin and Malin Head.

These outposts were an important factor in maintaining effective control of the people. The constable, in touch with the ordinary life of the community, gleaned all relevant information, and this was passed on to Dublin Castle. The fact that the rank and file of the force were Irishmen made it much more effective. From 1827 onwards Dublin Castle was fully informed of events in every part of Ireland, however remote.

GARDA STATIONS

The end of the British occupation meant the disbanding of the Royal Irish Constabulary. One of the first signs of the new order in the political field was the arrival of the Garda Siochana, in a distinctive uniform and unarmed.

Stations were established at Malin, Culdaff and Malin Head. The law-abiding ways of the residents later made possible the closing of Malin Head station, and the number of Gardai at Culdaff was reduced to one. The patrol car has now taken over some of the duties of the Gardai in the area.

DISPENSARIES

Man, from the beginning of time, has had to face constantly many threats to his existence. Diseases of many kinds have been an abiding problem and consequently the need for a remedy has always been present in every society. " Cures " of all varieties have evolved. Some have had a sound basis in a knowledge of the laws of nature, but others were mere superstitions. All, however, gave to the sufferer that hope which is so essential to maintain the will for survival. Indeed, in the case of certain ailments, whose origin and cause lay in the emotional area, recovery was possible through the belief of the patient alone.

The inhabitants of Culdaff and Cloncha were in no way different from people elsewhere. Nature and superstition played a part
in the curing of diseases. A writer in 1816[5] said of this area:

It is difficult to propose an adequate remedy for the errors which
prevail amongst the lower classes, respecting the treatment of diseases;
but if a dispensary could be established, under the management of a
skilful medical man, their prejudices on this subject would probably,
after some time, yield to reason and experience.

In speaking of diseases the same writer says:

Their treatment of these maladies often determines them to a fatal
issue, when they might otherwise have afforded hope of recovery. Stagnant air, innumerable visitors, unseasonable blood-letting and the unlimited use of ardent spirits constitute the regimen applied to all dis-
orders. Pleurisies and pulmonary complaints carry off great numbers;
and their predilection for quackery forms a most powerful auxiliary to
the malignity of disease. As soon as a patient appears to be dangerously
ill of any disorder, application is made to every person in the neighbourhood who pretends to medical skill. All the discordant prescriptions thus
obtained are combined and administered along with their grand specific,
whiskey, the quantity of which is increased in proportion to the exacer-
bation of the disease. Typhus, fevers and dropsy are to be met with in
this and the adjoining parishes; intermittents are extremely rare; scro-
fula is common; dyspepsia very prevalent, vaccination superstitiously
resisted.

The writer goes on to mention one custom in particular:

An infant at its birth is generally forced by the midwife to swallow
spirits, and is immediately afterwards suspended by the upper jaw with
her fore finger; this last operation is performed for the purpose of preventing a disease called the headfall. Many children die when one or two
days old, of the trismus nascentium or jaw-fall; a spasmodic disease
deemed peculiar to tropical climates; here, however, it is probably a
dislocation, caused by the above mentioned barbarous practice.

Up to recent times the midwife was a local " handy woman "
who had never undergone any training whatsoever other than the
traditional method of learning from the previous untrained midwife. Nevertheless, healthy babies were general and death of
either baby or mother was very rare indeed.

Certain families had traditional cures for specific diseases.
These cures were given freely to all in need but the secret of their
compounding was carefully guarded and handed down from generation to generation. The cures probably had their origin in the

171

monastic pharmacy and were part of the traditional herbal lore going back to the earliest times.

Up to the early part of the nineteenth century we had in North Inis Eoghain a community which lacked any medical service. Therefore, the patient had no other remedy than those current in the neighbourhood. The strong survived by the natural resistance of the body but the weak succumbed.

In 1825 a dispensary was established in each of the two parishes—one at Malin and one at Culdaff. The people were in no way reluctant to use the dispensary, as the following table shows: [6]

YEAR	NO. RELIEVED
1825	1,700
1826	1,630
1827	1,825
1828	1,904
1829	2,016

The dispensary was maintained in part by a grant from public funds and the balance by local subscriptions, e.g., in 1829[7] a grant of £50 was made from public funds and an equal sum was contributed locally.

Later a resident doctor was appointed. The Malin dispensary area covered most of the two parishes. It extended from Malin Head to Redford-Glebe. The remainder of the area was included part in Moville and part in Carndonagh dispensary area. This arrangement continues up to the present. Private doctors are now also available. There is no hospital in this area, and patients who require such attention go to Carndonagh, Letterkenny, Derry or Dublin as circumstances demand.

LOAN FUND[8]

The Culdaff Loan Fund was established in 1843, under the Acts of Parliament of 1836 and 1838, to give loans to industrious men of good conduct. It was responsible to the Commissioners of the Loan Fund Board of Ireland. The depositors who provided the money for the loan got interest of 6% *per annum*. The borrowers paid 6d. per £1 for twenty weeks—a charge of 6½%.

For the years in respect of which returns were published, the number of loans given annually and the capital invested were as follows:

172

YEAR	NO. OF LOANS	CAPITAL	NO. OF DEPOSITORS
		£	
1843	754	472	—
1844	2,006	1,167	31
1845	2,584	1,532	51
1846	2,570	1,539	48
1847	1,299	1,198	35
1848	1,656	751	18
1849	1,482	726	13
1850	1,061	522	14
1851	592	361	10

The Loan Fund ceased to function around 1940 and its affairs were wound up.

THE COASTGUARD SERVICE

The imposition of duty on certain goods at the end of the eighteenth century and the beginning of the nineteenth encouraged activities aimed at evading the duties and thus ensured a substantial profit to the smugglers. Outstanding examples of such goods were whiskey, tobacco and wine. The Government in London was forced to take preventive action. Efforts to eliminate illicit distillation are well-known. In the case of goods coming in by sea a coast watch was necessary—hence the formation of the Coastguard Service.

This service was established and controlled by the Customs up to 1858, when it passed to the control of the Admiralty. Its purpose was to control the landing of dutiable goods and in addition to prevent the distillation and export of whiskey made by unlicensed distillers.

Inis Eoghain, with its long coastline, its relation to the North Atlantic route and its remoteness from the point of central government, was a haven for smugglers. Here smuggling was widespread at the end of the eighteenth century and in the first half of the nineteenth. Every rank of society was involved in it. A report of 1822[9] shows that a boat with 805 lbs. of tobacco leaf was seized at Port Kinnagoe; 476 lbs. of tobacco leaf were taken at Malin Head and 1,430 lbs. at Greencastle. On June 20th, 1822, an American sloop of 38 tons called the *Orbit* was seized at Redford and the crew, consisting of three foreigners and one Irishman, arrested There is no doubt that a vast quantity in addition got in undetected at various ports.

The smuggling of tobacco went on around the Inis Eoghain area on so vast a scale that it was estimated that at this time the cost to the Treasury was in the region of £150,000 annually for this area alone.[10] A preventive waterguard was organised about 1820 but proved entirely inadequate. In 1822 a report to the Secretary of the Treasury suggested establishing a chain of stations around the northern coast, and especially in Inis Eoghain.[11] Among the recommendations was the placing of a station at Redford consisting of a force of twelve men. The report stated that a great deal of tobacco had been landed here over the previous year[12] and that it was a place of importance because of its closeness to the river and port of Culdaff. The report pointed out that building would be necessary to ensure adequate accommodation for the watchers.

The report went on to advise the placing of a station at Glengad Head because of its being the best anchorage on this side of the coast from Malin Head. It was usually the first place at which the smuggler called " when the wind was to the westward ". The landing was good and there was here " an abundant population eager to carry off the whole, and conceal it in glens and caves, which are very plentiful ". A station was also suggested at Malin Head, on the grounds that it was the most northerly point. Its situation was inviting to the smuggler because it had a good bay at either side. A vessel could take advantage of shelter from either easterly or westerly winds and so discharge in safety. Because of the traffic with Inis Eoghain, stations were suggested at Portstewart and Downhill. The flow of smuggled goods landed at Magilligan from Inis Eoghain could thus be averted.

The authorities considered the report and finally established within the parishes of Culdaff and Cloncha the following: lookout posts at Cruckameal, Redford, Dunmore, Culdaff-Glebe and two at Glengad. Stations were built at Bunagee and Malin Head. The coastguards at Redford lived at Meenawarra. The site of the look-out at Culdaff-Glebe can still be seen.

The look-out points were later closed when the smuggling had been eliminated but the stations at Malin Head and Bunagee remained in use until the period before the Treaty. The station at Bunagee was burned by the I.R.A. as part of the Republican policy of destroying the British administrative system.

Ballyhillin at Ardmalin and Culdaff-Glebe were areas whose inhabitants had a deep involvement in tobacco smuggling.

ROADS

While there is evidence that an elaborate network of roads

or tracks existed in Ireland from pre-historic times, there is little indication of any roads in the parishes of Culdaff and Cloncha before the eighteenth century. In the secluded society which existed here up to the English occupation long journeys were very rare. The townland environs set the limit of movement except for visits to church and market. Journeys were made on foot, or sometimes on horseback. Any other means of transport was well-nigh unknown.

In placenames here we have the mention of *cosan* (a footway), *ceasach* (a road over boggy ground), *roidin* (a path), *ath* (a ford), *cora* (stepping-stones) and *droichead* (a bridge), but the only suggestion of a more pretentious roadway is found in the town-land of Ballagh (*bealach*). There is also the townland of Drum-carbit, which may mean *droim carbad* (the ridge of the chariots). The word *bothar* does not occur.

The eighteenth century was in this area a period of intensive road-making and bridge-building.[13] During the middle of that century all the main roads of to-day were built. The bridge at Culdaff was built in 1737, but the bridge at Malin Town presented some difficulties. It was built around 1750 and fell as a result of a storm. The Grand Jury directed that a new bridge of stone and lime be built. It was arranged that the new bridge should be built in a different spot, nearer to the land side from the bay, and it was to consist of " four arches, two in the centre of fourteen feet wide and one at each end of ten feet wide ".

In 1815 we find that the roads were all in a bad state. A writer[14] stated:

They (the roads) have all sustained great injury, in consequence of a clause in a late distillery law, which prohibits the issue of money for the repairs of roads and bridges, so long as any of the fines imposed for illicit distillation remain unpaid.

In recent years, because of the tourist potential of this area, Bord Failte and the County Council have improved all the main roads and have widened and re-surfaced side-roads. Many seaside areas and other beauty spots have been made accessible to motorists.

METEOROLOGICAL STATION AT MALIN HEAD

The first station of this kind was established by the British Meteorological Service and was so controlled up to 1939, when the Irish service took over. Rainfall records for the Admiralty

Tower started in 1870. The service is a section of the Department of Transport and Power. The present building was opened in May, 1955.

The service records observations every hour of cloud cover, height and type, visibility, weather, wind direction and speed, and duration of bright sunshine. Readings are taken of extreme air temperatures and also temperatures in the ground at fixed times.

Upper wind measurements by pilot balloons are carried out daily. Observations of aurorae are performed hourly and more frequently if required during the hours of darkness. Copies of these records are sent each month to the Balfour Stewart Auroral Laboratory in Edinburgh for investigation and research. Full details of thunderstorms and hail showers are noted. Copies of the records are posted monthly to the Thunderstorm Census Organisation at Huddersfield in England. The Meteorological Station operates a tidal recorder at Portmore Pier on behalf of the Ordnance Survey.

1. *Mason's Statistical Survey*, 1816: "Culdaff and Cloncha," Edward Chichester.
2. *Parliamentary Papers, 1818*, Vol. 16.
3. *Parliamentary Papers, Session 1837-38.*
4. *Parliamentary Papers, Constabulary, 1830*, Vol. 29.
5. *Mason's Statistical Survey*, 1816: "Culdaff and Cloncha," Edward Chichester.
6. *P.P. 1830 — Dispensaries.*
7. *P.P. 1829 — Dispensaries.*
8. I, *P.P. 1844*, Vol. 30; II, *P.P. 1852*, Vol. 18.
9, 10, 11. *P.P. 1824*, Vol. 11: Commissioners' Appendix to Tenth Report of Commissions of Inquiry into the Revenue arising in Ireland. Appendixes No. 30 and 50.
12. *P.P. 1824*: *Seventh Report of Commissioners of Inquiry into the Revenue arising in Ireland.* Appendix. John Wright, Secretary to the Police Establishments, stated: "I think a great deal might be done if every gentleman was as active as Mr. Chichester was. I have heard of his going down and driving four or five hundred people from waiting for a landing of tobacco". It is worth noting that the port at Redford was only a hundred yards or so from Mr. Chichester's house and clearly within view of the nearby hill. The land adjoining the sea here was his property.
13. See Grand Jury Presentments for Donegal.
14. *Mason's Statistical Survey*, 1816: "Culdaff and Cloncha," Edward Chichester.

10
THE ISLANDS

THE VISITOR to Malin Head will notice an island rising out of the ocean. This is Inistrahull, a gaunt, grim, rock-fortress waging a ceaseless battle for survival with the relentless, restless sea. Lying five miles north-west of the Head, it is the most northerly outpost of Ireland's sovereignty. The townland of Inistrahull consists of an area of 113 acres, 3 roods and 37 perches. It is situated in the electoral division of Ardmalin and in the parish of Cloncha.

Did this island formerly belong to the parish of Culdaff? The Civil Survey of 1654, in its reference to Culdaff, says:

There is likewise belonging to this parish a small island being three leagues in the sea belonging to the Lord Chichester called Ensterhull containing two ballyboes of land: sixty acres arable, twenty pasture, 30 mountains and ten rocky.

Bishop Montgomery's Survey of Derry diocese in its report on Culdaff says:

There is an island in the sea called Strahull - 4 ballyboes.

The same mistake regarding location occurs when we find the island included in the Manor of Greencastle while the mainland nearby was in the Manor of Malin.

The island has been designated on various maps from the sixteenth century onwards. The form varies. Thus we have Daghall Ats Tralle, Daghall, Enis Daghall, Inistuathail, Strahull, Enesterhull and Illes d'Enesterhul[1]. The modern English spelling is Inistrahull. This represents the current and corrupt anglicised pronunciation.

What is the correct form? The topographer would note that the distinctive feature of the island, viewed from either Ireland or Scotland, is the two hills, one at each end of the area. The early observers, in both countries, were Gaelic speaking and called it Inis Dá Thul - the island of the two hills. A probable alternative name, also in use, was Inistuathail: a directional description in relation to the Irish mainland - the island to the north. One of the forms, given above, would suggest this.

The inlets on the island are Portban (white port). Portmore (big port), Portnahully (port of the burial), Portahurry (port of the

177

curragh), and Portaronan (the port of the seals).

When was the island first inhabited? Before examining this problem it is well to set out the signs of human activity insofar as these remain.

At the beginning of this century men carrying out digging operations found at a depth of eight feet an ornamented stone.[2] In general shape it resembles a Brazil nut. On the flat side is inscribed a circle nine inches in diameter. Within the circle there is a four-leafed pattern shaped like a cross, with expanding arms having curved sides. Towards the long end of the stone from the rim of the circle runs a shaft or staff design. Authorities who have examined it date it as around 750 A.D. and hold that it has a Christian association. It may have been taken from a church and later used as a " cursing stone ". Somewhat similar stones have been found elsewhere and had been put to superstitious uses of the same kind. The fact that the stone was found buried so deep shows that it was deliberately placed there, perhaps through the influence of clergy trying to eliminate the old pagan customs, which survived long into the Christian era. The stone is now on show at an hotel on the mainland nearby.

An old graveyard was found in recent years at the west end of the island. There is also a tall standing-stone on which is carved a cross. A relic of the Penal days is the cross-inscribed Mass Rock. Old quern stones are still to be found here also, as in many other parts of Donegal.

Evidence of more recent habitation can be seen in the graveyard and the school. There is no evidence that any place of worship ever existed here, apart from the Portnahully and Crucknahully already referred to.

The Hearth Money Roll for Co. Donegal compiled in 1665 makes no reference to the island. The householders are not listed in the Tithe Applotment Books in 1828. Evidently the inhabitants were not asked to pay tithes. Griffith's Valuation in 1857 shows that there were nine dwelling houses, of which six had land attached. The total annual valuation of rateable property was £23— £11. 5. 0 for buildings and the balance for land. The lighthouse occupied a space of three acres and 30 perches.

The family names here at the time were McGonagle, McLoughlin, Loughry and McKenny.

Donovan, writing in 1830,[3] mentions that there were then seven families and a population of about 50. The census of 1841 shows 54 people and seven houses while the census of 1851 shows a population of 68 and 11 houses. In neither case was there any vacant house.

From the slender evidence available it would seem that there were two separate periods of colonisation here. The older one would seem to have been followed by a period of complete absence of human habitation. There is a possibility that the Vikings used the island for a time as a base. The increase of population in the eighteenth century and the demand for land which followed led to the coming of a second group of inhabitants to the island. The entry of these people took place when Irish was still the spoken language of the people. This wild, inhospitable island was abandoned about the thirties of the present century, and only the light-keepers remain there to-day.

The only means of livelihood which the people had was fishing. The poor soil produced inferior crops and these were endangered by the storms and brine which swept over the island. The Congested Districts Board[4] established a station for curing cod, ling and saithe here in the years 1895, 1896, 1897 and 1898. Records show that the sea around yielded a rich harvest.

Local tradition says that the first modern settlers on the island were two brothers of the McLoughlin family from Malin Head. During a fishing expedition the brothers were on a boat which had to run before the wind to the Scottish coast for a safe port. On landing they were received with traditional Scottish hospitality and lodged at the house of the head of the clan. Here they made the acquaintance of the chieftain's daughter, and she and one of the brothers fell in love. The girl's father refused to consider a marriage between the two lovers, but the Irishmen were determined to have their way and outwitted the chieftain by going away quietly on their boat with the Scottish lass aboard. The lovers reached the island in safety and soon they were married.

One day the McLoughlin brothers saw two boats of armed men approaching the island from Scotland. Aware of the strangers' mission, they knew that there was no possibility of victory in open battle. The choice lay between surrendering the girl or resorting to a stratagem. A discussion took place and it was decided that the two men would hide in a secret cave where suitable weapons were left ready. The girl agreed to meet her relations and clansmen at the port, bring them to her house and appear to be eager to get back to her native Albain. She was to prepare a good meal and then produce a keg of good Inis Eoghain whiskey. It was hoped that when the Scots had drunk deep of the poteen it would be easy to deal with them.

The plan was successful and soon Mrs. McLoughlin was at the entrance of the cave to tell her husband and brother-in-law that the Scots were lying fast asleep in an inebriated state. The two brothers emerged and killed all the sleeping men. A large grave was made and here all the men were buried together. The chieftain waited in vain for the return of his men with his abducted daughter. In time the true story got through to Scotland and great was the rage of the chieftain and the members of his clan. The name McLoughlin of Inistrahull became anathema in the area. The slaughter was to be remembered for many a day in the Highlands.

About 1850 another boat was driven through storm to Scotland, where the crew was received with hospitality. On leaving, their names were written down by the clerk of the port. As one of the men said "McLoughlin of Inistrahull" an old fisherman who was standing nearby said: "If we had known you were the McLoughlins of Inistrahull 'tis little you would have got here. We should not let you go, you scoundrels! You are of the people who murdered our kinsmen". The men of Inistrahull returned to their island, marvelling no doubt at the long memories of their brother Celts.

The location of the cave mentioned above was a well-kept secret of the islanders and was handed down from one generation to another. Now its whereabouts is unknown.

The first lighthouse was erected here in 1812[5] and it first showed light in 1813. It began its operations on March 17th and has continued to the present day. The lighthouse tower[6] was situated on the eastern and highest hill of the island. The light was exhibited at a height of 180 feet and was visible for a distance of 19 miles. At the beginning the source of light was simply vegetable oil burned in wick lamps fitted in separate metal reflectors. A new lantern was fitted in 1863 and the light improved by the installation of an octagonal revolving optical apparatus of glass. In 1904 an oil burner was installed, which was fitted with an incandescent mantle about 2" in diameter. This formed a source of light of about 1,000 candles. The resulting beam from the optical apparatus was of about 200,000 candle-power. The duration of the flash was two seconds and it recurred every half-minute.

In the early part of this century[7] it was decided that a fog signal was necessary in this area. After careful consideration a site was chosen on the west side of the island. Here was erected a fog signal station, which commenced operations in 1905. There were then two separate establishments on the island, one at each end, requiring a complement of six lightkeepers in all. Two were on duty at each station and two on liberty ashore at any one time.

In 1952 investigations showed that the fog signal machinery had worn out. In addition, there was need for an improved light on this very busy shipping route. Consideration was given to a plan which would meet the two problems in the most economical manner possible. It was evident that it was desirable to ensure a saving in staff by placing both the lighthouse and fog station together. The fact that the buildings at the west end were in better condition, having been built much later than those on the east end, influenced the choice, and the final decision was to place the two stations together on the west end. A tower was built adjacent to the existing engine house, and in this was installed a lantern with electric light, above which was mounted the fog signal. A new air compressor and electric generating plant were installed. The overall height of the tower and lantern is 74 feet. It is based on a site 138 feet above the sea and the focal plane is 195 feet above sea level, somewhat similar to the height of the old lighthouse.

This, the first major lighthouse erected in Ireland since that on Rathlin in 1919, was completed in 1958 and was officially opened on October 8th of the same year by the Chairman of Irish Lights, Dr. J. H. J. Poole. The total cost was £31,601. The range of the new light is over 20 miles. Under favourable conditions the signal can be heard at 11 miles to the west, but only four and a half to six miles to the east.

The reliefs are now made once a fortnight, by a motor boat which is stationed at Portmore Pier. The contract for this service has been in the hands of the one family for over a century.

From the middle of the nineteenth century Lloyd's had a signal station on the island. This reported the arrival of ships from abroad by semaphore to the tower on the mainland, and the information was then telegraphed to London. The owners then informed the masters of the name of the port at which they should berth. Radio communication made this system obsolete, and the station was closed. Lloyd's, who owned the island, sold it to the Commissioners of Irish Lights for £100.

Geological authorities state[8] that the island is composed of Lewisian gneiss similar to the Lewisian outcrop of the Rhinns of Islay in Scotland. The rock formation of the island is entirely dissimilar in character to that of any other district of Inis Eoghain. The area in Scotland mentioned is about thirty miles from Inistrahull.

THE GARRIVE ISLES

This group of islands lies between Portmore and Inistrahull. There are five islands: Inisglas (the green island), Inisboillscinne (the middle island), Inisban (the white island), Carnban (the white rock) and Daughglass (the green sandbank ?). The last two are scarcely more than rocks. The other islands produce some herbage and in the summer sheep are left to feed there.

Around this area the direction of the tides causes a rough sea except in the calmest weather. This stormy sea is the origin of the name given to the group—*Na Garbh-Oileain*. In English this means " the islands of the rough sea " and is corrupted into the name given above. STUCKARUDAN *(Stuaic Ui Rodain*—the rock of O Rodden) lies a short distance off the mainland at Bree, Malin Head. There are no inhabitants. Sheep are brought here in summer to graze. CARRICKNAGALL *(Carraig na nGall*—the rock of the swans). This islet is situated in Culdaff river and is in the townland of Carthage. CARRICKEANAGH *(Carraig Eanaigh*—the rock of the birds). This islet is also situated in Culdaff river.

In addition to the islands listed above, there are many others too small and too numerous to be mentioned.

1, 2. *Romantic Inishowen*, H. P. Swan.
3. Ordnance Survey Name Books. Parish of Cloncha.
4. *Report of the Congested Districts Board of Ireland.*
5. *P. P.: Lighthouse, 1845.*
6. *Romantic Inishowen*, H. P. Swan.
7. *Transactions of the Institution of Civil Engineers* (1960-61).
8. *Geological Magazine*, 1930: "The Gneiss of Inistrahull," W. J. McCallien.

11

EDUCATION: 1600-1970

IN THE section which dealt with the monastic institutions it has been shown that religious foundations existed in this area from the sixth century onwards. As well as fulfilling their primary function these establishments were centres of learning. It can be easily seen, therefore, that the people of the area had opportunities for education while these institutions lasted. The families associated with the church maintained a tradition of learning to ensure that entrance into the clerical ranks was always kept within the sept. During the decline of the monasteries here the basics were taught within the family. For advanced studies the nearby monastery at Derry was available.

By the end of the sixteenth century we find that students from here had begun to attend the university at Glasgow.[1] This centre of higher studies was founded in 1451 by a bull of Pope Nicholas V at the request of King James II of Scotland. Because of the close association of this part of Inis Eoghain with Scotland, it was a natural development that when the educational institutions at home were breaking up because of the ceaseless wars those in search of learning would go to Scotland.

It is clear, therefore, that up to the beginning of the English occupation the tradition of learning had been maintained despite the disorganised state of other parts of Ireland. The high educational standard of the clergy here at this time is vouched for by British sources.[2]

With the beginning of the English take-over the position of the native Irish in the two parishes underwent a vast change. They were deprived of all their property. They were denied by law the right to maintain schools or educate their children. In a word, they were now being reduced to the position of ignorant serfs whose only purpose was to serve their English masters.

The records[3] show that in the seventeenth and early in the eighteenth century the Church of Ireland had organised schools for its own adherents. There was a school near the parish church in each case. The rector had the responsibility to see that it functioned properly.

What about the Catholic population ? The hedge school was the answer. Just as the Catholic parishioner worshipped God in secret, so he also acquired his learning in secret. The hedge school was from 1640 to 1780 the only means of education available at home for the Irish Catholic. The wandering scholar eager to impart his knowledge and anxious to earn a meagre livelihood set up his school in summer by the side of a hedge. One boy kept guard to warn the school teacher if the military were in the vicinity. In winter a cabin became the pupils' refuge, provided no person was compromised with the authorities.

To the visitor to these parishes the hedge school would have been a familar sight in the years between 1650 and 1750, and perhaps later. For example, the memory of this type of school lingers on in local tradition in Culdaff-Glebe and in Glacknadrummond, in each of which a hedge school was held. No doubt there were many others throughout the area.

The native Irish maintained through all the persecutions their love for learning and availed of every opportunity to become educated. The last quarter of the eighteenth century marked the beginning of improvement in the field of education in this area. In 1782 the Penal Laws were relaxed to permit Catholics to establish schools provided a licence for the school was obtained from the local Protestant bishop—in this case the Bishop of Derry. In 1793 Catholics were freed from this restriction and could now organise their own schools. The cost of building and maintaining and equipping the school and paying the teacher had to be met from local resources. However, it was an improvement and so from this date on we find Catholic schools beginning to spring up.

About this time a number of societies came into existence whose aim was to encourage the education of the poorer classes by grants and the supply of books, etc. At least four societies were active in this area. In the main these societies were proselytising in their aims.

In 1792 was founded the Association for Discountenancing Vice and Promoting the Knowledge and Practice of the Christian Religion.[4] It was incorporated by Act of Parliament in 1800. Its activities included the distribution of Bibles, prayer books and tracts and providing grants for the building of schools. Edward Chichester, the rector of Culdaff and Cloncha, was a member and he reports that the society was active in the area. There are no precise indications of the nature or extent of the activity of the society here. Its primary aim was to convert Catholics to membership of the Established Church.

In 1806 the Hibernian Sunday School Society for Ireland began its avowedly proselytising activities. Grants were given for the founding of schools, and spelling books and Bibles were given out free or at reduced prices. Between 1813 and 1829 seven schools were established in each parish.[5] These were attended by many Catholics. The activities of this society finally met strong opposition from the Catholic clergy. In addition, Catholic schools were established. By 1829 the society seems to have withdrawn from the area, though it may have for some time carried on its activities in a more subtle manner.

The Erasmus Smith School Trustees assisted by grants one school in the area. The benefactor, Erasmus Smith,[6] because of his financial contribution to Cromwell's war in Ireland, received grants of land amounting to 46,449 acres. He founded schools in his own lifetime and left part of the income from his land in trust for the education of the poor. This trust was primarily concerned with the education of Protestants, as the teaching of Scripture was a condition of the grant.

The Society for Promoting the Education of the Poor of Ireland[7] interested itself in the area during the first quarter of the nineteenth century. This organisation, which was popularly known as the Kildare Place Society, differed from the others mentioned above. It was not concerned with the religious denomination of the pupils and it made no effort to influence them in respect of their religious beliefs. Schools in the area received grants and in addition teachers from here were trained in the college set up by the society in Dublin.

The schools in question had no effect on the religious beliefs of the Catholics, who attended them in large numbers. They did not make a single convert. However, these organisations began the Anglicisation of the people of the area. English was taught to the children and the Irish language was now regarded as the sign of ignorance. Soon English became the language of the community and the native language was forgotten. Thus the English had their biggest success since their arrival in 1620.

The biggest event in the educational field was the setting up of a Board of Education in 1832. Soon most of the schools in the area came into the scheme. New schools were built and existing buildings replaced by better ones. The Catholics gave full co-operation to the new scheme and all their schools came under the control of the Board. Education was now available to all without distinction.

The educational programme hastened the Anglicisation of the people. Its aim was to make the pupils "happy English children". The story of Ireland—its history and its culture—was not a school subject. If the pupils did not hear the truth at home they did not hear it at all, unless some patriotic teacher risked his career by giving the correct version of history.

This educational system lasted for ninety years. By 1922, after three hundred years, the Celt was again master in at least part of his own land. Now the story of Ireland was a subject on the school syllabus and the native language was heard once again in places like Culdaff and Cloncha after a long silence. The slow and painful process of re-educating a nation now commenced. At present the Department of Education is aiming to provide an efficient educational system by closing one-teacher schools and transferring the pupils to larger schools. Transport is provided. In some cases the parents have accepted the new plan, in others there has been strong opposition.

There is no secondary school in the area. The children attend in the neighbouring parish, where there are secondary schools for boys and girls. Transport to and from Carndonagh is provided At Glengad a technical school has been erected to provide vocational education for the whole district.

Below is a brief note in respect of each school which operated in the parishes of Culdaff and Cloncha from 1620 onwards, insofar as information is available.

AGHAGLASSON:[8] This school was founded by the Hibernian Sunday School Society and functioned from 1813 to 1832. Records show that the numbers in attendance were 72 in 1824 and 43 in the following year.
AGHACLAY:[9] The first record of this school is in the Report of the National Commissioners of Education for 1835, when there was a total of 55 pupils on the rolls. For a time separate schools existed for males and females. In 1857 the female school was closed because the average attendance was not sufficient. In 1886 a new school was built, for which a grant of £224.14.0 was received from the Board of Education. The attendance here appears to have reached its maximum in 1895, when the total on rolls was 219. This school was closed in 1968, when the children were transferred to Malin school.
BALLAGH:[10] The Hibernian Sunday School Society founded a school here which existed from 1813 to 1832. The numbers in attendance for the years in respect of which data are available were: 1820, 108; 1825, 84; 1826, 74.

BALLYHARRY:[11] The records of the Hibernian Sunday School Society show a school at Termone from 1820 to 1828. This is probably the school which was sited at Cnoc an Amhairc. The numbers in attendance were: 1820, 77; 1821, 17; 1822, 12; 1823, 12. No data are available for the other years.

The Irish Education Inquiry[12] for 1826 shows that a school existed here, run evidently with the assistance of the parish. The teacher was John Doherty, whose recorded income was fifteen pence per quarter. The school itself was a building of 36 feet by 41 feet. The average numbers in attendance for the three months prior to the report were 44 Catholics and eight Presbyterians. The reports of the Commissioners of National Education[13] include references to this school from 1835 onwards. For a time two schools are shown — one for males and one for females. The female school was amalgamated with the school for males in 1863.

A new school was built in 1877, at a new location along the main road from Culdaff to Moville—the present location. The old school at Cnoc an Amhairc was abandoned. In 1933 the school was renovated and named St. Ultan's. At a meeting of parents and representatives of the Department of Education in 1967 it was decided to close the school and transfer the pupils of the area to Dristernan National School. This arrangement came into effect from June, 1968. The maximum in attendance here was the figure for 1862, when the total was 176.

From the reports of the inspector of the Board of Education one interesting point emerges. In his report for 1857[14] the inspector records that while he was present in the school a child spoke in Irish. The report goes on to assure the Board that the children "got no instruction through the medium". It is evident that in the homes here Irish was still the spoken language in 1857.

BALLYMAGARAGHY:[15] This school is mentioned in the Irish Education Inquiry of 1826. The teacher is shown as John McLoughlin and his annual income was £5.13.9. The school was a room 13 feet by 12 feet for which a rent of 20/- a year was paid. The number in attendance was 19.

BOCAN: The first references to this school is found in the report of the Irish Education Society for 1826.[16] The teacher was Michael Hassan, who earned £20 per year. The number of pupils at this time was 60, of which 41 pupils were Catholics and the balance Protestants. The school, which had no State support, was recorded as being in the "chapel". This school would seem to have been founded here early in the nineteenth century and was probably the first openly conducted by Catholics in the parish.

The Report of the Irish National Education Board[17] carries a record of this school from 1835 onwards. Its roll number was 160. Two separate schools, one for females and one for males, are recorded for the years 1850 to 1883. In practice these two schools were carried on as one. The two teachers had both boys and girls in their classes. The school was built in the chapel yard in 1832 and continued in use up to 1933. It was demolished and the ground included in the graveyard of the church at Bocan. A new school, called St. Buadan's, was built on the opposite side of the road. It is not clear whether there was an older building before 1832 or whether the school was held in the church.

For a long period this school was attended by all denominations. The name "McColgan" was closely associated with its teachers for two or three generations. We find the teachers often eligible for good service pay, and the Board of Education reports speak highly of the standard of education here. As far as records are available, the highest number of pupils in attendance was 297. in 1864.

187

Owing to a re-organisation of the primary educational facilities in the parish this school was closed in 1982. The pupils were transferred to Culdaff.

BREE: The Hibernian Sunday School Society founded a school here[18] about 1825 and maintained its association with the school until 1829. The number shown on the rolls for Sunday school attendance in 1825 was 112 and in 1826 it was 62.

The Irish Education Inquiry[19] records a school in operation here in 1826, when the teacher was Michael McKeevers, a Catholic, who earned £12 per year. The school was built of stone and mud and was in bad repair. The school attendance was 40, of which 23 were Presbyterians and 17 were Catholics. This school is not included in the Board of Education reports. It functioned well into the middle of the nineteenth century. The building is included in the 1857 Rate Valuation List and tradition says that local pupils attended here about 1850. The teacher was then known as "Donal the Master". He was supported by local subscriptions.

CARNMALIN:[20] The Hibernian Sunday School Society founded a school here in 1820. It seems to have lasted only up to 1823. The numbers in attendance were: 1820, 85; 1821, 104; 1822, 104, 1823, 104. The exact location of this school is not clear. It may have been Malin Head School.

CARROWMORE:[21] This was one of the earliest schools under Catholic control in the parish of Culdaff. It appears in the reports of the Board of Education from 1835 onwards and had 161 pupils. It probably existed before that time.

The highest number of pupils in attendance was 221, in 1840. Later a new school was built and this is still in use. William Canny, the teacher who taught here in the middle of the last century, was the recipient year after year of Good Service Premiums awarded by the Board of Education.

CARTHAGE: The Hibernian Sunday School Society[22] had a school here from 1813 to 1829. The number of pupils varied from the 89 (in 1820) to 32 (in 1822). The school is mentioned in the Irish Education Inquiry[23] of 1826, when the teacher was Daniel Farran, a Catholic, who earned £9.10.0 per year. The school building was of stone and was thatched. It cost £10. The number of pupils was 29 and of these six were Protestants.

The Board of Education report[24] mentions this school from 1850 until 1854, when it was struck off the records on the grounds that the building was unsuitable. The name of the teacher in 1852 was James Farran. The maximum on the rolls was 74, in 1854. The school was under the control of the parish priest of Cloncha.

CASHEL: A school organised by the Hibernian Sunday School Society[25] functioned here during the years 1813 to 1819. The number of pupils recorded is 34. The exact location of this school is not known.

CLONCHA: This school was built about 1760 by the Marquis of Donegall,[26] who made a yearly endowment of £10 towards the teacher's salary. Repairs were the responsibility of the parish. In 1809 a complaint was made that the cess imposed for the purpose of repairs was difficult to collect.

The Hibernian Sunday School Society[27] held a school here from 1813 until 1828, using the same building, presumably. The number of pupils in attendance varied from 36 in 1813 to 13 in 1822. The Irish Education Inquiry of 1826[28] shows that the school was then in existence. The teacher was Anthony Kane, who had been in training in 1822 under the scheme organised by the Society for Promoting the Education of the Poor of Ireland. He had commenced teaching here in 1804. His salary is shown as £22.5.0 a year. The number of pupils in attendance in 1804 was 60 — 40 Catholics, 16 Protestants and four Presbyterians.

The 1858 report[29] on Endowed Schools refers to this school under the heading of "Endowments not in Operation". The school was in bad repair and had been discontinued through lack of funds. The grant which the Society for Promoting the Education of the Poor had been making annually was discontinued because the Government had terminated its grant to the society. There is no information as to when the school finally closed. The reports of the Board of Education make no reference to it. It probably ceased about 1830, when schools were opened in the parish by the Catholic clergy.

The stones of the school building were taken away early in the present century. They were used to build a private house in Larrahirrel.

CRACKENAGH: This is probably the school which appears under the name "Templemoyle" in the reports of the Hibernian Sunday School Society[30] for the years 1813 to 1829. The number of pupils in attendance in the first year was 90. The Irish Education Society report for 1826[31] shows that the teacher here was John McLoughlin, who was in receipt of an income of £10 per year. The school building was in bad order and measured 15 feet by 11. The number of pupils was 20, all of whom were Catholics. It was supported by the parish.

The school at Aghaclay succeeded this one, both Crackenagh and Aghaclay being in the townland of Templemoyle.

CULDAFF: A school existed here from the seventeenth century onwards. Records[32] show that in 1686 the rector was also the schoolmaster. In 1693 the rector is warned that he must appoint a teacher. John Gill was schoolmaster in 1718. The location of the school is not stated. There is a reference in local tradition to the Fort School which existed here around the beginning of the nineteenth century. It was sited near the old fort in Culdaff.

The Hibernian Sunday School Society[33] had a school here from 1813 until 1829. The number on the rolls varied from 87 (in 1820) to 25 (in 1823). A new school was built in 1822. Records[34] of the Society for Promoting the Education of the Poor show that on the recommendation of the Rev. Edward Chichester the teacher, Alexander Moran, did a period of training as a teacher around 1820. He had already been teaching at Culdaff from 1814.

The Irish Education Society[35] report for 1826 shows that the teacher was still Alexander Moran. He was paid £10 a year. The school is described as a good house which cost £50. The number of pupils was 20, of which 18 were Catholics. The Kildare Place Society was a benefactor of the school, as well as the Hibernian Society.

The Irish Education Inquiry, 1826, shows that there was also a school for girls here, taught by Margaret Mitchell, who received a salary of £5. It was in a separate building and was described "as an excellent room". Mrs. Young, wife of the landlord, was the sponsor and she paid the teacher's salary. The number in attendance was 47 — 20 Catholics, 20 Protestants and seven Presbyterians. This school was subsequently merged with the other school operating in Culdaff.

By 1838, according to the Endowed Schools Commission of 1858,[36] the school had ceased to exist because of the establishment of a school at Bocan. The pupils left Culdaff and went to Bocan. The teacher emigrated. In fact, it is possible that the school had ceased much earlier. The school was subsequently re-opened and came under the control of the Board of Education[37] in 1880. The management was in the hands of the landlord, Young. The highest number of pupils was 87, in 1880.

The school was closed in 1970 and Protestants now attend school in the neighbouring parish.

A new school, St. Buadan's, under the management of the parish priest was opened in 1982. The number on the rolls in 1984 was 154.

CULKEENY: The first reference to this school is in the Report of the Commissioners of National Education[38] for 1835. From 1846 to 1856 two schools are shown, one for males and one for females. The separate school for females closed because "the school was not required and the teacher was irregular in attendance". The highest number of pupils was 260, in 1858.

The school was closed in 1969. A new school for the Glengad area was opened at Ballymena in 1969 — Scoil Cholm Cille.

DRISTERNAN: The earliest reference to this school is in 1820,[39] During the years 1820 to 1823, inclusive, a school operated here under the control of the Hibernian Sunday School Society. The total number of pupils varied from 62 (in 1820) to 22 (in 1823). It is evident that a school existed here at an earlier date. It was probably founded soon after the Penal Laws were relaxed to permit Catholics to have schools of their own.

The Irish Education Inquiry of 1826[40] records a school here taught by a teacher called Edward McConollogue. The school was a building 18½ feet by 13 feet. The people of the area paid the teacher and maintained the school. The total number of pupils was 77 — 56 Catholics, 11 Presbyterians and ten members of the Established Church.

Around 1835 the Board of Education[41] decided to give a grant for the building of a school here. At first the intention was to site the school in Moneydarragh but later we find it was decided to build the school for this area at Dristernan. A grant of £125 was made and £62.10.0 was collected locally. The school was in full operation in 1841. A grant was also allowed for the building of a school for females, but this did not materialise.

The highest number of pupils was 335, in 1843. The school is still in operation.

FALMORE: This school was built about 1869 and first appears in the Board of Education report[42] for 1870. The manager and the teacher were members of the Established Church. Later the school came under Catholic control. The highest number of pupils was 110, in 1874. The school was closed about 1930.

The school was built on the land of the local landlord, Nicholson, who was the first manager. The purchaser of Nicholson's estate, Edward O Brien, claimed ownership of the building when the school was closed. A lawsuit ensued between Mr. O Brien and the parish priest, Fr. John H. McKenna.

GLACKNADRUMMOND:[43] In the middle of the nineteenth century the Primitive Wesleyan Methodists started a missionary drive in Inis Eoghain. A school was founded at Glacknadrummond where the Methodist Church now stands. The land was given by George Young of Culdaff House. The school was opened in June, 1857. The building had accommodation for 200 pupils and included living rooms for the teacher. It cost £167.

GLENGAD: The reports of the Hibernian Sunday School Society[44] record a school here between 1813 and 1829. The number of pupils in 1813 was 93. In 1826 the Irish Education Inquiry reports[45] the existence of a school at "Ballyhan", Glengad. The teacher was John McLoughlin. The school was in bad repair and had been erected at a cost of £10. The number of pupils was 40, all Catholics. The school and teacher were supported by the local people.

Do both these references relate to the school at Culkeeny already mentioned ? "Ballyhan" may be a misprint for Balleighan, the townland in which Culkeeny is situated. The name "Glengad" is often applied to an area greater than the townland of Glengad.

GOOREY: The first reference to a school in this townland is found in the Irish Education Inquiry of 1826.[46] In a return dated 9th October, 1824, there is a record of the existence here of a school for females. The number in attendance was 24. The school was connected with the Society for Promoting the Education of the Poor. It would seem that the building was in course of erection during these years and was not completed for a few years. Did this building replace an earlier one ?

The school came under the control of the Board of Education[47] by 1841, when it was a school for both males and females. The management was in the hands of the Harvey family and the teacher was a Presbyterian. Around 1855 it was closed for a couple of years because the average attendance was too low, the building unsuitable and the teacher incompetent. These complaints were evidently remedied, as the school was soon in operation again.

A report of 1852 shows the religious denomination of the children in attendance as 33 Catholics, 31 Presbyterians and two members of the Established Church. The largest number of pupils on the rolls was 124, in 1845. The school was closed about the forties of the present century.

GROUSEHALL:[48] This school was built about 1840 through the activities of the Ball family of Grousehall. The cost was met in part by local subscriptions, in part by a grant from the Erasmus Smith Trustees and the remainder by a donation from the Misses Catherine and Grace Ball and Archdeacon Torrens. The building was large and well-finished and included a residence for the teacher. It was planned to accommodate 128 pupils.

The Trustees of the Erasmus Smith Fund continued to make yearly grants towards the teacher's salary until 1865. The reports of the inspectors show that the cause of the withdrawal of the grant was low attendance. The building was good and the standard of education excellent.

The number on the rolls in 1881 was 38 — 29 Protestants, five Presbyterians and four unspecified.

The school later came under the control of the Board of Education. The erection of the sign "Scoil Naisiunta Ghleann Daoile" showed the changing pattern of Irish history, but the school has been closed since the fifties of the present century.

INISTRAHULL: The first reference we can find to a school here is in the Board of Education report[49] for 1892, when the admission of this school is recorded. It had already been in existence for some time.

A new school building was erected in 1903. The school was closed when the inhabitants left the island in the forties.

The number of pupils in attendance in 1892 was 35. At the time the new school was built an attendance of 60 was envisaged.

KEENAGH: The Report of the Irish Education Inquiry for 1826[50] includes a reference to a school at Meedangormley, Keenagh. The teacher was a Catholic called Owen Rogan and the building was a thatched barn. The number of pupils was 23, of which 22 were Catholics. The school was supported by local subscription. It was already in operation for some time at the date mentioned. It had some connection with the Hibernian Society though its name does not appear in the records.

The school came under the control of the Board of Education[51] in 1840. Two schools, one male and one female, are shown around 1853.

There was, however, only one building.

The largest number of pupils was 283, in 1857. In 1852 there were 170 on the roll — 108 Catholics, 35 Presbyterians and 27 Protestants.

In 1857 the inspector states that the female teacher here had commenced teaching in 1822 under the London Hibernian Society. She had undergone a period of training in 1825 at Kildare Place. Her name was Anna Eliza Young.

This school was under the management of the Harvey family. In later times the teacher and pupils were Presbyterian, as the Catholics ceased to attend here. The school ceased from the second quarter of the present century.

KNOCKAMANY: 52 The Irish Education Inquiry records the existence of a school here in 1826. The teacher was Sarah Warden and her annual salary was £9.5.0. This was paid by local subscription. The number in attendance was 37 — seven Catholics, 27 Presbyterians and three members of the Established Church. The school was held in the teacher's own house. No further data regarding this school are available.

MALIN: The first record of a school here is in the reports of the Hibernian Sunday School Society.53 A school operated here from 1813, or earlier, until 1829. The highest number in attendance during this period was 135, in 1826.

The Irish Education Inquiry of 182654 shows that there were three schools here at that time. The first was in a stone and lime building given rent-free by the Marquis of Donegall, who also gave an annual grant of ten guineas. It was also assisted by the Kildare Place Society. The total in attendance was 75. This number was made up of both males and females and included Catholics, Protestants and Presbyterians. The teachers were Andrew and James Hewston, both of whom were Protestants trained by the Kildare Place Society.

The second school was held in a stone and lime building for which a rent of £2 per annum was paid. The teacher was James Diver, who was paid £15 a year. It was supported by the Hibernian Society and also received a grant of £5 a year from the wife of the local landlord, Harvey. It was a school for male pupils and was attended by all denominations.

The third school was held in a building 24 feet by 18 feet given free by Mrs. Harvey. This was for female pupils and was assisted by the Hibernian Society. All denominations attended this school also.

While it is not clear when these schools ceased as separate entities, it would seem that by 1841 the Board of Education55 had taken over to some extent. In 1852 the total number of pupils here was 151 — 94 Catholics, 36 Presbyterians and 21 Protestants. It was then a non-vested school under the management of Harvey. In the inspector's report for 1857 it is stated that the building consists of two storeys. The lower storey was the post-office and the upper one the school.

In 1890 it was decided to build a new school and a grant was given for a building large enough to accomodate 100 pupils — 50 male and 50 female. By 1894 the building was evidently completed, as the old school was taken off the list in this year.

The highest number recorded on the rolls here was 199, in 1858.

The Protestant school is now closed and the pupils attend a school in the parish of Donagh. A Catholic school was built in 1951 to serve the pupils of Malin Town and its environs, Scoil Threasa Naofa.

MALIN HEAD: The Irish Education Inquiry of 182656 records a school at Ardmalin taught by George Doherty. He earned a salary of £10 a year and taught in a building of stone and mud lent by a poor woman. He had 30 pupils — 28 Catholics and two Protestants. He was evidently supported by local subscription.

The school came under the Board of Education[57] in 1839. For a time two schools, one for males and one for females, existed. In 1843 the female school was closed and the pupils transferred to the other. The management was for a time in the hands of the local landlord, O Doherty, of the Park House. Around 1898 a new building was erected and the old school closed. The school has been rebuilt since in a different place. It is still in operation.

The largest number in attendance was 372, in 1847. This is the most northerly school in Ireland.

REDFORD: A school subsidised by the Hibernian Sunday School Society[58] operated here from 1813. It was sited along the lane leading into the Cloncha rectory, which was in the townland of Dun an Ghrianain. The number in attendance averaged 50.

The society reported on the school up to 1829. About this time the Society for Promoting the Education of the Poor of Ireland[59] became interested, through the action of the rector's wife, Mrs. Hamilton. An inspector of the Kildare Place Society visited the school in 1829 and as a result it received assistance. It would seem that Redford school ceased shortly after the re-organisation of Catholic schools in 1832.

STRATHRODDEN: A school was founded here in about 1829 by the Hibernian Sunday School Society.[60] No further details are on record of this school in the townland of Aghatubrid.

TULLY: The Ordnance Map of 1835 show that there was a school in the townland of Tullymore at that date. In 1841 the school came under the control of the Board of Education.[61] It was under the management of J. Harvey, the landlord. The largest number of pupils was 161, in 1852. The school was taken off the rolls in 1855 as the building was unsuitable. It probably ceased shortly afterwards.

The reports refer to this school as "Tully No. 2". Was there another school in the townland?

UMGALL: A school operated here during the years 1820 to 1823, inclusive. It was sponsored by the Hibernian Sunday School Society.[62] The average attendance was 60.

URBLEREAGH: This school was built in 1857 at a cost of £210, of which the Board of Education[63] gave £140; the balance was collected locally. It was built to accommodate 100 pupils and the management was for a time in the hands of the local landlord. The largest number in attendance was 249, in 1872. The school is still in operation.

———————————⊶⊷———————————

1, 2. *Analecta Hibernica*, Vol. 12: O Kane Papers.
3. *Derry Clergy and Parishes*, Leslie.
4. *Reports of the Association for Discountenancing Vice and Promoting the Knowledge and Practice of the Christian Religion.*
5. *Reports of the Hibernian Snnday School Society for Ireland.*
6. *Dictionary of National Biography*, Erasmus Smith.
7. *Reports of Society for Promoting the Education of the Poor of Ireland.*
8. *Reports of the Hibernian Sunday School Society for Ireland.*
9. *Reports of the National Commissioners of Education.*
10, 11. *Reports of the Hibernian Sunday School Society for Ireland.*
12. *Irish Education Inquiry, 2nd Report, 1826.*
13. *Reports of the Commissioners of National Education in Ireland.*
14. *Ibid.*, 1857.

15, 16. *Irish Education Inquiry, 2nd Report,* 1826.
17. *Reports of the Commissioners of National Education in Ireland.*
18. *Reports of the Hibernian Sunday School Society for Ireland.*
19. *Irish Education Inquiry, 2nd Report,* 1826.
20. *Reports of the Hibernian Sunday School Society for Ireland.*
21. *Reports of the Commissioners of National Education in Ireland.*
22. *Reports of the Hibernian Sunday School Society for Ireland.*
23. *Irish Education Inquiry, 2nd Report,* 1826.
24. *Reports of the Commissioners of National Education in Ireland.*
25. *Reports of the Hibernian Sunday School Society for Ireland.*
26. *Board of Education Report, 1809-1812:* English Schools of Private
Foundation.
27. *Reports of the Hibernian Sunday School Society for Ireland.*
28. *Irish Education Inquiry, 2nd Report,* 1826.
29. *Endowed Schools Ireland Commission, 1858.*
30. *Reports of the Hibernian Sunday School Society for Ireland.*
31. *Irish Education Inquiry, 2nd Report,* 1826.
32. *Derry Clergy and Parishes,* Leslie.
33. *Reports of the Hibernian Sunday School Society for Ireland.*
34. *Report of the Society for Promoting the Education of the Poor o
Ireland.*
35. *Irish Education Inquiry, 2nd Report,* 1826.
36. *Endowed Schools Ireland Commission, 1858.*
37, 38. *Reports of the Commissioners of National Education in Ireland.*
39. *Reports of the Hibernian Sunday School Society for Ireland.*
40. *Irish Education Inquiry, 2nd Report,* 1826.
41, 42. *Reports of the Commissioners of National Education in Ireland.*
43. I, *History of Methodism in Ireland,* Crookshank; II, *Derry Standard,*
June 11th, 1857.
44. *Reports of the Hibernian Sunday School Society for Ireland.*
45, 46. *Irish Education Inquiry, 2nd Report,* 1826.
47. *Reports of the Commissioners of National Education in Ireland.*
48. I, *Endowed Schools Ireland Commission,* 1858; II, *Ibid.,* 1881.
49. *Reports of the Commissioners of National Education in Ireland.*
50. *Irish Education Inquiry, 2nd Report,* 1826.
51. *Reports of the Commissioners of National Education in Ireland.*
52. *Irish Education Inquiry, 2nd Report,* 1826.
53. *Reports of the Hibernian Sunday School Society for Ireland.*
54. *Irish Education Inquiry, 2nd Report,* 1826.
55. *Reports of the Commissioners of National Education in Ireland.*
56. *Irish Education Inquiry, 2nd Report,* 1826.
57. *Reports of the Commissioners of National Education in Ireland.*
58. *Reports of the Hibernian Sunday School Society for Ireland.*
59. *Reports of Society for Promoting the Education of the Poor of Ireland.*
60. *Reports of the Hibernian Sunday School Society for Ireland.*
61. *Reports of the Comm`ssioners of National Education in Ireland.*
62. *Reports of the Hiber.iian Sunday School Society for Ireland.*
63. *Reports of the Commissioners of National Education in Ireland.*

12

POPULATION DATA

IN THE reign of King Charles II of England it was enacted that a tax be imposed on all householders. The basis of the tax was the number of hearths owned by each. The official description is as follows:

A Return of the severall Hearths, firing places and stoves within the county aforesaid by virtue of an Act of Parliament for establishing an additional revenue upon his Majesty, his heirs and successors for ever for the better support of his and their honour and dignity to us and others his Majesty's Justices of the Peace in the said county directed.

The chief value of the record is that it shows the names of the residents of each townland in Culdaff and Cloncha at a time when the native Irish were still largely undisturbed. The surnames of the Irish families are thus preserved and those of the earliest foreigners are shown.

PARISH OF CULDAFF
CASHEL: Knighton, John; Mac Cailin, Dualtach; Mac Rodaigh, Padraig; Mac Earcain, Toirealach; Mac Lochlainn, Donall; Mac Lochlainn, Sean; Mac Lochlainn, Eamann.

CARROWMORE: Mac Cailin, Donall; O Ceallachain, Uilliam; O Ceallachain, Aodh; O Ceallachain, Maghnus; Mac Congail, Sean; O Ceallachain, Maghnus.

BASKILL: Mac Cailin, Niall; O Cearnaigh, Eoghan; Mac Cailin, Muireartach; Mac Lochlainn, Diarmaid; O Brolchain, Eoghan; Mac Cailin, Eoghan; Mac Cairbre, Feidhlimidh.

OURT: Bunbury, John; O Coig, Aodh; Mac Conchuir, Eoghan.

AGHAGLASSON: O Siail, Brian; O Giollain, Niall; Mac Donaill, Eoghan; Mac Ceallachain, Sean; O Cearnaigh, Padraig; Mac Donaill, Brian Og; O Coileain, Niall; O Lonagain, Donall; O Dochartaigh, Brian; O Fearain, Cathal.

MUNEDARAGH: Mac Lochlainn, Brian; Mac Lochlainn, Donall; Mac Lochlainn, Sean; O Rodain, Aodh; O Laoghog, Conchur; O Dubhthaigh, Eoghan.

DRISTERNAN: O hEarcain, Sean; Mac Giolla Chomhain, Maghnus; Mac Cailin, Eoghan; O hEarcain, Aodh; Mac Seafraidh, Brian.

DRUMLEY: O Longain, Sean; O Galloglaigh, Conchur.

AGHATUBBER: Mac Lochlainn, Niall; Mac Cailin, Eoghan; O Cnaimhsi, Eamann; O Cnaimhsi, Maghnus.

BALLEIGHAN: O Cnaimhsi, Diarmaid.

BALLYHARRY: O Cathain, Toirealach; O Dochartaigh, Eoghan; Mac Ficheallaigh, Toirealach; O Laoghog, Brian; O Dochartaigh, Aodh; Mac Eoin, Sean; Mac Ficheallaigh, Feidhlimidh; O Cathain, Aodh.

BALLYMAGARAGHY: Mac Lochlainn, Eoghan; Mac Lochlainn, Eoghan Og; O Tomhnair, Ruairi; O Fearain, Eoghan.

TIRMACRORAGH: O Dubhthaigh, Feidhlimidh; O Cearnaigh, Eam-

ann; O Cearnaigh, Uilliam; O Cearnaigh, Donncha.
DUN AN GHRIANAIN: O Dochartaigh, Sean; O Coileain, Conchur.
DRUMAVILLE: Mac Cormaic, Feidhlimidh.
CEANN DROICHID: O Coigligh, Aibhne; O Coigligh, Donall; O Dochartaigh, Eoghan.
CULDAFF: Butler, George.[1]
LEITRIM: O Clathain, Eoghan; Mac Lochlainn, Eoghan; Mac Connmhaigh, Donncha.
BALLYCARRON:[2] Fleming, Robert; O Dochartaigh, Feidhlimidh; Mac Colgan, Donncha; O Fearain, Feidhlimidh; Mac Ficheallaigh, Eamonn; O Fearain, Toirealach; Mac Colla Eamann; O Dochartaigh, Ruairi.
GLENGAD: Mac Lochlainn, Sean; Mac Congail, Donncha; O Fearain, Seamas; O Dochartaigh, Donall; Mac Congail, Sean; Mac Colla, Donncha; Mac Colla, Cormac; O Brolchain, Conchur; Mac Colla, Aodh.
BALLEIGHAN: Mac Daibheid, Eoghan; O Ciaragain, Maeleachlainn; Mac Lochlainn. Eamann; Mac Daibheid, Toirealach; Mag Reannachain, Feidhlimidh; Mac Lochlainn, Feidhlimidh; O Cnaimhsi, Niall; O Cagair, Toirealach.
CREGCORR:[3] Miller, James; Intyre, John; O Dochartaigh, Cathal.

PARISH OF CLONCHA
LARRAHIRREL: Mac Colgan, Cathal; Mac Colgan, Diarmaid; Mac Lochlainn, Eoghan; Mac Colla, Eoin; O hEarcain, Brian; O Dochartaigh, Conchur.
DUNROSS: Butler, Robert; Breatnach, Sean: Mac Amhlaoibh, Niall; Wilson, Robert.
CARROWTEMPLE: O hEarcain, Sean; O Dochartaigh, Dualtach; O Loingseachain, Connlaodh; Mac Colgan, Eoghan; O hEarcain, Sean; O hEarcain, Uilliam.
DUN AN GHRIANAIN:[5] O Dochartaigh, Uilliam: O Fearain, Maghnus; o Giollain, Seamas.
GREALLAGH:[6] Mac Lochlainn, Seamas; Mac Lochlainn, Eoghan; Mac Lochlainn, Conchur; Mac Lochlainn, Niall Mor; Mac Lochlainn, Niall Og; O Dochartaigh, Diarmaid; Mac Lochlainn, Niall; Mac Lochlainn, Aodh; Mac Crosain, Niall.
BALLEIGHAN: O Ceallachain, Donall; Mac Colla, Connlaodh.
DRUMCARBIT: O Dochartaigh, Niall; Mac Amhlaoibh, Feidhlimidh; O Dochartaigh, Eoghan; Mac Lochlainn, Eoghan; O Maolmhuaidh, Eoghan; Mac Lochlainn, Ruairi.
CARROWMORE: Mac Lochlainn, Sean; O Gormain, Tomas; Mac Gabhann, Feidhlimidh; Mac Cionaoith, Aibhne; Mac Lochlainn, Sean; Mac Mathuna, Donncha; O Dochartaigh, —; O hEarcain, Padraig.
BALLELLAGHAN: O Brolchain, Sean; O Dochartaigh, Feidhlimidh; Mac Congail, Sean; O Brolchain, Toirealach; Mac Seafraidh, Maghnus.
BALLYCRAMPSEY: Mac Lochlainn, Feidhlimidh; Mac Lochlainn, Eamann; Mac Congail, Feidhlimidh; Mac Lochlainn, Diarmaid; Mac Lochlainn, Conchur; Mac Amhlaoibh, Eamann.
CARROWBEAGH:[7] Mac Lochlainn, Uilliam; Mac Lochlainn, Donall; O Cearnaigh, Sean; O Mongail, Eamann.
BALLAGH: Mac Lochlainn, Donncha; Mac Lochlainn, Dualtach.
BALLIEDOY:[8] Mac Lochlainn, Eoghan; O Baoill, Niall; O Doithe. Cormac.
BALLIKENNY: Mac Lochlainn, Eamann; O Dochartaigh, Toirealach; Mac Lochlainn, Aibhne; O Maolmhuaidh, Feidhlimidh; O hEarcain, Sean.
KINAGH: O Muiri, Donall; O Draighneain, Aindreas; O Dubhthaigh, Brian.

BRIGH:[9] O Dochartaigh, Tomas; O Dochartaigh, Eoghan; O Dochartaigh, Sean; O Maolmhuaidh, Brian; O Dochartaigh, Niall.
BALLIGORMAN: O Dochartaigh, Conchur; O Gormain, Eoghan; Mac Lochlainn, Aodh.
KULLOURT: O Dochartaigh, Ruairi; O Dochartaigh, Ruairi Og; O Ciaragain, Niall.
ARDMALIN: O Dochartaigh, Cathaoir; O Dochartaigh, Diarmaid; Mac an Bhreithiunaigh, Brian; Mac Lochlainn, Niall; Mac Cearain, Eamann.

An analysis of the list of householders shown above reveals that in 1665, apart from the Church of Ireland rectors, there were six Protestant householders in Culdaff and two in Cloncha.[10]

A tax of 2/- per hearth was imposed. In the case of Cloncha there was a total of 88 hearths—one to each householder. In Culdaff there were 105 householders and 108 hearths; John Bunbury of Ourt had three hearths and George Butler of Culdaff had two.

Comparison between the Hearth Money Roll and the census data for 1659 shows some differences, e.g., the census shows residents in Tully, Killin and Norrira but no names in respect of these townlands are recorded in the Hearth Money Roll. These householders may have been included in other divisions, as the townlands were not clearly defined until later.

CENSUSES

While the Bible records the taking of a census over two thousand years ago in the territories under Roman control, the practice is of comparatively recent origin in Ireland, as in Europe in general. The earliest attempt at enumerating the people of Ireland was made about 1659 and was associated with the Poll Tax. This census gave us the names then in use of the townlands, indicated the number of inhabitants—stating numbers of Irish and non-Irish—and named the people of standing in each locality. While it gives valuable information, it is not an absolutely accurate record.

Between 1670 and 1815 nine further attempts were made to determine the total population of the country. The first of these was that of Captain South in 1695 and this was followed by others at intervals up to the incomplete Government census of 1814. The first census which can be considered as reasonably accurate was that taken under the direction of the British Government in 1821. A census was then taken at intervals of ten years from 1821 up to and including 1911. The census due to be taken in 1921 was not taken because of the Anglo-Irish War. Under native rule a census was taken in 1926, 1936 and 1946 and thenceforward at five-yearly intervals. The latest census was that taken in 1971.

At the beginning data of a general nature only were recorded; for example the census of 1821 gave population data on a parish basis only. Later censuses went into greater detail and gave information for each townland. In 1926 population data ceased to be published on a parish basis and were given instead on the basis of the District Electoral Divisions.

The data available for the Poll Money Ordinance are set out *in extenso* below.[11]

PARISH OF CULDAFF

Per Record	Present English Form	Total	English and Scottish	Irish
Ballicarron	Carthage	29	—	29
Glangadd	Glengad	40	—	40
Bellichan	Balleighan	31	—	31
Culduff Glebe	Culdaff-Glebe	10	—	10
Teir Mac Crowra	Tirmacroragh	18	—	18
Bellicarry	Ballyharry	20	—	20
Bellimic Gargie	Ballamagaraghy	9	—	9
Drimbilly ½	Drumaville	4	—	4
Cashell	Cashel	21	2	19
Carrowmore	Carrowmore	22	—	22
½ of Waskell	Baskill	5	—	5
¾ of Waskell	Baskill	12	—	12
Augaglasson ½ qr.	Aghaglasson	15	—	15
3 Belliboes of Worth	Ourt	6	—	6
5 do.	Ourt	5	—	5
Leitrim, 2 Belliboes	Leitrim	8	—	8
Cregcorr	Crancor: Part of Culdaff v.	6	—	6
Cullduffe qr.	Culdaff	2	—	2
Munidaragh	Moneydarragh	23	—	23
Dromlee ⅓	Drumley	2	—	2
Dristernan ⅓	Dristernan	8	—	8
Aughatibert qr.	Aghatubrid	11	—	11
Kindroit ⅓	Kindroyhad	5	—	5
	TOTAL:	312	2	310

PARISH OF CLONCHA

Ardmalin qr.	Ardmalin	12	—	12
Brigh qr.	Bree	21	—	21
Belligorman ½ qr.	Ballygorman	10	—	10
Conlurt qr.	Kullourt	14	—	14
Kenagh ½ qr. and ye upper qr. of Cullurt.	Keenagh and Kullourt	19	—	19

Bellikenny qr.	Ballyheeney	15	—	15
Kenagh ¼ qr.	Keenagh	5	—	5
Tully One *Trian*	Tully	5	—	5
Bellidogh qr.	Lagg? See below			
¼ of Granny	Cranny			
Carrowbate	Not identified			
One Belliboe Drunge	Drung	16	—	16
One *Trian*				
Killin One *Trian*	Killin	10	—	10
Belliknawsie qr.	Ballycrampsey	21	—	21
Ballagh qr.	Ballagh	6	—	6
Ballileaghan qr.	Ballellaghan	15	—	15
Norire qr.	Norrira	13	—	13
Carrowmore qr.	Carrowmore	18	—	18
Drumcarbitt qr.	Drumcarbit	21	—	21
Belliraghan ½ qr.	Balleighan	16	—	16
Templemore qr.	Templemoyle ?	14	—	14
Drumovill qr.	Drumaville	17	—	17
Carrowtemple qr.	Cloncha ?	18	—	18
Laracrill qr.	Larrahirrel	16	—	16
Dunrosse qr.	Dunross	21	—	21
Dunogranan one *Trian*	Redford-Glebe	12	—	12
Dristernan One *Trian*	Dristernan	4	—	4
Menedaragh ⅓ of a qr.	Moneydarragh	10	—	10
Grellagh 2 ar.	Grellagh	6	—	6
	TOTAL:	355	—	355

The records name the *tituladores* or persons of standing in each parish. It is probable that these people were, in the case of the Irish, the rector, vicar and *airchinneach* and/or members of the ruling sept and, in the case of the non-Irish, the landowners of note. The names mentioned for Culdaff were George Butler and his sons for the townland of Ballycarron. Owen McDevitt, Balleighan, John Knighton, Cashel, and Donell McAllin, Carrowmore. The persons of standing listed for Cloncha were Cahir O Dogherty, Ardmalin, Thomas O Dogherty, Bree, Edmund Moder McLaughlin and Hugh McLaughlin, Tully, Rory O Dogherty, Kullourt, and Donnell Ballagh McLaughlin, Moneydarragh.

In the enumeration of the English and Scottish there are two recorded for Culdaff. These lived at Cashel and were evidently the family of John Knighton. While George Butler was named as living in Ballycarron, it would seem that he was regarded as Irish. He had probably come from another part of the country and was of the old Norman stock. All the residents of Cloncha were Gaelic Irish. It is clear that the number of planters at this date was very small, as the plantation of this area in large numbers did not commence until later in the century. This is confirmed by the Hearth Tax records taken somewhat later.

The names of the townlands give rise to some queries. The names and extent of these were not stabilised until the Ordnance Survey was completed in the first half of the nineteenth century. The townlands listed for Culdaff are, when allowance is made for spelling variations, almost the same as those of today. The modern townlands of Knock and Muff are not mentioned. "Cregcorr" has not been identified. It may correspond with the modern Muff or Knock, or more likely the townland of Crancor mentioned in the Down Survey map and register. " Cregcorr " is also given in Hearth Money Roll records. Confusion may have arisen through faulty orthography.

A comparison with the modern list for the parish of Cloncha shows that in the Poll Money Ordnance the following townlands are not listed: Dunagard, Meedanmore, Inistrahull, Knockamany, Knockglass, Umgall, Drumballycaslin, Glacknadrummond, Knockergrana, Goorey, Lagg, Drumnaskea, Lougherbraghey, Magheryard and Urbalreagh. It is probable that most of these areas were not then inhabited, the balance being included in the listed townlands. " Granny " is evidently the name " Cranny " which is now applied to a hill in the townland of Drung. " Carrowbate " is a name frequently found in documents of the period but not identified. " Bellidogh " cannot be traced (*Baile Drumhcha*, the town of the sandbanks—perhaps the modern Lagg, where sand abounds).

The townlands of Moneydarragh, Dristernan and Drumley were divided between the parishes of Culdaff and Cloncha. This explains the entry in both parishes of the first and second named.

Table A[12] below shows the total population for each parish insofar as data are available. The records for 1815 are estimated and are based on data supplied by the Rev. Edward Chichester, rector of Culdaff and Cloncha.[13] In view of the fact that he had, for tithe collection purposes, a complete list of the householders of both parishes, his population estimates are fairly reliable. The combined totals for both parishes are shown so that a comparison can be made with the data which follow for the District Electoral Divisions.

TABLE A

Year	Culdaff	Cloncha	Total
1650	312	355	667
1815	4,911	5,955	10,866
1821	5,530	6,130	11,660
1831	5,995	6,682	12,677

1841	5,883	6,778	12,661
1851	5,186	6,049	11,235
1861	4,895	5,929	10,824
1871	4,511	5,366	9,877
1881	4,224	5,066	9,290
1891	3,684	4,505	8,189
1901	3,321	4,142	7,463
1911	3,075	3,924	6,999

Table B shows the total population on the basis of Electoral Divisions from 1926 to 1966. It should be noted that all the divisions are within the two parishes except Termone. The last named includes the townlands of Ballymagaraghy (Moville portion), Leckemay, Carowbeg and Carrowmenagh, which are in the parish of Lower Moville.

TABLE B

E. D.	1926	1936	1946	1951	1956	1961	1966
Gleneely	964	888	884	828	750	667	600
Ardmalin	1,440	1,200	966	931	865	745	712
Carthage	1,114	1,099	1,028	1,048	1,037	956	888
Culdaff	1,099	969	884	945	852	659	660
Malin	941	841	702	787	766	635	601
Termone	818	735	601	537	503	454	430
TOTAL:	6,376	5,732	5,065	5,076	4,773	4,116	3,891

The religious professions of the population are shown in Tables C, D, E and F. Tables C and D show the data on a parish basis, while Table E gives the information on the Electoral Division basis. Table F gives a comparison on a percentage basis.

TABLE C: CULDAFF PARISH

Denomination	1815	%	1861	%	1881	%	1891	%	1901	%	1911	%
Catholics	4,493	92	4,291	87	3,717	88	3,215	87	2,900	88	2,723	88
Protestants	319	6	386	8	329	8	295	8	280	8	236	8
Presbyterians	99	2	178	4	130	3	117	3	92	3	77	3
Methodists	—		40	1	48	1	54	2	49	1	39	1
Others	—		—		—		3		—		—	
TOTAL:	4,911	100	4,895	100	4,224	100	3,684	100	3,321	100	3,075	100

TABLE D: CLONCHA PARISH

Denomination	1815	%	1861	%	1881	%	1891	%	1901	%	1911	%
Catholics	5,426	91	4,988	85	4,225	83	3,767	84	3,463	84	3,293	84
Protestants	270	5	317	5	245	5	220	5	219	5	197	5
Presbyterians	259	4	622	10	586	12	508	11	449	11	419	11
Methodists	—		2	—	10	—	10	—	9	—	8	—
Others	—		—		—		—		2	—	7	—
TOTAL:	5,955	100	5,929	100	5,066	100	4,505	100	4,142	100	3,924	100

TABLE E: Electoral Divisions; Religious Profession

1926	TOTAL	%	Gleneely	Ardmalin	Carthage	Culdaff	Malin	Termone
Catholics	5,547	87	823	1,319	1,069	931	679	726
Protestants	343	5	94	20	40	97	46	46
Presbyterians	415	7	31	97	5	45	205	32
Methodists	52	1	16	1	—	21	—	14
Others	19	—	—	3	—	5	11	—
TOTAL:	6,376	100	964	1,440	1,114	1,099	941	818
1936								
Catholics	5,073	88	771	1,125	1,064	812	631	670
Protestants	272	5	66	11	32	94	39	30
Presbyterians	330	6	33	60	—	45	167	25
Methodists	44	1	17	1	—	16	—	10
Others	13	—	1	3	3	2	4	—
TOTAL:	5,732	100	888	1,200	1,099	969	841	735

1961			
Ardmalin	745	698	47
Carthage	956	942	14
Culdaff	659	578	81
Gleneely	667	601	66
Malin	635	520	115
Termone	454	423	31
TOTAL:	4,116	3,762	354
PERCENTAGE:	100	91	9

TABLE F: (Percentage of Catholics and Others for Combined Area)

Year	Catholic	%	Others	%	Total
1815	9,919	91	947	9	10,866
1861	9,279	86	1,545	14	10,824
1881	7,942	85	1,348	15	9,290
1891	6,982	85	1,207	15	8,189
1901	6,363	85	1,100	15	7,463
1911	6,016	86	983	14	6,999
1926	5,547	87	829	13	6.376
1936	5,073	88	659	12	5,732
1961	3,762	91	354	9	4,116

The foregoing statistics require little comment. The steady downward trend of population in the whole area began after 1841. The ten-year period which included the Great Famine of 1847 showed the largest decline. This trend continued until 1946, when we find a slight increase between 1946 and 1951. The downward trend then resumed, until the latest census in 1966. The decrease on the figure for 1831, the highest shown, was

almost 70% by 1966. For every ten inhabitants in 1831 we had three in 1966 !
The data for the religious denominations of the area show that Catholics were 91% of the total in 1815—the highest until we reach 1961, when again Catholics and others were exactly 91% and 9% respectively. The non-Catholic section of the community held a stable percentage up to the beginning of the present century. The decline then set in even before the re-establishment of native rule. This continued to 1961—the 1966 census did not concern itself with religious denomination.

It may be noted that, of the non-Catholic denominations, Protestants predominated in Culdaff and Presbyterians in Cloncha. The religious persuasion of the landlord who, in each case, arranged the eighteenth-century plantations can thus be deduced.

TABLE G: Census

D.E.D.	1971	1979	1981
Ardmalin	693	707	746
Carthage	857	941	1002
Culdaff	621	745	769
Gleneely	565	635	648
Malin	552	569	542
Termone	390	375	374
TOTAL	3,678	3,972	4,081

IRISH SPEAKERS

The survey undertaken in 1926 by Coimisiun na Gaeltachta shows the following:

D.E.D.	Irish only	Irish & English
Ardmalin	—	127
Carthage	5	270
Culdaff	—	89
Gleneely	—	54
Malin	—	71
Termone	—	17
TOTAL:	5	628

These figures mean that almost ten *per cent.* of the people were still able to speak Irish as late as 1926. The total figure for Inis Eoghain Rural District at the same time was: Irish only, 22; Irish and English, 2,889.

TABLE A: Christian Names in Records up to 1665[14]

IRISH FORM	ANGLICISED OR LATINISED	FREQUENCY
AIBHNE	Uffney	4
AINDREAS	Andrew	1

AODH	Hugh	9
ARALT	Harold	1
BRIAN	Bernard	10
CATHAL	Charles	4
CATHAOIR	Cahir	1
——	Comedinus	1
CONCHUR	Nogher	9
CONNLAODH	Conleth	2
CORMAC	Cormick	2
DAITHI	David	1
DEASUN	Desmond	2
DIARMAID	Jeremy	4
DONALL	Daniel	12
DONNCHA	Denis	6
DUALTACH	Doalty	4
EAMANN	Edward	11
EOGHAN	Owen	26
FEIDHLIMIDH	Felim	16
SEOIRSE	George	1
ANRAI	Henry	1
MANUS	Manus	7
MAELEACHLAINN	Malachy	1
MUIREARTACH	Murtagh	1
GIOLLA NA NAOMH	Nemias	1
NIALL	Niall	15
PADRAIG	Patrick	8
PILIB	Philip	1
ROIBEARD	Robert	3
RUAIRI	Rory	7
SEAMAS	James	4
SEAN	John	1
SITRIC	Sitrig	1
SOLAMH	Solomon	2
TOIREALACH	Turlough	8
TOMAS	Thomas	3
UILLIAM	William	5

TABLE B: Surnames in Records up to 1665

IRISH FORM	ANGLICISED	FREQUENCY
——	Bunbury	1
BREATNACH	Walsh	1
MAC AMHLAOIBH	McCauley	1
MAC AN BHREITHIUNAIGH	Brehony	1
MAC CAILIN	Mac Callion	7
MAC CAIRBRE	Carbery	1
MAC CEALLACHAIN	Callaghan	1
MAC CEARAIN	Mac Carron	1
MAC CIONAOITH	Mac Kinney	1
MAC COLGAN	Mac Colgan	5
MAC COLLA	McCullagh	6
MAC CONCHUIR	McConnor	1
MAC CONGAIL	McGonigle	5
MAC CONNMHAIGH	McConnaway	1
MAC CORMAIC	McCormick	1
MAC CROSAIN	McCrossan	1

MAC DAIBHEID	McDaid	2
MAC DONAILL	McDonnell	2
MAC AN MHILE	McEvilly	2
MAC EOIN	Mac Keown	1
MAC FICHEALLAIGH	Mac Feeley	3
MAC GABHANN	McGowan	1
MAC GIOLLA CHOMHAIN	Kilcoyne	1
MAC EARCAIN	Harkin	1
MAC AN tSAOIR	McIntyre	1
MAC LOCHLAINN	McLoughlin	40
MAC MATHUNA	McMahon	1
MAG REANNACHAIN	McGrennaghan	1
MAC RODAIGH	McGroody	1
MAC SEAFRAIDH	Mac Sheffrey	2
MUILLEOIR	Miller	1
O BAOILL	O Boyle	1
O BROLCHAIN	Bradley	6
O CAGAIR	?	1
O CATHAIN	O Kane	2
O CEALLACHAIN	O Callaghan	5
O CEARNAIGH	Kearney	6
O CIARAGAIN	Kerrigan	1
O CLATHAIN	Clathan	1
O COIG	Quig	1
O COIGLIGH	Quigley	2
O COILEAIN	Collins	2
O CNAIMHSI	Bonner	
	Crampsey	5
O DOCHARTAIGH	O Doherty	29
O DOITHE	O Diff	1
O DRAIGHNEAIN	Dreenan	1
O DUFAIGH	Duffy	10
O FEARAIN	Farren	6
O GABHANN	Smith	1
MAC AN GHALLOGLAIGH	Gallogley	1
O GIOLLAIN	Gillen	2
O GORMAIN	Gorman	2
O hEARCAIN	Harkin	10
O LAOGHOG	Logue	2
O LOINGSEACHAIN	Lynchehaun	1
O LONGAIN	Lanagan	1
O MAOLMHUAIDH	Molloy	3
O MAONGAIL	Monagle	1
O MUIRI	Murray	1
O MAOILEAIN	Moylan	1
O RODAIN	Rudden	1
O SIAIL	Shiels	1
O TOMHNAIR	Tonner	1
O CUILL	O Quill	1
PLEAMANN	Fleming	1
DE BUITLEIR	Butler	2
MAC LIAM	Wilson	1
O DONAILL	O Donnell	1
DE LASA	Lacy	1
O MORAIN	Moran	1
O LAIBHEARTAIGH	Lafferty	1
O MUIREASAIN	Morrison	1

1. In the 1659 census George Butler is shown as residing in Ballycarron.
2. Carthage.
3. Crancor., now part of the townland of Culdaff.
4. Townland of Cloncha.
5. Townland of Redford-Glebe.
6. A district which corresponds with the modern townlands of Drumballycaslin, Drumaville and Templemoyle.
7. Probably the modern townland of Drung.
8. Probably the modern townland of Lagg.
9. Townland of Bree.
10. More accurately, there were eight householders who had non-Irish names. The fact that they were Protestants is verified in later records.
11. *Census of Ireland* circa 1659.
12. *Census of Population*, years 1821 to 1966.
13. *Mason's Statistical Survey*, 1816: "Culdaff and Cloncha," Edward Chichester.
14. I, Hearth Money Rolls, 1665; II, *Calendar of Papal Registars, 1417-1486*.

13
MEANS OF LIVELIHOOD

THE BASIC and fundamental urge of all animals is the quest for the food necessary to sustain life. In this regard the human animal is in no way different. The next requirement is a temperature in which life can be lived. Nature has fitted the lower order of animals with the necessary covering to ensure survival. Man, however, has to take deliberate steps to safeguard himself. Hence clothes and houses. When man has developed a society which assures him of the basics for survival—food, clothing and shelter —other desires of his higher nature begin to manifest themselves. In this way the arts develop in a society which has ceased to be pre-occupied with the quest for food and shelter.

In the parishes of Culdaff and Cloncha the inhabitants from the earliest times lived close to nature and drew directly therefrom food, clothing and shelter. It was a hard struggle and almost the totality of activity was involved in the securing of fundamentals. The earliest dwellers sustained themselves through the hunt, the wild fruits of the forest and the produce of the sea. In time the wild animals used for food were exterminated, the forests disappeared and man had to turn to the task of tilling the soil for his sustenance. Farming became the chief means of livelihood and so it remains to the present time.

RECLAIMING AND TILLING THE SOIL

The land was not particularly fertile here. While there was some clay, the greater part of the arable land was reclaimed from bog and marsh. Up to recent times the standard reclamation procedure was to make drains which consisted of a narrow passage two or three feet beneath the surface and covered by stone flags or sods. In clay land the sides of the drain consisted of stones carefully placed while in boggy land the sides were the portion of the soil left at each side undug. In both cases sods or flags were placed across the bottom of the drain, resting on the sides and leaving a narrow passage to allow the water to run into the main drain or stream. The soil was then filled in.

The land was dug with the spade. This digging was and still is called " delving " in this area. As required, sand and/or seaweed was added by being spread lightly over the soil. The land was then seeded and the crop grew. Oats was usually the first crop sown. It should be noted that even when ploughs were avail-

207

able the first turning of the sod was by means of the spade. With the advance of knowledge the plough was introduced—first the wooden and then the iron one. It is not clear when exactly it was introduced, but it was in use here before the year 1800.[1] While oxen were used here at times for ploughing, the horse was the more general. Many of the poorer people had only one horse. Since for many operations two horses were essential, two neighbours co-operated, each loaning his horse to the other in turn.

Man had, through experience, soon realised the importance of fertilising the soil to ensure a better yield of crops. Seaweed, farm manure and lime were used extensively. Along the coast the demand for seaweed was very great. The landlord and the Protestant rector had first claim on the available seaweed. When their requirements were satisfied the people in general had access to what was left. A close watch was kept on the shore and there was much rivalry among neighbours—" first come, first served ".

Burning of the top portion of the soil was done in certain areas here during the last century. It continued despite legislation forbidding it, but on a small scale. The intention was to increase fertility. This it did on a temporary basis but the overall result was harmful. Edward Chichester, writing in 1816, records a curious method of manuring land.[2] When it had been exhausted by a succession of crops and was again destined for potatoes, the middle of each ridge was dug up throughout its whole length and scattered over the surface of the field. The belief was that the soil at this point had retained a higher degree of fertility. He also states that at times peat moss was used as a fertiliser.

CROPS

The chief crops grown were potatoes, oats, barley, flax, cabbage, turnips and, on a very limited basis, rye. Potatoes and oats were largely for human consumption. Barley was grown extensively between 1780 A.D. and 1820 A.D. for distillation purposes and on a more limi ed scale later for animal feeding. Flax was grown for manufacture into linen for some time, but demand declined. A temporary boost was given to flax growing during the Second World War, but afterwards it was grown on a very restricted basis for thatching. Rye was grown on poor soil for human and animal consumption. Cabbage and turnips were grown for animal feeding.

The common rotation of crops around 1800 A.D. was

potatoes followed in successive years by barley, oats, oats again, flax and oats again.[3] At this point the cycle commenced anew. Later the benefits of putting the land out to grass became known and this was practiced generally. At the present time seed potatoes are grown by many farmers for export. The production is closely supervised by officials of the Department of Agriculture, who demand a very high standard. The disease-free soil is well suited to this product.

A noteworthy *lacuna* in the pattern of production here was and is the vegetable garden. The special nutritive qualities of vegetables were and still are largely unknown. Only a few households cultivate carrots, lettuce, onions and other highly valued vegetables.

Potatoes are now planted in drills but at the beginning of the last century the common practice was ridging. In 1815 the rector, Edward Chichester, was the only farmer who planted potatoes in drills in the parish of Cloncha and Norton Butler of Grousehall was the only one in the neighbouring parish of Culdaff.[4] The new method was soon adopted by the whole area.

SOWING

Oats and barley were sown in earlier times by the farmer from a sheet folded round his shoulder. He cast the seed by hand. This method required great care to ensure an even distribution. More modern methods have been in use since 1940.

In the last century potatoes were set by means of a long pole called a " kibber ". This implement was made of wood, pointed at the end and having a resting place for the foot about six inches from the narrowed end. The ridge was prepared and by means of the kibber a hole was made and the potato cut was placed in it. The implement was then withdrawn and the soil closed over the seed.

HARVESTING

The combine-harvester of to-day is indeed far removed from the implements in use a century ago. For reaping oats and barley up to the end of the last century the hook was used. The scythe followed and was succeeded by the horse-reaper about 1930 here. The combine-reaper followed.

The harvesting of the potato crop was a slow and laborious job until the advent of the digger. Up to the end of the first quarter of this centry the spade was in general use for digging potatoes. Potatoes were placed in well-clayed " pits " in the field until required.

Flax was pulled by hand. Farmers organised a *meitheal* when the crop was ready for harvesting. All the neighbours helped and at night when the work was finished a dance was held.

The stack garden was up to recent years a familar sight when the harvest of cereals was completed. The farmer's status was measured by the number of stacks of oats, etc., in his garden.

The separation of the grain was done in the last century by means of the flail. This was made up of a hazel handle and a striker made of holly. These were bound together by means of a thong of leather. The long winter nights were spent in threshing the oats, etc. The corn was then taken out to the top of a hill for winnowing by means of a hand fan.

The large farmers at the beginning of this century installed mills powered by horses. The smaller farmers took their produce to these for threshing and paid by giving a certain number of days' work, or in some areas a pint of poteen, for each stack threshed. The combine-harvester has now eliminated the horse-operated mill with its familar circular course.

INCREASE IN TILLAGE

In the last quarter of the eighteenth century the area under tillage increased at a rapid pace. Evidence of this can be found to the present day in the traces of ridges to be seen in areas which have now reverted to a wild and untilled state. The steady increase in population was the main cause.

Despite the increased tillage, however, farming methods did not improve. A writer in 1815[5] affirmed that the inhabitants still pursued modes practised in remote places at the beginning of the previous century. The rundale system was seen as an obstacle to development. There were no enclosures and cattle ran over the whole area in winter time, doing much damage.

SIZE OF FARM, 1800—1860

The increase of population led to the division again and again of the holdings, to such an extent that the people lived at bare subsistence level. In good years barely enough food was produced to sustain life at the lowest level and in years of crop failure— either partial or total—a condition of near famine existed. Each decade presented such a crisis.

The average size of holdings of all land, whether arable or

otherwise, can be seen from the data for these years in the nineteenth century:

YEAR	NO. OF HOLDINGS	AVERAGE SIZE (ACRES)
1815	1,894	206
1829	1,557	257
1857	1,841	228

In interpreting the above data it should be remembered that a substantial part of the area consisted of barren land. The average figure therefore included only a small proportion of arable land, say one quarter. The hardships faced by each family can be easily appreciated.

FARMING TO-DAY

The position to-day is the result of the inter-relationship of many factors. The smaller population has led to larger farms. The scarcity of labour has induced less tillage and increased the speed of mechanisation. The agricultural adviser, formerly scorned, is now welcomed. The farmer of to-day is more open to new ideas and is ready to learn how to run his farm better.

The beginning of the Second World War may be noted as a distinctive turning point. The farm labourer left the fields for more remunerative work in England or Scotland. The horse was replaced by the tractor. More generous grants by the Government, together with the arrival of a more sophisticated generation of young farmers, changed the whole approach to farming.

The son of the small farmer refused to marry and rear a family in the poverty-stricken environment of former generations. Many have remained unmarried and many others have gone abroad to earn an easier livelihood. Marriage and a family present less difficulty when a good steady income is assured.

THE FARM LABOURER

Up to the thirties of the present century the larger farmers each employed one or more labourers, who were hired on a yearly basis. The hiring fair was held in Carndonagh each November. Here the farmer and labourer met and agreed on a rate.

The conditions under which the labourer lived depended to a great extent on the attitude of the farmer and his wife. In some cases the labourer was treated as one of the family, sharing the same food at the common table. He had a good bed, clean clothes and good attention in the event of illness.

In other cases the labourer was treated as sub-human. Food was bad, work hard and unremitting, and sleeping quarters a loft in an outhouse. However, emigration and generally improved social conditions soon compelled such farmers to give better treatment to their employees. In time, also, the farm labourer found better conditions in other types of employment. By 1940 no-one was available any longer and farmers had to alter their methods of working. More mechanisation, and less tillage of troublesome crops such as potatoes, was the result. To-day the farm labourer has disappeared from this area.

LIVESTOCK

The livestock in this area are cattle and sheep. Formerly the horse was prevalent. The donkey is only rarely found here. Up to 1940 the horse was in general use for farm work and transport. The large farmers had a number of horses and even the smallest had at least one. The horse in general use was of the heavy type capable of hard work. The pony was used for human transport.

A writer[9] in 1815 stated that the horse then in use was small and ill-proportioned, but had great strength and swiftness. One of the items imported from Scotland at this time was horses.[10] These were evidently small as they were brought over in small boats. Sheep were described by the same writer as small in body, long-legged and coarse-woolled. These animals were kept in great numbers and were allowed to run wild.[11]

The Rev. Edward Chichester attempted to improve the type of sheep here by crossing the native with the Leicester introduced into the north through the action of the Protestant Bishop of Derry.[12] Through the influence of the Department of Agriculture new and better types of sheep and cattle have since evolved. The farmers can therefore secure the highest price available.

COTTAGE INDUSTRIES, ETC.

In the farming community the housewife played a very important part. Her skill and industry were a major contribution in maintaining a healthy balance between income and expenditure.

Poultry

Each farm had its poultry division, consisting of hens, geese, turkeys and ducks. For the purchase of the weekly supply of groceries the eggs produced on the farm were the only means of earning cash.

The older methods of production were often slow and uneconomic. The type of hen, etc., was not fitted to the area. The feeding was not suitable and hatching by hens was too slow. To-day expert advice is available and production is speeded up, at much less cost. Better strains, correct feeding and bulk-hatching all help to give a much better income.

Butter

Nowadays surplus milk is sent to the creamery and the monthly payment received is part of the regular farm income. No creamery was ever established in this area but transport is provided for carrying the milk to creameries outside the district. The sending of milk to the creamery is a modern development. Formerly the milk was churned at home. The churn staff and the old open churn were a familiar sight in each house. Considerable dexterity was needed to wield the staff without splashing the contents out. Some housewives in the second quarter of the present century introduced the small flapper-operated churn. This was more easily worked and time and energy were saved.

There was once a big demand for buttermilk for human consumption. Nowadays it is no longer available, because of the new method of milk disposal.

Spinning, Knitting and Weaving

Up to the early part of this century the spinning-wheel was a normal part of the household equipment. Socks, pullovers and cloth for apparel, etc., were home-produced to a great extent.

The fleece was cut from the sheep, washed carefully and teased by hand. The wool was then greased and carded into rolls. The rolls were spun into yarn on the foot-operated spinning-wheel. The yarn was doubled for knitting but the single strand was used for weaving. In the latter case the yarn was measured by being made into " cuts " on a revolving reel.

The weaver produced the cloth for blankets, suits and other uses. Each district had a weaver who earned his living in this manner and was paid in kind. The weaver has now disappeared. There was one at Malin Head up to 1930.

A fair for yarn and cloth existed at Malin in 1780.[13] About this time, because of the high quality of yarn in the area, a hosiery factory was established in Malin Town. The factory operated for a ten-year period.[14]

In the long winter nights the housewife spent her time in the preparation of wool and in spinning. At times a number of women met in the one house to spin and thus combine their working and social activities.

The Lime-kiln

The visitor to this part of the country will notice even to-day the lime-kiln. There is one on almost every farm. Lime has been used in Ireland for a long time.[15] The limestone was quarried in the area and broken up into small stones. These were placed in the kiln with turf and a fire was placed in the eye of the kiln. The stones were subjected to intense heat and so lime was produced.

The lime was used for white-washing the dwelling-houses and also in building and in land cultivation.

The lime-kiln is no longer in use. To-day crushed limestone is put on the land and the lime required for other uses is bought from large producers. In the earlier part of this century a few small farmers added to their income by burning limestone and selling lime to their neighbours.

Trees

Culdaff and Cloncha are poorly covered by trees. There existed among farmers a strong prejudice against tree growing. Their use as shelter belts was not appreciated. One of the few contributions made by the planters was the planting of trees around their demesnes. Thus, there are large plantings at Culdaff and Malin Town.

The trees most frequently seen here in the wild state are sycamore, elderberry and hazel. Malin Head is too exposed and consequently there are no trees in the tip of the peninsula. The forestry authorities encourage the growing of trees by grants and a free advisory service. Up to the present, however, little progress has been made in educating the farmer in the advisability of tree-planting.

The Production of Turf

Nature provided this area with plenty of bogland. Each family was able to provide the necessary fuel to ensure the provision of a good fire on the hearth for cooking and for heat.

By the end of May each year the scene of activity moved from the fields to the bogs. Each family had a right to unlimited turf. A bank was opened in a way that ensured the draining off of the water. The top layer, on which vegetation was growing, was cleared off. Then the cutter, using a special spade with a cow's horn on the top for a handle, lifted narrow blocks of the virgin bog and threw them on to the bank. A man stood here and spread out the turf in neat rows.

When the top surface was dry the turf was turned to allow the under-surface to dry. Later the sods were placed in " footings "—four on end and one on top. As the turf dried the " footings " were formed into " ricks ", which were made up of four or five footings. The turf was then carted home. The stack of turf was, and is still, to be seen at every country house in the area.

Where the bog was deep and of a certain texture " dabbing " was the method of cutting. A special type of spade was used, for cutting a down-stroke only. A man stood in the bottom of the trench and threw the turf out by hand to the bank, where another man spread the sods out.

When the weather was dry the amount of work involved in turf-cutting was considerably reduced, as some of the drying procedures, such as " footing " and " ricking ", could be omitted.

The method of turf production described above still prevails in this area. For the horse and cart the tractor and trailer have been substituted, but all else remains as in former generations. A vivid recollection of the early part of this century was the constant flow of carts laden with turf from the bogs to the houses scattered over the landscape, and the increasing size of the stacks of turf as load after load was added.

Fishing

Fishing was not, generally speaking, a main source of income for people in this area. It was done on a seasonal basis and provided for many of the small farmers living along the coast a much needed addition to the small income from their farms. Small boats were used and such fishing was attended by many hazards in all except the calmest weather. As a pastime there was fishing with the rod from rocks. On a smaller scale there was some fishing in the lakes and rivers.

The types of fish caught here are char, cod, wrasse, fluke, dogfish (*gubog*), *glasan,* bream (*garbhanach*), haddock, hake, halibut, herring, ling, mackerel, plaice, skate, pollack *(sileog)* and turbot. Seals were caught in Straghbreggagh and other areas and the oil extracted. Crabs and lobsters were also caught.

Some of the fish were retained for consumption by the fishermen's families and the balance were sold, either fresh or dried, in Moville and Carndonagh. From here the fish were sent to other inland towns or exported direct to Glasgow and Liverpool. Cur-

215

ing stations were established at various points. Certain families dried fish at home for use during the winter months.

The best known fishing banks were Dunmore Bank, the Hill and Hollow, Hempton's Bank, Giggan Bank, the Island Bank, Oiternagollapagh, Oitercarrigower and Oiternamweela. The fishermen were able to determine the correct location by landmarks on the mainland of Inis Eoghain.

In the records of the seventeenth century there are two fishing areas mentioned as in the " King's possession ". The right of fishing in Culdaff was one of these. This would seem to have been the property of the old monastery at Culdaff, as the Protestant Bishop of Derry claimed it. The second was Straghbreggagh Bay, which was granted to Sir Arthur Chichester. He leased it to Richard O Dochartaigh, the same person probably who held a freehold at Keenagh nearby.[16]

A report[17] on fishing prepared in the early part of the last century for the parish of Culdaff showed that the number employed was 200—men, 120, youths, 60, and boys, 20—on a periodic basis. The boats which were owned by the fishermen were " Norway yawls " and " square-sterned boats ". The yawls cost £8 each and the second type from £11 to £12. The boats were built " along the coast ". Where, was not stated.

To-day some fishing is carried out at Glengad but elsewhere it survives merely as an interesting pastime. Fishing was a hazardous pursuit because of the small boats and limited knowledge of weather trends. There were many drownings, the stories of which survived in oral tradition up to recent times. Many strange customs and superstitions were associated with fishing.

Distillation.

During the eighteenth, nineteenth and part of the twentieth centuries a considerable number from time to time engaged in illicit distillation to augment their slender income from farming. The number depended to a great extent on the activity of the law. As the pressure from the police lessened stilling increased and *vice-versa.*

Around 1815[18] it was estimated that one pound was made on each " run ". In 1930 an experienced stiller in Ballyharry disposed of his product on a wholesale basis and made a gross profit—labour charge not included—of 18/6 per gallon.

Seasonal Migration

Each year people from this area went to England and Scotland, where employment was secured for two months or so on farms during the harvesting operations. This custom ceased early in the present century.

Shirt-making

During the last century women earned some money by sewing shirts for manufacturers. The scheme was operated through middle-men and the work was done at home.

Emigrants' Remittances

When the older members of large families reached eighteen years or so the fare to the United States of America was secured either from a relative who had already emigrated or through a loan.

When the young people got employment, money was sent home to help parents pay off debts and provide food and clothing for the family. Up to 1940 almost every family had relatives in the United States and were dependent on the remittances sent from abroad.

Kelp

The making of kelp from a certain type of seaweed has been carried out in this district since the beginning of the last century and on a small scale up to the present. Around 1815 the kelp was exported to Glasgow through an agent, who paid the local producer from 3/6 to 5/- per cwt.[19]

Trade with Scotland

There was some trading early in the last century between Scotland and Culdaff.[20] Shetland ponies, herrings and barley were imported and whiskey was exported. The British revenue vessels stopped this trade when carrying out their campaign against illicit distillation.

Tourism

In the second half of the last century North Inis Eoghain, because of its good bathing facilities and beautiful scenery, was frequented by visitors from other parts of Ireland and also from England and Scotland. These visitors stayed in private houses. Little effort was made to develop this industry until after the Second World War. Over the past 25 years, thanks to Government encouragement and local initiative, the numbers coming have increased. Nowadays there are three hotels here and a number of guest houses. In addition, visitors are still catered for in private houses.

Safe bathing, beautiful scenery and a friendly and relaxed

environment are the main attractions for tourists here. Because of the short season—June, July and August—tourism can be regarded as a part-time operation only. Those engaged in it must have some other source of income.

Road Maintenance

A number of small farmers formerly earned a small income by contracting to maintain roads on a yearly basis. The County Council awarded the contracts to persons in each area at a specified sum of money. In practice this gave winter employment to the families who undertook the work. Stones were quarried and broken with small hammers. These were then spread as required, and the road was cleaned and ledged.

This method of contracting has been discontinued. The roads are now maintained directly by the County Council.

Pensions and other Government Aid

The introduction of the Old Age Pension at the beginning of this century was for the poor people a great improvement. The old person, formerly regarded as a burden and an extra mouth to feed, became an important source of income for the whole family. The family which had two old people in receipt of a full pension was regarded locally as being in a very strong financial position.

Nowadays practically every family has a source of income from public sources. This source may be one or more of the following: Old Age Pension, Children's Allowance or Unemployment Benefit.

CONGESTED DISTRICTS BOARD[21]

Under an Act passed in 1891 provision was made for giving help—financial and advisory—to the people of the poorer areas of the country. At local level the scheme was worked through a Parish Committee, which was made up of any or all of the following: clergy of all denominations, the Medical Officer, County Councillors, District Councillors and resident landlords.

A congested district was an area where at the commencement of the Act more than 20% of the population of a county lived in Electoral Divisions of which the total rateable valuation, when divided by the number of the population, gave a sum of less than £1.10.0 for each individual. County Donegal had 89 such Electoral Divisions, and among these were four in the parishes of Culdaff and Cloncha.

The exact areas were as follows:

ELECTORAL DIVISION	COMPRISING THE TOWNLANDS OF
Ardmalin	Ardmalin, Ballygorman, Ballyheeney, Bree, Kullourt, Dunagard, Inistrahull, Keenagh, Knockamany, Knockglass, Meedanmore, Umgal.
Carthage	Balleighan Lr. and Balleighan Upper in Cloncha Parish, Balleighan Lr. and Balleighan Upper in Culdaff Parish, Carthage and Glengad.
Culdaff	Cloncha, Drumaville, Drumballycaslin, Dunross, Glacknadrummond, Gort (Cloncha), Knockergrana, Larrahirrel, Redford-Glebe, Templemoyle, Culdaff, Culdaff-Glebe, Gort (Culdaff), Knock and Muff.
Termone	Ballyharry, Ballymagaraghy, Drumaville, Tirmacroragh.

The Electoral Divisions of Gleneely and Malin did not come under the Act.

The field of activity open to the Congested Districts Board extended to agricultural development, forestry, breeding of live-stock and poultry, sale of seed potatoes and seed oats, amalgamation of small-holdings, migration, emigration, fishing, meaving and spinning, agricultural banks and any other suitable industry.

To help the fishing industry a station for curing cod, ling and saithe was opened at Malin Head and on the island of Inistrahull a station for curing white fish, herrings and mackerel was established. A pier and breakwater were built at Portaleen Bay. A firm of fish merchants asked the Board to provide a qualified fish-curer to instruct the people at Malin Head in the curing of herrings. Only one person attended to receive the instruction, however.

An Agricultural Bank was founded at Ardmalin on the 6th of February, 1903. It had 42 members in 1904 and by 1907 the number had increased to 86. The number of loans given in 1906 was 77 and in 1907, 76.

A grant of £400 was given to a local committee which directed the widening and deepening of the river Ballyboe. Annually a considerable extent of land had been flooded because of defective drainage.

Courses in Domestic Economy were given at Culdaff and Gleneely and carpentry classes at Culdaff and Carrowmore. Lace and crochet classes were held in Culdaff and Gleneely. In 1914 the earnings from lace, crochet and embroidery at Gleneely were £125.10.0.

Grants to the parishes of Culdaff and Cloncha were given as set out below:

YEAR	CULDAFF	CLONCHA
1904	£30	£33
1907	50	75
1908	50	75
1910	45	140
1912	45	140
1913	75	140
1914	75	140

The Congested Districts Board was abolished soon after the end of the British occupation in 1922. The lasting results of its activities were negligible.

*A NOTE ON FISHING BANKS*22
Dunmore Bank affords good summer fishing in 15 to 20 fathoms. To locate the bank open Carriggannagh with Sliabh Sneachta over Dunmore Head. The point of departure is when Culdaff trees begin to open westward and Stuckarudden just appears along the heads.
The Hill and Hollow Bank is found by laying Stuckarudden up the valley of Carnmalin when Inisglass is barely open with Malin Head. When on the middle of the bed Sliabh Sneachta is down the valley of Glengad; then fish northwest until Dughlas is laid on Malin Head. Then the bank is lost in the sound and the boat is in deep water.
Hempton's Bank is considered to be a continuation of Inistrahull Bank, called Oitermore because there are but partial changes of depth upon it for above 20 miles north-eastward. Immediately off Illanaweelog, the easternmost point of Inistrahull, there are from 12 to 15 fathoms upon it. At about a mile there is very good fishing in from 18 to 20 fathoms and at five miles it is not 30 fathoms; and so north-eastward it shallows until the west end of the Croagh of Glengad is brought on Sliabh Sneachta. Eight or nine miles from Inistrahull the depth is from 20 to 22 fathoms and at ten to 13 miles, from 13 to 15 fathoms. It continues with soundings between 20 and 30 fathoms north-eastward until Dunmore Headh is brought upon the top of Sliabh Sneachta. Scotsmen say that it extends almost to the Scottish coast. The existence of this fishing bank was known without doubt to the earlier inhabitants of both Ireland and Scotland. Captain Hempton noted its location in 1778 and gave his name to it.
The Giggan Bank lies about four miles from the coast, running from a little west of Glengad Head to a mile or two east of Glenagivney Port. Fishers from the eastword ake station upon it when Binevna opens with Shroove Point or Inis Eognain Head and the signal tower of Malin Well opens with Stuckarudden. They sail westward and are on the middle of the bank when Sliabh Sneachta bears right up the valley of Glengad. Fishing can commence when Carthage House is brought on with Sliabh Sneachta and can continue eastward with the tide until Croaghdubh bears on the top of Sliabh Sneachta.
*Oiternagollapagh*23 lies south-westward from the Laeck of Inistrahull towards Carrigaveol Head. The bottom mostly shells, with soundings from 12 to 20 fathoms, and it is seldom without surf.

220

Oitercarrigower runs about two and a half miles from off about the middle of the south shore of Inistrahull towards the Garrive Islands and more westward off that direction towards the sound or Soois of Inistrahull.

FAIRS AND MARKETS

Among all peoples the assembly at which business was transacted and at which festivities of various kinds took place was an early development. In Ireland the *feis* and the *aonach* were occasions for buying and selling, athletic competitions and cultural exchanges among all levels of the people.

In Culdaff and Cloncha scant records have survived to inform us of the type or place of such meetings. In the Patent Rolls[24] of James I there is the grant of a yearly fair to Drung in Malin on the 30th October and the day following. The name *Drong* together with the royal grant indicates that there had been a custom of meeting here for business and other purposes. The licence for the fair here was later withdrawn.[25]

At Malin Well there was the custom of holding a meeting on the Feast of the Assumption. This gathering had a religious significance and was associated with the *turas* in honour of St. Muirdhealach. The meeting, known locally as Malin Well Fair, continued to be held up to the middle of the present century.

For a time a weekly market was held at Malin Town[26] for farm produce and yarn.[27] In the middle of the last century it was discontinued. Quarterly fairs were held here on Easter Tuesday, the 23rd of June, the 1st of August and the 1st of November.

At Culdaff fairs were held on the 10th of February, May, August and November. A local tradition says that the days on which fairs took place were invariably wet !

Of a much later date than the fairs at Culdaff and Malin was the quarterly fair at Gleneely Crossroads. This was held on the last Tuesday of February, May, August and November. For a time a grain fair was held weekly at Culdaff.

The development of a well-attended weekly market at Carndonagh tended to reduce the importance of the fairs at Gleneely, Malin and Culdaff. With the organisation of a mart at Carndonagh these fairs have now been discontinued. All the livestock from Cloncha and Culdaff is taken to Carndonagh, where buyers from all over the north attend.

Athletic contests have been held at Malin Head, Culdaff and

Termone. Formerly these were well attended but nowadays more sophisticated entertainment is sought.

———————————◦▒◦———————————

1. *Statistical Survey, Donegal*, 1802, McParlan.
2. *Mason's Statistical Survey*, 1816: "Culdaff and Cloncha," Edward Chichester.
3. *Statistical Survey, Donegal*, 1802, McParlan.
4, 5, 6. *Mason's Statistical Survey*, 1816: "Culdaff and Cloncha," Edward Chichester.
7. *Tithe Applotment Book*, 1829.
8. *Griffith's Valuation*, 1857.
9, 10, 11, 12. *Mason's Statistical Survey*, 1816: "Culdaff and Cloncha," Edward Chichester.
13. *Derry Journal*, March 3rd, 1780.
14. *Derry Journal*, May 22nd, 1792.
15. Colgan's **Tr. Th.** records that in 1163 the abbot of Derry built in the space of 20 days a limekiln 70 feet in dimensions every way to provide lime for the building of the abbey.
16. I, *Analecta Hibernica*, Vol. 3, Rawlinson; II, *Analecta Hibernica:* Ulster Plantation Papers, Vol. 8, P.292.
17. R.I.A.: Ordnance Survey of Ireland. Box 22: Statistical Enquiries on the Coast Fisheries, Culdaff, Documents A and B.
18, 19, 20. *Mason's Statistical Survey*, 1816: "Culdaff and Cloncha," Edward Chichester.
21. *Reports of the Congested Districts Board of Ireland.*
22. Donegal Ordnance Box, Royal Irish Academy.
23. *Oitir* means a bank in the sea.
24. *Irish Patent Rolls:* Patent No. 19, James 1.
25. *Irish Patent Rolls:* Patent No. 19, James I.
26. *Mason's Statistical Survey*, 1816: "Culdaff and Cloncha," Edward Chichester.
27. *Derry Journal*, March 3rd, 1780.

14

A NORTH INIS EOGHAIN HOMESTEAD IN 1930

IN GENERAL, historians and others concerned with the study and recording of the story of the nation have concerned themselves almost entirely with events of major national importance and with the people involved in them. Too little attention has been given to the life of the ordinary people. The so-called " ordinary people " not only constitute the majority of the citizens but are also the life and soul of the country. The throbbing pulse and the beating heart of the nation are found among the people who are concerned with the basics of living and surviving. These are in general the poor, the unknown and the downtrodden.

Anyone interested in the story of Ireland will note with dissatisfaction that practically nothing is known regarding the day-to-day life of past generations. This *lacuna* is a permanent hurdle to a full understanding of the real effect of national events.

In this narrative an effort is made to record some aspects of the life of a typical North Inis Eoghain family during the thirties of the present century. A description of the house, the family and how the latter lived is set out. While removed from us by only one generation, the pace of change has been so great that the intervening forty years have effected a transformation greater than any previously caused by the lapse of a century or more.

THE HOUSE

The visitor to North Inis Eoghain *circa* 1930 will have noted that the typical dwelling-house was a two-roomed, one-storey dwelling. Some had a slated roof but the majority were thatched with flax. The outer walls were white-washed with lime each year and a little patching was done oftener where the lime had been stained or washed away.

There was usually one outer door but in some cases there was also a back door. This last was unpopular because it tended to make the house colder in winter. At the door were placed large stone flags. These were known as the " door-stones " and were always kept washed and clean. From the door-stones a sort of open water passage led to a closed drain. This passage was made of paving stones laid side by side in the soil in such a manner as ensured an incline from each side towards the centre. The name " trinked " was applied to this passage-way, which was designed to take away from the house the water used for washing, etc.

The outer door led directly into the large room and was placed at the point in the outer wall where the inner cross-wall separating the two rooms touched. This large room was known as the " kitchen " and served as living room and dining room, and in many cases as a bedroom for some members of the family.

On entering one noticed that there were two windows, one in the front and a smaller one in the back. By 1930 in most cases the old clay floor had given way to cement but often the *leac na tine* had been preserved. This was a stone flag placed in front of the fireplace. Looking upwards one noted the *bac*—the main cross-beam of bog oak supporting the roof. The wattles and scraths supporting the roof were visible. Later the custom was to cover the inside of the roof with bags. These gave way to a ceiling of timber later again.

In the upper section of the kitchen, to the right of the fireplace, one noticed a bed surrounded by curtains. Here the boys of the house slept. In some houses a settle-bed was used instead. This was an item of furniture which served as a bed at night and a sort of couch by day. Around the kitchen seats were placed. These were known as forms or stools. There was no back support on this type of seating. Chairs were rarely used. By the fireside there was placed a low backless seat known as a " creepy ". This was made usually of a solid block of bog oak or fir. A plain deal table completed the furnishing of the kitchen.

Against the wall between the two rooms stood the dresser. On the upper portion of this was displayed the delph ware— bowls used for porridge and tea, plates and, on top, a row of large willow-pattern platters. The last-named were for display rather than use. The lower portion contained a cupboard in which such items as bread, tea and sugar were stored.

One also observed the churn and churnstaff, the spinning wheel and the reel. The last named was a device for measuring the yarn and forming it into " cuts " for despatch to the weaver.

THE HEARTH

The focal point of the house was the hearth. This was formed of paving stones placed edge to edge and was slightly raised above the level of the floor. The fire burned here constantly. The crane was fixed at one side and extended across the fireplace so that pots could be placed directly on top of the fire. The crooks attached to the crane allowed the pots to be positioned at different levels.

At night the fire was " raked ". Two red coals were laid on the hearth, turf was placed on each side and the ashes were piled over these. By morning the turf had become red coals as well and served to light the fire. Through the link established by the " rakings " the fire had continuity with the dead generations back to the time when first a fire was lit on the hearth. That primal fire was lit from that of an older house and so linked up with still earlier generations.

Here by the hearth at night, and especially in the winter, sat not only the family but also friends and neighbours. By this communal contact the story of Ireland and its folklore were transmitted orally by the story-tellers. Stories were told and re-told because time was plentiful in the long winter evenings of a leisurely age. No radio or television marred the peace and serenity of life in those days.

No memory remained so vivid in the mind of the emigrant in New York, Boston or elsewhere as that of the homely gathering by the fireside in an Inis Eoghain cottage during the winter. It was the scene of so many sorrows shared by sympathetic neighbours and of so many joys multiplied by the presence of friends. With longing the exile sang:

> Houses grand on a foreign strand
> Cannot be compared at all
> To a cottage bright on a winter's night
> In the hills of Donegal.

" THE ROOM "

The second chamber in the house was known as " the room ". Here usually the female members of the family slept. Two beds were placed along the back wall. Between the beds was formed a small room used as a wardrobe and above the beds was the " tester "—a sort of attic. This room was largely unused save as a bedroom. Important visitors were entertained here, however, and on Station Day the priest officiated in it. It became to a great extent the show-piece of he family.

THE WELL

Leading from each house could be seen a well-worn rodeen or footpath which indicated the position of the well. The clear water for human consumption was drawn from here. It was a well-cared-for spot, fenced around and protected from animals and any danger of contamination.

The well always had a special place in rural appreciation. Around it there was a certain indefinable aura: it was a sort of cult which went back to pagan times. The traditional " holy well " is well-known but it should be remembered that every well from which water was drawn for human consumption was given a unique ethos.

The value placed on wells and the particular mention of them in the Bible is a point worthy of note. While the scarcity of water gave a special primary reason in Israel for this well-honour there was an additional cult which seems to emanate from early times and which was common to Celt and Hebrew. Is there a suggestion that in early times pure water was regarded as a special gift from the gods who dwelt deep in the earth ?

THE FAMILY

The father concerned himself chiefly with the tilling and management of the farm. His field of activity was the " outside ", while within the house the mother was undisputed queen. Endless patience, careful planning and a good measure of foresight were all essential to ensure that a growing family had sufficient food and adequate clothing. At the same time, to present an appearance of modest prosperity in accordance with the norm of the age was vital for the status of the family. Money desperately required for food and/or clothing was often used to pay offerings at funerals or the priests' stipend. It was considered better to go hungry or barefoot than default where failure meant loss of face. " Keeping up with the Joneses " had its impact here too.

Some poet sprung from the heart of such a community as existed in Inis Eoghain in those days has yet to express in a full and fitting manner the work of the Irish mother placed in such an age, in such a time, in such a society. If he records rightly he will tell a tale of unselfish devotion, of hard, unceasing toil, of altruism of the highest order and of heroic patience in the midst of privations and frustrations.

The children were born into an atmosphere of high spiritual standards and of security. As families were large there was little of luxury, but affection and love made an adequate compensation. From their earliest years the children were taught the discipline of hard work. Each child, whether male or female, made its contribution to the farm work in accordance with seasonal demands.

FOOD

Neither the food itself nor the cooking of those days was of an order to satisfy either the appetite of the gourmand or the discerning taste of the gourmet. Yet it produced a people strong in body and clear in mind. Quantity was more important than the quality.

All the food was cooked on the open fire. The familiar utensils were the metal kettle for boiling water, the cast-iron pot for boiling potatoes and making porridge, the griddle for baking the large soda cake, the grid-iron for cooking the oaten cake, the bastible for baking and roasting meat and the old black-pan for making tea. The elegant teapot was still a vessel of the future. The delph bowl for tea and other liquids was in general use in place of the cup and saucer which came into vogue a decade or so later.

In a large bin with separate compartments flour, oaten meal and Indian meal were stored for human consumption. The oaten meal was produced from the corn grown on the farm and ground in the mill. It was the custom for each family to get a quantity of oaten meal ground each year about November to provide bread and porridge during the winter.

Breakfast, eaten about eight o'clock in the morning, consisted of tea, bread and sometimes an egg and/or butter. Very often, however, the eggs and butter were sold to secure such items as tea and sugar. The bread was home made and was either soda or oaten. Occasionally the housewife baked from potatoes a type of bread called " fadge ". The soda bread may have been made from flour or a mixture of flour and Indian meal.

" Ten o'clock tea " was a custom in most areas. Tea and bread constituted this collation, which was eaten in the field in the case of those working on the farm.

Dinner, at one o'clock, was eaten in the house together by all the family. Potatoes, milk and butter were the normal fare. Occasionally fish was available, but meat very rarely. The potato was the most important part of the diet. At times the potatoes were boiled in their jackets and at times they were made into " poundies " by peeling and mashing. If the potatoes were plentiful the family was assured of enough food throughout the year. Often, however, there was a lean period during mid-summer and many families suffered hunger, as money was not available to secure any alternative food.

At around five o'clock tea and bread were again taken. This collation was known as the " evening tea ". In summer this meal was brought to the men at work in the fields.

Supper was taken around ten o'clock. *Brachan*, made of either oaten meal or Indian meal, was eaten. Milk was added, and salt or sugar according to choice.

Meat was eaten two or three times each year. Fish was used more frequently and at times other edible foods from the sea, such as *bairnigh* and winkles. Crabs were also eaten. Apart from the potato, there was very little use made of vegetables.

EDUCATION

Many of the older people were illiterate, though not lacking in education in other senses. Generally parents encouraged children to attend primary school up to fourteen years, but no longer. The child at this age was needed urgently to work on the farm.

Apart from the pressing need for the children's labour on the farm, there was also the insurmountable hurdle of finance in the way of securing secondary education. Attendance at college meant a commitment in respect of board, lodging, fees and books which was far beyond the capacity of 98% of the people. The result was that these young people of North Inis Eoghain entered life ill-prepared. Despite such great qualities as intelligence, honesty and reliability, the young man or woman from this area had to accept abroad the most menial and lowest-paid jobs.

It is noteworthy that the children of these emigrants were, through the efforts and initiative of their parents, able to secure better education and thus passed into the middle-class society of the community in which they lived.

The parents of North Inis Eoghain, and also the community at large, were a powerful force in the character formation of the young. Hard work, self-discipline, a high standard of honesty and a strong religious sense gave them a good and firm foundation on which to build their lives. This gave to the country to which our young people emigrated valuable citizens.

RELIGION

In the life of the individual, the family and the community of the 'thirties religious beliefs were a powerful motivation. There was a total observance of external participation in public worship. Honesty and all the other virtues relating to human relations were observed even where such demanded sacrifice. Their deep awareness of eternity made the people conform to a high spiritual standard and enabled them to endure much hardship. Whether all fully accepted intellectually what was specified in matters of belief and morals is not clear. However, the community pressure was strong enough to ensure external acceptance and thus produced a very high standard in general.

The moral level was, in consequence, of a high standard. Illegitimacy was very rare and crimes such as theft and burglary were unknown. It must be admitted, however, that the community pressure was so strong that cases involving sexual aberrations of all kinds were kept a close secret. Each townland was jealous of its good name and so zealous in safeguarding it that sealed lips were presented in many cases of crimes to civil and ecclesiastical authority.

The clergyman held a high place in the community and his word was often law in matters far removed from his field. However, while there was profound respect there was not a blind acceptance. In matters of politics many refused to be influenced in any way by the clergy. This took place without in any way impairing their loyalty to the Church or respect for its ministers.

SOCIAL LIFE

The maintenance of healthy human contact is an expression of a normal and deep-seated human desire. This contact is essential for the development and preservation of a well-rounded personality. In the society under examination there were few formal gatherings but there was a highly-developed though informal social life. Each day, from early morning, neighbours dropped in for a chat in passing. The latest news was exchanged and discussed. At night, especially during the winter, *ceili*-ing was the custom. Each house had its quota of visitors who came around seven and stayed talking until eleven o'clock.

Radio and television were still in the future. There was but little contact with life outside the parish, and very few families took in a daily or weekly newspaper.

Other sources of human contact were the church on Sundays, the fairs and markets, an occasional visit to Derry, and to the corpse-house when a neighbour died.

A society of this kind had a certain stability, as there was little to make unfavourable comparison possible— a major factor in creating discontent. On the other hand, stagnation and dullness were a serious danger and could lead to discontent among

229

the young people, who rightly would seek more exciting activities.

A great limitation was the failure of those people whose position gave them a chance to act as leaders. The clergymen and teachers made no effort at leadership in fields outside their own day-to-day work. There was urgent need for such activities as would give the people an outlet for their talent and creative powers. The result was that the community made no contribution in the fields of sport or the arts.

BREAK-UP OF THE FAMILY

As the average farm was small, only one member of the family remained on the old homestead. Emigration was the only outlet in those days. Often five or more of one family would leave in turn for New York, Boston or some other part of the United States.

The break-up of the family had a more serious emotional effect in those days, when America seemed so distant and so few returned. The parents felt the separation keenly. The farewell party earned in some areas the doleful title of " Irish wake ".

CONCLUSION

As already pointed out, the pace of change in the forty years which have elapsed since 1930 has been very rapid. The Second World War directed the minds of the people outwards. Better communications have made them much more aware of the world in general, and by means of radio and television people are kept fully informed of national and international affairs.

The horse has given way to the tractor. The motor-car has drastically reduced distances. A new and more sophisticated society has evolved. Old customs are despised and the trend is to imitate what is seen abroad. The standard of living has vastly improved but the charm, dignity and simplicity of the older order are disappearing. Much that was distinctive of Inis Eoghain is passing and the community is much the poorer by the change.

15
SOME DISTINCTIVE MANNERS, BELIEFS AND CUSTOMS

THE DISCERNING onlooker will see in the customs and beliefs of North Inis Eoghain a mixture of the old pagan order and the Christian civilisation which followed. Paganism did not disappear, nor did Christianity replace it. Both merged, and many practices continued and many beliefs were entertained which would make the theologians—both moral and dogmatic—wince.

To-day a new generation is growing up which no longer believes in the old beliefs or practise the customs we relate. There are, however, areas where the beliefs and the practices are both still part of the pattern of living. But it is only a matter of time until the new and sophisticated order of things will prevail completely.

The full rich lore of the people in Culdaff and Cloncha is not recorded *in extenso*. A selection is made to show to some extent the customs observed and the beliefs held here.

NEW YEAR'S DAY

To ensure good luck during the whole year nothing was taken out of the dwelling-house. Ashes remained on the hearth and all water used for washing was saved in a large receptacle. Early in the morning water was taken from the well and salt was added. Each member of the family took three sips, invoking the protection of the Holy Trinity. The remainder of the water was given to the livestock. This was to protect family and animals from evil.

" LA 'LE BRIDE "

Rushes were cut on the afternoon of the eve of the feast. When darkness had fallen the head of the family went out and the door was closed. The head came to the closed door with the rushes in hand and, going on his knees, said in Irish: " A Bhrid na bratoige ! Oscail do shuile. Eist le Brid. Gabh ar do ghluine". From within the reply came: " 'S e do bheatha ".

The sheaf of rushes was spread on the table. Then a meal of mashed potatoes and butter was placed on top of the rushes for the whole family.

When the meal was eaten all the family took part in the making of the rush crosses. Sufficient crosses were made to allow one over each door and window in the dwelling-house and one for each outhouse. The crosses, together with a piece of cloth, were placed in a basket and left outside all night for the blessing of St. Brigid.

Early on the morning of the feast-day, the basket was brought into the house. Then the whole family went to Mass and on returning the crosses were placed in position. The cloth, known as the *bratog Bhride*, was kept for use in case of sickness.

" LA BEALTAINE "

In each townland it was considered that the house from which the smoke first ascended on the morning of May Day incurred all the bad luck for the year. On the other hand, the first at the well in the morning had the good luck for the following year. The result was that there was much competition to get early to the well and to be later than the neighbours in lighting the morning fire.

A maypole was erected and around it the young people sang and danced. On the eve a fire was lighted on the street and the cows were driven through the smoke and the embers.

HALLOW EVE

This was known as a night on which spirits of all kinds were abroad. In the evening a ceremonial supper was held at which the whole family was present. Salt and meal were mixed and rubbed into the crown of the head in the name of the Father, the Son and the Holy Ghost as a protection against evil.

ALL SOULS' NIGHT

It was the custom on this night to sweep the kitchen floor carefully and put on a good fire to welcome the souls of dead relatives who were still in Purgatory. On the following morning the discerning eye could see the mark of feet in the ashes. If the footprints indicated a person facing the fire all was well but if they pointed towards the door a death would take place in the family during the coming year.

EMIGRATION

To wish the emigrant going to America a safe journey it was usual for the neighbours to come and spend the night before the departure in the house. Dancing and singing continued until the morning. As each visitor brought a bottle of poteen, this type of function was know here as a " bottling ". The availability of so much whiskey had an exhilarating effect on the proceedings !

DISEASES

Many types of cures were available to the believing. For example, the cure for mumps was to put a donkey's bridle on the patient and lead him across a stream. The pair leading the patient were a man and wife who had the same surname.

THE SEA

Many were the customs associated with the sea and fishing. No wise boatman ever placed a white stone in his boat, because such a stone caused bad luck. It was unlucky to lift a dead body when out at sea. Stories are told of fishermen who refused to lift a body even though it was known to be the corpse of a neighbour or friend.

One story indicates that bad luck was associated with the drowned whether the corpse was on land or sea. A Malin Head woman residing at Dun an Ghrianain had a number of brothers engaged in fishing. Two of them were drowned and came in on the evening tide to Redford port. Her husband refused to allow the bodies to be brought into the house. A message was sent to the relatives at Malin Head and throughout the night the woman kept vigil alone by the side of the bodies lying on the seashore.

WITCHES

A typical story is related in various parts of North Inis Eoghain. Each area has its own localised version. One storyteller in Drumaville related that a hare was chased through the townland and was injured in the leg when passing through a pipe. The trail of blood was visible up to a named house in Ballymagaraghy . On the following day the old woman of the house was found in bed with an injured leg. She was reputed locally to be a witch. The current belief was that witches took the form of a hare to secure milk from the neighbours' cows.

LIVESTOCK

It was important to ensure good luck for cattle and other livestock. A horse-shoe was placed above the door of the byre and stable to protect against evil. A neighbour invited to look at the livestock always said " May God bless them ", as otherwise he would be suspected of " blinking ". Certain people were considered to be unlucky and if these looked at the livestock sickness and even death could ensue. Each area had its own two or three suspects.

Sometimes the fairies would " shoot " a cow or horse and illness would follow. However, there was always a man who could cure the animal by methods not known to the veterinary surgeon. One such was Tomas Mac Criostail, a man of skill and knowledge in dealing with the powers of evil.

Called to a sick cow in Gleann Tuaiscirt, he measured the cow " in her length and in her width with his right arm from his elbow to the tip of his finger ". He thus located the point at which the fairy shot entered. "How long is the cow sick?" asked Tomas. " About three days," said the anxious owner as he viewed the expert at work. " She will be sick as long until she is well," replied Tomas in his native Irish. He then asked the woman of the house to boil two half-pennies in the milk of a newly-calved healthy cow coloured black. Such a cow was found in Malin Glen and the owner was glad to oblige. The milk and coins were boiled and Tomas gave the mixture to the sick cow. Bestowing a blessing on all, Tomas set out for home on his cart. As he was travelling up the hill at Portaleen, the cow quietly died !

It is fair to state, however, that Tomas treated his share of healthier cows with greater success before and after.

A silver coin was always placed in the bottom of the bucket when milking a newly-calved cow. The wise housewife when churning placed the skin of a hare on the door or alternatively tied around the churn a rope made from the hair of a cow's tail.

PRESENTS

Care was taken when giving anything away to ensure that the giver was not disposing of his good luck as well. If the present was a fish, salt should be placed on its tail; if a neighbour came for a live coal, let him put a turf on the fire before he left.

DEATH

The customs associated with death were more numerous and have been observed much longer than any of the others mentioned.

Death was surrounded by awe, fear and mystery. Signs were evident among the neighbours and also at times visible to the members of the family concerned when death was coming—a wraith in the night, a warning dream, the person concerned seen at a distant place even though known to be in bed, and so on. The lore of the people abounded with suchlike warnings. The dull and unimaginative would miss the signs but the alert Celtic mind did not. The spirit world was as real to it as the potatoes and butter eaten at dinner.

When a death took place all the families in the townland were informed. Work in the fields ceased until after the funeral and the neighbours gathered in the house of the bereaved. Two of the men went to get the " dead-clothes " and the women began to prepare the corpse for the " laying-out ".

At the moment of death the clocks were stopped and all mirrors turned towards the wall. In some places the window nearest the death-bed was opened.

The " laying-out " consisted in washing the body, dressing it in the shroud and placing it on the bed, which was covered with linen sheets. All taking part in this function were compelled by custom to take a sip of whiskey.

The corpse was kept for two days and two nights after death. The day period was called the " corpse-hour " while the night vigil was termed the " wake ". Neighbours visited the house, sympathised with the relatives and prayed by the bed on which the corpse was laid. Refreshments in the form of tea, poteen and other beverages were available to all. Clay pipes filled with tobacco were given to the smokers. The wake was attended by the young people, who remained until the morning. The Rosary was said at midnight.

On the morning of the funeral the corpse was placed in the coffin in the presence of all the relations and the Rosary was said again. The " first and last lift "—the carrying of the coffin to the hearse at the house and the bearing of it later to the graveside from the church—were honours given to the nearest relations. The funeral went to the graveyard by the longer road if more than one way were available.

Inside the house the women were very active to ensure that all the arrangements associated with the laying-out were undone before the corpse had left the townland. All chairs on loan from neighbours were left outside the door and chairs on which the coffin had rested when brought outside the house were turned down on the street. A sip of whiskey was then taken by each one remaining in the house.

The coffin was brought into the church when the hearse arrived at the gate. Mass and funeral service followed Then offerings were collected from the people attending. The total collected was taken as a status symbol.

On the day following the funeral the " washing " took place. A number of women from the neighbourhood came and helped to wash all the sheets, etc., connected with the corpse.

It was the custom when the name of a dead person was mentioned for the speaker to say " May God rest him ". Great respect for the dead is a feature of this society and it is considered very bad form to speak ill of the dead. *De mortuis nil nisi bonum* was a rule carefully observed by all.

Keening the dead was a custom observed here until the early part of the present century. In the Drumaville area the corpse was carried to Ard na gCorp at Ballyharry. Here the corpse was placed on the ground and the professional lamenters chanted the *caoineadh*.

GHOSTS AND FAIRIES

To the mind of the older generation the world of spirits was all around. The souls of the dead did their Purgatory in the area in which they lived during life; fairies lived in every hill and dell and were constantly in touch with human beings, and the devil and his assistants were all the time on the watch. In the day-time nothing was visible but at night the whole spirit world became fully active. The lonely road and the empty house were spots to be avoided. Only the rash and the foolhardy went to such places.

Some fairies were good. Donall O Gallchoir and Sean O Gormain of Gortlesk in Ballygorman were making poteen at a wild and lonely spot at the bottom of the Bengorms. It was midnight. When the stilling was completed the two men sat quietly sampling the whiskey. Suddenly a small, red-haired woman appeared with a small tin pan in her hand. The two men regarded her, without fear, as a spirit. She asked for some whiskey, which was given to her. As she turned to leave she thanked them in Irish and told them that the police were coming. Then she disappeared.

The men hurriedly hid all the apparatus and, each with a keg of whiskey on his shoulder, went in haste up the bens by a devious route. At the top they secreted themselves for a while. Soon they saw a party of police go directly towards where they had been stilling. The men quietly went their way in safety to Gortlesk.

The person who died with a debt unpaid was doomed to remain in Purgatory unless someone on earth paid the amount due. There was in Ballyharry a man called Sean McColgan, who died. He was seen often at night by his neighbours and it was thus known that he could not rest. Why he could not was not clear.

One Sunday morning about midday, when almost all the people were at Mass, the widow sat alone in her house. Looking up she saw her dead husband standing outside the half-door which led into the kitchen. He pointed at his lips, as if to indicate that he could not speak. Then he looked towards an old cupboard and pointed at it in a fixed manner. Casting an anguished look at his wife, he suddenly disappeared.

The wife examined the cupboard carefully and found an unpaid bill for shoes Sean had bought years before. On the following day she travelled to Moville and paid the long-overdue account. Sean Mac Colgan was never seen again, as his soul had now found peace.

The dead returned at times to visit their former dwelling-place on earth. Seoirse Mac an tSaoir, a man of courage and not given to superstitious beliefs, was travelling by horse and cart from Moville. He had been delayed and it was after midnight when he reached Drumnagessan. As he rested the horse before going up the steep hill here a woman standing by the side of the road stepped up on the cart beside him. Her face was hidden and she sat at an angle. He was somewhat startled, but seeing that the woman meant no harm and had probably walked from Moville he continued his journey without further anxiety. No one spoke.

A mile further on there was the ruin of an old house in which had lived a family named Murphy. These had emigrated years before. As Seoirse reached the ruin the woman silently raised her hand as if to say " stop ". The horse stopped and the woman stepped on to the road and walked directly into the old house. As Seoirse watched in silence he recognised her as Mary Murphy, who had gone to America forty years before. She had long since died. What now brought her back to the scene of her early years ?

When a mother died and left very young children she still maintained from the next world a strong interest in her offspring. Seamas O Gallchoir married a girl from Ballyheeney named Caitriona Nic Lochlainn. On her wedding she came to live with her husband at Gortlesk, where both spent a year of great happiness. A son was born, but the mother died with a few days. When the funeral was over the young father faced the problem of caring for the child. The mother-in-law, Eilis Mhic Lochlainn, stayed a few days but then went home, refusing her son-in-law's request to take the child for a time.

Over the next ten days the husband looked after the child carefully, but the absence of a woman's care was very much felt. The child was restless and kept crying. One night about this time Eilis sat alone in her house awaiting the return of the other members of the family, who were out visiting. It was midnight and the door was open. The half-door was in position. Hearing a sound in the laneway leading to the house, Eilis looked at the door. There stood her dead daughter with her left hand resting on the half-door. The startled mother spoke: " Will you not come in, daughter ?" Caitriona looked at her sadly and said, " Since you will not take my child you will have no place for me ". The vision disappeared.

Putting her shawl around her, the grandmother set out alone in the middle of the night, taking the lonely road through Bree to Gortlesk. She knocked at the window and awakened her son-in-law. He arose, opened the door and admitted her. The mother-in-law said quietly, " I have come for the child ". No explanation was given. Seamas O Gallchoir and Eilis Mhic Lochlainn, carrying the child, set out forthwith for Ballyheeney, where the boy remained until he was 14 years of age.

Early in the present century there occurred at Malin Head a murder which affected profoundly the lives of four people. A young man had been in love with a neighbouring girl but for financial reasons married a woman of means. Later the old love affair was resumed and the girl involved was soon to have a child.

The crisis came on a stormy night at a wild and lonely spot. The woman and her illicit lover met to discuss matters. A row developed and the woman was killed; according to the evidence the man's attack had been planned. The man was hanged and his widow left the lonely dwelling-house which stood high on the face of the hill. Neighbours who came near at evening in search of straying cattle say that the cry of a child can still be heard in the deserted house.

A party of tourists out for an evening walk on the hill heard the crying proceeding from the house as they passed. One went to the door, opened it and shone his torch. The cry ceased on his approach. Desolation and decay were evident but there was no trace of a child. The story was told to the people who lived around and was heard without comment and with a knowing silence.

The *bean si* gave warning when a member of a family which had such a guardian spirit was about to die. One such family was called Mac Lochlainn and lived in Meenawarra. At the time of which we speak Seamas Mac Lochlainn, his wife and grown children lived on the family farm. One evening in late spring,

Mairead Bean Ui Ghallchoir was milking her cow in a house adjacent to the place inhabited by the Mac Lochlainn family. Suddenly the terrifying cry could be heard on the hill above the house of Mac Lochlainn. It continued for over half an hour. Every family in the townland save one heard the cry and came to the same conclusion. No member of the Mac Lochlainn family heard it.

At seven o'clock the following day a son of Seamas Mac Lochlainn knocked at each door in the townland. His father had died during the night. The *bean si* had given her timely warning.

When a hen crowed in the day-time it was a warning of a dire calamity. At four o'clock on an August afternoon a hen on the street of Neddy Brien's farm at Cnuckeen flew up on a cart. She crowed loud and long for ten minutes. Peig had gone to the seashore some time earlier to gather a *cnuasach*. By eight o'clock the men of the district were carrying her dead body on a door to her house. She slipped on a rock and fell into a deep pool.

When the devil appears to anyone in the night the Sign of the Cross will protect the person against his evil power. The evil spirit cannot cross running water. Often people in this area, when pursued by the devil—usually in the form of a black dog with glaring eyes—reached safety when they came to a bridge.

Do not visit a graveyard during the night, as the souls of the dead who are doing their Purgatory will be disturbed by your presence. Padraig O Cnaimhsi, the sexton at Bocan, usually locked up the church at nightfall. One night, because he had been at the market, he entered the graveyard late to lock up. It was midnight. As he left the sacristy he heard a loud, rebuking, firm voice saying, " What are you doing there ?" The voice was familiar. It was that of the previous parish priest, who had died about six months before.

LUCK—GOOD AND BAD

The concept of luck ran deep in the mind of the community of North Inis Eoghain. In the life of the people many forces, mysterious and unpredictable, were at work. Cattle got sick, people fell ill and crops failed. Good luck was at other times in control and man and beast were well and crops flourished.

Since bad luck very often meant complete disaster, every effort was made to avert it. Customs sanctioned by generations of experience were practised to protect and safeguard all against the powers of evil. The people did not hesitate to use pagan rites as well as Christian.

This was a community to whom the laws of nature were a mystery. The effects of germs and parasites on animal and plant were not yet known. Medical doctors and veterinary surgeons were unknown until the last century. The motto " any remedy is better than none " produced many extraordinary practices, but at least they sustained hope.

16
LEAC TINE[1]

SAMUEL STONE, the Protestant rector of Culdaff from 1769-1798, had the right to commute a death sentence once a year. Near Culdaff lived a blacksmith. He was called on late one night by an unknown horseman, who asked him to nail the front shoes of the horse. The shoes had become loose. The blacksmith set his fire going and lit his oil lamp. The shoes were soon affixed and the horseman continued his journey.

The time of which we speak was the turbulent years leading up to the rebellion of 1798. A late-working blacksmith was suspect, as the suspicion was that he was making pikes. Young, the landlord, thought so when he saw the light in the forge. He charged the blacksmith in court with pike-making. On Young's evidence he was sentenced to death. The blacksmith's wife appealed to Stone to intervene. Though Stone and Young were of the same religious persuasion, there was but little friendship between them.

Stone wrote from his house in Glebe to Young and asked him to spare the life of the blacksmith, but got the reply: " In spite of all the sticks and stones in Glebe the blacksmith will be hanged". Stone replied: " In spite of all the Youngs an dowls in Culdaff he will not". The parson exercised his prerogative and the life of the smith was saved.

✳   ✳   *

Willie Knox, who lived in Glack, was married to a mermaid. He had found her one day when fishing down at Dunmore. The mermaid sat combing her hair on a rock and was unaware of his admiring glance. Willie knew that if he got her tail she would be in his control. He advanced quietly and when he was close to her he put his hands around her and detached the tail. Willie brought her home and hid the tail in an old, dry drain behind the house.

Willie went to see the minister. The latter had some theological doubts about the validity of a marriage with a mermaid, but seeing the determination on Willie's face he decided to perform the marriage. He thought this better than to allow his parishioner to live in sin. The pair lived for years in tranquility and peace. The mermaid took the Christian name Mara.

She became a very efficient housewife and was popular among the neighbours. Four children were born in due course. Willie was fond of whiskey and regularly made a run of " wee still ". His wife acquired the art and helped her husband. Willie hid the stilling apparatus in various places outside the house. The worm was placed in the same dry drain as his wife's tail. With the coming of a certain Christmas Willie decided to make a " run ". He sent his wife out for the worm, telling where it was hidden. As Mara Knox reached into the drain for the worm what did she see but her tail ! It was as clean as it was on the day she lost it at Dunmore.

Now, if an ex-mermaid finds her tail again she reverts to type on the instant. Willie, her children and the poteen were immediately forgotten. Mara hastened to the sea, only half a mile away, and jumped in. She was never heard of again.

*   *   *

A fox which lived on Dunmore raided nightly the hen houses in the area around. Every morning the same story was related by a housewife in a different part of the district. Wanton destruction, and all done in the space of an hour or so. Dogs chased the marauder frequently, but all met the same fate. While the wise fox ran towards the edge of the steep cliff he managed, no one knew how, to get into his den on the face of the cliff. The stupid dogs ran over the cliff and were either killed or drowned as they fell.

The people of Glebe were so harassed that they held a meeting to organise the death of the fox. Andrew Knox finally came up with the right idea. The question was: " How did the fox manage to go over the cliff and escape the fall which led to the death of so many dogs?" Andrew said that someone should hide on the side of Dunmore and see what happened. Joseph Duggan undertook the task.

The following night Joseph selected his spot carefully, noting the direction of the soft breeze blowing at the time. As he sat there in the darkness the only company he had was the sound of the sea beating at the bottom of the bens and the intermittent flashes from the lighthouses on Inistrahull and the coast of Scotland.

In the stillness of the night the fox came and went on his thieving tour. An hour later Joseph heard him return, pur-

242

sued by two dogs. Now the watcher noted carefully what was happening. The fox came to the brink at speed, then it gripped a large briar which hung over the cliff and swung deftly into its den. The dogs ran on to their death.

All the important people in Glebe met again that night and a course of action was decided. Young Andrew Knox was appointed to watch that night. When the fox left the den he was to cut the briar. Andrew watched and when the fox left he did as he had been told. In due time the fox came back at speed, pursued as usual. As before, he came to the brink and attempted to grip the briar. Instead, he fell right down into the sea and was drowned.

*   *   *

A woman from Balleighan walked three miles to get lilies which grew on the shore of Lochbellthick. When she arrived at the lake she sat down to rest. As she sat there, out of the centre of the lake came an animal like a foal. The strange animal was friendly and came directly to the woman. She was frightened but did not move, and the animal lay down and rested its head on her knee. Soon the animal fell sound asleep. Its snoring could be heard a mile away.

The woman wanted to get away because she was very frightened. She unloosed her apron and laid the head of the sleeping animal carefully on it. Then she slipped quietly away. When she had travelled a few hundred yards she looked back. She saw the animal in a rage, standing and tearing the apron to shreds. The woman ran to get out of danger, and forgot about the lilies.

*   *   *

Advertisement in the *Derry Journal*, December 24th, 1776:

This is to give notice to the Revd. Dr. Torrens and the Revd. Dr. Elwood to take care in getting their Wigs from Mr. McGuigan, as he has already imposed on the former, a Wig of the late George Cary's, and the latter a Wig of the late Col. Knox's which were very much worn by each of the said gentlemen.

Derry. Neal Carlan.

Note: Elwood was rector of Cloncha from 1732 to 1785.

*   *   *

Roger McCann, a pilot who lived in Ballyharry, brought

243

Thomas D'Arcy McGee out in his boat and put him on a liner which was going to Canada. The boarding took place off Bally-harry. According to Harkin's history of Inishowen, McGee assumed the dress of a clerical student and remained in hiding at Kindroyhad until he secured a place on a boat going out from Derry.

❖   ●   *

Many shipwrecks are known to have taken place around the coast of North Inis Eoghain. Local tradition tells of the following:

The *A.C Beam* was wrecked off Ballyhillin about 1891. Only two Swedes were saved.

The *Cambria,* sailing from New York, foundered off the Garrive Isles in 1870.

The *Twilight,* belonging to Cook of Derry, entered by mistake the Bay of Straghbreggagh and was damaged on the bar around 1879. Part of this vessel can still be seen at low tide.

A ship called the *Bessi* or *Betsy* sailing from the West Indies for Greenock, was driven ashore by a storm and wrecked in Kullourt Bay.

The *Alcess* ran ashore at Claggan Bens. Another boat, name unrecorded, sank in Culdaff Bay with a cargo of slates.

The *Heckla* was wrecked in 1866 off Tremone Bay. She had a load of tin.

In March, 1891, the schooner *Westward,* with a cargo of bog ore from Lough Swilly, ran aground at Malin Head. The crew were all saved.

*   *   ●

Catherine Young, a member of the landlord family at Culdaff, was born in 1770. Her family arranged a match for her but she had secretly fallen in love with the drummer of the regiment in which her brother was an officer. His name was Murphy, a Catholic. Catherine eloped and married him. Two children were born: a daughter, who was given the same name as her mother, and a son, named Charles.

No doubt through the influence of the Young family, a farm was secured for the Murphys at Tirmacroragh, where a house was built, probably on the site on an older one, around 1850. The name Murphy was a permanent embarrassment because of its

Irish and Catholic associations. Charles joined the Army and went to India. He was in time promoted to the rank of major. He substituted the name " Murray " for his father's name and was known in Ireland and abroad as Major Murray. His sister Catherine took the name " Murfoy " and was called Miss Murfoy.

In 1850, through the efforts of Major Murray, the house now known as " Redford Cottage " was built. Here the family lived.

Catherine Young died in 1857. As she lay on her deathbed her son entered the bedroom and asked her would he send for priest or parson. She asked for the former and died as a member of the Catholic Church, of which she was probably a member since her marriage to Murphy, the drummer. While Major Murray tolerantly respected his mother's request for the priest, he did not permit her burial at Bocan, the burial ground for Catholics. She was buried by herself at Culdaff. The visitor entering the gate at Culdaff Church will notice to his right a simple headstone with the unusual inscription " My Mother, 1770-1857 ".

Major Murray was an eccentric and was greatly feared by his neighbours. When a cow belonging to a farmer named Bernard McSheffrey trespassed on Murray's land, Murray shot it.

Catherine Murfoy developed a relationship with a man who lived in Cnuckeen in the townland of Tirmacroragh. She had a family. Some said there was a secret marriage, but Miss Murfoy she remained until her death. This took place at Glebe in the house of Pat McDaid, where she had been living for some time before.

*   *   *

The name of Charles Stuart often occurs in the oral tradition of Inis Eoghain and the rest of Donegal. Apart from the fact that the Catholics here in the eighteenth century followed the Stuart cause in hope of improved conditions for themselves, the story is told that the Prince lived in Donegal for a time before his escape to the Continent after the debacle at Culloden. What evidence is there for this and why is the tradition, if correct, not supported by the historians of the period?

After the Battle of Culloden Prince Charles retreated in disguise to the Western Isles to await a boat for France. It has already been pointed out that there was a well established trading route between the west of Scotland and Culdaff in Inis Eoghain. As the advisers of the Prince faced the major problem of ensuring his safety, they must have feared that the British Navy might intercept any vessel on the way to France. Might not the friendly Scottish chieftains have suggested that the Prince be taken by small boat to Inis Eoghain? He could then be guided across the county to Glencolmcille, where a ship could call later and collect him. By this time the story would have circulated that the Prince was in France and there would be little likelihood, therefore, of the ship being molested. In addition, a ship would have a better chance of escape to the open sea if detected here than if found off the coast of Scotland. The most likely point of contact in Inis Eoghain would be Culdaff, not only because of the trading route but also because anywhere nearer to the Foyle would involve the risk of capture.

A letter of Valentine P. Griffith, rector of Glencolmcille, dated 22nd April, 1852, records in detail the tradition in the area regarding Prince Charles. It states that the Prince landed in Inis Eoghain and made his way with one attendant through Carndonagh to Sliabh Sneachta. Here he was expected and entertained in the house of one Gerald O Doherty, where he stayed for a few days. The writer of the letter visited this area in 1856 and found that the people here believed the Prince had stayed in the locality.

The Prince then went towards the Swilly and southwest to Letterkenny, says the account, where he stayed in the house of Robert Fletcher. Later he went to Glencolmcille, where he remained for a considerable time until a ship came from France for him. The letter gives the name of the family who kept him while he was in Glencolmcille.

The historians who deal with Prince Charles's flight are not clear about either the name of the ship or the time of his arrival in France. The reason would seem to be clear: he did not go direct from Scotland to France. Also, secrecy was essential, not only up to the time he reached France but afterwards, to ensure the protection of all those in Donegal who had helped him. It is interesting to note that at the time of the Stuart bid to regain the throne the landlord at Culdaff, George Young, had organised a troop of horse to hold the realm for the Hanoverians. Under his very eyes, early in a morning of 1746, the royal fugitive landed at Bunagee and passed probably within half a mile of the house in which Young lived.

246

Michael Harkin, in his historical work on Inis Eoghain, refers to the old church at Cloncha and records:

In this churchyard are also interred the remains of the Reverend Mr. Sheridan, a Roman Catholic priest who accompanied Prince Charles Stuart to the continent and returned with him when he made an unsuccessful attempt to regain the throne of his fathers. No stone marks the good clergyman's resting-place, though in life he was the attendant and companion of royalty.

Harkin was recording an oral tradition which unfortunately left much unanswered. The need for secrecy in the earlier generations meant that much was not spoken of to safeguard those involved in this historical episode. There is, however, in this reference an important link with the House of Stuart. It is the name Sheridan.

This surname is very rare in the parishes of Culdaff and Cloncha. It occurs once only. The Tithe Applotment Book for 1828 records one householder at Crackna. His name was James Sheridan. However, the Sheridan family, originating in Cavan, had a close association with the Stuarts from the days of King James II of England onwards.

The story begins in the diocese of Kilmore. The parish priest of Kildrumferton, Denis Sheridan, was very much influenced by the Protestant Bishop Bedell and conformed to the new religion. His son Thomas became an adherent of the House of Stuart and fought on the side of King James. Tradition states that he married an illegitimate daughter of the second James. (Authorities doubt this nowadays.) He was killed at the Battle of the Boyne.

King James took an interest in his young son, also called Thomas. This young man was educated abroad and later became the tutor of Prince Charles. Sir Thomas Sheridan accompanied Charles to Scotland in 1745. Another Sheridan, Michael by name, and a nephew of Sir Thomas, was also on the ship from France and was later involved in getting the Prince back safely to France after the defeat. There is no reference to a Fr. Sheridan. It is possible that one of this family was a priest who acted as chaplain to Prince Charles. Records show that this branch of the Sheridans had reverted to the old religion.

How did a reputed great-grandson of King James II find his final resting-place in so remote a part of Inis Eoghain? He may have fallen ill and died while the royal party made its way from the coast. In such circumstances he would be buried in utter secrecy, lest the English supporters in the area should know about Prince Charles.

Here the matter must rest pending the discovery of further evidence. The prudent judge will keep an open mind on this question. However, in the light of the data set out above it must be admitted that there are solid grounds for the belief that the fugitive Stuart passed this way some time in 1746.

✻   ✻   *

At Meenawarra lived a family called McCarron. This family had lived here since the seventeenth century and perhaps earlier. A member of it was in the army of Sarsfield and took part in the Battle of Aughrim. His sword was preserved up to the end of the last century.

✻   ✻   *

In the townland of Ballygorman lived Muintir Ghormain, a family which had a long association with the area. They were custodians of the Holy Stone of Malin and guardians of the shrine of St. Muirdhealach at Tobar Mhalann. At the end of the eighteenth century the head of Muintir Ghormain was Eoghan Cron Ua Gormain. He lived at Gortlesk with his wife Onora. In accordance with tradition, many pilgrims called at his house either for the blessing of the Holy Stone or to accompany them to Tobar Mhalann.

It was a night in early November, the eve of the feast of Saint Muirdhealach. Eoghan, his wife and family knelt and said the Rosary as was their custom. Because it was the vigil of the feast of the saint associated with Tobar Mhalann, Eoghan reverently blessed his family with the Holy Stone. He invoked the blessing of Muirdhealach on all for the coming year. The family then retired for the night.

At midnight, Eoghan Cron was awakened by a persistent tapping at the door of his house. Rising out of bed he opened the window. It was a clear, bright night. The full moon rode high in a sky untroubled by clouds. On the street stood a tall man with what looked like a staff in his hand. The face of the man startled Eoghan Cron. On one side it was normal but on the other it was horrible and somewhat diabolic. A voice, hollow and ghostlike, said: "*Eirigh agus tar liom go Tobar Mhuirdheal-aigh*".[2] The sound seemed to proceed not from the mouth, but rather from the chest. The timbre and resonance were scarcely human. Eoghan Cron was a man of courage. He had encountered many strange things, even the devil himself, in his time. For once, however, he experienced a very great fear.

Despite his anxiety, Eoghan Cron dressed in haste, went to the door and faced the stranger. The man advanced towards the door, leaving his staff leaning against the wall of the house. As he came nearer Eoghan Cron saw that the left side of the man's face was half-eaten away by a horrible cancer. The cause of the strange facial image and the distorted voice was now clear. Eoghan Cron lit a candle and asked the man to enter. The stranger did so. In the meantime Onora had entered the kitchen and she offered the stranger refreshment. He shook his head and in the same strange voice said: "*Nil mian bia na di orm—ta me i mo throscadh*".[3]

Without further conversation the stranger arose, went out and lifted his staff. Eoghan Cron went in front to show the way. It was then he discovered that the stranger was carrying not a staff but a crowbar. It could be heard hitting the road as they walked along. Every house in the townland was in complete darkness. There was an atmosphere of calmness and of peace everywhere, save in one place—the mind and heart of Eoghan Corn were sorely troubled. Was his midnight visitor mad and was his own life in danger?

Along the road the pair walked in silence towards Bulibin and over the top of Drumnakill. As they neared the sea the beat of the waves rolling over the pebbles towards the shore could be heard—there was no other sound, save their own footsteps and the metallic ring of the crowbar. A weird and nightmarish impression hung over Tobar Mhalann at this late hour. As the pair approached the area adjacent to the old church the stranger took the lead. He turned sharply to the left and went directly to the bottom of the cliff. Leaving aside the crowbar, he went down on his knees and felt with his hands on the ground. Working with speed and precision he cleared from the surface of a stone slab a thin layer of soil and vegetation. Shining in the clear moonlight Eoghan Cron could see a flag-stone measur-

249

ing about six and a half feet by three feet. At one end a cross was neatly incised.

The stranger's intention could now be understood—he intended to open the grave. Lifting the crowbar, he deftly placed it under one end of the flag-stone. Eoghan Cron watched in horror. It was a monstrous crime to interfere with the dead. What was he to do? What could he do? The stranger soon brought Eoghan Cron to attention by signalling in a most peremptory manner for help in lifting the stone. Working together, they removed the flag-stone to one side. Within, clearly visible in the moonlight, lay the intact skeleton of a very tall adult. The skull, with the full set of white teeth still in place, lay there grinning in a most gruesome and fearful way.

As Eoghan Cron watched in terror he asked himself was this experience which he was going through a nightmare or a reality? The bright moon above, the murmuring sea behind and the firm earth beneath all spoke of actuality. Yet as he looked at the open grave and the strange man he wondered.

The stranger now stood in silence for a few moments at the foot of the open grave. Making the Sign of the Cross on himself, he knelt down and kissed with great respect the feet of the skeleton. Then he stood erect and walked towards the head of the grave with slow, deliberate steps. As Eoghan Cron watched he was reminded of the priest at the altar. There was the same precision, the same dignity and the same profound respect. As he reached the head of the grave the stranger knelt down and slowly, deliberately and reverently lifted a tooth from the jaw of the skeleton. He took from his pocket a clean handkerchief, wrapped the tooth therein and placed the relic in his pocket.

The stranger now signalled to Eoghan Cron and together they placed the flag-stone in its correct position. Not a single word was spoken. The two then retraced their steps towards Gortlesk. At the end of the *cosan* leading to Eoghan's house they parted. The stranger, absorbed in thought and carrying the crowbar, went down towards the main road. Eoghan returned to his house and went to bed.

Exactly one year later, Eoghan Cron, his wife and family had said the Rosary and had carried out the customary observances connected with the vigil of the feast of Muirdhealach. They retired to bed. It was a night of Stygian gloom—inky darkness permeated the whole land as the lights were one by one extinguished in the area from Kilnoxter to Ardmalin. There was not a breath of air stirring.

At midnight, Eoghan Cron was roused from sleep by a loud knocking at the door. He arose, lowered the window, peered out and challenged the disturber of the night. He soon recognised the stranger of the previous year. To Eoghan's query the man replied: " *Eirigh agus tar liom go Tobar Mhuirdhealaigh* ". But this time there was a difference: the voice that spoke was full, pleasant and human.

Despite the extreme darkness, Eoghan was surprised to see that in some mysterious, inexplicable manner the man was clearly visible. The crowbar was in his right hand. From his left hand there seemed to radiate a diffused and extraordinary brilliance which illuminated his whole person. Looking at the stranger's face, Eoghan was astonished to see that the full bloom of health was evident on both sides. The revolting cancer was gone.

Eoghan dressed, lit a candle, opened the door and invited the stranger to enter. As he entered, Eoghan Cron noticed that he held his left hand in front of him. Through the loosely clenched fingers Eoghan saw the tooth taken from the skeleton at Tobar Mhalann the previous year. The man sat down in silence.

When Eoghan was ready for the journey the man arose and said commandingly: " *Biodh an lochrann leat* ".[4] Eoghan placed a lighted rush candle in his weather lantern and the two went off without further delay. When they reached the grave the lantern was placed adjacent to the flag-stone. Its faint light dispelled enough of the surrounding gloom to allow the work of opening the grave to proceed. When the stone was removed the stranger, following the same ritual as before, reverently replaced the tooth in its proper place in the jaw bone. The grave was then carefully closed.

The two men returned to Gortlesk in silence. No word was spoken when they parted. As Eoghan Cron stood at the end of his loneen he could hear the footsteps of his extraordinary visitor receding down past Craig Mor and Caislinn. The accompanying clink-clank of the crowbar could be heard as the strange

man faded into the darkness, and forever out of the life of
Eoghan Cron Ua Gormain.

———————————✠———————————

1. These stories are a selection of the folklore of the district. They were
   told and re-told around the hearthstone when neighbours gathered together.
2. "Arise and come with me to Malin Well."
3. "I desire neither food nor drink—I am fasting."
4. "Take the lantern with you."

252

17
NOTE ON THE TOWNLANDS

THE LARGEST townland in this area is Moneydarragh, with an acreage of 2,596 acres, and the second largest is Glengad, with a total of 2,569 acres. The smallest townland is Drumballycaslin, which has 53 acres and the second smallest is Tullybeg, with 72 acres.

The area from Kullourt to Lagg had different names in 1660 from those we have to-day. In place of Kullourt, Knockamany, Lagg and part of Drung, we had Tullyarden, Downa, Balliedogie, Grangeah and Carrowbate. The exact limits of the townlands were defined about 1830 by the Ordnance Survey team. They are, however, based on old Gaelic divisions.

PARISH OF CULDAFF

TOWNLAND	ACREAGE	MEANING OF PLACE-NAME
Aghaglasson	2,119. 0. 39	ACHADH AN GHLAISIN: the land of the stream.
Aghatubrid	576. 2. 7	ACHADH TIOBRAIDE: the land of the well.
Balleighan Lower	639. 1. 35	BAILE FHIOCHAIN: Feighan's homestead.
Balleighan Upper	1,006. 2. 9	do. do.
Ballyharry	996. 1. 22	BAILE AN CHURRAIGH or BAILE AN CHORA: the town of the marshy land or town of the stepping stones.
Ballymagaraghy	387. 0. 25	BAILE MHIC GEARACHAIGH: the homestead of Mac Gearachaigh.
Baskill	686. 2. 15	ASCALL: the small territory or FASCHOILL: the grove. This townland is spelt "Waskill" in earlier records.
Carrowmore	798. 1. 34	CEATHRU MHOR: the large quarter-land.
Carthage	1,497. 2. 21	NEW CARTHAGE: name given by the seventeenth century planters to commemorate the old city of this name in North Africa. The correct name is *Baile an Chairn:* the townland of the cairn.
Cashel	761. 3. 21	CAISEAL: the stone building or fort.
Culdaff	244. 3. 36	CUIL DA ATH: the corner between two fords. This townland includes two older townlands, Carrowtemple and Crancor.
Culdaff-Glebe	158. 1. 21	GLEBE: a clergyman's benefice. The correct and older name is *Dun an*

253

			Ghrianain: the fortification of the summer palace.
Dristernan	508. 2. 5		Dristearnan: the place of brambles.
Drumaville	369. 1. 12		Droim an Bhile: the ridge of the sacred tree.
Drumlee	630. 2. 29		DROIM LIATH: the grey ridge.
Freehold	218. 1. 30		A recent name referring to the tenure. It is situated on the bank of the Gleneely river between the townlands of Ourt and Baskill.
Glengad	2,549. 0. 33		GLEANN GAD: the glen of the withes.
Kindroyhad	414. 1. 7		CEANN DROICHID: the head of the bridge ("bridgend").
Knock	164. 1. 1		CNOC: a hill.
Leitrim	806. 1. 4		LIATHDROIM (Liatroim): grey ridge.
Moneydarragh	2,596. 3. 0		MUINE DARACH: the shrubbery of the oak.
Muff	470. 0. 4		MAGH: a level district.
Ourt	754. 3. 13		FUARGHORT: cold field.
Tirmacroragh	664. 2. 38		TIR MHIC RUAIRI: McRory's land.

PARISH OF CLONCHA

Ardmalin	1,980. 1. 13	ARD MHALANN: the top of the brae face.
Ballagh	606. 2. 9	BEALACH: the way.
Balleighan Lr.	265. 2. 30	BAILE FHIOCHAIN: Feighan's homestead.
Balleighan Upper	97. 3. 30	do. do.
Ballellaghan	668. 3. 0	BAILE ILEACHAIN: the homestead of Ellachan.
Ballycrampsey	146. 3. 19	BAILE CHNAIMHSI: the homestead of Crevshey.
Ballygorman	799. 2. 36	BAILE GHORMAIN: the homestead of Gorman.
Ballyheeney	278. 3. 24	BAILE UI CHIONAOITH: O Kenny's homestead.
Bree	1,151. 1. 12	BRI: a brae.
Carrowmore	839. 0. 22	CEATHRU MHOR: the large quarterland.
Cloncha	781. 3. 34	CLUAIN CATHA: the meadow of Catha.
Kullourt	987. 1. 5	CUIL FHUARGHOIRT: the corner of the cold field.
Drumaville	1,298. 1. 39	DROIM AN BHILE: the ridge of the sacred tree.
Drumavohy	187. 3. 22	DROIM AN BHOTHAIGH: the ridge of the hut.
Drumballycaslin	53. 2. 33	DROIM BAILE CHAISLEAIN: the ridge of the town of the castle or DROIM BAILE CHAISLIN: the ridge of the homestead by the stream.
Drumcarbit	742. 3. 19	DROIM CARBAD: the ridge of the chariots. The old road to Malin passed through this townland.

Drumnaskea	314. 2. 17	DROIM NA SCEACH: the ridge of the bushes.
Drung	197. 2. 30	DRONG: a place of meeting. A fair was held here in pre-plantation times. This townland was also known as Carronvleigh/*Carn Bleithe*: the heap of the grinding or grain.
Dunagard	289. 0. 20	DUN NA gCEARD: the fort of the skilled workers.
Dunross	603. 1. 36	DUN ROIS: the fort of the copse.
Glacknadrummond	576. 0. 26	GLAC NA dTROMAN: the hollow of the dwarf elders.
Goorey	203. 1. 19	GUAIRE: a sandbank above high-water mark.
Inistrahull	110. 3. 26	INIS DÁ THULL: the island of the two hills.
Keenagh	226. 2. 10	CAONACH: moss
Killin	287. 3. 37	CILLIN: little church.
Knockamany	306. 3. 7	CNOC NA MANACH: the hill of the monks.
Knockergrana	161. 0. 11	CNOCAR GREANACH: the gravelly hills.
Knockglass	158. 1. 2	CNOC GLAS: Greenhill.
Lagg	348. 3. 36	LAG: a hollow.
Larrahirrel	364. 3. 28	LATRACH IRIAIL: the rough land of Irial.
Lougherbraghey	595. 3. 35	LUACHAIR BHRACHAIDH: the rushy land of Brachey.
Magheryard	413. 3. 25	MACHAIRE ARD: the high plain.
Meedanmore	341. 3. 16	MIODAN MOR: large meadow.
Norrira	489. 3. 31	AN FHORAOIR: a sandy beach.
Redford-Glebe	474. 1. 21	BEAL AN ATHA DEIRG: the mouth of the red ford and *glebe*: clergyman's benefice. The correct name is *Dun an Ghrianain*.
Templemoyle	1,011. 3. 6	TEAMPALLL MAOL: the roofless church.
Tullybeg	72. 1. 27	TULACH BHEAG: the small hill.
Tullymore	176. 2. 29	TULACH MHOR: the large hill.
Umgall	461. 2. 36	IOM-SCAL: the area around the hut or shelter perhaps. This townland is divided in two portions.
Urbalreagh	545. 3. 39	EIREABALL RIABHACH: the grey tail —of land—a reference to the shape of the townland.
Tullyarden	—— - —	TULACH ARDAIN: the hill of the terrace.
Doona	—— - —	DUNADH: a fortress — probably Dunargus.
Balliedogie	—— - —	BAILE DUMHCHA: the homestead of the sandhills.
Carrowbate	—— - —	CEATHRU BEITH: the quarterland of the beeches.
Grangeah	—— - —	GRAINSEACH: a monastic granary.

Charles Macklin

CHARLES MACKLIN, ACTOR AND DRAMATIST

George Faulkner's *Dublin Jounral*, in its edition of July 18th, 1797, recorded the following:

Died on Tuesday last, at his apartment in Tavistock Row, London, Mr. Charles Macklin, the Veteran Actor.

Charles Macklin was born in the year 1699[1] at Gortanarin, in the townland of Templemoyle, parish of Cloncha[2] and County of Donegal.

Early Years and Education

The actor started life as Cathal Mac Lochlainn. His name was Anglicised to Charles McLaughlin and later in life he adopted the name Charles Macklin. Under the last name he became famous " throughout the Three Kingdoms ". The name Mac Lochlainn was an honoured one in Ulster. It was the cognomen of a former royal line, which was also for a time the ruling family in Inis Eoghain.

Cathal was born at a time of defeat and despair for supporters of the Irish cause and of the Catholic Church. The defeats of Derry, Aughrim and the Boyne were very fresh in the minds of the people of Inis Eoghain. Young men from Culdaff and Cloncha had been soldiers in the army of King James. These men, among whom was William McLaughlin, the father of Cathal, had participated in the war between two foreign kings for an alien throne. It seemed to these Irishmen the best way available of serving their faith and country.

Irish was the spoken language in the area where Cathal grew into boyhood. Around the hearths in Templemoyle he would have heard participants in the recent struggle tell the story of what took place during the siege of Derry and the battles of Aughrim and the Boyne. He would have shared their sorrow because of the defeats and their hopes of victory in the days to come. On Sunday mornings he would have walked to the Mass Rock at Aghaclay and on his way he would have seen the ruins of the church at Greallach, where his ancestors had worshipped for centuries.

As the early years passed Cathal must have had some dim awareness of the fact that being either Irish or Catholic was a handicap to progress in the Ireland of the time. The young man who was both had a well-nigh insurmountable obstacle to overcome. A person of Cathal's temperament and character must have become increasingly aware of these things as he moved around. The rudiments of learning were received in the hedge school nearby. He would have acquired some knowledge of English, if not from his teacher, very likely from his father.

He would have been well aware of the state of servitude in which his parents and neighbours lived, as these proceeded regularly to the agent of the Protestant bishop, their landlord, to pay rent for their own land. Templemoyle was part of the old church-lands of Greallach and these were now in Protestant hands.

Here it is well to consider the character of Charles Macklin so that we can more fully understand the reasons underlying his behaviour and his ceaseless urge to impress all with whom he had contact. He had a violent temper wedded to an overbearing manner. He riled all his associates by his dogmatic, haughty, vain attitude. His one-track mind left no room to consider the opinions of others, no matter how well-informed the other party might be. He made no effort to win goodwill by kindness. He overawed instead, so that people would fear and admire him. He was at ease only among those whom he considered his inferiors. To these defects add rudeness and a total disregard for age or sex[3] in his words and actions. It is easy to understand that the direct result of such attributes was a history of quarrels and legal involvements. Few could maintain an even relationship with him for long. He was a bully who was in his element when exhibiting himself in a superior role. Ambition to excel was an ever-present urge.

Nature gave him a clear, sonorous and strong voice, together with a stalwart frame. His face had a rugged and corrugated appearance—a man who could not escape notice in a crowd. A person with such a character, such a voice and such an appearance could find fit expression on the stage alone. Given the correct character-part, Macklin was able to express himself fully using all his talents and undisciplined urges to the fullest extent. Each night on the stage was truly for him an emotional catharsis, making life livable for his own family thereby.

Macklin's family, because of the military background of the father, did not settle down in Templemoyle. The knowledge of another way of life and better opportunities elsewhere made the parents decide to move southwards in the early years of Charles's life.[4] The exact date is not known. The family spent some time in or near Drogheda and later moved to Dublin. His father died in 1704 and the widow married Luke O Meally, landlord of the Eagle Tavern at Werburgh Street. Later Mr. and Mrs. O Meally went to live at Cloncurry, 15 miles from Dublin.

Charles seems to have been in England for a short time, but he came back to Dublin, where he attended the Island Bridge Academy for a few years and completed his education. His gift of mimicry soon began to manifest itself, to the amusement of his school friends. To his schoolmaster, a Scotsman called Nicholson, he was a source of trouble. Charles had few pleasant memories of this teacher. Some attribute his later dislike for Scots and Scotland to this early experience.

During these years Charles visited his mother at week-ends. Indeed, one of his few attractive traits was his devotion to his mother. He kept in touch with her until her death and he treasured her memory deeply until his own end in 1797.

About his twenty-sixth year he crossed to England and soon found an opportunity to show his histrionic ability in a strolling company which he joined. He took the part of Richmond in *Richard III* on the stage at Bristol.

It was probably around this time that he became a Protestant. Was it a " marriage of convenience "? He was not noted for any strong religious devotion, and he was concerned chiefly with advancement in his chosen career in a land hostile to the religion of his youth.

His Irish accent attracted unfavourable attention and proved to be an obstacle to his acting. For six months he resided with a Welsh clergyman who had an English wife. He assiduously practised an English manner of speaking and eliminated every trace of his native accent. To perfect his acceptability to his English public he altered his surname. " MacLaughlin " was too Irish, so he substituted " Macklin ". Cathal Mac Lochlainn, the Irish-speaking Catholic, was transformed into the " respectable " Charles Macklin, Protestant and speaking the King's English with an excellence which the average Englishman might envy.

It must not be assumed that Macklin was *totally* ashamed of his Irish background, but he took great caution to make it eminently respectable. He hid his early association with Inis Eoghain and instead " created " a background of substance and power.

The story he told was that his father was a member of the landed gentry in Co. Down and that his mother came from a similar stratum of society in Co. Westmeath.[5] His position on the stage and in English society cost a considerable amount of hard work and the compromising of many principles and convictions.

The rest of Macklin's life is chiefly a story of great success as an actor and dramatist in London and Dublin. He had, however, time for many other activities, getting as a result a fair share of publicity outside the theatre.

The Actor[6]

Nature and hard work brought Charles Macklin to the top in the theatre. For years he laboured in inferior roles in strolling companies up and down the length of England. All through those years of toil he aimed at full participation in the highest role in the centre of the world of acting, London. Thoroughness and intense application were Macklin's tools in taking on any major role. He studied the history and background of his subject and endeavoured to think and feel like the man he represented on the stage. As a result he brought to each role an originality and naturalness which after some hesitation were accepted as a new and forceful contribution to the stage.

His first London appearance was at Lincoln's Inn Field in October, 1725, as Alcander in Dryden and Lee's *Oedipus*. His part here was not a success but he continued to play as a regular member of a London company. He was on the stage at the Drury Lane and Haymarket Theatres. In 1733-4 he got the first-rate parts at Drury Lane because of a quarrel between Highmore, the manager, and the principal actors. The quarrel was over in 1734 and Macklin lost the parts which meant so much to him. He was offered, and accepted, a part at the Haymarket in *Don Quixote in England*, but in September he was back at Drury Lane, where he remained until 1748.

It was in the role of Shylock at Drury Lane that Macklin showed his great talent for interpretation. He appeared in this role 22 times between the months of February and May of 1741. Despite the misgivings of the management, Macklin went ahead with his ideas and the result was a major triumph after a long and arduous preparation. He won the unqualified applause of an appreciative and critical audience.

Kirkman, one of Macklin's biographers, recorded an anecdote which illustrates the appreciation of the people of the time that

Shylock was well-interpreted by this great actor. At a party where Pope, the poet, and Macklin were present, a lady told Pope that he must write Macklin's epitaph when the time came. "That I will, Madam," said Pope. "Nay, I will give it to you now:

Here lies the Jew
That Shakespeare drew.

And Kirkman concludes: " The whole company highly approved of this Epitaph, and Mr. Macklin often related this anecdote in our hearing with great glee; and a more just, comprehensive and concise inscription never was written ". The story is probably apocryphal.

Macklin went to Dublin in 1748 and played at Smock Alley, which was at that time under the management of Thomas Sheridan. After a quarrel he returned to London and for a period of two years he quit the stage. He returned to it in 1755 and continued his acting for a space of 35 years. He entertained numerous audiences at Drury Lane and Covent Garden in London, and in Dublin he appeared at both Smock Alley and Crow Street. His fee in 1785, when he was acting in Dublin as Shylock, was £50 per night.

His long career on the stage came to an end on May 7th, 1789, in the well-loved role of Shylock. He got confused on this occasion and forgot his part. He left the stage without finishing and never acted again. For a man so devoted to his art this must have been a sad occasion.

During his years on the stage Macklin acted in 161 main roles. These included, in addition to Shylock, the roles of Iago, Mercutio, Macbeth, Polonius and Richard III. He also appeared in his own plays. Among these was *The True Born Irishman*, in which the major part of Murrough O Dogherty was acted by Macklin himself. His roles were both comic and serious, but he excelled in the former.

Macklin gave lessons in acting for private pupils and he took the greatest pains in their training and advancement. It was a labour of love and he gave himself unsparingly.

In 1787 he played the roles of Sir Archy and Sir Pertinax before the King and Queen of England. When Macklin was presented he replied, in response to the King's query about his age, that he had been born in the last century, served His Majesty in this one and hoped to do so in the next.

The Dramatist[7]

While the name of Macklin will be forever associated with acting, he also secured a measure of success in the writing of plays. His first, written in 1746, was entitled *King Henry VII or The Popish Imposter*. It was not a success. In 1746 he also wrote *A Will and no Will* and in 1747 *The New Play Criticised*. Neither of these received any worthwhile notice.

In 1759 he wrote a very successful farce called *Love a la Mode*. This was produced at Drury Lane and critics noted that it was a great improvement on his earlier writings. The following year he wrote and produced *Married Libertine*, which ran only nine nights. In 1763 he produced at Smock Alley Theatre his *The True Born Irishman*. It was well received there but when produced in Convent Garden under the title of *Irish Fine Lady* it was a failure, because the humour of a London audience was different to an Irish one. Macklin had learned another lesson in the hard school of experience.

In 1764 he wrote *The True Born Scotchman*, which was produced at Crow Street on February 7th, 1766, and at Capel Street Theatre. The Dublin audiences gave the play a very warm reception. Macklin later did three revisions of this comedy and altered the title to *The Man of the World*. The approval of the Lord Chamberlain was secured after a long delay and the revised play was produced to a London audience at Covent Garden on May 10th, 1781. It was a major success. *The Man of the World* is the best of his works. Other plays were *The Whim* (1765) and *A Lick at the Buckeens* (1772).

Macklin had to maintain constant vigilance to ensure that his plays would not be plagiarised. He took drastic action against anyone attempting to do so.

In recent years a re-awakened interest has developed in Macklin's plays. In 1967 Radio Eireann produced *The Man of the World*. In 1968 a London firm of publishers issued *Four Comedies* by Charles Macklin. The plays included were: *The True Born Irishman, Love a la Mode, The Man of the World*[8] and *The School for Husbands*.

The Man of Many Quarrels

A man of Macklin's temperament and character inevitably ran

into conflict with many of those with whom he came into contact. His professional life, his social life and his domestic life are all a record of ceaseless conflicts.

In 1735 he had a violent dispute with a fellow actor called Thomas Hallam.[9] The immediate cause of the quarrel was a wig which Hallam had taken. When challenged about the wig, Hallam took it off and threw it at Macklin with a scathing remark. Hot words were exchanged and finally Macklin used his stick, which entered Hallam's eye. The wounded man was taken to a nearby hospital, where he died the following morning. Evidently the stick had gone deeply into his head. Macklin was charged with murder. After careful preparation, the actor conducted his own defence. The court found him guilty of manslaughter only and he seems to have escaped without any punishment. The episode gave him a taste for the law.

David Garrick became a great friend of Macklin and for a period they were inseparable. Their friendship developed to the point where they took a house together at Bow Street. Garrick and Macklin, together with other actors, took part in a strike against the management of Fleetwood. Later the strike was settled and Garrick was re-employed at better terms, but Macklin was made the scapegoat and dismissed. Macklin considered, probably rightly, that Garrick had let him down. A lifelong feud was the result.[10]

When Macklin attempted to appear as Macbeth in 1773 at Covent Garden there was a determined opposition to him.[11] This was organised by a number of actors who through jealousy objected to his taking on the role. The press joined in the barrage against him. Against all Macklin fought back with determination. He brought the matter into court and was awarded damages and expenses. Macklin offered to settle for less. The judge expressed admiration of his conduct and remarked: " You have met with great applause to-day: you never acted better ". Macklin had conducted his own case with great ability. By now he was becomaware of his ability in the forum.

In Dublin he quarrelled with Thomas Sheridan at Smock Alley and in London with the actor Quin. The same atmosphere of conflict was found in his domestic life.[12]

Macklin and his Family[13]

The life of a strolling player in eighteenth-century England was by no means conducive to respectable living. Macklin spent years in this environment and had a relationship with an actress called Mrs. Anne Grace, the widow of a Dublin hosier. She was born Ann Purvor in Ireland. In 1733 a daughter was born and named Maria. In 1739, when their daughter was six years old, the pair were married. Mr. and Mrs. Macklin appeared on the stage together at times. Mrs. Macklin had a measure of fame in her own right. In 1750 a son was born to them and named John.

On the 28th December, 1758, Mrs. Macklin died. By September, 1759, Macklin had married Elizabeth Jones from Chester. She had been housekeeper at the Macklin home while the previous Mrs. Macklin was alive. There was a hint of some sort of *liaison* between Macklin and his housekeeper while his first wife was alive. Maria, his daughter, had objected to this. The second Mrs. Macklin survived him. She died in 1808 and was buried with her husband.

Maria Macklin early followed the profession of her parents. She began her stage career in 1742 at the age of nine and continued to act for almost 25 years. She was evidently a good actress, reliable and easy to get on with. Her retirement from the stage took place in 1776 after a dispute with her father. The strain of sharing the same house with him proved to be too much for her. She took separate apartments and shared with a friend. Her death took place at Brompton on July 3rd, 1781, at the early age of 48. Evidence of the depth of the estrangement from her father is the fact that while she left around £2,000, none of it was bequeathed to her father. Her assets had been acquired through success in a lottery.

John Macklin received the best education his father could secure for him. Macklin had great hopes of seeing his son successful and thus adding glory to a name which had already received notice. In 1769 John was on his way to India, where his father's influence had secured a job for him with the East India Company. On the same boat travelled a young man called Warren Hastings—a name later known throughout the whole of England. John enjoyed the trip and lost almost all his money on gambling. He landed with practically no funds and soon his father was receiving begging letters. Then one day in 1775 John returned to London and Charles had to do further planning for the future of his 25-year-old son.

The veteran actor, now in his seventies, had gained considerable knowledge of the law through his lawsuits. Indeed, he must have regretted that he did not get an opportunity in his early years to follow the legal profession. What he was denied his son could now attain. John was now enrolled to study law at the Middle Temple on October 25th, 1775.

John's application to study was poor and his love for a free and easy life among his friends was great. He sold his law books and next we find him in America. His grandfather had fought in Ireland to secure the Stuart succession and now John was fighting in America to ensure the success of the cause of a Hanoverian. He soon tired of the tough army life, however, and managed to get a discharge. He came back directly to England, in disgrace for a second time. What his father said we know not, but he must have been sorely disappointed.

John must have become associated with the stage, as we find him in Dublin with his father in 1785. He returned to England the same year. There is no record of any success in this field. The next record we have of him is that of his death of lockjaw on April 14th, 1790, at the age of 40. Charles Macklin, now in his nineties, was left to spend his last years alone save for the company of his second wife.

Macklin in Business[14]

In 1753 Macklin quit the stage and in March of the following year he had opened a tavern and coffee-house under the Piazza in Convent Garden. A distinctive feature of this venture was the three-shilling ordinary—public meal—over which the actor himself presided.

Later in the same year, at Hart Street, Covent Garden, Macklin began a function which was called " The British Inquisition ". The entertainment, which commenced at seven o'clock in the evening, consisted of a lecture followed by a debate.

Both ventures failed, however, and bankruptcy resulted. But in time Macklin paid all claims in full and enhanced his name thereby. By now the actor had found that he was not a business-man and he returned to the stage, where he was to remain to entertain another generation.

Macklin and Dr. Johnson[15]

Macklin and the famous Johnson met in 1761. This was the first of many contacts. One report of a meeting has been recorded for us. These two men were famous in their day but in different spheres. Nevertheless, whenever they met each tried to outshine the other.

265

Johnson, during a celebrated encounter, felt that Macklin was getting the better of the exchanges. The lexicographer addressed the actor in Hebrew. " What is that, Sir ?" queried Macklin. " Hebrew," said Johnson. The actor replied, " But what do I know of Hebrew ?" " But a man of your understanding, Mr. Macklin, ought to be acquainted with every language." Dr. Johnson felt he had scored a point very successfully. " Och neil en deigen vonshet ham boge vaureen "! replied Macklin (sic). Johnson was now placed at a disadvantage, but managed to ask the name of the language. " Irish, Sir," said Macklin. " Irish !" roared the doctor. " Do you think I ever studied that ?" Back came the reply, " But a man of your understanding, Dr. Johnson, ought to be acquainted with every language !"

Macklin was also acquainted with Johnson's biographer Boswell.

The Closing Years

Despite his substantial income, Macklin had more than once in his life endured the inconvenience of poverty. His most acute financial shortage, however, was experienced in 1790 on the death of his son. All his savings had been spent in John's education and in clearing up the various involvements in which he found him.

His friends became aware of his need and organised the publication of his best plays, *The Man of the World* and *Love a la Mode*.[16] A total of £1,582. 11. 0 was collected. To ensure a certain income while he lived, an annuity of £200 was purchased and a yearly sum of £75 payable to Mrs. Macklin in the event of her surviving her husband was included in the contract. The balance of the fund was handed over to Macklin. Lord Loughborough, a former pupil, gave an annuity of £20. The veteran actor could now rest free of financial worries.

Senile decay set in but still Macklin kept in touch with the theatres which had seen the days of his triumphs. A seat was always reserved for him while he lived and he was able to come and go as he wished.

Macklin's Death

Between the hours of nine and ten on the morning of July 11th, 1797, Charles Macklin died. His life corresponded almost with the entire eighteenth century. He was buried in a vault under the chancel of St. Paul's Church, Convent Garden. His coffin bore the simple inscription:

Mr. Charles Macklin,
Comedian,
Died the 11th July, 1797,
Aged 97 years.

St. Paul's was a fitting resting-place for the great actor. Around him lie buried many other famous men and women—authors, painters and actors. Each, like Macklin, had excelled in his or her chosen field. The visitor to St. Paul's can still see the memorial tablet erected to the memory of Macklin. Above the tablet was placed a carving of the two masks, comedy and tragedy. The tragic mask had a dagger thrust through the eye—a reference to the fatal dispute. The inscription reads:

Sacred to the Memory
of Charles Macklin, Comedian.
This Tablet is erected
(with the aid of Public Patronage)
by his affectionate Widow
ELIZABETH Macklin
Obiit 11th July, 1797, Aetatis 107.
Macklin! the father of the Modern Stage
Renown'd alike for Talents and for Age,
Whose Years a Century and Longer ran,
Who liv'd and dy'd as may become a Man.
This lasting Tribute to thy Worth receive,
'Tis all a grateful Public now can give
Their loudest Plaudits now no more can Move
Yet hear! thy Widow's still final voice of Love.

An Assessment

Critics state that Charles Macklin had high merit as a dramatist and that he excelled in stage-management. While he secured fame in the roles of Shylock and Macbeth, it is agreed that he found the best expression for his talent in comedy.

Nature had given him a forbidding appearance. Quin, a fellow actor, said of him: " If God writes a legible hand that man is a villain !" And on another occasion: " Mr. Macklin, by the cordage of your face you should be hanged".[17] This helped in many roles, but especially that of Shylock. His appearance in the trial scene was so fearful that it was reported that George II, in a discussion with Walpole over the control of an unruly House of Commons, said: " What do you think of sending them to the theatre to see that Irishman play Shylock ?"[18]

Macklin never ceased to be an Irishman. As already stated, he often visited Dublin and indeed at the end of his career he intended for a time to settle down in Ireland. Are Macklin's sentiments expressed in his play *The True Born Irishman* ? The leading character, in reply to the taunt of his snobbish wife, " You are true Irish to the very bone of you," says: " Indeed I am, and to the marrow within the bone too, and what is more, I hope I shall never be otherwise ". Note also the *laudatio* on the name of O Doherty in the same play.

The influence of his native Inis Eoghain can be seen in the names of some of the characters, *e.g.*, O Doherty aforementioned and O Brollaghan—both surnames common here.

Macklin's Biographers

Charles Macklin's impact on the mind of the people of his time can be seen by the fact that before he was ten years dead three full-length biographies of him had been written. In 1798 appeared the work of Francis Aspry Congreve, considered by all as the most accurate and trustworthy.

In 1799 was published the second biography. The author was James Thomas Kirkman, reputed by some to have been an illegitimate son of Macklin. Kirkman said of himself that " he was a near relative, bred up and living for upwards of twenty years with the actor ". Despite the fact that he was in a good position to give a true record, Kirkman's two-volume work is regarded as fiction rather than fact.

The third biography was printed in 1804 and its author was William Cooke, a man who knew Macklin in London. This work is not regarded as trustworthy either.

In 1891, almost a century after his death, a biography was written by Judge William Edward Abbott Parry. A great number of articles and pamphlets was also published. Interest in Macklin has continued to the present time. In 1960 a full-length biography was published by Harvard University Press. The author was William W. Appleton. This work is well-documented and is beyond doubt the most satisfactory biography to date.

HENRY DOHERTY[19]

Among those who tc ok part in the Williamite Wars was a young man from the townland of Muff, in the parish of Culdaff, named Henry Doherty. He was born about 1665. Despite the restrictions of the time, he managed to secure a good education. He had a good command of the Irish language.

Henry Doherty soon came under notice and was appointed secretary to Patrick Sarsfield. At Limerick he drew up in Irish the articles of the Treaty of Limerick. After the defeat of the Irish cause Henry Doherty returned to his native parish, where he remained until his death in the eighteenth century. His descendants lived in Muff until 1867, when the last of the family, another Henry Doherty, emigrated to America.

SHANE O DOHERTY[20]

Shane O Doherty was a poet who was born in Malin about 1700. He was nicknamed Mac Avergy. He went to live in the nearby parish of Clonmany, where he died in 1764. None of his works has survived.

WILLIAM ELDER, EDITOR AND POLITICIAN

In the townland of Norrira, near Malin Town, in the parish of Cloncha, was born on July 22nd, 1823, William Elder.[21] His name as an orator, parson, editor and politician was famous in New Brunswick.

The Elders were one of the Presbyterian families which in the eighteenth century had come from Scotland as planters. In 1799 we find a William Elder signing the petition to King George asking for the speedy implementation of the Act of Union.[22] In the Tithe Applotment Book[23] we find the name John Elder as a landowner. The last-named was evidently the father of William Elder and the signatory of the petition would have been his grandfather.

William attended the local school. He was well served with primary education facilities, as there were at this time three schools in nearby Malin Town. The young boy was well-gifted intellectually and advanced rapidly in his studies. When he had passed through all the grades he was appointed assistant teacher at Malin. Coming from a devout religious background, he decided to study for the Presbyterian ministry. To enable himself to get the necessary higher education he worked in a Derry solicitor's office in summer and in winter carried out his studies at the university, where he qualified as a Doctor of Laws. Then he emigrated to St. John, New Brunswick, where he had care of a congregation. He soon attracted attention by his ability to speak in public and to write in the newspapers.

He was for a time editor of *The Colonial Presbyterian* and *The Morning Journal*. Later he was proprietor and chief editor of the St. John *Daily Telegraph*. He was elected a member of the State Legislature of New Brunswick in 1878 and was re-elec-

269

ted at the next election, in 1882. His death took place in 1882, in his sixtieth year.

SIR WILLIAM McARTHUR[24]

William McArthur was born at Malin on the 6th July, 1809. He was the fifth child of John McArthur and Sarah Finlay. John McArthur was a Wesleyan minister who had served for a time on the Newtownstewart circuit. He had travelled for 12 months in 1793, during which year he had been called out. He retired in 1818 to Ardstraw, Co. Tyrone, and died in 1840. It is not clear why the family was at Malin at the time William was born.

The boy went to a school at Stranorlar taught by a man called McGranaghan. Here he had as a fellow-pupil Isaac Butt, who later became famous in the Home Rule movement. At 12 William left school and went to work as an apprentice at Enniskillen with Hugh Copeland, a woollen draper. Four years later, in 1825, he went to Lurgan to work, at £45 *per annum*, for a manufacturing tobacconist and spirit merchant called William Johnston. Here for five years he served as salesman and bookkeeper. In his spare time he did some writing for the local paper, the *Imperial Reporter*. In 1830 McArthur went back to the woollen trade for a short time in Dublin. For four years, from 1831, he was in partnership with Joseph Cathar in the same trade in Derry. The partnership was terminated in 1835 and McArthur continued in the business alone. In 1841 he became a member of the town council. His flair for business and politics was becoming evident.

A chance event had a profound effect on McArthur's business career. His brother Alexander went to Australia for health reasons and while there William sent him goods from England. The transaction was successful and Alexander commenced business as an import agent in Sydney. It was the period of the gold rush in Australia, and business prospered. Branches were opened in various parts of the continent and soon the McArthur brothers were wealthy men. William transferred the headquarters of the business from Derry to London, and by 1857 he was resident at Brixton.

In 1865 William again began to take an active part in politics. Standing as a Liberal for Pontefract, he was unsuccessful in his ambition to become a member of parliament. However, he was successful in 1868 in getting elected as representative for Lambeth, which seat he held until 1885. At the dissolution he failed to secure re-election to the House of Commons. In 1886 he became a Liberal Unionist. In colonial matters he was a strong supporter of the imperial policy of expansion. He led the movement in favour of the annexation of Fiji. He achieved this despite the strong opposition of Gladstone.

While in the House of Commons he gave his attention to educational matters and also the various problems affecting his own country. He is recorded as having supported the controversial grant to Maynooth. He became Sheriff of London in 1867; alderman in 1872 and Lord Mayor in 1880. Queen Victoria honoured him in 1882 by making him a Knight Commander of the Order of St. Michael and St. George.

His death took place suddenly in 1887 while travelling on the Underground Railway in London. He is buried at Norwood Cemetery. Sir William McArthur had in 1843 married Marianne, only child of Archibald McElwaine of Coleraine. She died in 1889.

Throughout his life he had remained a faithful member of the Methodist Church. He contributed liberally to many Methodist causes and at death he left £150,000 to charities chiefly connected with that Church. His memory is still revered by the Methodist communion, one of whom, the Rev. T. McCullough, wrote his biography.

ROBERT A. WILSON, JOURNALIST[25]

The Wilson family were resident at Malin Head when their son Robert was born in 1820. Mr. Wilson, Senior, was in the Coastguard Service. Mrs. Wilson was an educated woman. She gave her son the rudiments of an education and imparted to him a life-long interest in and love for literature. The family later moved to Falcarragh, where his mother died. Robert emigrated to the United States, where his literary abilities secured him a post on one of the leading papers. He seemed assured of a very successful career in this field, but his health failed. To recuperate he returned to Ireland and spent the remainder of his life in his native land.

On his return he made a study of current political questions to prepare himself for the continuance of his career as a journalist. He made himself acquainted with the Tenant Right campaign and for a couple of years was on the staff of the *Nation*. Another period of convalescence followed. When he recovered he joined the staff of the *Fermanagh Reporter and Enniskillen Advertiser* He was the contributor of the famous letters which appeared regularly under the name of " Barney Maglone ". Later, when he went to Belfast and joined the *Morning News*, he continued his famous letters. His flair for satire and humour got full scope for expression, as well as his ability as a poet.

He had a marked facility for languages. Irish he had acquired in his early years at Malin Head and Falcarragh. Later he added Latin, Greek, Italian, German, Spanish and French. Thus he opened for himself and others the vast literary treasures which those languages contained. His pen was ever active in defending the poor and downtrodden people of his day. He was very popular with his fellow-workers and others.

On his death on August 10th, 1875, his many friends erected a memorial over his grave in Belfast. The inscription reads:

In memory of the late Robert A. Wilson, an able journalist, a gifted poet, a fearless advocate of the rights of the people. *Obiit* 10.8.1875.
"Then his dust to the dust
And his soul to its rest.
But his memory to those
Who can cherish it best."

SEAMAS MAG REANNACHAIN

Seamas Mag Reannachain, poet, was born at the Bishop's Hill, Glacknadrummond, in the parish of Cloncha, in 1866. His parents were Donall Mag Reannachain and Brid Nic Lochlainn. Farming was the family occupation. The known poems of this Cloncha poet are: " Inis Eoghain," " Marie McSheffrey," " Kevin Barry," " St. Martina," " Big Still versus Wee Still ".

He married a local woman called Sarah Doherty, who predeceased him by 12 years. He carried on business for a time as a shop-keeper in the village of Culdaff and later retired to Dunross.

He died in 1933 and is buried in Bocan. His grave is marked by a simple headstone.

FREDERICK YOUNG, FOUNDER OF THE GHURKAS[26]

Frederick Young was born at Culdaff in 1786. His ancestors were planters who had come to Culdaff around 1630. The Young family were granted lands on lease from the Marquis of Donegall and the Protestant Bishop of Derry.

Frederick Young went to India at the age of 14 and took up a career in the British army there. He became a general. During his term in India he succeeded in establishing good relations with the hill tribes and founded the famous Ghurka Regiment.

After half a century in the Indian occupation-army he retired in 1854 to live at Fairy Hill, Bray. Owing to the failure of the bank in which his money was lodged he had to sell his house and move to Ballybrack, where he died in 1874.

MAOL IOSA O BROLCHAIN, POET AND PROFESSOR

In the early part of the eleventh century, in the north of Inis Eoghain, a son was born to the family of O Brolchain. The place of birth is not certain but was probably in the present parish of Culdaff. The name by which this child was known was Maol Iosa —it is not clear whether the name was given at baptism or later taken in the religious community he joined.

The life of Maol Iosa spanned the greater part of the eleventh century. This was the period which saw the end of Danish power in Ireland and efforts to establish a more organised system of native rule. It was in this century that the first steps were taken to overhaul the structure of Irish Church government and eradicate many of the abuses which hindered the fulfilment of the Church's mission.

Maol Iosa sprang from a family[27] which had a long tradition of culture and learning and which could trace descent from a great royal progenitor—Eoghan, founder of Cineal Eoghain. The family of O Brolchain was directly descended from Suibhne Meann, who was King of Ireland from 615 to 628 A.D. Members of it held high positions at Derry, Armagh and Iona.

At an early age[28] Maol Iosa began his studies at the famous monastery of Both Chonais[29]. It is highly probable that his family was closely related to the abbot or that his parents were *manaigh* on the monastic lands in the district. As the child advanced in age he also grew in learning so that he subsequently held a position of importance in the monastery.

Maol Iosa became famous throughout the whole of Ireland for wisdom, learning and piety. He was also recognised as a poet of standing. Colgan writes[30] of him as a man of virtue and holiness of life famous afar in his own day. The same authority goes on to state that there was no one to equal him in the standard of his knowledge. He excelled in all the sciences. The *Annals of Ulster*[31] speak of him as a " master of wisdom and of piety and in poetry in either language " (*i.e.*, Irish and Latin). The *Annals of Clonmacnoise*[32] (surviving only in translation) say:

Moyle Issa O Brothloghann, the ealder and sage of Ireland, was soe

273

ingenious and witty, and withall soe well learned, that he composed great volumes containing many great Misteryes and new sciences devised by himself . . .

The *Martyrology of Donegal* includes him among the Confessors of the Faith and states that his feast-day is January 16th.

Maol Iosa did not spend his whole career at Both Chonais. It is probable that he visited and lectured at most of the great foundations of his time. That he spent some time at Armagh and Lismore is confirmed.[33] On the 16th of January, 1086, after a lengthy illness,[4] Maol Iosa died at the monastery of Lismore, where later an oratory was erected to his memory.[35] The annalist records:[36]

The seventeenth of the Kalends of February
The night of the feast of Fursa fair,
Died Mael-Isu Ua Brolchain,
Alas who is there to whom it is not grevious plague sore?

Earlier writers[37] speak of a cult of Maol Iosa in North Inis Eoghain and reference is also made to the survival of some of his manuscripts. Nowadays his name is completely forgotten, however, and there is no evidence of the existence of any manuscripts. The oral tradition associated with him died, it would seem, with the disappearance of the Irish language. His memory survived so long firstly because of his standing as a learned man who was proficient in many sciences, secondly by reason of his repute for holiness and finally because of his religious poems. Many of these[38] escaped the ravages of the Norman and English conquests, but it is a matter for regret that many others were lost.

It is a tribute to Maol Iosa's standing that his poems were, in his own time, circulated throughout the whole country. Indeed, he was the most outstanding poet of the eleventh century, though his works are not regarded as possessing high literary merit. They indicate, rather, a man of deep and simple spirituality. A close study of the psalms is indicated and his acceptance of the intercessory power of the angels is clear. A natural and non-puritanical approach to human roblems is also evident. For instance—
In " Achaini an Ghra ":

Deus meus, adjuva me,
Tabhair dom do shearc, a mhic dhil De,
Tabhair dom do shearc, a mhic dhil De,
Deus meus, adjuva me.

In " Prionsa na nAingeal ":

A Aingil,
Beir, a Mhichil mhorfheartaigh,
Go dti an Tiarna mo phaidir.

In another poem:

Guard for me my feet
On that good land of Ireland
That they lose not rest
On useless journeys.
Guard my male organ
As regards chastity and purity
May lust never overcome me,
Never approach me, never near me.

Maol Iosa played a notable part in the life of Ireland in the eleventh century. The upheavals and turmoils caused by the course of history have in the past hindered the research and other work necessary to ensure that this great man got due recognition. The time is now opportune to take action. An up-to-date and accurate edition of all his poems[39] is needed and the people of his own peninsula should see that a fitting memorial is erected to his memory. Will the ninth centenary of his death in 1986 see a revival of interest which will produce results along the lines suggested ?

1. The exact date of Macklin's birth is disputed. Some give 1690 and others a later date. 1699 is favoured, as Macklin is stated to have spoken of himself as 88 years old in 1788. (Ref. Appleton.) His widow, however, had inscribed on the memorial tablet that he was 107 years at his death.
2. The local tradition is that he was born in the district stated above. This is supported by:
   (a) Edward Chichester in *Mason's Statistical Survey*: "Culdaff and Cloncha". While he states Culdaff parish, the actual place of birth is located in the parish of Cloncha a short distance from Culdaff village. Chichester was writing within 20 years of Macklin's death. As he was rector of both Culdaff and Cloncha he was in close touch with local tradition.
   (b) *Inishowen*, "Maghtochair". The author interviewed the people of the area, but he made the mistake of placing Gortanaren, because of its proximity to Culdaff, in the same parish. His evidence is important.
   (c) Congreve, the most reliable of Macklin's early biographers, states that the actor was born in Inis Eoghain.
   (d) *Inis-owen and Tirconnel*, William James Doherty, 1895. He states that an enquiry carried out by the Rev. Philip O Doherty into the

275

local tradition had confirmed the exact place of birth as stated above. Unfortunately, the data on which this judgement was based were not given.

3. *Dictionary of National Biography*: Macklin, Charles.
4. *Inis-owen and Tirconnel*, William James Doherty.
5. *Life of Macklin*, Kirkman.
6, 7. *An Actor's Life*, Appleton.
8. *Irish Times*, Oct. 26th, 1968.
9. *Dictionary of National Biography*: Macklin, Charles.
10, 11, 12, 13. *An Actor's Life*, Appleton.
14. *Dictionary of National Biography*: Macklin, Charles.
15. *An Actor's Life*, Appleton. The incident was recorded by Kirkman.
16, 17. *Ibid.*
18. *Dictionary of National Biography*: Macklin, Charles.
19. *Inishowen*, "Maghtochair". The author recorded the oral tradition of the area in the second half of the last century.
20, 21. *Inis-owen and Tirconnel*, William James Doherty.
22. George Faulkner: *The Dublin Journal*, December 14th, 1799.
23. Tithe Applotment Book, 1829: Parish of Cloncha.
24. I, *Dictionary of National Biography;* II, *History of Methodism in Ireland*, R. Lee Cole, M.A.; B.D.
25. *Inis-owen and Tirconnel*, William James Doherty.
26. *Three Hundred Years in Inishowen*, Young.
27. *Acta Sanctorum Hiberniae*, Colgan.
28. *Crinoc*, a poem by Maol Iosa, has the following verse. He refers to his psalter, saying "When you slept with me, valiant of the sharp wisdom, I was a pure-hearted, quiet, uncomplicated lad, a gentle boy of seven sweet years."
29, 30. *Acta Sanctorum Hiberniae*, Colgan.
31. *Annals of Ulster*: entry for 1086.
32. *Annals of Clonmacnoise*: entry for 1084.
33. *The Annals of Inishfallen*, in an entry for 1086, state: "Mael Isu Ua Brolchain of the community of Ard Macha, the venerable senior and eminent sage of Ireland, rested in Les Mor Mo-Chata".
34. In his poem, *Atlochar duit, a mo Ri*, Maol Iosa says, as he lies in his bed in Munster: "I give thanks to you, my King, who look after our welfare in this world; it is six months from yesterday that I have been lying on my sick-bed".
35. *Adamnan's Life of St. Columba*. Edited by Reeves, P.405. The oratory was burned in 1116.
36. *Annals of Ulster*.
37. I, Colgan in *Acta Sanctorum Hiberniae;* II, *Inishowen*, "Maghtochair".
38. List of extant Poems: *Achaini an Ghra; Spiorad na Firinne; Prionsa na nAingeal; Rop soraid in set-sa; A choimdhe baidh . . . non — geibh fot comm; A choimdiu, nom-chomet . . . non-chomet a choimdiu; Buaidh crabuidh, Buaidh n-ailithre . . . tuc damh na ceithre buadha; Dia haine ni longad . . . ocus garseclae; Crinoc; Atlochar duit, a mo Ri; Mo chinaid i comtaine.*
39. Vide: Maol Íosa Ó Brolcháin, Muireann Ní Bhrolcháin, An Sagart, Maigh Nuad 1986.

NOTE: Due acknowledgment is made to the authors of *Ri na nUile* — Sean S. O Conghaile, C.S.S.R., and Sean O Riordain — for extracts from their translation into modern Irish of *Achaini an Ghra* and *Prionsa na nAingeal;* to Diarmaid O Laoghaire, S.J., for an extract from the poem *Guard for me my feet* in his work entitled *Old Ireland and her Spirituality;* and also to Frank O Connor for an extract from the poem *Crinoc* in his book *King, Lords and Commons.*

19

THE STORY OF MOORE O CONNOR

ON THE 2nd of May, 1851, Moore O Connor was instituted in
the Church of St. Buadan as rector of the parish of Culdaff. He
had succeeded John Sheal and held the benefice until 1857. At
the time of his departure his name was well-known not only in
the diocese of Derry, but also in every part of Ireland. Born in
Tralee[1] about the year 1820, he began life with the very Irish
name of Muireartach Diarmaid O Conchuir. This was Anglicised
" Murtagh Jeremiah O Connor " and later changed by the bearer
to " Moore O Connor " to ensure a better public image for himself.

Like so many other men of note and notoriety, the early years
of O Connor are vague. It is certain that he was born in Tralee.
His father was a tradesman—some say a blacksmith and others
a coffin-maker.[2] Probably he secured his livelihood by both trades.
His parents were Catholics and as a member of this denomination
young O Connor lived his early years. Nearby, a family of means
and influence lived, and this family took a special interest in
Moore O Connor.[3] As a result he secured a good education and
an insight into the manner of life of the richer and more substantial residents of Tralee and its neighbourhood.

Before the story of Moore O Connor is told it is important to
give a picture of the man. He was endowed with great intellectual
ability, a pleasant personality and a great ambition to succeed in
life. His education enabled him to express himself with eloquence
whether in debate or in the pulpit. His pen was facile, colourful
and, when necessary, virulent. His acquaintance with the richer
people in Tralee gave him a great hankering for the " good life ".
The ruthless element in his character made him use without
scruple all his ability to achieve his ends. He enjoyed controversy
and attacked his enemies with a reckless courage. He lacked
religious conviction almost entirely. Catholicism he cast aside
when he found it a barrier to his plan, while for the Established
Church and all its institutions he had complete contempt.

Around 1838, when still in his teens, he left Tralee and made
his way to Dublin, where he secured a post as an assistant teacher
with the Rev. William Sturgeon, who had a school at Portobello.[4]
He enrolled as a medical student; in what institution we know
not. About this time, to lessen the Celtic content of his name, he

assumed the name of Moore O Connor and ceased to profess the religion of his birth. The medical studies were of short duration. At the end of 1839 O Connor went off to London, but before leaving Dublin he provided himself with excellent references—all forgeries.[5]

The first document, in O Connor's own handwriting, reads as follows:

I have been requested by Mr. O Connor to state my opinion of him. I consider him to be a religious, conscientious, diligent and trustworthy young man who has been labouring most creditably and zealously for his own advancement and I have every confidence that he would discharge faithfully the duties of every situation for which he may be seeking. I can also add unhesitatingly that I consider him to be a critical and excellent classical scholar.
(Signed): G. Sidney Smith, Clerk, F.T.C.D. 1st Dec., 1839.
I fully subscribe to the above.
(Signed): Thomas Luby, Clerk, F.T.C.D. 3rd Dec., 1839.

The text of the second document was as set out below:

It is with great pleasure that I can state my opinion of Mr. Connor from a long and intimate acquaintance with him in the university. I look upon him as a person of sound judgement, of extensive reading, of a disciplined mind and of a heart the most amiable and purified I have ever met. His manners ever since I knew him have been marked with decorum and consistency. He has attended all his terms in the university and has been the prizeman of his division for some time.
(Signed): Thomas Miller, Clerk, M.A., M.R.I.A., T.C.D. April 27th, 1840.

The third document read:

With a very great pleasure I have heard of your determination to devote yourself to the service of the Lord Jesus Christ by becoming a minister of the Gospel and most gladly I contribute my testimony to your character and fitness for that important duty. I have had the pleasure of being a long time acquainted with you. I know that your literary attainments are of a very high order. So far as ever came to my knowledge your character is irreproachable and has always been marked with consistency and I have ever considered your temper and disposition as naturally kind and amiable and zealous for good. With these feelings I have no hesitation in pronouncing you well adapted to fill the sacred calling of a minister of Christ and I trust that with the blessing of the Lord your ministry will be eminently successful.
I am,
My Dear Sir,
Faithfully yours,
William Sturgeon, M.D.,
Clerk.
Portobello. Oct. 4th, 1839.
To Mr. J. M. Connor.

Both G. Sidney Smith and Thomas Luby later affirmed that the documents purporting to be signed by them were fraudulent and their signatures a forgery.[6] The certificate in the name of Thomas Miller was also fraudulent, as it was established that at the date shown there was no such man as Thomas Miller a Master of Arts of the University of Dublin or a member of the Royal Irish Academy. With regard to the document signed by William Sturgeon, it was confirmed that the text was in Sturgeon's hand-writing but that the words "To Mr. J. M. Connor" were not. O Connor had stolen the reference in Sturgeon's handwriting, which was intended for another person.[7]

These documents give us an indication as to his intentions. He failed to succeed in medicine and now proposed to seek ordination in the Anglican Church. He could thus secure a benefice and attain that standard of living he so eagerly sought.

On arrival in London Moore O Connor secured employment as a teacher in a school in Putney run by the Rev. Edward Trimmer. Here he became acquainted with the incumbent of St. Mary's Church, Putney, Christopher Robinson. In the eyes of both Trimmer and Robinson, the young Irishman was a model Christian, and O Connor carefully imparted his desire for admission to the ministry to these two clergymen.[8] After discussions with Trimmer, Robinson contacted an organisation called The Society for the Propagation of the Gospel in Foreign Parts. An appointment was obtained and an approach was made to the Bishop of London to ordain O Connor as a deacon. "Excellent certificates" were produced to show his fitness for the office.

The legislation provided for ordinations of this kind on condition that the candidate made a solemn declaration to serve abroad. On the 19th December, 1840, with 15 others, O Connor signed the following:

We whose names are hereunto subscribed to be admitted to the Holy Order of deacon by the Right Honourable and Right Reverend Father in God Charles James Lord Bishop of London do hereby declare that we propose to take upon ourselves the cure of souls or to officiate in a spiritual capacity in Her Majesty's colonies or foreign possessions and to reside therein and we do hereby severally engage to perform the same.

On the following day Moore O Connor was ordained a deacon of the Anglican Church in a Westminster church by the Bishop of London.[9] The first major step had been taken towards his goal, though his desire to secure a benefice in Ireland still had two obstacles to overcome: he had to secure ordination to the priesthood and a special permission to officiate in an ecclesiastical capacity in Great Britain or Ireland.

An indication of O Connor's character can be found in the fact that while in Trimmer's employment he had converted to his own use money collected from the students to buy books. This was discovered after he left, when the bookseller presented the account for payment to the school.[10]

Early in 1841 O Connor was back in Ireland and secured a position as a curate in St. Andrew's Church in Suffolk St., Dublin. When the Bishop of London wrote to remind him of his solemn engagement to serve in the Colonies, he firmly refused to go. The facts of his case got to the ears of the Archbishop of Dublin, and O'Connor's curacy was terminated.[11] The Bishop of London wrote to the Archbishop of Dublin and Armagh informing them of the position and requested them to advise all the suffragan bishops.[12] However, because of the delay in issuing due notice, Moore O Connor secured another success.

The diocese of Derry was ruled from 1831 to 1858 by Richard Ponsonby, a prelate noted for his lack of spirituality and his administrative inefficiency.[13] As O Connor left Dublin he went to Derry to seek a post. It is not clear whether the decision was based on luck or design. In any case it was the ideal place for him. A curacy was obtained at Fahan, where he carried out his duties fittingly.[14] The zealous young curate next applied to the Bishop of Derry for letters dimissory to get ordained. The latter issued the necessary documents and armed with these O Connor got ordained, on June 27th, 1841, as a minister of the Anglican Church by the Bishop of Lichfield.[15]

It is clear that there was some blundering along the way, but exactly where cannot be easily determined. Ponsonby was at fault in failing to make due enquiries before allowing O Connor into his diocese. It would also seem that neither the Bishop of London delayed in notifying the Primate or the Primate was slow in warning Derry. In any case, O Connor was ordained before the cautionary letter reached Derry.

The Rev. Moore O Connor came back to Derry after his ordination and acted as licenciate curate in Fahan Lower from 1843 to 1846.[16] The security of a parish was still his aim and he constantly planned to attain this position. His efforts to get into the diocese of Down and Connor were frustrated by the bishop there.[17] In 1846 O Connor went back to England. During his five years in England he failed to get any permanent appointment, although he successively held eight curacies. As to his conduct, we have one hint: while acting as a curate in Richmond, he was detected in some false statements and expelled from the diocese by the Bishop of Winchester. Nevertheless, representing himself as a B.A., T.C.D., he got an *ad eundem* degree from Cambridge.[18]

All the while, O Connor kept closely in touch with the diocese of Derry, and finally got the chance he sought. John Sheal, a kindred spirit it would seem, agreed to sell his benefice in Culdaff. An agreement was drafted and signed, and the sum of £450 was paid over.[19] It was a simoniacal agreement, involving both in conflict with ecclesiastical law, but it meant that in May, 1851, Moore O Connor was in possession of a secure income and a post which gave him a definite standing in the community. At the age of 31 he had achieved his ambition. Richard Ponsonby at Derry ratified the institution of the new rector at Culdaff without any investigation. Good luck was O Connor's in full measure.

Culdaff was then, as now, a place of peace and beauty where a man could enjoy a peaceful and untroubled existence. The rector had a small flock, who made few demands on their spiritual father. The weekly service was the only regular duty and only a minimum of administrative work was involved. Indeed, as Moore O Connor moved around his glebe in those early days he should have felt at peace. Whatever prudence and wisdom he possessed must have counselled him to pursue a quiet, peaceful course and attract no attention to either himself or his parish. This, precisely, he failed to do. Some restless urge within him led to a course of action which directed the nation's spotlight on Culdaff and its flamboyant rector. The result was disastrous for Muireartach Diarmaid O Conchuir.

The first two years of his rectorship corresponded with the last years of the episcopacy of Richard Ponsonby. During this time the rector of Culdaff was almost entirely free from supervision. By 1853, however, William Higgins was in control of the diocese. The new bishop was an able and firm administrator. Culdaff got his attention in due course and Moore O Connor soon realised that critical and discerning episcopal eyes were focussed on his parish.

The image projected by O Connor during his six years as rector may now be noted.

He soon found that his income was not sufficient and he got into debt.[20] To meet his requirements he got money from the Church Commissioners and converted it to his own use. His handling of the material affairs of the parish was unsatisfactory. He appointed as churchwarden and later as parish clerk an illiterate labourer called John Knox. Knox held a small parcel of land in Culdaff-Glebe, where he was a tenant of the rector. Bishop Higgins found matters so unsatisfactory that he had Knox dismissed from the post of parish clerk.[21]

In addition, O Connor associated with the local Catholic clergy, while the doctrine he preached to his flock gave rise to concern because of its " Romish tendencies ".[22] In fact, of course, the incumbent of Culdaff had never had any formal course of divinity and the only knowledge of Christianity he had was that obtained when he was a Catholic boy in Tralee. There are suggestions that he treated some of his parishioners in a cavalier fashion[23] and thus made enemies who ensured that a stream of unfavourable reports circulated to all interested in such information.

Letters began to appear in the Derry newspapers under various pseudonyms, e.g., *Hibernicus, Hibernicus Junior*. One appeared under the name of " John Knox ", the deposed parish clerk. These letters were virulent in tone and unrestrained in language. Even bishops were not spared. It soon became known the writer was the resident of the rectory at Cregnasole—Moore O Connor.

A glimpse of O Connor's domestic life, about which little is known. He had married an English girl, who had died in childbirth. It is not clear whether she had ever come to Culdaff. A rumour was circulated that the rector had been giving strychnine to his wife, but it would seem that there was no truth whatsoever in this.

His way of life came to the notice of the local papers, and some animosity developed between him and the *Derry Sentinel*. This paper published, on January 5th, 1855, the following:

It would fill a volume were we to record the many instances of unclerical conduct on the part of Mr. O Connor. We know far more of his history than he imagines, and we could trace it out pretty accurately from the day when, bearing the unaristocratic name of Jerry Connor, he quitted the domicile of his respected sire, the coffin-maker of Tralee, down to the present moment when he assumes the style, title and dignity of the Rev. Moore O Connor, Rector of Culdaff.

It would be a long and not very edifying story to tell how, after being employed as a messenger in a newspaper office in Dublin, he, on false pretences, obtained ordination from the Bishop of London; how he remained in Ireland instead of proceeding to Canada, on the plea of ill-health.

How he stealthily obtained a curacy in the country, from which he was driven by the Bishop of London; how he proceeded next to Buncrana as curate and tutor; how he gave out, while there, that he had been a captain of dragoons, a graduate of Oxford, etc.; how he attempted to pawn the poetry of American and British poets on the public as his own; how he got possession of the property of certain elderly ladies, and afterwards treated them unhandsomely; how when he obtained a curacy in England, he pretended that he had at the same time a valuable living in Yorkshire, and by his representations was enable to form a connexion in a respectably family, which terminated in a very brief period.

These are only a few of the incidents of the same kind in the career of this man who has the audacity to plume himself on his spotless character, and to vilify persons infinitely his superior in every respect.

Originally a Papist himself, he does not scruple to imitate the example of his quondam instructor, the Romish priest, and dares to denounce any of his parishioners who contravene his behests. Truly it is a most calamitous circumstance that such men are permitted for a moment to have the spiritual oversight of a large district of country.

This was a devastating attack, and it is a matter for conjecture as to why the newspaper published the statement. Was the editor concerned with the good name of the Church of Ireland or was it only spleen ? It is clear that the newspaper had secured the facts of O Connor's background, and now everyone in the diocese was fully informed. O Connor's standing with the clergymen of his own denomination was severely damaged. The rector at Donagh, Nicholas Columbine Martin, was the only friend he had among them.

For two months there was silence. Then, under the name of " John Knox ", the following letter appeared in the *Derry Journal* in its edition of March 6th, 1855.

"Our hungry *Sentinel* scribbling fills its purse
With petty pilfered thoughts, and makes them worse,
Like gypsies, lest the stolen brat be known,
Defacing first, then claiming for its own."
Sir,
I believe that the last number of the *Sentinel* displayed a degree of turpitude unexampled in public journalism.

Its hashed-up re-heated falsehoods as regards the Rector of Culdaff I shall not condescend to notice, further than to observe that they are subtle and unscrupulous, with just a little colour of an occasional semblance of truth to give them zest.

"Whenever passion," as Bacon says, "wishes to disgrace and destroy, it charges without proof, and traduces without shame," and such is the invariable operation of hatred and revenge, more especially when the objects of these are honest men and worthy men, commanding the esteem of all who know them.

Your readers, no doubt, remember Captain Gulliver, who called, some years back to Laputa, where he saw pure ideas converted into animal filth in a college hall. For my part, I never see or read a number of this curious print that I do not think of the famed Captain Gulliver, and ask myself what else doth the lying, know-nothing *Sentinel* office work, distorter of the public news, a deserter from Christian charity, a temporisor in religion, and a violator of private correspondence; it may not rank with the college-man in Laputa for the creation and concoction of moral filth; it has taken its diploma of B.A. in scoundrilism — B-lackguard in private, and A-postate in public life.

It has called to its aid against the Rector of Culdaff no less a personage than Dr. Bloomfield, successor to wicked old Ridley in the See of London. So far at least as the temporalities are concerned, for in no other respect has it any existence.

For my part, I laugh at the "Crambe repetita" of Bishop Bloomfield and O Driscoll!!! It is quite absurd that any peccadillo of the Rector of Culdaff, quite venial, if one at all, should be hoarded against him for nearly two decades of years back. "Tontarne animis coelestibus irae." But the animosity of this "Dead Body Bill" — see Cobbett's Legacy — Bishop of Irishmen is well known, his altercations with Archbishop Magee, Dr. Thorpe, Rev. L. Prior, etc., etc. As Dryden, in his translation of Virgil, says of the hatred of Juno towards the Trojans:
"She persecutes the ghost of Troy with pains
And gnaws even to the bones the last remains."
These "bones" shall one day or other break the cannibal's teeth. Palaces for the prelates and penury for the curates. "Quosque, tandem patienter nostra abuteris Catalina." How long will prelacy monopolise the treasury of the Church, and hide itself in baronial enjoyment to gorge itself on the spoil?

We fear evil days are in store for the Establishment, and that her fine liturgies and simple teachings will contrast the more fearfully with her prelatical plunderings.

It would be a long, long tale to indite all the vagaries of this Bishop Bloomfield. From the period, 1809, when, as tutor to some hereditary legislator, he drank tea with Cobbett at his house in Botley, up to the present time. How rugged had been the course of the immortal Cobbett — how thickly had his path been strewn with thorns. How smooth, how flowery, how pleasant the career of Charles James London! Yet here we are as Cobbett says: "You, with a mitre on your head, indeed, and a crozier in your holy hands — I at the end of my rugged and thorny path, in a situation to have a right in the names of millions of this nation to inquire not only into your conduct, but into the utility of the very office you fill". But we must give a sketch of this holy man! It must not be in the immortal verse of a friend of ours —
"He stalks in fatness, what a sight
For Christian climes and Christian eyes!.
His coat as 'Hunt's Jet Blacking' bright
A rich silk apron o'er his thighs,
His cheeks in that plethoric plight,
That Lent to Popish priest denies."
No! No! We shall give it in plain prose, and your readers on reading

it will imagine that they are reading a sketch in the life of some railway speculator, or an old Bailey advocate. Here it is "Non hic est meus sermo". Another Right Reverend Father in God.

The bishops are the chief pastors of the Church. They are called the successors of the apostles. Think of the apostles and think of them — Alas!! it is fearfully true — so true that it is plain to all conscientious men to speak of it — that our bishops live and act as men of the world but no more.

O Connor's anger was directed first at the *Derry Sentinel* and then at the Bishop of London, the prelate who had ordained him a deacon some fifteen years before. Whatever about the name signed to the letter, there was no doubt about the identity of the author.

In June, 1855, the *Derry Sentinel* returned to the attack and published the following news item:

Rumour — Clerical Changes in Carndonagh.
It is an old adage and a true one, that "misfortunes makes us acquainted with strange bedfellows". But if a report we have heard be true, every doubt existing on the matter will be dispelled. The Rev. Michael Magill, one of the Roman Catholic curates, has been removed from the parish of Donagh to another sphere of labour and it is stated as one of the reasons, indeed the principal one, his great intimacy with one old friend, the Rev. Jerry Connor, Rector of Culdaff. Report says that these worthy divines were in the habit of spending many jovial evenings together at the family altar of Father Mick and when their devotions and mystic rites had been duly and fully celebrated to the jolly god, it was their practice to occupy the bed of their host together as very dear and fraternal friends on such occasions should do.

The *Derry Sentinel* was clearly keeping a close eye on the rector of Culdaff. O Connor, who was working closely with the rector of Donagh, kept his vitriolic pen in action—more letters to the papers. Thereby he was building up a case for those whose aim was to expose and destroy him.

The redoubtable Moore O Connor kept up the battle for his rights with zeal and vehemence, not only in word but in action. On the 27th March, 1856, the new church at Gleneely, built through the efforts of the Misses Ball, was due for consecration by the Bishop of Derry.[24] The Rev. John McClintock was appointed to act as curate here, in an area within the pastoral care of the rector of Culdaff, who was neither asked to officiate in the new church nor consulted about the appointment.

On the day of the consecration the following notice was displayed on the wall of the church:

To all whom it May Concern — I, the Rev. Moore O Connor, rector of Culdaff in the diocese of Derry, do hereby respectfully and publicly declare that as such rector, it is my right to preach and perform Divine Service in this church, situate at Gleneely within my said parish of Culdaff, and that no person has any right to officiate therein without my consent first had and obtained; and that I hereby formally protest against the appointment of the Rev. John McClintock as curate thereof by the Bishop of Derry, or any other person or persons whatsoever. Given under my hand, this 27/3/1856.

As the Bishop was about to commence the consecration service O Connor and the rector of Donagh advanced from the door of the church and went to the Communion rails. Here O Connor read the notice given above. On completion he handed a copy to the Bishop. Then the rectors of Donagh and Culdaff withdrew to a distant part of the church.

After careful consideration, and consultation with advisers, O Connor decided to take an action for libel against the *Sentinel* for its reports of January and June, 1855. The case was held in the Court of Common Pleas in Dublin on June 30th, 1856, and the following day. The defendant held that the statements made were true and had brought a formidable array of witnesses from Ireland and England to prove the reports. However, on the advice of his legal representatives O Connor exercised his right to refrain from entering the witness box and from giving evidence. This prevented the defendant's counsel from either cross-examining O Connor or taking the evidence of his client's witnesses. After an absence of about half an hour the jury returned with a verdict for the plaintiff and awarded O Connor over £300 in damages. It was, however, a pyrrhic victory, as further developments will show.

In the course of informal discussions at the court in Dublin during the days of the libel action between O Connor and the *Derry Sentinel*, the Rev. Thomas Luby, who had been summoned as a witness by the defendant, was shown the document on which his signature appeared and which was one of the references given to the Bishop of London by O Connor at the latter's ordination to the deaconate. Luby denied that the signature was his.[25] After the case had ended, a full report was made to the Bishop of Derry. As a result of Luby's statements the Bishop decided to hold a full enquiry into the circumstances of O Connor's admission to the ministry. The Bishop's chaplain, the Rev. William Edwards, was sent to the office of the Bishop of London to secure copies of all documents concerning Moore O Connor. The documents were checked by contacting the persons who were alleged to have given the references where this was possible. The registrars of Trinity College and of the Royal Irish Academy were consulted. The full picture became clear to William Higgins in the months following the libel case as information flowed into the Episcopal Palace at Derry.[26] The disturbing truth was that Moore O Connor had never been legally rector of Culdaff. Higgins decided on immediate action to remove him.

The exact course of action required careful consideration. The Bishop sent a comprehensive report to Dublin Castle and asked for advice from the Attorney-General. It was decided that the ecclesiastical court would deal with the breaches of Church law and later the civil court would handle the serious offence of forgery. While in Derry early in January, 1857, O Connor was served by an agent of the Bishop with an inhibition forbidding him to officiate in any spiritual capacity within the parish of Culdaff or any part of the diocese.[27] The order forbade him to collect tithes and any other ecclesiastical emolument. Mr. Harvey of " The Cottage ", Culdaff, was appointed lay administrator. A copy of the inhibition was posted on the door of the church in the village of Culdaff, and the Rev. John McClintock was appointed to conduct the Divine Services for the time being.

As the parishioners proceeded to the church from the different parts of the parish of Culdaff for the midday service on Sunday, January 11th, 1857, there was some doubt as to who would be the officiating clergyman that morning or indeed, whether there would be a service at all. A contemporary newspaper report states:[28]

The Rev. Mr. McClintock, the nominee of Dr. Higgins to the Chapel of Ease at Grousehall, and whose authority as curate has never been admitted by the Rector, accompanied by his father and a few more friends entered the edifice. At this time Mr. O Connor, being in canonicals and in the reading desk, was about to commence the service, it being precisely twelve o'clock. Mr. McClintock, junior, then came up to the reading desk and said that he appeared at the request of the Bishop of Derry to perform the service of the church and to preach. In reply Mr. O Connor, apparently unmoved, said that he would not allow him — that the Bishop in this case was acting most illegally, and that there was no occasion to disturb the performance of divine service. Mr. McClintock still insisting, Mr. O Connor then felt it necessary to call on the police to remove him, as being likely to disturb the service. The elder Mr. McClintock then asked Mr. O Connor did he object to his son's preaching; whereupon Mr. O Connor distinctly and calmly said that he

287

did. The parties then retired after which the rector proceeded with the services.

The morning psalms were most appropriate for the occasion. The "Miserere Mei Deus", "Be merciful unto me, O God, for man goeth about to devour me — is daily fighting and troubling me," was read most feelingly by the Rector, as also was the Litany. The Gospel and Epistle for the octave of the Epiphany then followed, after which Mr. O Connor preached a most beautiful and deeply impressive sermon from the 20th Chapter of the Acts of the Apostles, verses 17th to 38th. As the subject was the valedictory address of St. Paul to the Church of Ephesus, and by some thought to be that of Mr. O Connor to the Church of Culdaff, it was listened to by all with profound attention and many were visibly affected.

The month of February, 1857, saw two legal actions involving O Connor. On the 10th the Consistorial Court of Armagh sat to hear the case of the Bishop of Derry against him. The charges were:

1. He had secured ordination to the deaconate by false representations.
2. He had obtained the degree *ad eundem* from Cambridge by false pretences.
3. He had secured the benefice of Culdaff by a simoniacal contract.
4. He had got money from the Ecclesiastical Commissioners of Ireland (evidently on false statements).
5. Disobedience to the Bishop of Derry.
6. Obstruction of the Rev. John Samuel McClintock.

The case was adjourned to the following day because the defendant did not appear. O Connor did not attend the sittings held on the following day or on February 26th either. When the court opened on March 5th, 1857, however, Moore O Connor was present. He stated that he had no money and consequently could not pay any legal representative to defend him. The court arranged for his defence.[29]

O Connor's inability to attend the earlier sittings at Armagh was caused by the fact that he was attending another case in Dublin. The *Derry Sentinel* had appealed the libel case held in the previous year. The appeal was held in Dublin on the 12th of February, 1857. The judge allowed a full hearing and commented that the letters written by O Connor under the *nom de plume* of *Hibernicus* " were such as nobody would approve of ". The jury found for the *Sentinel* and thus the former judgement was reversed,[30] to the extreme annoyance and disappointment of O Connor.

Moore O Connor was now compelled to give careful attention

to his future. The years of planning to get a secure position had achieved success when he was inducted as rector of Culdaff, but his own imprudent actions had undone all this. The evidence which he knew was now available to the Consistorial Court would and could lead to only one conclusion—his removal from the incumbency. Then he would be charged before the civil court for forgery, and a term in gaol would be the result—not a pleasant prospect for such an ambitious man.

He was now in his late thirties—not too old to try another way of life abroad. In July, 1857, Moore O Connor wrote a letter of resignation to the Bishop of Derry and also informed His Lordship that " the purifying wave of the Catholic Church " had passed over him.[31] Was this a Parthian shot at the prelate just to annoy him, or was he genuinely returning to the Church of his birth ? It is a matter for speculation.

Moore O Connor then quickly left the rectory at Cregnasole. Where he went or what happened him afterwards is not recorded. The charge of forgery was not proceeded with, as he could not be found.

The Consistorial Court of Armagh met in October, 1857, and the judgement of the Primate was delivered. He was found guilty of the charges and deprived of the orders of deacon and priest.[32]

In November, 1857, a meeting was held at Derry.[33] The meeting was attended by the Protestant clergymen of the diocese and its purpose was to congratulate the Bishop on his firmness and perseverance in bringing the action against O Connor to a successful conclusion. One parson, the Rev. M. Knox, stated: ". . . At the same time I can testify that while a curate in Buncrana, Mr. O Connor was both zealous and active and although there was a cloud over him, he had then done his duty as well as any clergyman in the diocese ".

Here ends the story of Murtagh Jeremiah O Connor, the colourful and flamboyant rogue from Tralee. He provided the *cause celebre* of the 1850s, and a mighty headache for the Establishment.

——————————·✸·——————————

1. *Derry Clergy and Parishes*, Leslie.
2. *Derry Standard*, 3rd July, 1856.
3. *Memorials of the Dead of Ireland*, Vol. V. Article by Dr. R. S. Young.

289

4, 5, 6, 7, 8, 9, 10, 11, 12. State Paper Office, 1857. 647, Carton 759. Report of Bishop of Derry to Dublin Castle.
13. *Derry Clergy and Parishes*, Leslie.
14. *Derry Standard*, Nov. 12th, 1857.
15, 16, 17, 18. *Derry Clergy and Parishes*, Leslie.
19. State Paper Office, 1857. 647, Carton 759. Report of Bishop of Derry to Dublin Castle.
20. *Derry Clergy and Parishes*, Leslie.
21. *Derry Standard*, July 3rd, 1856.
22. *Derry Clergy and Parishes*, Leslie.
23. *Derry Standard*, July 3rd, 1856. See report of libel action from which the substance of what follows is drawn except where otherwise stated.
24. *Derry Standard*, April 3rd, 1856. Full report of incident at Grousehall.
25, 26. State Paper Office, 1857. 647, Carton 759. Report of Bishop of Derry to Dublin Castle.
27. *Freeman's Journal*, Jan. 16th, 1857.
28. *Derry Standard*, Jan. 15th, 1857. The paper quotes from a *Derry Journal* report.
29. *Derry Standard*, Feb. 12th, 1857; Feb. 26th, 1857; March 5th, 1857..
30. *Derry Standard*, Feb. 12th, 1857.
31. *Derry Standard*, July 16th, 1857.
32. *Derry Standard*, Oct. 29th, 1857.
33. *Derry Standard*, Nov. 12th, 1857.

20
AN ASSESSMENT OF THE COMMUNITY IN 1970

THE INDIVIDUAL, with all his uniqueness and all his rich versa-tility, is the cell which, coalescing with others, forms the com-munity. In isolation he is a solitary star in outer space, unseen and unproductive. In association with others, all the potential of his being can be developed and the richness of his individuality can be placed at the disposal of the people as a whole. The im-pact on the life of a parish and nation of a community in which the individuals give their maximum is dynamic and revolutionary in the best sense of the word.

In its rudest and most inchoate state, the community can be defined as a body of people living in the same locality. In its higher and more perfect form the community is an organised, social body. It has a clearly defined and publicly expressed ideal and a dynamic, imaginative leadership.

The true community is in a constant state of change under the healthy stimulus of competition and of progress. It is con-tinually being formed by the pressure of events, directed and con-trolled by careful planning and inspired leadership. Its members are profoundly aware of the strength of united effort, and the result is that they live at a higher level, intellectually and cultur-ally. As a united group they achieve results of the highest order, and make a far-reaching impact on the life of the nation as a whole.

CULDAFF AND CLONCHA: A TRUE COMMUNITY

It can be immediately stated that since the residents of this area are a group living in the same land space they form a com-munity in its most primitive form. Does this group go further and constitute a true community as defined ?

A close examination shows that there is no common purpose, no real leadership and no stimulating activity. In place of change there is stagnation, and the whole society is passive to the trend of events. The vast creative force of the individual is left un-developed, and frustration and apathy are the results.

The clear answer is that the people here do not merit the name of a true community. Occasional expressions of activity merely show the untapped potential and the unconscious desire of many for a better organised and more productive, dynamic way of life. The absence of any worthwhile results is our best evidence of the dormant conditions which operate here.

What are the causes of this barrenness ?

WHAT IS AN IDEAL IRISH COMMUNITY ?

For high achievement and substantial effort a goal is needed for the individual, the community and the nation. It is the function of leadership to formulate the ideal, 'to create unbounded enthusiasm for its attainment and finally to plan carefully the steps towards complete fulfilment. Our aim is to establish a perfect Ireland for our people.

Those entrusted in Ireland to-day with the leadership of a community, whether through the office they discharge or the special qualities they possess, should aim to create an original society which will draw the best from our past, retain what is good in the present, and extract from outside what is useful to attain the aim of a perfect country (or as near as may be in human terms). We want to ensure for all a high cultural and intellectual level, together with a standard of living comparable with that obtaining in any modern civilised country. Poverty, whether of mind or body, must be eliminated.

Each citizen will be made fully aware of our past history and the part which his own area played in the life of the nation. He will know of our achievements in the field of literature, whether Gaelic or Anglo-Irish. He will be fully acquainted with the works of our greatest artists in every order. This will enrich the mind of each individual so that he can appreciate what is good and make a contribution of the highest order in his society. Such a person will reject what is shoddy and second-rate, wherever it comes from.

HOW DOES THIS COMMUNITY MEASURE UP?

This community lacks direction. The powerful force which gives a people as a whole and every member of it a goal at which to aim is totally lacking. The young people have no incentive to improve either themselves or the area. The adults are frustrated, indifferent and apathetic.

There is no real leadership in the area itself. In such a society the natural leaders are the clergymen, the teachers, the political party leaders, the professional men and to some extent the middle class.

In examining the role of the priest in this community, we can see the profound and far-reaching effect of leadership. When the old Gaelic order collapsed, and with it the natural leaders in the general field of activity, a vacuum was created, with disastrous results. However, in the religious sphere leadership remained and the native Irish responded fully. There was no break in the continuity of organised parish life. At the Reformation the priest was dispossessed of the Church buildings and property. He remained, however, among his people, serving them without break. When the Penal Laws were rigorously applied, he ministered in secret to his subjects and when the laws were relaxed he came out in public to carry out his spiritual functions. The result was that the people, as a whole, remained true to the old religion and rejected with contempt the efforts made to convert them to the reformed edition of Christianity. The credit is due almost entirely to the priests.

However, with a few exceptions, the priests have failed completely to give any leadership outside the religious sphere. An energetic, imaginative priest could transform this society in a short time, because the people would respond readily to leadership from this quarter. Such a man has yet to come.

The school teacher in a small community can wield a strong and persuasive influence. In our community the teachers are not as active or dynamic as one might desire. Are they muted by our managerial system, or by the poor community response, or by the general national inertia in the field of education ?

The educational system itself is faulty. No effort is made to create a pride in one's own area. While history is taught regarding national events, pupils are not shown how these affected life at local level. It is an extraordinary state of affairs that children will learn of ancient Rome and classical Greece yet hear nothing about the ruined abbey or old castle which they pass each day on the way to school. The fault does not lie entirely with the teachers, however. In truth, both teacher and pupil are the victims of a short-sighted and unimaginative Department of Education.

No effort is made to create an awareness in the minds, of school children regarding their community responsibilities. The idea is fostered that everything should be left to the Government and the Civil Service. The creative urge is strangled. Is it surprising that the people, ignorant of their local history, fail to take any pride in their district ? In the light of inadequate education is it not easier to understand the poor civic response ?

The party leaders here have, without doubt, something of the *elan* which is a sign of some superior quality. They fail because in the nature of things party politics are divisive. In addition, these men lack education, training in community organisation and a true, unselfish identification with the best interests of the people.

The only professional man is the medical doctor. His close contact with the life of the people places him in an unique position to act as a consultant and adviser to those who would undertake and discharge the functions of leadership. Yet this great reservoir remains unused and the community as a whole is left impoverished. The service which the resident doctor can give to this community in a role outside his purely medical field has yet to be recognised and used.

While we have here a society which might be loosely described as classless there is a small group which can be termed the middle class. These, through lack of education and true national identity, fail to give any lead. Their tendency to ape what is British, American and second-rate ill-equips them for any real service to their own community.

While the people occupy and share a common area there is no consciousness of a common bond or a mutual interest. The dynamic force of a common interest in the area, which would make each person concerned with the general weal, is totally lacking. The quality of life in every field here is affected and impoverishment is the tragic result.

A community which has no ideal, which lacks leadership and which has no unity of purpose must remain stagnant and unproductive. No standard of values is present to guide its members as to what to accept or what to reject. Such a group of people will drift whither events and circumstances impel it. A realistic definition of the community under review is that of a rudderless ship on an uncharted sea subject to the blind forces of wave and wind. The continuance of this state of affairs will end in extinction and annihilation.

One of the surprising features of our community is that its people have but a dim consciousness of the fact that they are Irish. It is true that a minority are correctly orientated but the majority are not. This can be seen in their attitude to the Irish language. Many are unaware that Irish was the spoken language of our people since the dawn of history and they fail to see that its revival is a vital matter for the survival of the true Irish nation.

The failure to identify themselves with their own nation has led to a contempt for not only the language but also Irish music, Irish history, both national and local, and their own traditions. These people accept blindly what comes from abroad, and reject what is the expression of their own historic and cultural past. No effort is made to develop their own resources. Lacking the will to act for themselves, they look to the Government to do everything for them. The healthy motto " God helps those who help themselves ", which produced such good results in past generations here, has now ceased to motivate. While co-operation with the Government schemes to develop farming is lacking, there is a large queue each week at the local post offices to collect unem ployment benefit.

However depressing the picture, there is reliable evidence to indicate that the people have in them still the unconscious will to better themselves if only an incentive is given under dynamic leadership. One such example which bore fruit recently can be cited.

In 1970 Malin Town secured first place in Ireland in the Tidy Towns Competition. This magnificent achievement was the result of over ten years' work. The early workers faced apathy and in- difference. They persevered year by year, gradually raising the standard, sponsoring greater participation and finally securing the whole-hearted involvement of the entire community. Here was leadership in action. The achievement of this small group of people could be regarded as a pilot scheme. Perhaps we have in Malin Town's victory the initial step leading to a transformed society.

It is also important to note how the people here take an in- terest in party politics. The fever of election time can involve, on one side or other, almost everybody. Could this not be repea- ted in other spheres ?

However, the best means to measure the life of any com- munity is to establish what it produces in every field of activity, whether cultural, intellectual or economic. Applying this yard- stick to our area, what is the answer ? Nothing . . . silence in every field of the arts and barrenness in community out-put speak louder than anything that can be said.

APPENDIX I
Sinn Fein: Note on the Period 1917-1921

The national re-awakening which began at the end of the last century and continued with increased tempo in the new century had its impact even in the remote and isolated district of North Inis Eoghain. The Gaelic League, the National Volunteers and the Redmondite party all had some following here.

On the summit of Cruckaughrim in 1915 a large meeting was addressed by Tomas Mac Donnchadha. His inspiring words were remembered by many of his hearers here when this good Irishman was executed by the British in the following year. In life and in death he made his contribution to the kindling of national fervour in our area.

The news of the Easter Rising reached North Inis Eoghain in the spring of 1916. The majority were largely indifferent but to the patriotic minority the news was a source of great joy. Another generation of Irishmen had challenged the British in arms. The outcome was awaited with fear and hope.

SINN FEIN CLUB

The abortive rising was soon over and hope was replaced by despair. Maxwell, however, soon roused the anger of the Irish nation. The people of Culdaff and Cloncha responded surprisingly and shared in the anguish which swept the country. Meetings were held and in 1917 Eamon de Valera addressed a rally in Carndonagh. There was a ready response among the people in joining the new organisations. In Culdaff a Sinn Fein club was formed. This was known as the O'Rahilly Sinn Fein Club, and the members met regularly at the old Carrowmore school.

The officers were: Sean Mac Daibheid, Glenkeen, Chairman; Seamas O Dochartaigh, Cashel, Secretary; Liam Mac Cionaoith, Bootagh, Assistant Secretary; Micheal Mac Conaill Oig, Carrowmore, Treasurer.

Among the members were: Seoirse Mac Cuindlis, Gleneely; Padraig Mor Ua Cnaimhsi, Meenawarra; Sean O Loingsigh, Gleneely; Sean Mac Cailin, Gleneely; Aindreas O Dochartaigh, Cloncha; Seamas O Ceallaigh, Ballyharry; Padraig O Donaill, Garrareagh; Padraig O Dochartaigh, Cnoc; Niall O Dochartaigh, Cloncha; Seamas Mag Reannachain, Dunross; S. Mac Siomoin, Carrowmore; Micheal Mac Lochlainn, Carrowmore; Sean Mac Lochlainn, Carrowmore; Sean Mac Colgan, Culdaff; Niall Mac Lochlainn, Cashel; Seamas O Dochartaigh, Bootagh.

IRISH REPUBLICAN ARMY

A unit was formed on a parish basis in July, 1919, and was called "The Culdaff Company". The officers were: (Captain) Liam Mac Cionaoith, Bootagh; (First Lieutenant) Padraig Mac Colgan, Tirmacroragh; (Second Lieutenant) Padraig Mac Ficheallaigh, Bootagh; (Adjutant) Seamas O Dochartaigh, Bootagh; (Quartermaster) Aindreas O Ceallaigh, Ballyharry.

The following were Volunteers: Padraig Mac Ficheallaigh, Bootagh; Donall Mac Cionaoith, Bootagh; Padraig Mac Cionaoith, Bootagh; Cathal O Dubhthaigh, Ballyharry; Padraig O Dubhthaigh, Ballyharry; Padraig Mac Canna, Ballyharry; Padraig O Dubhthaigh, Drumaville; Sean Mac Congail, Tirmacroragh; Risteard Mac Congail, Tirmacroragh; Risteard Mac Congail, Tirmacroragh; Michael Mac Ficheallaigh, Ballyharry; Sean O Dochartaigh, Tirmore; Riobard O Dochartaigh, Tirmore; Pilib O Dochartaigh, Belnagran; Michael Mac Cailin, Dristernan; Michael O Ceallaigh, Ballyharry; Aindreas Mac Seafraidh, Ballyharry; Micheal Mac Conaill Oig, Carrowmore; Micheal Mac an Ghoill, The Holmes; Sean O Dochartaigh,

Bootagh; Proinsias O Gallchoir, Culdaff-Glebe; Donall Mac Diarmada, Drumley; Sean MacColgan, Culdaff; Brian Mac Cionnaoith, Bootagh.

The Intelligence personnel were: Padraig Ua Cnaimhsi, Meenawarra; Niall Facnar. Culdaff.

CUMANN NA mBAN

A branch was formed in the parish and courses in first aid were given. Some of the members were:

Proinsias Anna Nic Colgan, Termacroragh; Nora Nic Colgan, Termacroragh; Grainne Nic Lochlainn, Drumaville; Sorcha Nic Canna, Ballyharry; Caitriona Ni Dhonaill, Ballyharry; Brid Ni Dhonaill, Ballyharry; Cait Ni Dhochartaigh, Ballyharry; Aine Ni Dhochartaigh, Ballyharry.

SINN FEIN COURT

The Irish Republican Army issued a warning to all the people of the parish to avoid using the British courts. The instructions were carefully obeyed—some doing so through fear, but many because they realised that the British courts had no moral right in Ireland.

The Sinn Fein Court met in the old school at Carrowmore at night as required. The I.R.A. acted as a guard. The judges were: Brian Mac Lochlainn, Ballintroohan; Padraig Mac Loclainn, Drumley; Padraig O Ceallaigh, Ballyharry; the clerk of the court was Seamas O Dochartaigh, Cashel.

GENERAL

The I.R.A. drilled regularly at Ballyharry school. The only noteworthy activity in which the local members were involved was the collection of arms. The owners of guns at this time were mainly Protestants. Some gave their weapons willingly and some protested; all realised that the old order which gave them a position of privilege was at an end.

The parish priest, Fr. McCullagh, and his curate, Fr. McGlynn, encouraged their parishioners to support the Sinn Fein organisation. Men "on the run" from other areas were given board and lodging here. Houses of hospitality were located at Culdaff, Meenawarra, Tirmacroragh, Larrahirrel and Glengad.

The General Election of 1918 was very keenly contested. Every voter on the register recorded his preference. The supporters of the Redmondite party also were very active. In Culdaff the Tricolour was flown on the day of the election. When the booth closed the Sinn Fein representatives went to get a meal. During their absence the Redmondite supporters in Culdaff village took down the Tricolour and burned it, and bicycles belonging to the Sinn Fein supporters were broken.

In 1920 Liam Mac Cionaoith of Bootagh was chosen to contest the District Council Election for the Termone area. He headed the poll; Sinn Fein candidates were successful everywhere in this area.

298

APPENDIX II
Independence: 1921—1970

The Treaty issue became a major point of controversy here, as elsewhere in Ireland. The parish priest led the Pro-Treaty supporters and he became so much invoived that he tore down Anti-Treaty posters. Those in favour of acceptance were made up of the old Redmondites and those Sinn Fein followers who took their political guidance from the clergy. The Anti-Treaty group was made up of those who were uncompromisingly seeking a free, united Ireland.

The element here who rejected the Treaty were in the minority in those years and they were regarded as outcasts from society and from the Church. These people required great courage to withstand the opprobrium of the local clergy and the fulminations issuing from the hierarchy. They stood firm, however, and in time many of the timid, frightened earlier by the clergy, returned to the support of the Republican party.

In later years the party alignments followed the Treaty division. Fine Gael was supported by the Redmondites, as well as the more pro-British section of the community, while Fianna Fail tended to secure its support from the extreme and middle-of-the-road Republicans. It is note-worthy that when a Unionist candidate contested the area many Catholics gave him their support. These were people who had had close associations with the "Big House".

The decision of the British to concede defeat and withdraw from the area now governed from Dublin was received with dismay by the non-Catholic section of the community here, who had great fears about their future. Indeed, in view of the trend of events in the period which followed the signing of the Treaty, there was ground for such concern. The more discerning saw also that for them the days of privilege were at an end. While there was no general exodus of non-Catholics from the area, a number of families sold their farms and went to live in the Six Counties. Their descendants there will be faced with a similar crisis when the re-unification of the country takes place, as it undoubtedly will.

As if to give solid grounds for non-Catholic fears, a group of men arrived at the residence of the Young family, descendants of the principal landlord in this area, on the night of May 26-27th, 1922. Those in residence were asked to leave and then petrol was sprinkled and the building was set afire. This was a reprisal for the action of a member of the Young family in the Six-County area.

On that May morning, as the sky and the surrounding area were illuminated by the burning building, to many of the native Irish the scene was deeply symbolic and the act savagely just. The edifice crumbling under the heat symbolised the end of three centuries of injustice. The balance was being restored and ten generations of despotism and oppression were at an end. The generation of the Young family alive in 1922 suffered for the sins of their ancestors.

The 'Thirties were years of poverty and privation for the people of this area. The general economic depression throughout the Continent, accentuated by the Economic War with England, tended to make farming very unattractive. From these years can be traced the change from intensive tillage to other methods of farming.

The Second World War was followed with keen interest. Many of the people here sought a British defeat and, consequently, rejoiced in each German victory. "Lord Haw Haw" was listened to with great atten-

299

tion and interest. On the other hand, many were intensely pro-British, but it is note-worthy that none of these joined the British Army, even though such action was not opposed by the Irish Government!

Many of the young men volunteered for service in the local defence forces, and the girls joined the Red Cross unit. A number of look-out posts was established along the coast so that information could be quickly passed to the central intelligence service.

In 1957, when the I.R.A. conducted one of its intermittent campaigns against the British occupation of the Six Counties, this area featured in a small way in rendering assistance to that force.

One day a message came through the grapevine to a small farmer who lived alone at Ballyharry. He was asked to give lodgings to a number of men who were planning a raid on the British Army post at Magilligan in County Derry. Inis Eoghain, because of its location, was an ideal base for planning and carrying out such an attack. The I.R.A. stayed here for a fortnight. A reconnaissance was carried out at Magilligan by one of the men. Target practice took place at the shore, bombs were made and the attack was planned in the greatest detail. Finally, a friendly boatman at Greencastle provided the means to cross the narrow water.

On the night selected a car owner in the area provided a vehicle and the men were taken in two runs to an agreed spot along the Foyle. Two small boats, with oars, lay ready. Soon the men were over, had placed the bombs and had lit the fuses, which allowed time to re-embark before the explosion took place. All went ahead as planned, save for one miscalculation. While the men were placing the bombs, etc., the tide receded and left one of the boats half-full of water and aground in soft sand. It was impossible to move the vessel, so all got into the other boat. As they rowed across in haste the explosion went off. The men landed safely and the waiting car soon brought them all back to Ballyharry.

Before the attack it had been agreed that it was too dangerous to remain any longer in the house in which they had been lodging. A message had been sent to a house in Meenawarra where lived an elderly couple. Here preparations had been carried out, with the help of neighbours, to lodge and feed the I.R.A.

When the men returned to Ballyharry all signs of the preparation for the raid were cleared away. Guns and ammunition were taken to Meenawarra, where they were securely hidden. The men then had a meal and went to bed.

Meanwhile, the R.U.C. had alerted the Civic Guards and the Special Branch. The boat lying by the side of the Foyle indicated that the raid had been carried out from Inis Eoghain. The Civic Guards soon established the owner of this boat but got no further information. The eastern portion of the peninsula, from Greencastle to Culdaff, was placed under intensive surveillance. In some way the Guards discovered that the men had stayed in the house at Ballyharry and a raid was carried out — exactly 24 hours after the men had left.

In carrying out their investigations in Ballyharry and elsewhere the Guards met with complete silence. Everyone refused even to discuss the matter. No one would incur the odium of being an informer in such circumstances. Meanwhile, the men relaxed in peace in Meenawarra.

Around midnight a friendly watcher saw a police car arrive in Meenawarra. It stopped for some time but went off without taking any action. In the house all were asleep and no light was showing. It was now clear that it was too dangerous to remain here any longer. The men were roused from sleep and brought into a nearby bog for safety until the morning. In the meantime, a friendly contact was alerted in Buncrana to ensure food and lodging and the party set out on foot. On the way through Glentogher they asked for a meal at a house. The meal was served but the woman of the house notified the Garda Station. The unsuspecting men went on their way, but in separate groups. As they approached the house at Buncrana they were arrested. One escaped and the rest were sent to internment in the Curragh.

On the evening following their departure from Meenawarra the house in which the men stayed was surrounded by armed detectives. With guns at the ready they entered but nothing more menacing was found than two octogenarians sitting by the fireside. The old pair were subjected to an intensive questioning but they kept a prudent silence. Finally the detectives left without establishing any evidence. This incident indicates the temper of the people. Anyone attacking British forces will have the support and protection of many of the people here. In such circumstances no information will be given to the State. This attitude is the result of the moulding of many generations.

APPENDIX III
The Parish of Culdaff: A Community Study in 1982

INTRODUCTION:

Those engaged in research relative to local history often experience disappointment and frustration because of the dearth of information regarding the ordinary day-to-day life, in the past, of the people in the area chosen for investigation. A contributory factor to the absence of suitable data is the view that the daily routine of current life is too trivial and commonplace to deserve written attention.

How inaccurate is this trend of thought can be seen if one speculates about a resident of any area in Inis Eoghain in the year 982, that is one thousand years ago, who had had the imagination and initiative to record the manner of daily life in his habitat. Information about food, clothing, social conditions and all that went to make up the full pattern of daily life then would now be of absorbing interest.

The student of local history could well ponder on two facts: society is constantly undergoing change and the present is as much a field for attention as the past. The present essay was undertaken with this in mind.

POPULATION:

The community of Culdaff Parish in 1982 consists of three hundred and fifteen households of which two hundred and seventyfive are of the Catholic persuasion. The balance is made up of Protestant householders which can be sub-divided into Anglicans, Methodists and Presbyterians. The total population is about 1300 of which 85% are Catholics.

Regarding the surnames found in the area the traditional Gaelic names, in an anglicised form, still predominate. In order of frequency these are O'Doherty, MacLaughlin, MacDermot,[1] Harkin, McDaid, Ruddy, McGonigle, McColgan, MacCallion, Farren, MacConalogue, MacGrenaghan, Lynch, MacFeely, Carney, Mooney and Donaghy. Together these constitute upwards of 50% of total while O'Doherty and MacLaughlin together represent about 20% of the total population. Other surnames are Long. Houten and Mills. In allocating the Christian name to the newly born the custom heretofore was to select from the names in use within the families respectively of the two parents. The first born got the name from the father's side, next from the mother's side and so on alternatively. Usually only one name was given. The traditional pattern has now been generally abandoned. Practically all get two and a few three names. These are selected from any country according to the whim of the parents. The Irish forms of the names selected are rarely used. However a glance at the names used during years 1977 - 1981 inclusive shows some exceptions: Róisín, Úna, Ciarán, Éanna, Seán, Niall, Conhúr, Caoimhín, Diarmaid, Siobhán, Déaglán, Niamh, Brian, Ros, Fiona, Fionnuala, Orlaith, Aisling, Catríona, Colm & Pádraig.

The birth rate over the same years stood at an average of three per cent. Female births exceeded the males. The population is further augmented by the return of a number of retired people born in the parish and who had spent most of their working life in Great Britain or the United States.

ORGANISATIONS:

The individual reveals an important facet of his character in the company he keeps and in the clubs of which he/she is a member. In the same way a community is assessed by a look at the organisations which have developed to meet the needs of the people. The common interests of each group in an area thus finds an adequate expression.

The residents of the parish under review have a choice of more than a score. Those interested in party politics can decide between the Fine Gael

303

Branch operating for the whole parish, three Fianna Cumainn viz Culdaff, Gleneely and Ballyharry and the Independent Fianna Fail Cumann. The Parish Council under the chairmanship of the Parish Priest ensures an harmonious awareness of the feelings and attitudes of the people in matters pertaining to ecclesiastical affairs among the Catholic section of the Community. The members are elected by the people.

The overall affairs of the parish are served by the Community Council whose members are also chosen by universal suffrage. In addition there are two Development Associations, one at the village of Culdaff and one at Gleneely. There is also a branch of the Irish Country Women's Association with a membership of twentytwo. Its activities are social, cultural and utilitarian.

The farmers have established an active branch of the Irish Farming Association. There are over one hundred members who are enabled to keep abreast of all development in relation to their means of livelihood. The world of entertainment is catered for through a Youth Club, Boy Scouts, two Football Clubs, one at Gleneely and a second at Culdaff, a Tennis Club, a Badminton Club and a Dart Club. The Drama Group provides plays and concerts.

The ascetical and·the pious find an outlet respectively in the Pioneer Total Abstinence Association and the Legion of Mary. Catholics attend the Church at Bocan where there is daily Mass and on Sundays two Masses. Anglicans have a church at Culdaff. There is a weekly service conducted by the minister of the combined parishes of Clonmany, Donagh, Cloncha and part of Culdaff. The members of the Methodist persuasion have a weekly service at their church situated in the townland of Glacknadrummand. Presbyterians attend at the Hillhead, in the neighbouring parish of Donagh.

WHAT THE PEOPLE READ:

In the field of communication the people have a wide choice. All the government radio stations in Ireland and Great Britain are within range. In the case of television they have access to all the British stations and Radio Telefis Eireann. Very few houses here now lack either radio or television equipment.

Just as the body is repaired and sustained by the use of food, so also the mind is informed and stimulated by what is read. As the parish of Culdaff lacks a library service it is not possible to record the choice of reading matter in the field of books. Thus attention is confined to newspapers and periodicals.

One household in three takes in a daily newspaper. Half of these choose an English paper, the *Daily Mirror* being the favourite. Of the Irish dailies the *Irish Independent* has the highest circulation, followed by the *Irish Press*. The *Irish Times* is a poor third. The only twice-weekly paper available here is the *Derry Journal*. The Tuesday edition is bought by one quarter of the households. The Friday edition reaches practically every household in the area and is read by all denominations. Thus anyone wishing to communicate with the whole parish should select the Friday edition of the *Journal*. Even the advertisements are news!

The weekly publications on demand are the *Farmers Journal, Donegal Democrat, People's Press, Derry People, Derry Sentinel, Ireland's Own* and *Woman's Way*. The first named has a circulation of over one hundred; the others together do not reach more than one third of the households. The *Irish Catholic* is circulated through the parish authorities.

The Sunday papers are in wide demand. Half of the households takeι more than one paper. More than half of the papers are Irish. Here the *Sunday Press* has a good lead followed by the *Sunday World*. In the case of the English papers chosen the *News of the World* and the *Sunday Mirror* tie for first place. These are followed closely by the *People*. Indeed these three English papers together provide Sunday reading for almost half the households. The *Sunday Times* and *Observer* combined get entry into about half-a-dozen houses.

THE PARISH STRUCTURE:

The community is served by two Post Offices viz Gleneely and Culdaff. A daily delivery of letters is provided from Monday to Friday inclusive. One in three of the householders has had a telephone installed. The local Post Offices have not yet been connected with the national automatic system. However the Department of Communications plans to link up north Inis Eoghain within the next couple of years.

Eight public house licences are held and of these six are active. Four are located in the village of Culdaff. There is one supermarket and five of the old type grocery shops. A weekly house delivery is also provided by one shop owner.

For pupils of the Catholic persuasion three primary schools function. These are located at Gleneely, Carrowmore and Culdaff. During this year Bocan school was closed and the pupils were transferred to the newly opened school in the village of Culdaff. For children of other denominations transport is provided to bring them to a primary protestant school in the neighbouring parish of Donagh. All protestant parents except one family avail of this service. The exception insists on attendance at the nearest Catholic school where their children follow the normal course except in the case of religious instruction.

Facilities for secondary education are available at the Community School at Carndonagh. Almost all avail of these. The children of protestant parents in general go to Carndonagh. The few exceptions attend at the Royal School in Raphoe. The number going forward to third level is minimal.

School transport is provided for attendance at both primary and secondary schools except where the pupil's distance from the respective centre renders it unnecessary.

The people here live close to the soil and from it draw to a considerable extent the means of livelihood. The present trend in farming is away from tillage and towards the production of cattle, pigs and sheep. Seed potatoes for export are also a source of income. Most of the householders get their fuel supply locally, but, the peat bogs are by now almost exhausted.

The community as a whole is subsidised by the Department of Social Welfare through pensions, unemployment benefit and assistance and children allowances. This type of income circulates quickly as any visitor to Culdaff or Gleneely on Tuesdays and Fridays will note. Thus the business people benefit as well.

ASSESSMENT OF THE COMMUNITY:[2]

If one uses contrast as a yardstick by which to assess the people of Culdaff parish anyone who moves around the whole country and meets the general run of inhabitants will see them as dour, puritanical and somewhat parsimonious. The spontaneous gaiety, the openness and generosity which are found in the West and South are lacking.

There is a low national identity balanced by a strong feeling of local identity. The people have a sturdy under-lay of independence. The leaders of Church and State are kept firmly in their place. Despite threats or orders the native judgement will assert itself and determine the line of action the people decide to take. They will brook no interference.

The modern rat-race finds no place here. The people are easy-going and are content with the simple things of life. Their mental attitude insulates them against much that is promulgated through the media. It is virtually impossible to communicate a new idea to the older generation .

Their interests lie almost entirely within their own ambit. A local radio station on the lines of Radio na Gaeltachta and a newsheet covering day to day events within the parish would be more acceptable than what is provided by the media at present. The Friday edition of the Derry Journal comes nearest to the people's needs.

During the year under review a state of war developed between Great Britain and Argentina. As the war progressed it was clear that the majority of the people were pro-Argentinian. Each victory scored by the South American State was welcomed. The close observer could see that what really lay beneath the surface was a strong antipathy to the British. For those whose recollections extended to the Second World War it was reminisient of the pro-German sentiments of the people here in the 1939-1945 period.

As already mentioned the parish is heavily subsidised by the State. Since the majority of the people are farmers with small holdings the contribution in taxes to the Irish Exchequer is minimal. It could be described almost as a tax free haven. Most now live in good houses many of which have been built in the last decade. A bathroom with indoor toilet is found now in the majority of the dwelling houses.

Emigration to the United States and Great Britain has ceased. Those who leave to seek employment are more likely to be found in some other part of the country.

Farmers here in general keep up-to-date with developments in their own field though a few can be found with their feet and minds firmly fixed in the ethos of 1882.

The members of the community here are of course subject to all the weaknesses of which flesh is heir. Discreetly beneath the surface are kept the aberrations which the conventions of the society demand all to frown on. The inner gossip circles have many morsels to feed on and to enjoy. Meanwhile the mantle of respectability is presented to the public.

Finally one can observe that whatever the media says about economic recessions in Ireland or abroad there is in this year of grace no sign of gloom in the parish of Culdaff.

The traditional role of the married male in this society calls for a special mention. He deems that his work is completed when provision is made for food, clothing, shelter and the procreation of the species. It is accepted and expected that his wife will wait "hand and foot" on him for twentyfour hours per day. She will also carry the financial management function together with all that pertains to the education and training of the growing family. Instead of discharging his role as head of the house he serenely smokes his pipe and adopts the pose of a neutral observer.

This in turn is balanced by the compensating position of the married female. She is the dominant partner setting her stamp firmly on the children especially the sons. To some extent here is a matriarchy. The daughters seem to escape from this unbalanced environment unharmed. The sons however experience at least some emotional damage.

In ordinary conversation poverty is applied in the restricted sense of a lack of material goods. The term has however the wider meaning of the absence of anything needed to develop fully the individual and the community to which he belongs. Poverty in the sense of lack of goods can be said to be largely absent from the parish nowadays. There is a great poverty in the fields of art, culture and in those areas which pertain to intellectual development and stimulation. Social life is also lacking.

The interested observer will immediately pose the question "why". The society of today would seem to be suffering from some great upheaval which has left it dispirited and impoverished. The cause can be identified with the conditions created by the British invasion. Dispossession of goods led to material poverty and the loss of the Irish language with the rich culture enshrined therein produced cultural indigence.

The institutions concerned with education have done little to remedy the problem. Their leaders have failed to distinguish between the mere imparting of knowledge in school and college and the maturing and development of the pupils entrusted to their care. A person can answer an examination paper and secure full marks and be totally incapable of integrating his knowledge into the judgements and the practical problems in his daily life. Literacy and the possession of knowledge are not in themselves education though they can help.

The people here take a great interest in party politics. Fidelity to ones party is almost as strong as adherence to ones religion. An election is seen as a bit of diversion no one believing or expecting any real change whatever party is in office or in opposition. The majority support Fianna Fail in its two versions viz official and independent.

Since we are dealing with a relatively stable community one can indentify to a great extent the ethos of the supporters of the main parties. Fine Gael draws its support from the descendants of the Redmondite party, from those areas directly influenced by the local "Big House", those associated closely with the Royal Irish Constabulory and the Protestant section. The last-named regard Fine Gael as a tolerable second, always giving absolute preference to a Protestant candidate. The national loyalty is low among Fine Gael adherents. Indeed their attitude is well expressed by more than one of these in the remark made to the writer. The speaker was indifferent to what flag flew over the country. Indeed the preference would be for the Union Jack.

The republican ethos is strong varying between the extreme, supporting Sinn Fein to the middle-of-the-road category. The former regard Fianna Fail as second best. In general the republican supporters are the descendants of the old Gaelic section which never accepted the British presence.

A deeper scrutiny shows that all the party adherents support a name rather than a real political philosophy. For example, the Fine Gael philosophy of today is far removed from the conservative right wing doctrine of the Thirties and Forties. The existence of a pseudo-liberal wing today and the significance thereof goes unperceived. Similarly the republican supporters fail to see how careerism[3] has taken over in the upper echelons of all parties. Lip-service is given to the ideals of Éamonn De Valera. Conviction is lacking. All fail to see that while the label is the same the contents are vastly altered.

The Protestant section of the Community can largely be identified as the descendants of the planter stock who came to the parish in the seventeenth and early eighteenth centuries. While the religion they profess has kept them apart as a separate section, they are in no way different from the rest of the people in manners, speech and customs. They hold a greater proportion of wealth than their numbers would warrant in an equitable distribution. While they secured a better basis through being given the more fertile lands confiscated from the native stock their comparatively more wealthy position has been secured through their own initiative. Their enhanced position in this respect began during the First World War when they availed of the high prices for farm produce given by the British Government. The materialistic philosophy entwined with their religion also played a part in their success.

Despite their integration into the Irish setting the Protestants do not feel at home in an Ireland which is largely Catholic and Gaelic. As a group they really find their true identity in the British setting but by no means in a provocative, flag-waving manner. However they are somewhat confused when they go across the Irish Sea and find that the English regard them as full-blooded Gaels. They reject the land in which they were born and are in turn rejected by the nation with which they identify.

Ecumenism has got a somewhat frosty reception here from all denominations. Any efforts made by the clergy were ignored. The general view was and is that each person should follow his/her conscience and respect his neighbour's right to do likewise. The Ne Temere was accepted by all without cavil. It was clear and decisive. All denominations saw where they stood and no mixed marriages took place. There was no bitterness and no resentment.

The post Vatican II period has produced a change in the attitude towards mixed marriages. A survey of the parish in 1982 shows the following:

A. No of mixed marriages   11
B. I Each party retained own religion   6

II	Catholic party became Protestant	4
III	Protestant party became Catholic	1
C.	I Family baptised Protestant	5
	II Family baptised Catholic	5
	III No religion	1
D.	Married in both churches	2
	Married Protestant church only	4
	Married Catholic church only	5

The change, it is feared, could cause friction in the community. The majority of both denominations prefer the days of the Ne Temere ruling. They have history to support them. Harmony prevailed.

THE FUTURE:
This parish in common with other rural ones in Ireland has now been, through modern communication and improved transport, brought into contact with the whole outside world. Its society is at present undergoing a period of rapid change.

The older generations were born into a stable order where everything was conditioned by tradition and outside influences were minimal. The accepted pattern of the community life had a high moral tone. Honesty and integrity were the norm. The people had a balanced sense of values between the material and the spiritual orders. Thus anyone born into it was unconsciously moulded and without much effort was carried along in the stream of its life. Neither great knowledge nor deep conviction was required.

Those born within the last quarter of a century live in an entirely different environment. Through a higher educational standard they are more literate and are put in touch with the flood of ideas being circulated through books, periodicals and newspapers. Their personal contacts come from a wider and more diverse field. To all this add radio and television.

The general trend of this wider area of communication is largely materialistic, pagan and destructive of the traditional Christian outlook which obtained in the community in the past. The older people will remain largely unaffected. The younger will not. The latter require a greater knowledge of their religion and a deeper conviction about the truths of Christianity if they are to stand firm to the traditions and values of their fathers.

The older people have a feeling of unease but seem unaware of what corrective course to initiate. They are concerned and well-disposed but lack any inspired leadership. At national level over the past thirty years our leaders in Church and State failed to see where the developments in the communication field were leading and thus were unprepared for the crises today. Consequently, can one be too critical of the parents and leaders in Culdaff unprepared for the problems facing them in 1982.? What lies before the community which has here been analysed.?

REFERENCES:

1. The Irish form is Ó Duidhíorma, the name of the ruling family in Gaelic times of the sub-kingdom of Bredagh which included the parish of Culdaff.
2. For their help when I was collecting the necessary data my thanks are due to the following:-
David McCandless, Kevin McLaughlin, Brian Deeney, W.J. MacConallogue, Bernard McGuinness & Patrick O'Connor. However the judgements made and the opinions expressed, if any, are entirely those of the writer.
3. The extent to which careerism rather than conviction dominates can be seen from the following episode for whose veracity the writer can vouch. A dynamic young graduate thinking of entering politics consulted a priest friend as to which party he should join. The priest indicated a certain party saying that in it there was a better chance of quick promotion. The young man acted on his advice, applied for membership and was accepted. At the following general election he secured the nomination for a constituency and was elected to Dail Eireann. The new Taoiseach impressed by the young man's ability gave him a portfolio in the Cabinet. The rank and file are ignorant of the realities of Irish party politics.

APPENDIX IV - DOCUMENTS REGARDING THE ASSASSINATION
OF NORTON BUTLER

Two documents in the State Papers Office give an interesting sidelight in respect of William McGuinness's betrayal. The friends of the McGuinness family had a handbill printed and circulated to expose the base deed of Sean McEleney. The document was on sale at all the fairs and markets. The text is as follows:

"A Full, True, and Impartial Account

of the apprehending of William Maginnis, brother of the late Dan Maginnis, who was executed sometime ago for the murder of Norton Butler, Esq., Grousehall, County Donegal, barony of Ennishowen.

I, William Maginnis, agree that I was accused of being in company with my brother at the murder of the above gentleman and a reward was offered for apprehending me with others which caused me to leave the country for a time until the people would be more settled. When I returned it was well-known, by many of the general neighboured who never minded me and imagined they thought there was blood enough shed in our unfortunate barony. I began to do some work and was employed by my judas betrayer Shaun McAleney who engaged me to cut turf for three days which was nearly performed, on that evening I was most cowardly betrayed by the said Shaun McAleney who came up to me - judas like - in these words "well William Maginniss, you are a clever fellow and has a good pistol, will you let us see how far the would carry a ball" and thinking no danger from the man who employed me, I immediately discharged the piece, when in a moment I was arrested by gentlemen and constables, and to make the business more easy for my betrayer he and I were tied on a car and carried to Lifford when I now remain to await the sentence of my God, my King and my Country, wishing no harm to any person in the world."

In June 1818 G. Gregg, a Government Official at Derry, was in the public market and found a street hawker named Joseph McDonagh selling the handbills. Gregg bought a copy and sent it to Tristram Carey, a landlord and magistrate resident at Castlecarey.

Carey had MacDonagh arrested and sentenced him to a month in Derry gaol. The seditious leaflets were confiscated and burned. Carey wrote to Dublin Castle as follows:

June 12, 1818

"I therefore take the liberty of calling your attention again to the propriety of rewarding the person through whose means William Magennis has been taken and of securing his safety in the way least likely to be attended with future inconvenience to him, the receipt of this I endeavoured to prove before and a further assignment may be found to the activity that is used by Magennis's friends in pointing out this person to the odium of all those who hold an informer infamous. This is plainly evinced by the paper I enclose which to ensure a readier sale has been disposed of at a lower price than the printer could sell at. Its intention clearly is to remove any doubts that can at present be entertained of McAleney being accessary to the apprehsion of Magennis and to hold him out as an object of popular vengeance.

I hope therefore it is thought conducive to the public service that he is provided for, a weekly allowance may be made for his support."

Signed: Tristram Carey, Castlecarey.

LIST OF PROTESTANT HOUSEHOLDERS 1740[1]

Parish of Culdaff

Location	Names
Aghaglasson	William Hutchinson, Adam Carrothers, Samuel Carrothers, William Carrothers
Ballyharry	William Clarke, Andrew McIntyre, Thomas Magee, James Crawford, Widow Wallace, Alexander Smith
Baskill	Donall McCauley, Michael O'Carolan, John Thompson, Alexander Riddalls, Widow McClintock, Patrick O'Carolan, Thomas Lawson, Mrs. Butler, Andrew Thompson, John McCauley
Calhame	Mark Carr, William Wilson, Matthew Hemphill
Carrowmore	David Hood
Cashel	Thomas Morrison, Alexander Morrison, William Alcorn, Daniel O'Carolan
Culdaff	Robert Young
Culdaff-Glebe (Cragnasole)	William Brown
Dristernan	George Chittock, George Gill, John Johnston
Drumlee	George McCandless, Alexander Johnston, Alexander Bonnettan, Widow McCandless
Garrowleane	William Lawson
Goorey	Samuel McCauley, William Hamilton, Moses Moore
Kindroyhead	James Mitchell, Robert Mitchell, Widow Gillen, Matthew Gill, John Gill, Art O'Gillen, Thomas Flynn
Lisdarragan	George Alcorn, John Alcorn
Straroddin	William Wilson, James Guthrie, John Wilson
Terrawee	Walter Butler
Tiranaoire	John McFarland
Tirmacroragh	Charles Newcomb, Robert McAteer, Samuel Crawford, William Crawford
Treanatubber	James Balfour

Parish of Cloncha

Ardmalin	Ludovick Houston
Ballagh	John Glendenning, John Smith, William Heslitt, James Colhoun, John Scott, Ninian Boggs
Ballellaghan	Mr. Fulton, John Nutt, Hugh Park, Andrew McAteer, John Fulton, Mr. Harvey, John McAteer
Ballycrampsey	John Hunter, John Moore, Robert Colhoun
Ballylinn	Matthew Murray, James McIntyre
Bree	Thomas Miller, Arsabella Campbell, George Platt, Robert Miller, John Molloy, John Platt, John Moore

Carrowmore	John Scott, Widow Moore, Francis McKenry, John Patterson, Matthew Patterson, Patrick Porter
Cloncha	James Read, William Read
Drumballycaslin	John Strawbridge
Drumcarbit	Jonathan Bind, David Colhoun, James Elder, Matthew Platt, John Carswell, Thomas Johnston, Robert Starott, Margaret Colhoun, William Hamilton, Richard Scott, Robert Wilson, John McKeague, James McConohy
Dunross	George McAteer, Samuel McAteer, Ranall McDonald, Andrew McAteer, John McAteer, James McAteer
Evishnagarr	Widow Fulton, Thomas Fulton, Patrick Colhoun, William Porter, William Houton, William Moore, Alexander Moore, Henry Scott
Goorey	John Montgomery, Hugh Crawford, James Cameron, Joseph McCorkill
Keenagh	Mr. Moore, William O'Carolan, Philip Maguire, James Nelson, Alexander Nelson
Killin	Widow Boggs, John Boggs, Francis Boggs
Knockamany	Matthew Brown, John Turner, John Crawford
Knockglass	William Beggs, John O'Carolan
Kullourt	John Elder, Alexander Richie, Joseph Henderson, Widow Alexander, Matthew Merchant
Lagg	Mr. Alexander
Larrahirrel	Widow McNeill, Robert Loam, Walter McKinley, Robert Long, William McClean, Walter McAteer, William Caldwell, John McNeill
Letterore	Arsabella Alexander, David Moore
Meedanmore	Robert Elder, John Crockett
Milltown	John Hutchinson, John Adams
Norrira	James Mackey, John Mackey, John Richie, Joseph Scott, Robert McFarland
Redford-Glebe	William Elwood, Edward Jones, Robert Cooper
Umgall	James Merchant, John Merchant, Alexander Moore, John Crow

[1] G.O. Ms 539

312

INNISHOWEN

Sweet Innishowen, you're renowned in story,
Your silvery brooks and your rippling rills.
In St. Patrick's time, were Owen's glory.
While life remains I will love thee still.

Slieve Snacht, I ween, is your highest mountain,
A cap of snow its head doth crown.
Cruck-na-noineen has crystal fountains
That to the Foyle go a-dashing down.

Round the Meentagh Loch and the Lake of Shadows
My spirit lingers to pause awhile.
Fair Culdaff! you have emerald meadows,
Where feathered singers the time beguile.

Malin Glen and Strabreaga's waters
Claim your attention, as you pass by,
The Isle of Doagh has lovely daughters.
The law of prudence they don't deny.

There are pleasant headlands around fair Clonmany:
Sweet Magher-a-Shamrock and old Dunaff.
I must confess you're as fair as any:
I'll ne'er deny you, bright fair Culdaff!

Your dark green lanes and heath-clad mountains,
Your beauteous summits and golden strands,
Your shady glens and glistening fountains
Proclaim the work of Dame Nature's hand.

Proud Bin-ee-Kinney looks down defiant
On Elwood's waves, as they fall and swell.
The Cuckoo's Rock stands up like a giant
Where the bees may feast on the heather bell.

The hills of Croragh have purple heather,
Enough to cover the lark and more.
'Tis sweet to sit there in summer weather
To gaze on Redford and grim Dunmore.

I well might call you the glen of echoes.
I mean you Redford, the seat of sway.
The rocks ring time as Port Elwood's waves
Go out and in at the close of day.

Behind Dunmore, where the dookers slumber,
The azure sea croons a lonely song.
From Glebe to Esklin, four coves in number,
Bid echo the waves along.

Your pardon for praises of my childhood home:
'Tis Glacknadrummond 'neath the Bishop's Hill,
Whence the eye o'er vistas far may roam
By Lough Swilly, Derry and sweet Moville.

Dear Innistrahull seems to be quite near
And, beneath, the village of loved Culdaff.
The Highland Hills stand out when the day air is clear
And you can see the head of lone Dunaff.

At night are seen the bright lights of Derry,
Beyond Drung Hill, twenty miles away.
When the sun shines bright, cross Greencastle ferry,
The Antrim hills stand in grim array.

Carn town is seen and the grove at Collon
And Malin Bridge, with its arches nine;
Rasheney, Leenan and lovely Pollan
And Malin banks when the sun doth shine.

Look northwards! Now see the Coastguard Station,
Glengad's tall cruach and Bunagee.
See Young's demesne with its vast plantations:
A prettier picture you cannot see.

Turn to the east. See McGlinchey's cottage,
You must here ponder! 'tis holy ground.
You almost seem in a state of dotage.
Each lovely scene doth your thoughts confound.

Your thoughts must linger round Redford dwelling,
If e'er you visit its lovely grove,
Once there, you will surely keep telling
Of scenes romantic and dreams of love.

Round the Altar Hill there are rich pines growing,
Where the blackbirds sing and the cuckoos call.
From Redford bog there's a river flowing
Bound on each side by an earthen wall.

315

Look further east and see Ballyharry.
See Bootagh Rue and its waters cool.
On winters' nights, be they dark or stormy,
You will see the lights of the little school.

Sweet Innishowen, I must leave thee mourning,
Alas! he's gone who gave thee name.
If ancient honours are not returning,
Why hold the hero, then to blame?

Séamas Mag Reannacháin (1866-1933)

INDEX

317

319

320

Macklin Memorial at Culdaff

AN tÚDAR

323